Religion and Law

Religion and Law: Biblical-Judaic and Islamic Perspectives

edited by
Edwin B. Firmage
Bernard G. Weiss
John W. Welch

Eisenbrauns
Winona Lake

1990

Library of Congress Cataloging-in-Publication Data

Religion and law: Biblical-Judaic and Islamic perspectives/edited
by Edwin R. Firmage, Bernard G. Weiss, John W. Welch.
p. cm.
Originally papers presented at a conference held Mar. 5–8, 1985
under the joint sponsorship of the University of Utah and Brigham
Young University.
Includes bibliographical references and indexes.
ISBN 0-931464-39-0
1. Law (Theology)—Biblical teaching. 2. Bible. O.T.—Criticism,
interpretation, etc. 3. Islamic law. I. Firmage, Edwin Brown.
II. Weiss, Bernard G. III. Welch, John W. (John Woodland)
BS1199.L3R45 1989
291.8′4—dc20 89-34612
CIP

Acknowledgment of permission to reprint certain
illustrations will be found at the end of this book.

Contents

Editors' Introduction

In the Bible, as in Jewish thought since the end of the biblical period, law is understood to be inseparable from religion. In Christianity, despite the complexity of Christian thinking about the place of law within the divine economy, a similar attitude prevails. When Christian writers, beginning with those who wrote the New Testament, speak of law in the context of such topics as "law and grace," they generally mean the Holy Law that Moses received at Mount Sinai. Islam, the dominant religion of the Middle East and the world's most widespread religion after Christianity, shares the same point of view: all law worthy of the name comes from God.

Indeed, from a strictly monotheistic point of view, there is logic in this way of thinking. If there be indeed a single and all-powerful creator of the universe, this divine being cannot but be sovereign over people and all living things. Sentient creatures such as humans should therefore seek to know whether this being makes any demands upon them. When such demands are discovered, whether through prophets or other channels of revelation, those demands necessarily constitute the law by which creatures are *ultimately* to be governed. The notion of a holy law is thus inherent in all monotheistic religion. When taken seriously, it can only mean that human beings will look to a holy law to discover the principles according to which a society should be governed.

This ancient biblical idea, though maintained for centuries in the three greatest monotheistic religions, has been challenged by the advent, in the Western world, of a secularist view of law and the social order. Millions of people whose cultural heritage includes the holy law idea as a central ingredient have, in consequence, been caught up in a debate over whether law in the present world is to be kept in close relation with religion or detached from it. Most of the Western world has opted for the latter alternative, but not always without some misgiving. The people of the Middle East, on the other hand, are experiencing a revival of interest in the former alternative. Both Israel and its Muslim neighbors have been witnessing a clearer drawing of the line between modern secularist and traditional views concerning the relation between religion and law, with those who stand on the side of tradition gaining an ever increasing voice.

A meaningful account of this debate requires a reasonable understanding as to how the two terms *religion* and *law* are to be defined. The term religion, though a bugbear within the field of religious studies, is the less problematic of the two terms in the present context. Since the relation between religion and law will here be treated as a problem arising among adherents or heirs of the above-mentioned monotheist faiths, the term religion will be understood to embrace those religions that entail belief in a divine being who enters into communication with the human race through prophets or similar vehicles of revelation. The term law, on the other hand, is not so easy to nail down. This is in large part due to the debate over its meaning that has been carried on within Western jurisprudence. Owing to the pervasiveness of the positivist understanding of law within Western intellectual culture, most speakers of English, upon hearing the word law in ordinary conversation, do not usually take it to be a reference to holy law. Thus speakers learn to distinguish law in the everyday sense of the term (as in "the law requires that seat belts be fastened") from holy law. The unqualified use of law will be understood to be a reference to the latter only in specialized contexts, such as sermons in churches or synagogues. The positivist spirit that underlies most everyday use of the word law sees coercion as a definitive factor in law. However much positivists may wish to further refine their definitions of law, they generally see law as emanating from the agency that possesses the supreme instruments of coercion, namely the state. As a consequence, they frequently place holy law, which does not have coercion as one of its definitive elements, within the larger category of morality, separating it from the sphere of law as such.

Accordingly, how one understands the relationship between law and religion will depend in part on how one understands law. If one understands this term to be a reference to holy law, then one's view concerning the relationship between law and religion can only be that law is inseparable from religion: in fact, being authored by God, it is as inseparable from religion as God himself. If, on the other hand, one understands law to be a reference to the law that emanates from the state, then one's view may or may not be that law is inseparable from religion. In a perfectly theocratic system of government, law in this positivist sense would indeed be inseparable from religion; but, then, it would in such a system be indistinguishable from holy law. In situations where the state is clearly not theocratic (whether because it falls short of the theocratic ideal or repudiates that ideal), law in the positivist sense is clearly separable from religion. The two things now constitute, or belong to, separate spheres: law is not a part of religion but something that exists over and against it.

Two distinct views of the relationship between law and religion now become possible. One may regard religion either as seeking to influence the law or as having no concern with the law. To speak of religion as seeking to influence the law will generally be tantamount to speaking of religion as seeking to bring the law (in the positivist sense here intended) into conformity with the holy law. To say that religion has no concern with the law, on the other hand, is to mean one of two things: either that law in the sense of holy law is not a part of religion (or is only a marginal element in it) such that there is nothing religion would seek to bring ordinary law into conformity with, or that holy law belongs to a sphere (either a dimension of present human life or a future millennial age) distinct from the sphere in which ordinary law operates, and owing to the evilness of the latter sphere one should not expect the holy law to be operative in it.

The chapters in this volume, all of which are concerned in one way or another with the relationship between religion and law, were originally papers presented at a conference held on 5–8 March 1985 under the joint sponsorship of the University of Utah, through its Middle East Center and the College of Law, and the Brigham Young University, through its J. Reuben Clark Law School, the David M. Kennedy Center for International Studies, and the Richard L. Evans Chair of Judaeo-Christian Studies. Many of the papers were expanded or revised on the way to final publication as chapters in this volume.

All of the chapters, with one exception, are primarily concerned with the concept of holy law as developed within the Bible and the great monotheistic faiths. They all therefore take the fusion of law and religion as a starting point, not questioning its validity but concentrating rather on exploring some aspect or consequence of it. The one exception is the chapter by Delbert R. Hillers, who sees the legal life reflected in certain ancient documents as essentially secular, calling in religion only to fill in certain gaps. The other authors generally have in mind, when speaking of law, *written* (some might prefer to say statutory) law as represented by collected law found in the Bible, the Talmud, or in the Islamic legal texts. An exception to this is Bernard S. Jackson, who pays special attention (found nowhere else in this volume) to the judicial process in ancient Israel as distinct from written law. The law that emerges out of this judicial process is, however, not necessarily distinct from holy law, since the charisma, or spirituality, of the Israelite judges gave to the justice that they dispensed an aura of sacredness. By and large, the following chapters, however much they may be applicable to the modern situation, do not deliberately deal with that situation but rather discuss their chosen topics within an ancient or medieval framework. Exceptions are the chapters by Izhak Englard, J. Clifford Wallace, and George E. Mendenhall. The first two are concerned with the debate, mentioned above, between modern secularist and traditional views of law in the context of modern Israel, while Mendenhall deals in part with the relevance to the modern situation of the age-old notion of a covenant with deity.

Although the contributors to this volume were, as participants in the original conference, not tightly bound to a format of specified topics but were allowed to choose their topics more or less freely within a framework of suggested themes, most of the chapters that follow may nonetheless be seen as forming a number of clusters. The first three chapters (Weinfeld, Weiss, Mendenhall) share as a common theme the idea of covenant—that agreement between God and humanity from which the binding force of the Holy Law derives. Chapters 4–14, which form the largest cluster, may be said to be concerned in one way or another with the question of what constitutes the underlying principles of, or spirit behind, the holy law. Wherein, in other words, lies the *value* of the holy law? To a large extent, these chapters, whether consciously or unconsciously, are seeking to explore how adherence to the law may, if at all, be defended against the charge of constituting a meaningless or mechanical legalism. The value of the law may be established in a number of closely related ways: by disclosing its social ideals (Greenberg, Welch), by treating it as indispensable to spirituality or holiness (Falk, Sanders), by articulating its ethical foundations (Jacob Milgrom, Wright, Denny, Giffen), by integrating it into a mystical vision (Ayoub, Alishan), or by granting autonomy to the judicial process (Jackson). Within this group of papers is a subcluster (Jacob Milgrom, Wright, Denny, Giffen) that deals with the concerns just described primarily with reference to ritual law. Chapters 15 (Jo Milgrom) and 16 (Hallet) are somewhat related to the preceding chapters, except that they are concerned with the meaning and value of a single provision of the law, namely the prohibition against images as it relates to a single field of human endeavor, namely the visual arts. Of the five remaining chapters, chapters 17–19 (Freedman, Paul, Hillers) take up three different historical topics that have a bearing on the relationship between religion and law, while chapters 20 (Englard) and 21 (Wallace) treat this general theme of the book from within a contemporary context.

In the notes at the beginning of each chapter, the editors endeavor to bring out more fully and clearly the underlying continuity that runs through all twenty-one chapters of this volume.

While the original conference included fifteen papers and fifteen responses, six of the responses have been molded into chapters in this volume by virtue of the substantive contributions that they made to the general themes of the conference.

Two of the editors have contributed chapters to this volume, and information about them may be found in the editorial notes preceding their chapters. The third editor, Edwin B. Firmage, was the principal initiator, organizer, and moderator of the original conference. Professor Firmage teaches constitutional and international law at the University of Utah College of Law. He received the J.D., LL.M., and S.J.D. degrees from the University of Chicago where he was on the editorial board of the *Law Review*. He served on the staff of Vice-President Hubert H. Humphrey with responsibility in civil rights. He was named United Nations Visiting Scholar in 1970–71 and Fellow in Law and Humanities at Harvard Law School in 1974–75. In 1978 he received the Distinguished Teaching Award from the University of Utah and in 1987 was invited to deliver the Reynolds Lecture, *Ends and Means in Conflict*. His books include *To Chain the Dog of War: The War Power of Congress in History and Law* (with Francis Wormuth), and *Zion in the Courts: A Legal History of the Church of Jesus Christ of Latter-day Saints* (with Collin Mangrum).

The editors express gratitude not only to participants, many of whom traveled around the world to attend this conference, but also to Scott Hagen, Blake Ostler, and Stephen Clark for research assistance. Lora Lee Petersen performed in her usual professional and pleasant manner in typing manuscripts with more than the usual foreign words and variations of style. Thanks are due also to Gary P. Gillum, librarian in charge of ancient studies materials at the Harold B. Lee Library of Brigham Young University, who prepared the indexes, and to David P. Aiken, the editor for Eisenbrauns, who proofread the entire manuscript of this volume with impressive expertise, provided many helpful suggestions, and made stylistic adjustments that have given this multiauthored volume in its final form a high degree of internal consistency. Finally, Edwin Firmage, Jr., a student of Jacob Milgrom at the University of California at Berkeley and of Moshe Weinfeld at the Hebrew University of Jerusalem, provided help in the selection of participants. Without his original conception of such a gathering, this conference would not have occurred.

Edwin B. Firmage
Bernard G. Weiss
John W. Welch

Religion and Law

Moshe Weinfeld

The Decalogue: Its Significance, Uniqueness, and Place in Israel's Tradition

THE FOCUS OF THIS ESSAY is, appropriately, upon the Decalogue, the most famous collection of laws ever promulgated. Weinfeld shows why, despite the existence of similar collections of laws in the Bible itself and despite of the presence elsewhere in the Bible of nine of its ten commandments, the Decalogue is unique: it has a special connection with the covenant whereby Israel's relationship with God is established. Certain features of the decalogue, which Weinfeld outlines, make it especially suited to have this special connection. Because of its centrality to the covenant, the Decalogue occupies a primary place in the ceremony of covenant renewal that occurred during the Feast of Weeks and that Weinfeld believes to be reflected in Psalms 50 and 81. This opening chapter brings the reader face to face with the proposition, common to the monotheistic faiths, that law owes its origin and its authority to a covenant with God.

Moshe Weinfeld is Professor of Biblical Studies at the Hebrew University of Jerusalem. He is a member of the editorial board of *Vetus Testamentum* and editor of *Shnaton*. Among his many important publications are *Deuteronomy and the Deuteronomic School* and *Justice and Righteousness in Israel and the Nations.*

Each of the Ten Commandments, except the last one,[1] be it affirmative or negative, appears in a similar form somewhere else in the Pentateuch. The prohibitions against idolatry and swearing falsely, the commandments to observe the Sabbath and to respect parents, the prohibitions against murder, adultery, theft, and bearing false witness—all these appear again and again in the various laws of the Pentateuch. For example, the ancient collection of laws called "The Book of the Covenant" (found in Exodus 21–23, adjoining the Decalogue) opens with the laws concerning idolatry: "With me, therefore, you shall not make any gods of silver, nor shall you make for yourselves any gods of gold" (Exod 20:23 [Hebrew 20:20]). In this same collection of laws most of the other commandments of the Decalogue are also found: observance of the Sabbath (23:12), respecting parents (though formulated in the negative; 21:15–16), murder (21:12), kidnapping and theft of property (21:16; 22:1–4 [21:37–22:3]), and false witness (23:1).

Parallels to the Ten Commandments in Other Parts of the Pentateuch

The first two commandments, "You shall not have other gods . . . , you shall not make for yourself any sculpture and image [*psl wkl tmwnh*]," and "you shall not bow down to them and you shall not worship them [*lʾ tštḥwh lhm wlʾ tʿbdm*]," are paralleled in the various codes and legal passages of the Pentateuch. For example:

1. "You shall not bow down to any other god [*lʾ tštḥwh lʾl ʾḥr*]" (Exod 34:14). This has the same motive clause as does the second commandment: "because YHWH . . . is a jealous god [*ʾl qnʾ hwʾ*]"; (cf. Exod 20:5, Deut 5:9b).
2. "You shall not make with me gods of silver nor shall you make for yourselves gods of gold" (Exod 20:20[23]).[2]
3. "You shall not bow down to their gods and you shall not worship them" (Exod 23:24).
4. "You shall not make molten gods [*ʾlhy mskh*] for yourself" (Exod 34:17).

[1] See below, pp. 15–16, on the tenth commandment.

[2] For this "paralleling of doubled prohibition," see M. Paran, "Literary Features of the Priestly Code: Stylistic Patterns, Idioms, and Structures" (Ph.D. diss., Hebrew University, Jerusalem, 1983) 91.

5. "You shall not make molten gods [*ʾlhy mskh*] for yourselves" (Lev 19:4).
6. "You shall not erect for yourselves a sculpture or pillar [*psl wmṣbh*]" (Lev 26:1, cf. Mic 5:12).

The pair *sculpture* (*psl*)/image (*tmwnh*) is found only in Deut 4:16, 23, 25 and in the Decalogue; however, this does not justify placing the origin of the expression in Deuteronomy. On the contrary, Deuteronomy diverges significantly from Exodus in its use of this pair. In contrast to Exodus, which expresses this pair with a conjunctive (*psl* and *tmwnh*), Deut 4:16 conjoins the pair in a construct: "a sculpture *of* any image [*psl kl tmwnh*]," which is in line with the usage of Deut 4:23, 25, "a sculpture of the image of anything [*psl tmwnt kl*]." Note also the pleonastic usage of Deut 4:16: "sculpture of any statute image [*psl tmwnt kl sml*]."[3] Deuteronomy actually makes an abstract out of two concrete objects: any *imagery representation.*[4] This is based on the deuteronomic theology expressed in Deut 4:15: "because you have not seen any image on the day God spoke to you."[5] In mentioning "sculpture and any image," the second commandment turns out to be the most radical among the pre-deuteronomic sources, suiting perfectly the categorical nature of the commandments of the Decalogue (see below). The deuteronomic version of the Decalogue made the commandment even more radical.

The phrase "of the heaven above and of the earth below" is an interpretative gloss that might be deuteronomic, but it could also be

[3] On the construct of synonyms in the Bible, see Y. Avishur, *The Construct State of Synonyms in Biblical Rhetoric* (Jerusalem: Kiryat Sepher, 1977) [Hebrew]; on the case of *pesel/tĕmûnāh*, see esp. p. 104.

[4] F.-L. Hossfeld's argument (*Der Dekalog: Seine späten Fassungen, die originale Komposition und seine Vorstufen* [Orbis Biblicus et Orientalis 45; Göttingen: Vandenhoeck and Ruprecht 1982]) that the deuteronomic version of this commandment (as well as others) is the original one and that the Exodus version is secondary, is forced and cannot be accepted. Cf. recently C. Levin, "Der Dekalog am Sinai," *Vetus Testamentum* 35 (1985) 165–91.

[5] This notion may have its origin in Exod 20:23, where the prohibition against making gods of silver and gold comes next to the statement that God spoke from heaven (Exod 20:22); cf. A. Toeg, *Lawgiving at Sinai* (Jerusalem: Magnes, 1977) 134–35 [Hebrew]. Exod 20:23 is not deuteronomistic as E. Nicholson argues in "The Decalogue as the Direct Address of God," *Vetus Testamentum* 27 (1977) 422–33. On the contrary, Deut 4:36 is dependent on Exod 22:23. Exod 20:22 has no deuteronomic clichés; calling/speaking from heaven is also found in Gen 21:17; 22:11, 15. On the other hand the notion salient in Deuteronomy that God spoke from amidst the fire is not attested in Exodus. See also Hossfeld, *Der Dekalog*, 179.

considered a genuine phrase of the Decalogue that has strongly
influenced Deuteronomy.[6] The same applies to the phrase "house of
slaves [*byt ʿbdym*]" in Exod 20:2 (Deut 5:6).[7]

The prohibition of bowing down and worshiping in Exod 20:5
(Deut 5:9) refers to "other gods" as well as to "sculptures and images"
(for the phrase of "worship sculpture" [*ʿbd psl*] cf. Ps 97:7; 2 Kgs
17:41; 2 Chr 33:7), and there is no justification to see Exod 20:4 (Deut
5:8) as an interpolation.[8] In fact, the polemic against "fetishes" in the
Bible is based on the notion that the idol is identical to the god it
represents.[9]

The third commandment is paralleled in Lev 19:12: "You shall
now swear falsely by my name," and in the framework of casuistic
law in Lev 5:22, "If he swears falsely regarding any one of the various
things."[10] These differ in that the formulation of the third commandment, "to take God's name [*nśʾ šm yhwh*]," has a much broader
connotation than "to swear [*hšbʿ*] by his name," and might imply not
to use God's name for any declaration and oath at all, as was
understood by Philo (*On the Decalogue*, 84–91) and the Rabbis
(*b. Ber.* 33a).

The fourth commandment (observance of the Sabbath) has its
parallels in the Covenant Code and the Priestly Code:

1. "Six days you shall do your work [*tʿśh mʿśyk*] but on the seventh
   day you shall abstain from work [*tšbt*] so that your ox and your
   ass may rest and that your bondman and the stranger may
   refresh" (Exod 23:12). The motive clause here reminds us of the
   motivation of the Sabbath law in the deuteronomic version of the
   Decalogue (Deut 5:13–14).
2. "Six days shall you work [*tʿbd*], but on the seventh day you
   abstain from work [*tšbt*]; you shall abstain from work at plowing
   time and harvest time" (Exod 34:21).

[6] I suggest that it is deuteronomic in my *Deuteronomy and the Deuteronomic
School* (Oxford: Clarendon, 1972) 331 n. 1.

[7] See N. Lohfink, *Das Hauptgebot* (Analecta Biblica 20; Rome: Biblical Institute,
1963) 100ff. On the dependence of Deuteronomy on the Decalogue, see S. A. Kaufman,
"The Structure of the Deuteronomic Law," *Maarav* 1 (1979) 105–58.

[8] As argued by W. Zimmerli, "Das zweite Gebot," *Festschrift Alfred Bertholet* (ed.
W. Baumgartner et al.; Tübingen: Mohr, 1950) 550–63; *Gottes Offenbarung: Gesam-
melte Aufsätze zum Alten Testament* (Munich:: Kaiser, 1963) 234–48.

[9] Cf. M. Greenberg, "The Decalogue as Reflected in Biblical Criticism," *The
Decalogue throughout the Generations* (ed. B. Z. Segal; Jerusalem: Magnes, 1985) 81.

[10] Cf. Ps 24:4: "who has taken a false oath by my life [Qere: "his life"; *lʾ nśʾ lšwʾ
npšy/npšw*] or sworn deceitfully."

3. "You shall keep my Sabbath [*ʾt šbtty tšmrw*], . . . for it is holy for you . . . [*qdš . . . lkm*]. Six days may work be done [*yʿśh mlʾkh*] but on the seventh day there shall be a sabbath of complete rest (*šbt šbtwn*)" (Exod 31:12–17).
4. "Six days work [*mlʾkh*] may be done but on the seventh day you shall have a sabbath holy to the Lord. . . . You shall kindle no fire" (Exod 35:1–3; cf. 16:29–30; Lev 19:3; 26:2; Num 15:32–35; Jer 17:21–27).
5. "Six days work may be done, but on the seventh day there shall be a sabbath . . . a sacred occasion [*mqrʾ qdš*]. You shall not do any work [*kl mlʾkh*]" (Lev 23:3).

The commands of the Priestly Code (3, 4, and 5) stylistically resemble the sabbath formulation of the Decalogue. The following elements are common in each formulation: the phrase "keep the sabbath [*šmr ʾt hšbt*]," the concept of 'holiness' of the sabbath (*qdš*), the word *mlʾkh* for work, and the characteristic feature of the Decalogue, its comprehensiveness and totality: "You shall not do *any* work [*kl mlʾkh*]."

The fifth commandment (respecting parents) has parallels in the affirmative as well as in the negative formulations (see below): "You shall each fear [revere, *tyrʾw*] his mother and his father" (Lev 19:4); "He who strikes his father or his mother shall be put to death" (Exod 21:15); "He who reviles [*mqll*] his father or his mother shall be put to death" (Exod 21:17); "If any man reviles [*yqll*] his father or his mother he shall be put to death" (Lev 20:9); "Cursed be who insults [*mqlh*] his father or his mother" (Deut 27:16, cf. 21:18–21).

Reviling or cursing (*qll*) father and mother is the opposite of respecting or honoring father and mother, as an Akkadian document from Ugarit shows: "the one of my sons who dishonors [*ša uqallil*] . . . his mother . . . and those of them who honor [*ša ukabbit*] . . . his mother."[11] Compare also Matt 15:4: "For God said, Honor your father and mother; and he that curses [*kakologōn*] his father or mother shall surely die." The *piʿel* form of *qll* 'curse' in the Bible usually means to utter a curse, in contrast to the *nifʿal* and *hiphʿil* forms, which express contempt (see, e.g., 1 Sam 2:30, 2 Sam 6:22, 19:44; and cf. *qlh* in Deut 27:16).[12] Nevertheless, it should be admitted

[11] E. Thureau-Dangin, "Trois Contrats de Ras-Shamra," *Syria* 18 (1937) 250ff. (Ras Shamra tablet 8.145, lines 24–25).

[12] Cf. my article "*qllh*" in *Encyclopaedia Biblica* (Jerusalem: Bialik, 1976), 7:186ff.; also see my comments on Deut 27:16 in *Deuteronomy and the Deuteronomic School*, 277–78.

that the basic meaning of *qll* is like the Akkadian *qullulu, gullulu,* 'to despise esteem lightly'; and it is not impossible that *qll* in the Bible also means 'to despise, to dishonor'.[13] Such a meaning seems most likely in the story of Naboth the Jezreelite, where *brk,* 'to bless', appears instead of *qll,* 'to curse' (1 Kgs 21:10, 13). What is meant here is not an actual 'curse', but the dishonoring of God and king. (See also 'God's curse' [*qllt ʾlhym*] in Deut 21:22–23, and compare the Temple Scroll phrases concerning traitors: "and he dishonors [betrays = *wyqll*] his people and the people of Israel," and "despised [*mqwlly*] by God and people.")[14]

The sixth commandment's prohibition against murder, with its casuistry, is attested several times in the law codes of the Pentateuch: Exod 21:12, Lev 24:17, Num 35:30–34, Deut 19:11–13.

The seventh commandment concerning adultery with all its ramifications is dealt with in Lev 18:20, 20:10, Deut 22:22; cf. Num 5:11–30.

The eighth commandment (theft) is to be compared with Lev 19:11: "You shall not steal [*lʾ tgnbw*]." The casuistry of the eighth commandment is developed in Exod 22:1–12.[15]

The ninth commandment (false witness) has its parallels in Exod 23:1: "You must not carry false rumors [*šmʿ šwʾ*], you shall not join hands with the guilty to act as a malicious witness [*ʿd ḥms*] . . . keep far from a false charge [*dbr šqr*]"; and in a casuistic setting in Deut 19:16–19: "When a malicious witness [*ʿd ḥms*] comes forward to give false testimony [*ʿnwt srh*] against a man . . . the judges shall make a thorough examination, if the man who testified as a false witness [*ʿd šqr*] giving false evidence against his fellow-man [*šqr ʿnh bʾḥyw*] . . . You shall do to him as he schemed to do to his fellow."

The common expressions in all these commands are *ʿd šqr/šwʾ*, *ʿd ḥms*, and *ʾnh brʿ/bʾḥ*.[16] It seems that the deuteronomic version of

[13] See H. C. Brichto, *The Problem of "Curse" in the Hebrew Bible* (Philadelphia: Society of Biblical Literature, 1963).

[14] On Deut 21:22–23 see my *Deuteronomy and the Deuteronomic School,* 51 n. 4; on the Temple Scroll see Y. Yadin, ed., *The Temple Scroll* (Jerusalem: Israel Exploration Society, 1983), 2:244, col. 64, lines 7–13.

[15] According to the Rabbis "you shall not steal" in the Decalogue refers to kidnapping (*b. Sanh.* 86a), as some modern scholars also claim. See A. Alt, "Das Verbot des Diebstahls im Dekalog," *Kleine Schriften* (Munich: Beck, 1953) 333–40; M. Goshen-Gottstein, "Du sollst nicht Stehlen," *Theologische Zeitschrift* 9 (1953) 394ff. But see M. Klein, "Verbot des Menschendiebstahls im Dekalog," *Vetus Testamentum* 26 (1976) 161–69; see generally B. Jackson, *Theft in Early Jewish Law* (Oxford: Clarendon, 1972). For kidnapping, cf. Exod 21:15; Deut 24:7.

[16] *šwʾ* is synonymous to *šqr* and *mrmh,* see, e.g., Ps 24:4 (*šwʾ//mrmh*); 144:8, 11; Job 31:5; and cf. Exod 23:1 (*šwʾ*) with 23:7 (*šqr*). However, *šwʾ* is also combined with

the Decalogue used the unusual combination *ᶜd šwᵓ* in order to prohibit not only false witness but also testimony circumventing or evading true evidence.[17]

Nine of the ten commandments are then spread all over the law codes of the Pentateuch.[18] Wherein lies, then, the uniqueness of the Decalogue, and how did it become the crowning event of the encounter of the God of Israel and the people of Israel? Why is it that precisely this group of commandments is claimed to have been spoken to the people directly by God (Exod 20:1, 18–19; Deut 4:12; 5:4, 21) and to have been written by God's finger on the tablets of stone (Exod 31:18; 32:16; 34:1, 28; Deut 4:13; 5:19; 9:10) and were placed in the Ark of the Covenant (Deut 10:1–4)?

If one should say that this was due to their antiquity, it can be replied that neither the content nor the style of the Decalogue proves them to be older than other laws of the Pentateuch. The short commandments, "You shall not murder," "You shall not commit adultery," "You shall not steal," are not exceptional; similar commandments are to be found in Lev 19:11, 13: "You shall not steal, you shall not deceive, . . . you shall not defraud your neighbor, you shall not commit robbery [*lᵓ tgnbw, wlᵓ tkḥšw . . . lᵓ tᶜšq ᵓt rᶜk wlᵓ tgzl*]." Likewise, the variegation in the contents of the Decalogue is not unparalleled; similar compilations are found in Leviticus 19 and in Deuteronomy.

On the other hand, just as there is no proof for the antiquity of the Decalogue, there is nothing to prove them later. The notion of a quasi moral-prophetical nature that assumes the late origin of this set of commandments has been obsolete ever since H. Gressman refuted it and is thus no longer accepted.[19]

Great importance is attributed to the particular divine revelation of the Decalogue. As is well known, this event is commemorated in Judaism annually on the Feast of Weeks, Shabuoth, the celebration of the giving of the Torah. It may be asked, however, whether this event

---

'vanity' (*hbl*) and is thus broader in its connotation than *šqr*, cf. Jonah 2:9, Zech 10:2, Ps 31:7.

[17] Cf. E. König, "Zur Erklärung und Geschichte des Dekalogs," *Neue kirchliche Zeitschrift* 12 (1901) 378; J. J. Stamm and M. E. Andrew, *The Ten Commandments in Recent Research* (Studies in Biblical Theology 2/2; London: SCM, 1967). Hossfeld (*Der Dekalog*, 85–86), who considers the deuteronomic version as original, argues that the Exodus version changed *šwᵓ* into *šqr* in order to make a more profound distinction between the third prohibition (false oath) and the ninth prohibition (false witness). This explanation, of course, is in line with his thesis, but is not convincing.

[18] The tenth commandment is discussed below, pp. 15–16.

[19] H. Gressmann, *Mose und seine Zeit* (Göttingen: Vandenhoeck and Ruprecht, 1913) 437ff.

was celebrated in earlier times as well. If so, what was the role of the Decalogue in the cult ritual? The Mishnah reveals that during Second Temple times, the Ten Commandments were read daily together with the *Shema*^{c} in the Temple (*m. Tamid* 5:1) and were it not for the heretical sects they would still be read today.[20] To be sure, the Decalogue is to be spoken daily in accordance with the Palestinian practice as reflected in the Cairo Genizah, and to this day pious Jews read the Decalogue daily at the end of prayer.[21]

I will try to answer these questions by reference to biblical and external sources that help determine the significance of the Decalogue.

The Decalogue—A Basic Formal Affirmation in the Religion of Israel

Let me first state the particular and most characteristic features of the Decalogue.

The ordinances of the Decalogue apply to every individual in Israelite society. This contrasts with the ordinary laws, whose enactment depends on particular personal or social conditions. For example, sacrifices are conditioned on certain circumstances of the individual (vows, sin offerings, etc.) and of the community (the temple service); other ordinances are dependent on specific circumstances, such as the laws of purity, release of land and liberation of slaves (*Shemiṭṭah* and Jubilee), the civil code, laws of matrimony, the priestly dues, etc. Every Israelite, on the other hand, commits himself or herself not to practice idolatry, not to swear falsely, to observe the Sabbath, to honor parents, not to murder, not to commit adultery, not to steal, not to give false witness, and not to covet. Everyone is likely to commit such things, no matter one's personal status nor the environment or period when one lives; and therefore all are warned to abstain from them.

The Decalogue is for the most part formulated in the negative; even the "positive" commandments—observance of the Sabbath and

[20] *Y. Ber.* 1:8, 3c; *b. Ber.* 12a; "One in fact ought to read the ten commandments daily. Why do we not do so? Because of the claims of the heretics that they might not say: 'These alone were given to Moses at Sinai.' " See E. E. Urbach, "The Status of the Decalogue in Worship and Prayer," *The Decalogue throughout the Generations* (ed. B. Z. Segal; Jerusalem: Magnes, 1985) 127–46 [Hebrew], on the background of the heretics' claim.

[21] Cf. J. Mann, "Genizah Fragments of the Palestinian Order of Service," *Hebrew Union College Annual* 2 (1925) 299; "Changes in the Divine Service of the Synagogue Due to Religious Persecutions," *Hebrew Union College Annual* 4 (1927) 288. For references concerning this custom, see Urbach, "The Status of the Decalogue."

honoring parents—are in fact prohibitives.[22] The observance of the Sabbath is clarified explicitly by way of prohibition: "Six days you shall work . . . but the seventh day is a Sabbath . . . you shall not do any work" (Exod 20:9-10). Similarly, the main object of the commandment to honor parents is to prevent offense or insult, as is seen in the various and related laws in other law-collections: beating (Exod 21:15), cursing and disgraceful conduct (Exod 21:17, Lev 20:9, Deut 27:16), rebellion and disobedience (Deut 21:18-21). In Leviticus 19, which refers to the Decalogue (see below), the command is indeed formulated in the negative by the opposite of "honor": "You shall each fear his mother and his father" (v 3).[23]

The inclination toward a negative formulation is due to the overall character of this group of commandments, which sets forth the basic conditions for inclusion in the community of Israel, conditions transmitted to the people through the prophet who first conveyed God's word and God's will to them. These conditions determine what a member of this special divine community is to refrain from doing.

A similar state of affairs can be found in the set of commands that Jonadab son of Rechab, father of the house of the Rechabites, passed on to his sons: "You shall not drink wine . . . and a house you shall not build and a seed you shall not sow and a vineyard you shall not plant . . . so that you may live many days on the land you inhabit" (Jer 35:6-7).[24] A parallel from the Hellenistic world provides a set of

[22] Accordingly, some have incorrectly tried to change the formulation of these two commandments; see, e.g., K. Rabast, *Das apodiktische Recht im Deuteronomium und im Heiligkeitsgesetz* (Berlin/Hemsdorf: Heimatdienstverlag, 1949) 35ff. E. Nielsen, *The Ten Commandments in New Perspective* (Studies in Biblical Theology 2/7; London: SCM, 1968) 84ff.

[23] Ancient Near Eastern documents indeed express the son's obligation toward his parents with the verbs *kabātu* 'honor' as well as *palāhu* 'fear'; see M. Schorr, "Urkunden des altbabylonischen Zivil- und Prozessrechts," *Vorderasiatische Bibliothek* 5 (1913) 13a: *ipallaḫ ukabassi*, "and he shall fear and honor her" (= *Cuneiform Texts from Babylonian Tablets in the British Museum* [London: British Museum, 1896-], 2:35:8). This subject matter of this law is connected with economic support and ancestral duties after death: "He shall clothe him, feed him and if he dies he shall eulogize him and bury him." Cf. *b. Qidd.* 31b: "He honors him while alive and honors him after death . . . he feeds him . . . clothes him, brings him in and takes him out." For the meaning of honoring father and mother in the Bible compared to the son's obligations to his parents in the ancient Near East, see R. Albertz, "Hintergrund und Bedeutung des Elterngebots im Dekalog," *Zeitschrift für die alttestamentliche Wissenschaft* 90 (1978) 348-74.

[24] The Rechabites also observed their laws because they were "the commandments of their father" (vv 14, 16, 18); cf. E. Gerstenberger, *Wesen und Herkunft des apodiktischen Rechts* (Wissenschaftliche Monographien zum Alten und Neuen Testament 20; Neukirchen-Vluyn: Neukirchener, 1965), no. 17.

prohibitions given by the god to the founder of the temple, a set of prohibitions to which all the worshipers oblige themselves with an oath (discussed below).

The commandments of the Decalogue are precisely and concisely formulated and contain a typological number (ten) of commands. As has been noted already, the text of the Decalogue has with time undergone expansion and revision. This process is most conspicuous with respect to the commandment of the Sabbath. The explanation for the observance of the Sabbath in the book of Deuteronomy is completely different from that found in the book of Exodus.[25] Other examples of expansions and revisions in the present form of the Decalogue as a whole could be given.[26] The original Decalogue can be reconstructed as follows:[27]

1. I, the Lord, am your God, you shall have no other gods beside Me.[28]
2. You shall not make for yourself a sculpture and image.
3. You shall not swear falsely by the name of the Lord your God.

[25] Since the explanation in the book of Exodus is connected with the creation as found in the priestly tradition (Gen 2:1–3; Exod 31:17), scholars of Wellhausen's school, who view P as late, are forced to assume that the form of the Decalogue in Exodus 20 was later than that of Deuteronomy 5. But as early as 1883, K. Budde (*Die Biblische Urgeschichte* [Giessen: Ricker, 1883] 493f.) sensed that Exod 20:11 reflects an ancient tradition; because of his adherence to Wellhausen's analysis, however, he reversed conclusions and claimed that the late P was influenced by the Decalogue in its explanation of the Sabbath. See my comments in "God the Creator in Gen 1 and in the Prophecy of Second Isaiah," *Tarbiz* 37 (1968) 109 n. 22. On the explanation of the Sabbath in the book of Deuteronomy, see my *Deuteronomy and the Deuteronomic School*, 222.

[26] For a recent discussion of the problem, see Stamm and Andrew, *The Ten Commandments in Recent Research,* 18ff. On the deuteronomistic expressions present in the form of the book of Exodus, see my *Deuteronomy and the Deuteronomic School,* 318 n. 2.

[27] See Greenberg, "Decalogue," *Encyclopaedia Judaica* (Jerusalem: Keter, 1971), 5:1443–44, and "The Decalogue as Reflected in Biblical Criticism."

[28] The division proposed here between the first and second commandments is found as early as Philo (*On the Decalogue,* 50ff.) and Josephus (*Ant.* 3:91–92). Jewish tradition accepted the view that "I the Lord am . . ." (v 2) is the first commandment and vv 3–6 "You shall have no . . ." (on idolatry) constitute the second commandment; see "Mekhilta of Rabbi Ishmael" (tractate *Ba-Ḥodesh* §6; *Mekhilta de-Rabi Yishmaᶜel,* ed. H. S. Horovitz and I. A. Rabin [Frankfurt, 1931; repr. Jerusalem: Bamberger and Wahrmann, 1960]), "Mekhilta of Rabbi Simeon ben Yoḥai" (*Mekhilta de-Rabi Shimᶜon ben Yohai,* ed. J. N. Epstein and E. Z. Melamed [Jerusalem: Shaᶜare Rahamin]), and other medieval Jewish commentators. Nevertheless, it is possible to find traces of Philo's and Josephus's division in Jewish tradition. Thus, for example, in "Sifrei to Numbers" §112a: (*Sifrê de-ve Rab̄: Sifrê al Sefer Bammidbar veSifre Zuta,* ed.

4. Remember to keep the Sabbath day.[29]
5. Honor your father and mother.
6. You shall not murder.[30]
7. You shall not commit adultery.
8. You shall not steal.

H. S. Horovitz [Leipzig: Fock, 1917] 121): "R. Ishmael says . . . 'Because he has spurned the word of the Lord' [Num 15:31]—who spurned the *first commandment* as said to Moses by the Great One: 'I the Lord am your God; you shall have no other gods beside me'." The rabbinic saying "'I am' and 'there shall be no' were heard from the mouth of the Great One," may also indicate that these are one commandment; and, to be sure, this tradition is advanced in *b. Hor.* 8a in the name of a Tanna of R. Ishmael's school (cf. *b. Mak.* 24a).

The reading of the Decalogue according to the "superior accents" (*ṭʿm ʿlywn*) divided according to commandments and not according to verses also reflects, in my opinion, the division of Philo and Josephus. With all the many difficulties involved in the development of the accentual tradition of the Decalogue (see M. Breuer, *The Aleppo Codex and the Accepted Text of the Bible* [Jerusalem: Kook, 1977] 55-66 [Hebrew]), one thing is clear: according to the superior accents, v 2 never receives accentuation as the end of a verse, but is a *rebia* or an *athnach,* which shows that the first commandment included "I am the Lord" and "You shall have no."

According to the plain meaning as well, "I, the Lord, am your God" functions as a subordinate clause to the following prohibition; cf. esp. Judg 6:8-10 ("I, the Lord, am your God. You must not worship the gods of the Amorites"), Hos 13:4, Ps 81:8-10[9-11]. For the understanding of "I the Lord . . ." in the Decalogue and the meaning of *ānōkî* and *ānî* at the beginning of sentences in Akkadian and Semitic inscriptions, see A. Poebel, *Das appositionell bestimmte Pronomen der 1 Pers. Sing. in den westsemitischen Inschriften und im Alten Testament* (Assyriological Studies 3; Chicago: Oriental Institute, 1932). Poebel rightly claims that such sentences cannot be interpreted as self-presentation: not "I am the one who led you out" but rather, "I, who led you out, (command you): You shall have," etc.

[29] In the version of Deuteronomy, *šāmôr* 'observe'. The verb *zkr* in Deuteronomy has only an historical meaning: 'remember'. See the deuteronomic motivation of the Sabbath observance: "Remember that you were a slave in the land of Egypt" (v 15), while in other sources and especially in P *zākar* had a meaning of 'commemoration'. Cf. W. Schottroff, *"Gedenken" im Alten Orient und im Alten Testament* (Wissenschaftliche Monographien zum Alten und Neuen Testament 15; Neukirchen-Vluyn: Neukirchener, 1964) 117-25. The Sabbath in Exodus 20 is conceived as a sacral commemoration intended to dramatize God's resting on this day, whereas in Deuteronomy 5 the observing of the Sabbath is seen as historic recollection, "because you were a slave in the land of Egypt." The author of the book of Deuteronomy thus distinguishes between 'remember' and 'observe'. Concerning the observance of the commandments, Deuteronomy speaks of 'observation' (*šmr*) whereas 'remembrance' (*zkr*) is reserved for the historical notion. See my *Deuteronomy and the Deuteronomic School,* 222.

[30] The order of these three commandments (murder, adultery, theft) is different in Philo (*On the Decalogue,* 121ff.; *On the Special Laws,* 3:8; *Who is the Heir,* 173), in part of the New Testament (Luke 18:20; Rom 13:9; unlike Matt 19:18-19 and Mark 10:19), in Codex Vaticanus of Deut 5:17-20, and in the Nash Papyrus (see M. Z. Segal, *Massoret uBiqqoret* [Jerusalem: Kiryat Sefer, 1957] 230). In those texts the order is

9. You shall not bear false witness against your neighbor.
10. You shall not covet.

True, there is no uniformity of rhythm here, and the commandments can be divided into three groups according to their length:[31] (1) commandments with four stresses or more (the first, second, third, and ninth); (2) commandments with three stresses (the fourth and fifth); and (3) commandments with two beats (the sixth, seventh, eighth, and tenth). However, there is no reason to view the whole, on this basis, as secondarily and artificially contrived. The length of the sentence and its rhythm depends on its content, and some topics cannot be fully expressed in only two words. Moreover, formal heterogeneity itself is no indication of an eclectic and secondary compilation, as certain scholars assume; original collections of sayings of varying length are found in the Bible and in the literature of the ancient Near East. Accordingly, there is also no justification to reformulate the two affirmative commandments in the negative in order to attain a unity of form.[32] On the other hand, the structure of the Decalogue does reveal some unifying features: their short form, the typological number ten, and the arrangement into two groups (commandments concerning the individual and God and commandments concerning the individual and his or her neighbor, discussed further below). These features testify to the oneness of the unit. A form and structure of this kind enables the engraving of the commandments on stone tablets and their learning by heart; this intimates that these commandments comprise a set of fundamental conditions that every Israelite was obliged to know and learn.

---

adultery, murder, theft. According to M. Weiss (*The Bible from Within: The Method of Total Interpretation* [Jerusalem: Magnes, 1984] 256–59) this order, which deviates from the MT, preceded Jeremiah, who quoted it in a chiastic manner:

Jer 7:9	*Philo, NT, Nash Pap.*
theft	adultery
murder	murder
adultery	theft

[31] See G. Fohrer, "Das sogenannte apodiktisch formulierte Recht und der Dekalog," *Kerygma und Dogma* 11 (1965) 49–74; *Einleitung in das Alte Testament* (12th ed.; Heidelberg: Quelle & Meyer, 1979) 73–74. According to Fohrer and others the original version of "you shall not covet" was longer: "You shall not covet the house of your neighbor." In my opinion, the original form of this commandment was identical to that of the sixth through eighth commandments.

[32] See H. Cazelles, "Les origins du Decalogue," *Eretz-Israel* 9 (1969) 16 n. 27; see also n. 22. According to Cazelles (p. 16), the Sabbath commandment originally read: "You shall do no work on the Sabbath day," whereas the commandment "you shall honor" was added later under the influence of wisdom literature.

The commandments are essentially "categorical imperatives" of universal validity, above time and independent of circumstances.[33] No punishment is prescribed, and no details or definitions are given. Accordingly, it is doubtful whether these commandments would satisfy the needs of the legislator, the citizen, or the courthouse itself. One might ask what kind of theft is treated in the eighth commandment and what would be a thief's punishment; whether murder applies to fellow citizen only or to any human being; what kind of work is prohibited on Sabbath (contrast Exod 34:21, 35:3; Num 15:32-36). But such questions are irrelevant, since these commandments are not intended as concrete legislation, but as a formulation of conditions for membership in the community. Anyone who does not observe these commandments excludes herself or himself from the community of the faithful. This is the function of the Decalogue. Although the definition of laws and punishments is given later in various legal codes, this is not the concern of the Decalogue, which simply sets forth God's demands of his people.

Most instructive in this respect is the last commandment, "Do not covet." As B. Jackson has shown there is no justification for challenging the traditional interpretation of *lʾ tḥmd* as lust and intention.[34] The verb *ḥmd* by itself does not connote taking or appropriating. When it does so, it joins verbs like 'take' (*lqḥ*; Deut 7:25; Josh 6:18 [LXX], 7:21), 'rob' (*gzl*), or 'carry' (*nśʾ*; Mic 2:2).[35] The verb *ʾwh* in Deut 5:21[18], which stands in parallel to *ḥmd*, is even more difficult to interpret as 'to appropriate', as noted already by Ibn Ezra on Deut 5:16. It is true, lusting for something is usually a precondition for using or appropriating, and therefore the verb *ḥmd* may involve also appropriating. But as it stands, it denotes coveting, and that is what is implied in the Decalogue. From the practical halakic angle, it could not be interpreted as an abstract postulate without practical consequences, and therefore the Rabbis gave it a pragmatic meaning.[36]

This is a command that cannot be enforced and hence is not punishable by human. This command concerns the violation of

[33] See Alt, "Die Ursprünge des israelitischen Rechts," *Kleine Schriften*, 1:321-22.

[34] Jackson, "Liability for Mere Intention in Early Jewish Laws," *Essays in Jewish Comparative and Legal History* (Leiden: Brill, 1975) 202-34.

[35] See Greenberg, "The Decalogue as Reflected in Biblical Criticism," 86.

[36] See Mekhilta of Rabbi Ishmael (tractate *Ba-Ḥodesh* §8): "Perhaps even if he covets with speech, therefore Scripture teaches: 'You shall not *covet* the silver and gold upon them, and *take* it for yourself' [Deut 7:25], just as there he must perform an action, so here he must perform an action." See also the Mekhilta of Rabbi Simeon ben Yoḥai on this same verse.

ethics, which can be punished by God only. In other words, this is not law in the plain sense of the word, but the revelation of God's postulate, and so are the other commands of the Decalogue.

Indeed, the commandments are called *dĕbārîm* 'words' and not *ḥuqqîm* 'laws'.[37] Furthermore, in rabbinic literature the ten commandments are named *ʿaśeret ha-dibbᵉrôt. Dibbᵉrôt* is the plural formation of *dibbēr,* a noun that has the meaning of 'divine prophetic revelation', as may be learned from Jer 5:13:[38] "the prophets shall prove mere wind, and the *dibbēr* [divine *word*] is not in them." The "words" of the Decalogue were therefore conceived not as the other laws of the Pentateuch but as divine commands given by revelation, different altogether from the "laws," which could be enforced by an earthly court.

The commandments are formulated in the second person singular, as if they were directed personally to each and every member of the community. Philo astutely indicated that an individual might evade a command given to a whole group, "since he takes the multitude as a cover for disobedience" (*On the Decalogue,* 30); this is not the case with a command addressed to the individual. Philo thus stresses the I-Thou relationship, whose importance is expressed in the writings of Martin Buber.[39] Buber did, in fact, apply the idea to the Decalogue, but he did not use the literary-critical criterion with respect to the character and origin of the apodictic style of biblical law.[40] A. Alt's distinction between the casuistic and apodictic forms of biblical legislation has deepened the understanding of the style of biblical law. He pointed out the uniqueness of the apodictic style, and more precisely the peculiarity of the prohibitive and prescriptive commandments in the legislation of the Bible.[41] Unlike the casuistic style typical of both ancient Near Eastern and modern law, the apodictic formulation, either negative or affirmative, is alien to the

[37] A. B. Ehrlich, *Randglossen zur hebräischen Bibel* (Leipzig: Hinrichs, 1908), 1:340.

[38] Greenberg, "The Decalogue as Reflected in Biblical Criticism," 67–68; cf. also M. Gruber, "On the 'Ten Commandments'," *Bet Miqra* 88 (1982) 16–21 [Hebrew].

[39] M. Buber, *I and Thou* (New York: Scribner's, 1937). For the development of this work, see R. Horowitz, "The Development of Buber's *I and Thou,*" *Proceedings of the Israel Academy of Sciences* 5:8 (1975).

[40] In *Darko Shel Miqra* (Jerusalem: Bialik, 1964) 100–102 [Hebrew].

[41] Alt, "Die Ursprünge des israelitischen Rechts." Alt included in the apodictic category both commandments formulated in the third person and declarations in the participial form (one who hits . . . etc.). Later studies further sharpened distinctions, showing that the commandments in the second person cannot be placed on the same plane with the above-mentioned commandments; cf. my article "The Origin of the Apodictic Law," *Vetus Testamentum* 23 (1973) 63–65.

legal sphere. It seems now that it originated in a covenantal ritual in which the king stood before his subjects and imposed upon them their duties.[42] The Decalogue is indeed considered as the obligations of the king, who appears personally, as it were, before his subjects, and imposes upon them his commandments.

The Decalogue is not a set of abstract moral rules like those found in other law-corpuses, such as "love your neighbor as yourself" (Lev 19:18), "You too must befriend the stranger" (Deut 10:19),[43] "Justice, justice shall you pursue" (Deut 16:20); accordingly, there is no justification for the claim that the Decalogue constitutes the epitome of Israelite morality. The Decalogue is, rather, a fundamental list of concrete commands applicable to every Israelite, comprising the essence of God's demands from his confederates. The first part of the list expresses the people of Israel's special connection with their God. This relationship requires connection with their God, a relationship that requires exclusive loyalty (as opposed to the multiple loyalty of idolators), the prohibition of sculptured images and of the false swearing by God's name, and the obligation to observe the Sabbath and to honor parents. The second part of the list has a socio-moral character and includes the prohibition of murder, adultery, theft, false witness, and coveting of another's wife and property.

Honoring parents is well suited to serve as a connecting link between the two sets of commandments, those dealing with human-God relations and those dealing with human-human relations, since father and mother belong to an authority higher, and they constitute an authority to be respected, similar to God and king. To be sure, an offense against one of these three authorities, God, king, and father and mother, is punishable by death; cf. the curse of God and king (in the Naboth story) and curse of father and mother (Exod 21:15, 17).

Philo indeed says that the first set of enactments (i.e., the first five commandments), begins with God, the father and maker of all, and ends with parents, who copy God's nature by begetting living persons (*On the Decalogue,* 61). In another place he says that the commandment of honoring the parents was placed on the borderline between the two sets of five: it is the last of the first set, in which the most sacred injunctions are given; and it adjoins the second set, which contains the duties of human to human. He explains that the reason for this is that the parents by their nature stand on the borderline

[42] Weinfeld, ibid., 70–71.

[43] Deut 10:19 is apparently drawn from Lev 19:34: "The stranger who resides with you shall be to you as one of your citizens; you shall love him as yourself, for you were strangers in the land of Egypt."

between the mortal and the immortal (*On the Decalogue,* 107). Similarly, the Rabbis compare honoring parents with honoring God ("Sifra to Leviticus" [tractate *Kedoshim* §1]).

The medieval commentator Ibn Ezra discerned a gradation in the second set of injunctions: first is murder, which entails destruction of body; second is adultery, which is violating another's body; then comes taking another's property by force; afterwards, crime against another's property not by physical force, but by mouth; and finally comes coveting, which is neither by force nor by mouth, but through mere intention.

Other Law Collections that Resemble the Decalogue

In the framework of their investigation of the Decalogue, scholars have often compared these commandments to other collections of laws and instructions in the Bible,[44] but it is apparent that none of these collections possess the same uniqueness that characterizes the Decalogue. Consider here the most prominent of these collections.

Leviticus 19

A set of commandments similar to the Decalogue is also found in the Pentateuch in Leviticus 19, the only chapter of the Holiness Code (Leviticus 17-26) that contains a combination of religious and moral laws such as those of the Decalogue.[45] The other chapters of this code are not so heterogeneous; each chapter treats a specific law.

It must be admitted that the common denominator of all the laws in this chapter is the idea of holiness, nevertheless it is clear that the chapter as a whole is based on the Decalogue. The Rabbis, in fact, learned from Lev 19:1 ("Speak to the *whole* Israelite congregation") that this chapter was proclaimed in full assembly (*bĕhiqāhēl*).[46] Indeed, the revelation on Mount Sinai is called 'the day of the Assembly' (*yôm haqāhāl*; Deut 9:10, 14; 18:16, and see below). In the later midrashic discussions are indications of the connection of this

[44] See the preface of Stamm and Andrew, *The Ten Commandments in Recent Research,* 22-75 and the references there.

[45] For an analysis of this chapter, see B. Schwartz, "Leviticus 19: A Literary Commentary to a Pentateuchal Legal Passage" (M.A. Thesis, Jerusalem, 1980 [Hebrew]).

[46] Attributed to Rabbi Ḥiyya in "Sifra to Leviticus" (tractate *Kedoshim* §1) and "Leviticus Rabbah" 24:5 (*Midrash Wayyikra Rabbah,* ed. M. Margulies [Jerusalem: Ministry of Education and Culture and the American Academy for Jewish Research, 1953-60] 647). The homily is influenced by Exod 35:1: "Moses then convoked the whole Israelite community." See also Schwartz, "Leviticus 19," 26.

chapter to the Decalogue: "Why was this proclaimed in full assembly, because the essential parts of the Torah hang on it. Rabbi Levi said: 'Because the ten commandments are included in it'."[47]

Indeed, Leviticus 19 opens with a reference to the fifth, fourth, first, and second commandments of the Decalogue:

> You shall each fear his mother and his father, and keep my Sabbaths: I the Lord am your God. Do not turn to idols or make molten gods for yourselves: I the Lord am your God (vv 3-4).[48]

The reference is chiastic (i.e., in reverse order), as is common with quotations from (and reference to) other texts.[49] The author opens with the fifth commandment (honoring parents), continues with the fourth (Sabbath), and concludes with the second (idolatry). Even within the sentence he changes the order of the components: the object precedes the predicate (not "you shall [each] fear his father and mother," but "[each] his father and mother shall you fear"; and similarly also concerning the Sabbath). Even the order of the objects themselves is interchanged (not "his father and mother," but "his mother and father").

These three topics recur, with slight variations, toward the end of this section, in vv 30-32: observance of Sabbath, appealing to ghosts and to soothsayers, and respecting the elderly.[50] That two of these topics (Sabbath and idolatry) conclude the Holiness Code in Lev 26:1-2 testifies to their central importance in the world-view of the author.[51]

In the continuation of chap. 19 are found commandments concerning theft, false witness, and oaths (vv 11-12). The Rabbis found allusions in this chapter to murder:[52] "Do not stand against the blood of your neighbor" (v 16);[53] and adultery: "Do not degrade your

[47] See the rabbinic sources cited in n. 46. Cf. the similar phrasing in Matt 22:40 (concerning the commandments "Love the Lord" and "Love your neighbor as yourself"): "On these two commandments hang [*krematai*] all the law and the prophets."

[48] On the relation between "fear" and "honor," see n. 23 above.

[49] See M. Seidel, *Hiqrei Miqra*, 1978: 1-97 [Hebrew].

[50] On the structural-stylistic similarity of vv 30-32 to vv 3-4, see Schwartz, "Leviticus 19," 92-94. Honoring parents and honoring the elderly are included by Philo (*On the Decalogue*, 165-67) in the fifth commandment.

[51] Note that Ezekiel constructs his admonition in chap. 20 around these two sins: idolatry and desecration of the Sabbath (vv 16, 18-20, 24).

[52] See "Leviticus Rabbah," 24:5.

[53] This law follows an injunction against slander (*hlk rkyl*) and it seems then that standing against someone's blood here means being involved in a plot against somebody by endangering his or her life; cf. Ezek 22:9: "slanderers [*ʾnšy rkyl*] were amidst you to shed blood."

daughter and make her a harlot" (v 29). It is possible that "You shall not commit adultery" is also the basis for the laws of mixing of kinds (*kilʾayim*), having intercourse with a slavegirl, and the law of *ʿorlah* 'uncircumcised fruits' (first fruits of the tree) contained in this chapter (vv 25–29)? In Deut 22:9ff. the laws forbidding mixture of kinds are found next to laws on adultery;[54] this may explain the proximity of the laws on mixture of kinds and intercourse with a slavegirl in Lev 19:19–22. It seems probable that the law on "uncircumcised fruits" was attached to these laws by way of concatenation, a common way of arranging laws in the ancient Near East.[55] If the assumption of S. A. Kaufman regarding the connection between the falsification of measures and weights in Deut 25:13–16 and "You shall not covet" is correct, then Leviticus 19 concludes in a way similar to the Decalogue (cf. vv 35–36).[56]

It should be added that like the Decalogue, which opens with the self-presentation of God, thus conferring authority to the laws that follow, the commandments of Leviticus 19 similarly open with "I the Lord am your God" (v 2), and this formula is repeatedly affixed to the various laws of the chapter.

In view of all this, it seems clear that Leviticus 19 fills a gap in the priestly literature of the Pentateuch. In contrast to the deuteronomic legislation, which repeats the Decalogue as it appears in the book of Exodus, the Decalogue is not found in the priestly legislation, even though it explicitly declares that it transmits the laws and rules given by the Lord "through Moses on Mount Sinai between himself and the Israelite people" (Lev 26:46; cf. 27:34). The absence of any reference to the Decalogue in the priestly legislation gives the impression that the main point is lacking. Accordingly, Leviticus 19 comes to fill this lack by giving us a "Decalogue" in a reworked and expanded form of its own.[57]

[54] According to Kaufman, "The Structure of the Deuteronomic Law," 138–39, the whole legal section in Deut 22:9–23:19 relates to "you shall not commit adultery." The laws of this group are: the mixing of sorts, forbidden sexual relations, the exclusion of groups from religious communion with Israel (23:1–9), purity of the camp (23:10–15), and cultic prostitution (23:18–19)—all of which relate to sexual matters.

[55] On this phenomenon, see S. M. Paul, *Studies in the Book of the Covenant in the Light of Cuneiform and Biblical Law* (Vetus Testamentum supplement 18; Leiden: Brill, 1970) 106f., and Kaufman, "The Structure of the Deuteronomic Law," 115.

[56] Kaufman, ibid., 143–44.

[57] See Abrabanel's comments on Leviticus 19: "What is correct is that God ordered Moses to convoke the whole Israelite community that he warn them concerning these commandments and remind them of the Ten Commandments and the principal laws, since all this was preparation for the making of a covenant which is written at the end of this book in the section '*ʾim beḥuqotai*.' The Ten Commandments are not mentioned

Yet it should be emphasized that though this chapter is essentially a variation of the Decalogue, it does not replace it. Substantially, it is different from the Decalogue itself. As I have said, the main characteristic of the Decalogue is its applicability to each and every individual regardless of circumstances. This is not the case in Leviticus 19. Except for the laconic laws (vv 3-4, 11, 13), which are paralleled in the Decalogue, all the other laws in this chapter are contingent upon the special circumstances in which they were given. The law of *piggūl* 'unclean sacrificial objects' (vv 5-8) relates merely to one who sacrifices a well-being offering; the law of gifts for the poor (vv 9-10) obligates the landowner only; the warning against perverting justice (vv 15-16) concerns only the judge; the laws against mixed kind (v 19) concern a field or vineyard owner. The same holds true for the law of the ravished slavegirl (vv 20-22) and the law of forbidden fruits (vv 23-25). The remaining commandments concerning idolatrous practices and the like (vv 26-29) are also accompanied by a detailed statement of the circumstantial background, and accordingly they deviate from the "categorical imperative" characteristic of the Decalogue, as I have shown above (pp. 15-16). The sections on hatred in one's heart and love of one's neighbor (vv 17-18) are essentially parentic and constitute an appeal to the conscience. As I have emphasized, there is no place for such in the Decalogue, which contains realistic rules devoid of abstraction. Finally, unlike the Decalogue, which does not include ritual laws at all (see below), Leviticus 19 does contain such laws (vv 5-8, 21-22, 24-25). Accordingly, this chapter cannot be placed on the same plane with the Decalogue.

Deuteronomy 27:15-26

This collection of "curses" contains warnings whose content (idolatry, incest, murder, dishonor of parents) somewhat coincides with the provisions of the Decalogue, but on the other hand differs from the Decalogue in its orientation, form, and character.

These warnings are not obligations imposed on the whole community but are aimed rather at those who commit their crimes in secret. This is the common denominator of this chapter, as Ibn Ezra and others have observed. This chapter treats transgressions that are generally committed in secret, in a way difficult to discover, such as adultery (vv 20-23), trespassing against and misleading a blind person

---

as they were mentioned and given to Israel, because they do not come nor are they mentioned here in order to announce them, as they were given to Israel, but . . . only to be explained here. . . ."

(vv 17–18), dishonoring parents (v 16),[58] perverting justice and taking bribes (vv 19, 25). As for the two offenses generally not committed in private (idolatry, v 15, and murder, v 24), the explicit focus here is only on those committing such crimes in secret (*bstr*). What is dealt with here is a cultic ceremony that purges the community of criminals over whom it has no control, and accordingly the punishment is transferred to the authority of God. By receiving a curse, the offender is excommunicated from the community, thereby diverting the collective punishment of the entire community.[59]

No categorical commandments here (as in the Decalogue) lack circumstances and details of punishment. On the contrary, the character of the offense is described in detail, the accompanying punishment being simply "cursed be." Similarly, warnings are directed to landowners (v 17) and those standing trial (vv 19, 25). This is unlike the Decalogue, whose commandments apply to each and every individual of the community (see p. 10 above). Needless to say, from the aspect of form and style, Deut 27:15–26 greatly differs from the Decalogue. Unlike its apodictic commandments, "you shall" and "you shall not," we find here the present participle form is found, along with the prefixed "cursed be." This form is similar to the commands of Exod 21:12–17 ("He who strikes . . . shall be put to death," etc.), also formed with the present participle plus punishment.[60]

Ezekiel 18 and 22

Ezek 18:5ff. contains a set of basic moral-religious obligations that resemble the Decalogue. The passage deals with a righteous man who does what is just and right:

> He does not eat on the mountains [a pagan practice], he does not raise his eyes to the idols, he does not commit adultery, he does not lie with a menstruous woman, he returns the debtor's pledge, he does not steal and does not cheat, he does not lend at interest, he abstains from evil and executes true justice between man and man, and moreover, he even gives bread to the hungry and clothing to the naked (vv 15–17).

[58] *mqlh ʾbyw wʾmw.* On the difference between *mqll* 'curse' and *mqlh* 'dishonoring', see above, pp. 7–8.

[59] From the religious aspect the ceremony fits the ancient, pre-monarchic period when the community felt a collective religious responsibility and the existence of one wrongdoer in their midst could have endangered the whole community (cf. the story of Achan in Joshua 7).

[60] See my treatment of this issue in "The Origin of the Apodictic Law," 63–65.

Even though certain details here correspond to the Decalogue (idolatry, adultery, and theft), it should be noted that certain moral virtues (the giving of bread and clothing to the needy) appear here and in wisdom literature and the prophets (e.g., Isa 58:7), but not in the laws of the Pentateuch. Also, this passage mentions the lending with interest and adjudication, matters intended for property owners and judges, not for everyone. This is unlike the Decalogue, whose commandments are intended for all. It should be added that murder is not mentioned here, an indication that this passage also does not deal with fundamental human obligations, as do those of the Decalogue.

Alongside these moral issues are found cultic matters, such as "eating on the mountain" and lying with a menstruous woman (v 6), that are not found in the Decalogue. The list is characterized by a beginning and ending that define, in effect, the person who avoids these transgressions: "If a man is righteous and does what is just and right" (v 5), "he is righteous, such a man shall live" (v 9). What is dealt with here, therefore, are the qualities of a righteous person who not only refrains from evil deeds but also is benevolent to the poor. In this respect this list is similar to lists of moral-religious virtues in Psalms 15 and 24 (discussed below) intended for those who wish to approach the Temple precincts and the sphere of the Divine.[61]

From the aspect of form as well, this list is different from the Decalogue in that, in contrast to the latter's categorical formulation with no elaboration, in Ezekiel 18 the matters are defined and detailed.

A similar list is found in Ezek 22:6–12, which contains even more items corresponding to the Decalogue than found in Ezekiel 18, such as Sabbath and honoring parents (vv 7–8) and bloodshed and incest (vv 9–11). But alongside these are bribery and fraud (vv 7, 12), interest (v 12), as well as matters of sancta and cult (vv 8, 9) and purity (v 10). In fact, there is a considerable correspondence here to Leviticus 19. This list begins with the matter of honoring parents (v 7), similar to the opening in Lev 19:3. After the exhortation against exploiting a stranger and defrauding an orphan or widow (cf. Lev 19:33–34), there follows: "You have despised my Holy things and profaned my Sabbaths" (v 8); this is essentially the same as the commandment of Lev 19:30: "You shall keep my Sabbath and venerate my sancta."[62] The

[61] See my article "Instructions for Temple Visitors in the Bible and in Ancient Egypt," *Studies in History and Literature of Ancient Egypt* (ed. S. Groll; Scripta Hierosolymitana 28; Jerusalem: Magnes, 1982) 224–50.

[62] *mqdšy* is not necessarily the Temple; it often indicates holy objects in general. See, e.g., Lev 21:23; Num 18:29.

next sentence, "informers in your midst were intent on shedding blood" (v 9), is but an allusion to Lev 19:16: "Do not spread calumny about your fellows. Do not stand against the blood of your neighbor," referring to slander and bloodshed.[63]

Like Leviticus 19, this list also does not represent a compilation like the Decalogue.[64] Here, matters of cult and purity are mentioned—matters that are wholly absent from the Decalogue. Moreover, here are found, as in chap. 18, lending with interest and bribery, directed at property owners and people of standing, not at each and every person, as in the Decalogue. In fact, the prophet explicitly states that the list of sins is aimed at the princes of Israel (v 6). And here also the formulation of the items is not absolute and categorical, as in the Decalogue, but includes details and definitions. It may be that, as with Leviticus 19, the Decalogue stands in the background of this list in Ezekiel 22, but the prophet developed his exhortations far beyond the scope of the Decalogue and adapted them to the particular reality that applied to the princes of Israel.[65]

Psalms 15 and 24, Isaiah 33

S. Mowinckel found a relation between the Decalogue and Psalms 15, 24, and Isaiah 33:14-15, which he terms "entry liturgies."[66] In these psalms the entry and dwelling in the House of the Lord are conditional upon the fulfillment of moral commandments, such as innocence and purity of heart; avoiding slander, false oaths, and contempt of friends and relatives; honoring the God-fearing; not accepting bribes or taking interest. These lists open with a question: "Who may ascend the mountain of the Lord?" (Psalm 24), "Who may stay in your tent?" (Psalm 15), "Who of us can dwell with the devouring fire?" (Isa 33:14). Accordingly, Mowinckel sees in these psalms a reflection of the entry ceremony into the Temple. In his view, in a later period these moral demands—under the influence of

[63] Cf. n. 53 above.

[64] Cf. Greenberg, *Ezekiel* 1 (Anchor Bible 22; Garden City, NY: Doubleday, 1983) 342ff. Greenberg rightly stresses the Ezekielian priestly character of the lists of virtues in Ezekiel 18 and 22.

[65] Bloodshed here is not actual murder but actions of rulers that lead to murder. Most instructive is the sentence "Slanderous men in your midst were intent on shedding blood" which is parallel to Lev 19:16 (see n. 53 above). In Leviticus 19 the sentence is incorporated in a set of laws dealing with judges (vv 15-16) and it refers to judges whose reliance on slander might lead to blood guilt. On the relations between judge and officer see Weinfeld, "Judge and Officer in Ancient Israel and in the Ancient Near East," *Israel Oriental Studies* 7 (1977) 65-88.

[66] S. Mowinckel, *Le décalogue* (Paris: Félix Alcan, 1927) 141ff.

prophecy—were removed from the sphere of the cult, and thus the way was paved for the collection of the Decalogue as we know it.

But there is, in fact, no justification for the comparison of these psalms with the Decalogue. These psalms mention only refined moral demands; gross sins such as murder, theft, and adultery, found in the Decalogue, are not referred to at all. Unlike the Decalogue, which contains national-religious laws, these psalms are on a purely universalistic level. As I have shown elsewhere, these psalms came to define the "righteous" who are entitled to dwell in God's tent, not the average Israelite.[67] The fact that identical demands are found on the doorposts of the gates of Egyptian temples explains the questions at the opening of the lists in the Bible: "who will dwell," "who will ascend," etc. These psalms, then, are of general moral demands, not a set of obligations cast upon every Israelite, like those of the Decalogue or the similar ones of Leviticus 19 and Ezekiel 18 and 22. The stylistic features as well are completely different from those of the Decalogue and the other lists.

Book of the Dead and *Šurpu*

The commandments of the Decalogue used to be compared to the "negative confession" contained in chap. 125 of the Egyptian *Book of the Dead* and to the Mesopotamian *Šurpu* incantations.[68] However, these compositions, too, differ significantly from the Decalogue in both form and content. As to form, the *Book of the Dead* is a sort of confession of the deceased before entrance into the next world, whereas the *Šurpu* are a set of incantations meant to free the sick from every possible sin and thus bring about their recovery. As to content, the sins of the *Book of the Dead* include murder, adultery, and theft, but also lesser transgressions, such as the falsifying of weights and measures, slander, and insulting one's neighbor. Alongside these are cultic sins, such as cursing the gods, negligence in the divine service, desecration, and sacrilege. Similarly, the sins of the *Šurpu* incantations include murder, adultery, theft, false oath, gossip, hypocrisy, oppression, falsifying weights and measures, trespassing, not clothing the naked. Also included are cultic sins such as eating forbidden foods, desecration of sancta, contact with the banned, and the like. These are, then, clearly literary efforts to encompass every possible

[67] See my article mentioned in n. 61.

[68] On the *Book of the Dead*, see M. Lichtheim, *Ancient Egyptian Literature* (Berkeley: University of California, 1976), 2:124–32; on *Šurpu*, see E. Reiner, *Šurpu: A Collection of Sumerian and Akkadian Incantations* (*Archiv für Orientforschung* supplement 11; Graz, 1958; repr. Osnabrück: Biblioverlag, 1970) 13ff. (Tablet II).

sin; there is little similarity with the collection of commandments of the Decalogue.

The collection of the Decalogue is thus different from all the other collections of commandments. It is distinguished by incorporating a set of concise basic obligations directed at a member of the Israelite community, which is connected by a special covenant with God. This set is a sort of Israelite creed. In this respect it is similar to the *Shema*ᶜ, a declaration also composed of an easily remembered verse that contains an epitome of the monotheistic idea and serves as an external sign of identification for the monotheistic believers. It is no accident that both the Decalogue and the *Shema*ᶜ occur close to one another in Deuteronomy and were read together in the Temple (*m. Tamid* 5:1).

Just as the monotheistic principle expressed in the *Shema*ᶜ is realized in many legal particulars (such as the destruction of idols, the ban or excommunication of inciters to worship foreign gods, the excommunicated city) detailed in the various law codes, so also the religious and moral principles of the Decalogue take form in various laws of the Pentateuch. As I have shown, attempts to construct units and sections of laws around the Decalogue, which become essentially its commentary, are also found in biblical literature. Jewish philosophers like Philo and Saadia Gaon have indeed tried to base all the Pentateuch's commandments on the Decalogue.[69]

The Decalogue was solemnly uttered by every faithful Israelite as the God of Israel's fundamental claim on the congregation of Israel, and it became the epitome of Israelite moral and religious heritage. That is why, among all the laws, the list of commandments contained in the Decalogue came to be regarded as primary and basic in the establishment of the relationship between God and Israel. Only the Decalogue was heard as directly spoken by God, and accordingly it is the Decalogue that serves as the *testimony* of the relationship between Israel and its God.

The Renewal of the Obligation— The Decalogue in Worship

In the last fifty years the view has become increasingly accepted that the event at which God pronounced his words at Sinai was not

[69] On Philo, see Y. Amir, "The Ten Commandments according to Philo of Alexandria," *The Decalogue throughout the Generations* (ed. B. Z. Segal; Jerusalem: Magnes, 1985) 95ff. [Hebrew]; generally, see E. E. Urbach, *The Sages* (Jerusalem: Magnes, 1979) 315ff.

regarded as a once and for all event but as an occurrence that repeated itself whenever the people of Israel assembled and swore allegiance to their God. The motivation for this view was given by Mowinckel in his book, *Le Décalogue*. In the course of an investigation of Psalms 50 and 81, he concluded that Israelite assemblies were held at which the revelation at Sinai was reenacted and celebrated. These psalms, which allude to covenant rites and a festival day, quote the opening of the Decalogue: "I am the Lord your God and you shall have no other gods," etc. (50:7, 81:10–11). In Psalm 50 there is reference to three of the last commandments: theft, adultery, and false witness (vv 18–20). Psalm 50 is composed against a background of God's revelation in Zion (v 2), his appearing in a storm, and, while sounding true justice for the pious, making a covenant with a sacrifice (vv 5–6);[70] all this resembles the giving of the Law at Mount Sinai by means of a sacrificial covenant (Exod 24:1–8). Psalm 81 is composed against the background of the festival, accompanied by the trumpeting of the Shofar while proclaiming that God set up the law and justice and testimonies for Israel (vv 4–5).

If evidence of both psalms is combined with the giving of law and justice (including quotations from the Decalogue and the revelation at the festival) the assumption that these psalms relate to a festival in which the event of the giving of the Law is celebrated, as Mowinckel assumed, is indeed reinforced. However, these psalms were not meant to mark the event of covenant renewal but to admonish the people. Psalm 50 admonishes a people against making sacrifices while disregarding God's commandments (vv 8–13); it likewise admonishes the wicked hypocrite who indeed bears the words of the covenant on her or his lips but does not uphold it (vv 16–21).[71] Similarly, Psalm 81 mentions the giving of the Law and the Decalogue in order to admonish the people who do not hear God's voice and do not walk in his ways (vv 12–16). Reproofs of this type based on the Decalogue are also found in the prophecies of Hosea and Jeremiah.[72] Both prophets complain about the breaking of the basic commandments of the

[70] "The heavens proclaimed His righteousness, for he is a God who judges" (Ps 50:6). Justice and righteousness in this context of a covenant refers to the giving of the Law, cf. Ps 99:4, "You who worked judgment and righteousness in Jacob," which appears there alongside *testimony and law* given to Moses and Aaron (vv 6–7); see Weinfeld, *Justice and Righteousness in Israel and the Nations* (Jerusalem: Magnes, 1985) 109–12 [Hebrew].

[71] See B. Schwartz, "Psalm 50: Its Subject, Form, and Place," *Shnaton* 3 (1979) 77ff. [Hebrew].

[72] Cf. F. I. Andersen and D. N. Freedman, *Hosea* (Anchor Bible 24; Garden City, NY: Doubleday, 1980) 336–37.

Decalogue and do so in proximity to polemics against the priests and sacrifices. Hosea complains about the absence of "knowledge of God" in the land (4:1), expressed in the verse "[False] swearing, lying, murdering, stealing, and committing adultery" (4:2). The prophet then proceeds to condemn the priests who reject the knowledge of God and forget his law, while eating the sin offering (vv 6-8). Similarly, Jeremiah admonishes the people when they come to the Temple gates to worship the Lord (7:2), while he refers to five of the Ten Commandments: "Will you steal and murder and commit adultery and swear falsely, and sacrifice to Baal, and follow other gods?"[73] Later on the prophet turns to polemics against the sacrifices:

> Thus said the Lord of Hosts, the God of Israel: Add your burnt offerings to your other sacrifices and eat the meat! For when I freed your fathers from the land of Egypt, I did not speak with them or command them concerning burnt offerings or sacrifice. But this is what I commanded them: Do my bidding, that I may be your God and you may be my people; walk only in the way that I enjoin upon you, that it may go well with you (Jer 7:21-23).

I have shown elsewhere that this statement of Jeremiah that the people of Israel were not ordered to make sacrifices when they left Egypt can be understood only on the assumption that Jeremiah was referring to the Decalogue, which, to be sure, does not mention sacrifices at all.[74] According to Deut 5:19ff., God spoke only the Decalogue to the people of Israel at Mount Sinai, whereas the other laws were then spoken to Moses only and he made them known to the people close to his death in the desert of Moab.

Psalms 50 and 81, which relate to the event of the law-giving at Sinai, are in the main psalms of admonition and thus are similar to the admonitions of Jeremiah and Hosea, which appear against the background of the Decalogue. It seems to me that the combination of revelatory event and reproof in these psalms can be explained in that the reprovers chose to voice their reprimands precisely at the festival that celebrates the giving of the Law and during which the Decalogue was publicly read as part of the festivities. In relation to the reading of the Decalogue in an assembly, the prophets and poets admonish the hypocrisy of the people who do not practice what they preach (cf. Ps 50:16-21). Likewise they reject the abundant sacrifices, which are not

[73] On the chiastic correspondence of Jeremiah's words to the Decalogue, see Weiss, *The Bible from Within*, 256-59, and n. 30 above.

[74] Weinfeld, "Jeremiah and the Spiritual Metamorphosis of Israel," *Zeitschrift für die alttestamentliche Wissenschaft* 88 (1976) 52-55.

mentioned at all in the Decalogue.[75] The difference between the prophets and the poets of the psalms is that the former, whose main interest is admonition, have no need to describe the ceremony at which the admonition is voiced, whereas the temple poets, whose main interest is liturgy, describe and exalt the ceremony of covenant renewal and mention alongside it words of reproof concerning those who do not observe the conditions of the covenant. Thus, Psalm 50 opens with the revelation at Zion, in language similar to that of the revelation at Mount Sinai.[76] This demonstrates that the event of revelation was transferred from Sinai to Zion.

The fire and the storm that appear in these psalms are signs of theophany (Ps 50:3, 81:8), and the pious followers who make a covenant with sacrifice (Ps 50:5) call to mind (as already noted) the revelation at Mount Sinai (Exodus 24). Psalm 81 clarifies another side of the picture. The text refers to the historical background of the festival, which celebrates the giving of the Law, "justice" of the God of Jacob, and testimonies to Joseph (81:6).[77] It describes the Exodus from Egypt, the history of the people on their way up to Massah and Meribah, following which description is a quotation from the Decalogue.[78] The sounding of the Shofar mentioned in connection with the giving of law and justice in Jacob (vv 4–5) refers apparently to the Shofar heard at the giving of the Law at Mount Sinai (Exod 19:16, 19) and sounded at the ceremonies of covenant renewal in Israel, as seen in 2 Chr 15:14.[79]

[75] Cf. Amos 5:25: "Did you offer sacrifice and oblation to me those forty years in the wilderness," mentioned in connection with festivals: "I loathe, I spurn your festivals" (v 21).

[76] Compare Deut 33:2, "The Lord came from Sinai . . . he appeared from Mount Paran," with Ps 50:2, "From Zion . . . God appeared."

[77] Compare S. E. Loewenstamm, "The Bearing of Psalm 81 upon the Problem of Exodus," *Eretz-Israel* 5 (1958) 80–82.

[78] "I shall answer you concealed in [*bstr*] a thunder" means an answer in the cloud accompanied with God's thunder and lightning; cf. Ps 18:12–14: "He made darkness his concealment [*strw*] . . . then the Lord thundered from heaven." The answer in the cloud can be interpreted as God's speaking to Moses out of the cloud; see Exod 19:18–19: "Now Mount Sinai was all in smoke . . . and the whole mountain trembled. . . . As Moses spoke, God *answered* him in thunder." Cf. also Ps 99:6–7: "Moses and Aaron . . . when they called to the Lord *he answered them.* He spoke to them in a pillar of cloud—they obeyed his decrees, the law he gave them." However, it is possible that the answer in a cloud may be related to the redemptive events of the Red Sea in Exod 14:20, 24. On the ambiguity of the testing at the waters of Meribah (on the one hand God tests Israel, and on the other hand Israel tests God), see Loewenstamm, "The Bearing of Psalm 81 upon the Problem of the Exodus."

[79] In late Jewish tradition, which knows only sounding the Shofar on Rosh Hashanah, this psalm was, to be sure, related to this festival (*b. Roš Haš.* 8a–b, 34a,

The order of events in Psalm 81 coincides with that of the book of Exodus, where the giving of the Torah comes after Massah and Meribah (Exodus 19 after Exodus 17). If so, the festival reflected here might be Shabuoth, the festival of the giving of the law (as discussed further below).

The linguistic usages found in these psalms in relation to the recital of the Decalogue by God are of great importance:

Psalm 50:7	*Psalm 81:9–10*
Hear, my people, and I will speak, O Israel, and I will instruct you.	Hear, my people, and I will instruct you; Israel, if you would but listen to Me! You shall have no foreign god, you shall not bow to an alien god.
I am God your God.	I am YHWH your God who brought you out of the land of Egypt.

The expressions "hear my people" and "Israel" preceding "I am YHWH your God" recall the declaration "Hear, O Israel! YHWH [is] our God, YHWH is one" in Deut 6:4 and may shed light on the proximity of the *Shema*^{c} to the Decalogue as it appears in Deuteronomy 5 and 6. The combination of *Shema*^{c} with the beginning of the Decalogue is actually reflected in a Jewish liturgical tradition of fourth century B.C.E.:

> From where did Israel get the recital of *Shema*? Rabbi Phinehas the son of Hama said: From the giving of the law at Sinai did Israel get the recital of *Shema*^{c}. You find that the Holy One, blessed be he, opened like this, he said to them: "Hear, O Israel, I am YHWH your God." Then all responded and said: "YHWH [is] our God, YHWH is one," and Moses said: Blessed be the name of his glorious kingdom forever and ever ("Deuteronomy Rabbah" 2:31).

R. Kimmelman (who kindly informed me of this source) suggested that this tradition demonstrates the way *Shema*^{c} was recited in the synagogue at that time. The cantor recited the words ascribed to God: "Hear, O Israel, I am YHWH," etc., while the congregation responded: "YHWH [is] our God, YHWH is one."

Most instructive in the quoted passages from Psalms 50 and 81 is the verb *hē*^{c}*īd* (< ^{c}*wd*). When joining the preposition *b*, the verb usually has the meaning of 'warn', but in certain contexts this

---

etc.), but this is Midrash. In accordance with the Midrash, the motif of sounding the Shofar at the revelation at Mount Sinai (Exod 19:16, 19) penetrated the Rosh Hashana liturgy (the "Atta Nigleita" prayer); see below, n. 114.

verb has the connotation of 'instruct'. Thus in 2 Kgs 17:15 this verb, combined with the noun in plural *ᶜēdwôt* 'testimonies',[80] has undoubtedly the meaning 'to teach/impart', as may be learned from its parallel: "the commands and the covenant imposed upon their fathers." The same applies to Neh 9:34, which reads: "They did not listen to your commandments [*mṣwh*] and to your *ᶜēdwôt*, which you imparted [*hᶜydt*] to them." To be sure, recent studies make it likely that, in addition to the usual meaning of the verb *hᶜyd b* 'warn', this verb indicates the imposing of laws on one hand, and teaching on the other hand.[81] Thus, the connection between law-giving and admonition is also reflected in Psalms 50 and 81. Also, the verb *hzhyr* reflects this double meaning: 'law giving' ("and enjoin [*whzhrt*] upon them the laws and the teaching," Exod 18:20) and 'warning' as well (2 Kgs 6:10, etc.).[82] The connection between law-giving and warning is not without reason, for the essence of a law is in fact a warning against transgressions. It is thus not surprising that admonition is bound up with law-giving in Psalms 50 and 81. This integration is reflected in Jeremiah 11, when the prophet, who is ordered to spread the words of the covenant in Jerusalem (v 6), formulates his words as a threat: "Cursed be the man who will not obey this covenant" (v 3). In this context, the clause "For I repeatedly and persistently warned your fathers [*hᶜd hᶜdty hškm whᶜd*] from the time I brought them out of Egypt to this day, saying, 'Obey my commands'" (v 7) leads me to understand the verb *hᶜyd* here not just to mean 'warning' but also an admonitory command. This speech may be compared with that of Moses in Deut 32:46: "Take to heart all the words with which I have warned you [*mᶜyd bkm*] this day. Enjoin them upon your children, that they may observe faithfully all the terms of this Teaching." These verses together may show that the giving of the Law and admonition are in fact two sides of the same issue, and this accounts for the connection of the two in Psalms 50 and 81.

As demonstrated below,[83] the Festival of Shabuoth served in Second Temple times as an occasion for an 'assembly' (*ᶜaṣeret*) to

[80] The "*Shemaᶜ* Israel" prayer was considered a *testimony* by the Rabbis; see *b. Ber.* 14b.

[81] T. Veijola, "Zur Ableitung und Bedeutung von HEᶜID I im Hebräischen," *Ugarit-Forschungen* 8 (1976) 343f.; B. Couroyer, "Un Égyptianisme dans Ben Sira 4.11," *Revue biblique* 82 (1975) 206ff.

[82] LXX translates *whzhrth* ('enjoin' in Exod 18:20) with the same verb as it translates *hᶜyd* in Ps 50:7 and 81:9: *diamartyromai*. It is interesting to note that the medieval liturgy surrounding the Decalogue was called *azharot* 'enjoinments'. See I. Elbogen, *Der jüdische Gottesdienst in seiner geschichtlichen Entwicklung* (3d ed.; Frankfurt am Main: Kauffmann, 1931; reprinted Hildesheim: Georg Olms, 1962) 217. This term apparently has a long tradition behind it.

[83] See p. 39.

renew and reconfirm the Sinai covenant; this festival was the background of these psalms. Mowinckel sensed the festival rite as the background of these psalms, but because of his fervor to find everywhere a reflection of the New Year holiday, he found it here too, though without any basis. The festival to be envisaged here could well be Pentecost. The Pentateuch does not give a date for the festival of Pentecost, but according to the Book of Jubilees and the writings of the Qumran sect, the festival was celebrated on the fifteenth day of the month (see below). Accordingly, the *ksh* of Ps 81:4 would conform also to the festival of Shabuoth, a festival on which the people annually renew their covenant with their God.[84] The yearly renewal of a covenant is known from the ancient Near East, from the beginning of the second millennium B.C.E. up to the Hellenistic and Roman eras, and is explicitly found in the Qumran "Rule of the Community" in regard to the annual entering of sect members into the covenant (col. 2: 19; see below).[85]

The Tradition of the Decalogue and its Evolution

In endeavoring to reconstruct the development of the tradition of the Decalogue, I propose the following process:

At the dawn of Israelite history the Decalogue was promulgated in its original short form as the foundation document of the Israelite community, written on two stone tablets, which were later called "the tablets of the covenant" or "tablets of the testimony."[86] The tablets

[84] *ksʾ* is the day of the full moon, as seen in Phoenician and Akkadian where *kusiu* means the aureola of the moon, apparently originating from *kasû* III 'to tie [the crown]' (cf. L. Koehler and W. Baumgartner, *Lexicon im Veteris Testamenti Libris* [Leiden: Brill, 1985], s.v. *ksh*). Scholars maintain that the calendar of the Bible and especially the calendar of the Priestly source is identical to that of the book of Jubilees and that of the sect of the Judean desert. Cf., e.g., Jaubert, "Le calendrier des Jubilés et de la secte de Qumrân: ses origines bibliques," *Vetus Testamentum* 3 (1953) 250–64; "Le calendrier des Jubilés et les jours liturgiques de la semaine," *Vetus Testamentum* 7 (1957) 35–61. H. Cazelles ("Sur les origines du calendrier des Jubilés," *Biblica* 43 [1962] 206) even proposed to see *ksʾ* and *ḥdš* in Psalm 81 as parallel concepts, both indicating the day of the full moon.

[85] On the Hellenistic and Roman eras, see my "The Origin of the Apodictic Law: An Overlooked Source," *Vetus Testamentum* 23 (1973) 72 n. 1; and "The Loyalty Oath in the Ancient Near East," *Ugarit-Forschungen* 8 (1976) 393–94.

[86] 'Covenant' (*bĕrît*) and 'testimony' (*ʿdwt*) are parallel; cf. "ark of the covenant"/ "ark of the testimony." The word 'testimony', *ʿdwt,* is etymologically identical with Aramaic *ʿdn* and Akkadian *adê,* both meaning 'covenant'; cf. my article "*bryt,*" *Theological Dictionary of the Old Testament* (ed. G. J. Botterweck and H. Ringgren; Grand Rapids: Eerdmans, 1974–), 2:253–79.

functioned as a testimony to Israel's commitment to observe the commandments inscribed upon them. They were placed in the ark of the covenant, which, together with the cherubim, symbolized God's abode. The cherubim were considered the throne, and the ark God's footstool.[87] Hittite documents contemporary with Moses' time indicate that nations used to place the covenant documents at their gods' feet, that is, at the feet of their divine images.[88]

This analogy to covenant practices in those days explains Moses' breaking of the tablets when he saw the children of Israel worshiping the golden calf. For the nations of the ancient Near East (mainly Mesopotamia), the breaking of the tablet meant the cancellation of the commitment. The classic Mesopotamian expression of this matter is *ṭuppam ḫepû* 'break the tablet' (cf. the Roman *tabulae novae*, which was written after prior obligations were canceled).[89] It is thus likely that Moses did not act out of weakness or anger, but with forethought.[90] The violation of the first two commands of the Decalogue (apostasy and the making of sculptured images) necessarily entailed the breaking of the tablets on which the commands were inscribed.

[87] Cf. M. Haran, "The Ark of the covenant and the Cherubim," *Eretz-Israel* 5 (1958) 87-88 [Hebrew].

[88] So, e.g., in Ramses II's letter to the king of Mirah in the north: "See, the writ of covenant which I have made for the great king of Heth, has been laid at the (storm) god's feet, the great gods will be witnesses to it. . . . And behold, the writ of covenant which the great king of Heth, made for me, has been laid at the god Ra's feet, the great gods will be witnesses to it." B. Meissner, "Die Beziehungen Ägyptens zum Hattireiche nach hattischen Quellen," *Zeitschrift der deutschen morgenländischen Gesellschaft* 72 (1918) 58 [= *KBo* 1 24 rev. 5ff.]. For additional references see V. Korošec, *Hethitische Staatsverträge* (Leipziger Rechtswissenschaftliche Studien 60; Leipzig: Weicher, 1931) 100ff.

[89] See *The Assyrian Dictionary of the Oriental Institute of the University of Chicago* (Chicago: University of Chicago, 1956–), vol. Ḫ, pp. 171-72. It seems to me that this is the origin of the rabbinical expression *šbr*, meaning to annul the validity of a marriage contract or debt. In certain places we can still interpret "breaking" as used by the Rabbis in its plain meaning, such as: "If she said 'I am unclean', she breaks the [ostracon on which the] Ketubah [was written]" (*m. Soṭa* 1:5). In the course of time, when the custom of writing receipts (of debt repayment) developed, this receipt annulling the validity of the commitment was called *šobar* and is derived from the denominative "break" meaning "writing a receipt," cf. the phrase *šwbrt ʾl ktwbth* in *t. Ketub.* 4:11, 9:1. The mishnaic terms for documents, such as *geṭ*, 'bill of divorce' and *šeṭar* 'bill, note', are taken from Akkadian. In my article "The Decalogue: Its Significance and Evolution in Israel's Tradition," *Reflections on the Bible* (ed. E. Hamenachem; Tel-Aviv: Don, 1976), 2:116 n. 17 [Hebrew], I established the Akkadian origin of *šobar*, and only later discovered that A. Gulak, *Das Urkundenwesen im Talmud* (Jerusalem: Mass., 1935) 148 n. 1, came to the same conclusion even though he did not adduce any supporting data from Akkadian literature.

[90] Cf. the rabbinic tradition that Moses preached *a minori ad majus*: "If about Passover, a single commandment, it says 'No uncircumcised person may eat of it,' how

Ibn Ezra correctly perceived this matter in his comment on Exod 32:19: "And from overwhelming zeal Moses broke the tablets which were in his hands like a certificate of evidence, and thus he tore up the certificate of conditions, and this was in view of all of Israel, for thus it is written [i.e., Deut 9:17] 'and I broke them before your eyes'."

It should be assumed that the Decalogue was read in the sanctuaries at ceremonies of covenant renewal;[91] and the people would commit themselves each time anew, as seen in the usual ancient Near Eastern custom of renewing covenants annually.[92] Psalms 50 and 81 do indeed testify to such rituals, as I have tried to show above; and in my view, these rituals took place on the Festival of Shabuoth, the festival of the giving of the Law.

In Second Temple times, the Decalogue was read daily in the Temple, together with the *Shema*ᶜ prayer, close to the time of the offering of the Daily Offering (*m. Tamid* 5:1). In the Nash Papyrus, discovered in Egypt, the Decalogue preceded the *Shema*ᶜ passage, a text that reflects a liturgical form.[93] In phylacteries found at Qumran, the Decalogue is found next to the *Shema*ᶜ, and according to the testimony of Jerome this was the custom in Babylonia up to a late period.[94] Josephus testifies in regard to the Decalogue: "These words it is not permitted us to state explicitly, to the letter" (*Ant.* 3:90), apparently meaning to say that it was forbidden to pronounce them in improper circumstances because of their sanctity.

Rituals of the ancient world may illuminate this process of evolution of the religious custom. In a private sanctuary of the first century B.C.E. in Philadelphia, Asia Minor, the sanctuary's foundation

---

much more the Torah which contains all the commandments" and "R. Yishmael taught, the Holy One, Blessed be he, told him to break them" (*y. Ta*ᶜ*an.* 4:7, 68c and parallels).

[91] Psalm 50 was read in Jerusalem as v 2 shows. On the other hand, Psalm 81 belongs to a northern tradition (cf. "a decree upon Joseph," v 6) and apparently originated in one of the sanctuaries in the north; on northern Psalms, including Psalm 81, which was transferred to Jerusalem after the destruction of Samaria, see N. M. Sarna, "The Psalm Superscriptions and the Guilds," *Studies in Jewish Religious and Intellectual History Presented to Alexander Altmann* (ed. Siegfried Stein and Raphael Loewe; University, Ala.: University of Alabama, 1979) 288ff.

[92] See n. 85 above.

[93] Cf. M. H. Segal, "Papyrus Nash," *Lešonēnu* 15 (1947) 27–36 (reprinted in his *Massoret uBiqqoret*, 227–36 [Hebrew]).

[94] On Qumran, see Y. Yadin, "Tefilin from Qumran," *Eretz-Israel* 9 (1969) 60–85 [Hebrew]; on phylacteries generally, see A. M. Haberman, "The Phylacteries in Antiquity," *Eretz-Israel* 3 (1954) 174–76 [Hebrew].

inscription was discovered;[95] it details the commandments of the goddess Agdistis, to whom the sanctuary was dedicated. The man who initiated the inscription, Dionysius, received as it were a revelation in a dream in which Zeus gave him the commandments written in the inscription. The commandments oblige all this sanctuary's visitors or whoever belongs to this house (*oikos*) to swear to observe them.[96] The commandments are (1) not to destroy an embryo and not to use means to abort a fetus,[97] (2) not to rob, (3) not to murder,[98] (4) not to steal anything, (5) to be loyal [*eunoeîn*] to the sanctuary. If somebody commits (a transgression) or plans (to commit one), he shall not be allowed to and it will not be kept silent, but they will make it known and punish him.[99] (6) A man shall not lie with a strange woman except for his wife . . . not with a boy and not with a virgin. The last item is:

> A man or a woman who committed one of these transgressions shall not enter this sanctuary, since here great gods sit [on their seats] who watch against these transgressions and will not tolerate transgressors. . . .[100] The gods shall pardon the obedient and grant them blessings, and they will hate those who transgress [against the commandments] and impose upon them great punishments. . . .[101] The men and women who are

[95] O. Weinreich, *Stiftung und Kultsatzungen eines Privatheiligtums in Philadelphia in Lydien* (Sitzungsberichte der Heidelberger Akademie der Wissenschaften, Philogisch-historische Klasse, 1919:16; Heidelberg: Winter, 1919).

[96] For a discussion of a parallel to these instructions in the teaching of the twelve apostles (Didache), see Weinfeld, "The Genuine Jewish Attitude toward Abortion," *Zion* 42 (1977) 129–42 [Hebrew].

[97] On this issue, see my "The Genuine Jewish Attitude toward Abortion."

[98] Based on the reconstruction *m[ē harpagmon mē] phonon*. However, in F. Sokołowski's edition, the reconstruction is *m[ē allo ti paido]phonon* (*Lois sacrées de l'Asie mineure* [Paris: Boccard, 1955] 20ff., no. 20, 11); if so the sentence relates to infanticide. However, the reading of Keil-Parmerstein, on which Weinreich based his *Stiftung und Kultsatzungen*, has been generally accepted. See also A. D. Nock, "Early Gentile Christianity and its Hellenistic Background," *Essays on the Trinity and the Incarnation*, ed. A. E. J. Rawlinson (London: Longmans, 1928) 72ff. (= Nock, *Essays on Religion and the Ancient World* [ed. Z. Stewart; Cambridge: Harvard University, 1972], 1:65ff.).

[99] For the understanding of *eunoeîn* as loyalty, see my "The Loyalty Oath in the Ancient Near East," 383–84; for references on the extraditing of violators ("make it known") of the covenant and agitators in covenant documents (cf. Deuteronomy 13), see Weinfeld, ibid., 389–90.

[100] Compare in the Decalogue: "A jealous God visiting guilt . . . for the Lord will not clear . . ." and in Josh 24:19: "Because he is a holy God, a jealous God, he will not forgive your transgressions and your sins."

[101] Compare the blessings and curses at the conclusions of covenants in the Bible, and see Weinfeld, "The Loyalty Oath in the Ancient Near East," 397–99.

certain of their uprightness shall touch the inscribed pillar every month and year at the time of offering sacrifices.[102]

Without relating to the Decalogue, A. D. Nock compared this inscription to Pliny's epistle to Traianus (*Ep. ad Traianus* 10:96:7) concerning the Christians who get up at dawn (*ante lucem*) in order to sing canons (*invicem*, a sort of precentor and choir),[103] afterwards they commit themselves with an oath (*sacramentum*) not to steal, not to commit adultery, not to betray confidence, and not to deny any deposit.[104] After Nock's article, the assumption was raised that Pliny's epistle referred to the Decalogue.[105] To be sure, as known, the reading of the Decalogue and the *Shema*ᶜ prayer every morning were considered acceptance of the yoke of the heavenly kingdom, a kind of commitment by oath.[106]

Even though the sanctuary of Philadelphia in Asia Minor dates from the first century B.C.E., no doubt the custom discovered there has

[102] This is a sort of "swearing on the Bible" or other holy object that was customary in the ancient Near East and Greece. See my comments, "Greek and Roman Covenantal Terms and their Affinities to the East," *Lešonénu* 38 (1977) 232 and n. 5 there.

[103] Nock, "The Christian Sacramentum in Pliny and a Pagan Counterpart," *Classical Review* 38 (1924) 58f. In "Early Gentile Christianity" Nock indicates that O. Casel ("Zum Worte *sacramentum*," *Jahrbuch für Liturgiewissenschaft* 4 [1924] 285) already saw before Nock the parallel in Pliny's epistles. The epistle dates from 112 B.C.E.; see A. N. Sherwin-White, *The Letters of Pliny* (Oxford: Oxford University, 1966) 327ff. In my opinion this singing is akin to the Psalms (*Pĕsûkê dĕ-Zimrâ*) recited before the *Shema*ᶜ and its blessings in the daily liturgy (see my "Traces of *kedushat yoẓer* and *pesukey de-zimra* in the Qumran Literature and in Ben-Sira," *Tarbiz* 45 [1976] 23ff.). A good example of the worshiper's response in morning psalms is Psalm 145 from Qumran: after every verse is the response, "Blessed be the Lord and blessed be his name for ever and ever" (see ibid., 24–25).

[104] For *sacramentum* meaning an oath of allegiance in a religious context see Weinfeld, "The Loyalty Oath in the Ancient Near East," 406–7. The oath reads: *Ne furta, ne latrocinia, ne adulteria commiterent, ne fidem follerent, ne depositum apellati abnegarent.*

[105] C. J. Kraemer, "Pliny and the Early Church Service," *Classical Philology* 29 (1934) 393ff.; S. L. Mohler, "The Bithynian Christians Again," *Classical Philology* 30 (1935) 167f.; and C. C. Coulter, "Further Notes on the Ritual of the Bithynian Christians," *Classical Philology* 35 (1940) 60ff. The last two items in the oath are apparently parallel to the two last commandments: "You shall not bear false witness against your neighbor" and "You shall not covet." In Mark 10:19 *mē aposterēsēs* means "You shall not defraud," which was found in Lev 19:13 in a unit based on the Decalogue; cf. also Lev 5:21, which deals with abnegation of a deposit or a pledge. According to a possible interpretation all these items are included in "You shall not covet," discussed above (cf. also Coulter, "Ritual of the Bithynian Christians," 60f.).

[106] See the discussion in my "The Loyalty Oath in the Ancient Near East," 406ff.

roots in an ancient Near Eastern religious tradition.[107] This ancient custom can serve as a sort of background for understanding the evolution of the tradition of the Decalogue in Israel. I assume that the beginning of the tradition of the Decalogue is grounded in a reality similar to that found in Philadelphia in Asia Minor. The old community was unified around the ark, which contained the tablets of the covenant. The believers were sworn to observe the Decalogue written on the tablets, given by revelation to Moses, the founder of the community and its cult. Dionysius of the Philadelphian sanctuary thus appears to have fulfilled a role parallel to that of Moses in Israel.

The tablets containing the Decalogue thus constituted a kind of binding foundation-scroll of the Israelite community (a constitution?). With the disappearance of the ark and the tablets of the covenant, the Decalogue was freed from its connection to the concrete symbols to which it was previously attached. At festive assemblies and every morning in the sanctuary, the Decalogue was customarily read, and all those present would commit themselves to them by covenant and oath.[108]

On the importance of the tablets inscribed with the traditions under discussion it is worth recalling here Pausanias's story about a holy place in Greece (Arcadia) where two stones stood with the sacred books placed between them (cf. the book of the Torah that was placed "beside the Ark of the Covenant" in which the tablets of the Law were set, Deut 31:26); the worshipers would take oaths by these stones (*Description of Greece* 8:15:2).

Despite the similarity in background between the Decalogue tradition and the oaths of the worshipers at the temple in Philadelphia, the decisive difference between the placement of the Decalogue in Israel and the place of the ordinances among the worshipers at Philadelphia should be pointed out. In contrast to the Israelite conception of the Decalogue as a set of obligations put upon every Israelite wherever he or she may be, in the pagan tradition what is

[107] See Nock, "Early Gentile Christianity," 74ff. On the consciousness of sin bound up with confession in Near Eastern and Asian peoples, see R. Pettazzoni, "Confession of Sins and the Classics," *Harvard Theological Review* 30 (1937) 1-14; on confession in Egypt, see my "Prayers for Knowledge, Repentance, and Forgiveness in the Eighteen Benedictions," *Tarbiz* 48 (1979) 196-97 n. 56, and also my article "Instructions for Temple Visitors."

[108] *ʾemeth we-Yaṣṣib*, which was said in the Temple after the Decalogue and the *Shemaᶜ* prayer (*m. Tamid* 5:1), is a kind of obligation by oath to fulfill the demands included in the Decalogue and the *Shemaᶜ* (see my "The Loyalty Oath in the Ancient Near East," 405ff.).

dealt with are obligations upon a group of *temple visitors* who are required to strictly observe ritual purity in order to prevent the desecration of the holy site. In this aspect, the Philadelphian oath is similar to the conditions of entrance for temple visitors in Israel and in the ancient Near East mentioned above. Needless to say, the basic religious demands particular to Israel that are included in the first half of the Decalogue are not found and are not expected to be found in the Philadelphian oath.

The Rabbis indeed felt that in contrast to the first five commandments, which are of specific Israelite nature, where the name YHWH is often mentioned, the last five commandments are of universal nature, without mention of the Tetragrammaton at all.[109]

The Revelation at Sinai and the Festival of the Giving of the Law

The festival at which it was customary to dramatize the revelatory event at Sinai and to make a renewed oath, as it were, on reception of the Law, was the Feast of Weeks; and in my view, this rite is reflected in Psalms 50 and 81 (discussed above). In Second Temple times, this festival was called 'Assembly' (*ᶜaṣeret*), and it is so called by Josephus (*Ant.* 3:252).[110] This term can be explained by realizing that the Feast of Shabuoth was a day of assemblage together, or in biblical language "the day of the Assembly" (*yôm haqqāhāl*); this indicates the day on which the people assembled together in order to receive the Word of God, as expressed in the Decalogue (Deut 9:10, 10:4, 18:16).[111] On this festival the wonderful event was apparently dramatized in a ritual, and the people took the Decalogue upon themselves by covenant and oath.

Exod 19:1 indicates that the Israelites reached the wilderness of Sinai in the third month. The account of the preparation for the revelation at Sinai follows immediately. Following Mowinckel, some scholars have correctly assumed that the rites of sanctification and the

[109] Cf. "Pesikta Rabbati" 21:18 (*Pesikta Rabbati Midrasch*, ed. M. Friedmann [Ish-Shalom] [Vienna: privately printed, 1880] 99a).

[110] See Targum Onqelos and Targum Pseudo-Jonathan to Num 28:36 (*bšbᶜwtykm* 'your Feast of Weeks' = *bᶜsrtykwn* 'in your assembles'); cf. Targum Neofiti I on Deut 16:10 (*ḥgh dšbwᶜyh hyᵓ ᶜṣrth* 'the Feast of Weeks, which is *ᶜṣrth*').

[111] See D. Hoffman's thorough discussion of this problem in his commentary *Das Buch Leviticus* (Berlin: Poppelauer, 1905–6), 2:158ff. Note that *Targum Pseudo-Jonathan* and *Targum Neofiti I* both translate *bywm hqhl* as "on the day of the assembling of the community" and Deut 18:16 as "on the day of assembly of the tribes to receive the Torah."

flowing of Shofar described in this chapter reflect the course of a ritual customarily performed during covenant renewal ceremonies. The preparations for the revelation at Sinai are in fact preparations for a divine encounter, which comes about at every assembly held at the Temple. Similar to the preparations described in Exod 19:10, 15 (namely sanctification, washing of clothes, and abstention from women), in Gen 35:1-3 Jacob commands his household to purify themselves and to change clothes before going up to Beth-El.[112] The "setting of bounds" around the mountain and the distancing of the people from the most holy site found in Exod 19:11-13, 21-24 are also characteristic of the restriction placed on access to a holy site.[113] The blowing of the Shofar indicated an occasion of oath and commitment, and indeed in the covenant of Asa in the third month (2 Chr 15:14), the Shofar was blown at the time of oath making. A. B. Ehrlich already concluded from this that the Jewish custom of accompanying an oath with the sound of the Shofar is based in the Bible.[114]

It thus appears that just as the Feast of Passover and the Feast of Unleavened Bread came to dramatize the event of the Exodus, and as the Feast of Tabernacles, involving sitting in "booths," came to dramatize the booths in which the Israelites lived in the wilderness (Lev 23:42-43), so also the Feast of Shabuot commemorates the revelatory event at Mount Sinai.

That the Feast of Shabuoth was a day on which the people assembled at the Temple can be learned from Josephus and from the Book of Acts in the New Testament. Josephus tells of two assemblies in Jerusalem on the Feast of Weeks—one in connection with the

[112] Similar restrictions for visitors of a sanctuary were found in ancient Greece. See M. P. Nilsson, *Geschichte der griechischen Religion* (3d ed.; Munich: Beck, 1974), 2:74. The inscription in the Temple of Zeus Kynthios is instructive. It requires all the temple visitors to be pure, to be clad in white clothes, and barefoot. They must also have abstained from sexual relations and not be unclean by contact with the dead.

[113] Nachmanides already pointed out the similarity between the bounding of Mount Sinai in Exodus 19 and the warnings concerning approaching the tent of Meeting (see his preface to the book of Numbers and his preface to Exodus 25); cf. J. Milgrom, *Studies in Levitical Terminology* (Berkeley: University of California, 1970), 1:44ff.

[114] Thus, for example, the Shofar were blown at the inauguration of a king, when all the people obligated themselves to be loyal to the new king (see 2 Sam 15:10, 1 Kgs 1:39, 2 Kgs 9:13, 11:14). On the sounding of the Shofar accompanying an oath, see the article *hst* in A. Kohut (ed.), *Aruch completum; sive, Lexicon, vocabula et res, quae in libris Targumicis, Talmudicis et Midraschicis* (reprinted New York: Pardes, 1955), 3:224: "And they blow the Shofar with the oath." See A. B. Ehrlich, *Mikrâ ki-Pheshutô* (3 vols.; Berlin: Poppelauer, 1899-1901); reprinted New York: KTAV, 1969), on 2 Chronicles 15.

invasion of the Parthians in 40 B.C.E.: "When the feast called Pentecost came round, the whole neighborhood of the temple and the entire city were crowded with the country folk" (*War* 2:43; cf. *Ant.* 17:254). The assembly served as a cover for the rebels, but it was itself strongly motivated by the traditional observance of a day of popular, mass assembly (cf. *War* 2:73). Similarly, in Acts 2 the crowd that gathered during the Feast of Weeks, contained Parthians, Medes, Elamites, inhabitants of Mesopotamia, Judea, Cappodocia, Pontus, Asia, Phrygia, Pamphylia, Egypt, and the districts of Libya around Cyrene (Acts 2:9–11).[115] Acts 20:16 reveals that the Feast of Weeks was an especially important pilgrim festival. There it is told that Paul makes an effort to arrive in Jerusalem for the Feast of Weeks, an arrival that reminds us of what is said concerning Judah the Maccabee (2 Macc 12:31–32), who returned from Scythopolis in time for the Feast of Weeks.

Philo calls the Feast of Weeks a festival observed in the most national/popular way, *dēmotelestatē heortē* (*On the Special Laws* 1:183). When he describes the celebration of the Feast of Weeks by the therapeutae, he calls this festival a 'very great festival', *megistē heortē* (*De Vita Contemplativa* 65).

The following older sources give further testimony concerning the observance of covenant renewal ceremonies celebrating the giving of the Law on the Feast of Weeks:

2 Chr 15:8–15 states that in the third month of the 15th year of the reign of Asa, men from Judah, Benjamin, Ephraim, Manasseh, and Simeon assembled together in Jerusalem in connection with the rededication of the altar.[116] They offered sacrifices, entered a covenant to seek the Lord with all their heart and soul, and made oaths in a loud voice, to the accompaniment of blasts from trumpets and Shofars. The oath, an oath of covenant, calls to mind the covenant at Sinai, also made with the offering of sacrifices (Exod 24:3–4).[117] The oath is made rejoicingly, *with all the heart and willingness*, this gives more validity to the obligation. The joy, however, may also refer to a

[115] *Ta megaleia* (Acts 2:11) means 'the great works' or 'the great visions'; cf. *mwrʾym gdwlym* (Deut 4:37) and *mrʾ gdwl* (Deut 26:8), which is interpreted as a vision and revelation in LXX (*en horamasin megalois*), the Aramaic translations (*ḥzwnyn rbrbyn*), and the Samaritan Pentateuch and rabbinic homilies (*wbmrʾ gdwl*, referring to the revelation of the Divine Presence according to "Midrash Tannaʾîm" to Deuteronomy).

[116] The Targum adds in v 11: *bḥgʾ dsbwʿyʾ* 'on the Feast of the Weeks', cf. A. Sperber, *The Bible in Aramaic* (Leiden: Brill, 1959), 1:45.

[117] On *bryt* and *ʾlh* and its congruency with the *bryt* and *sbwʿh* see my "הברית והחסד," *Lešonénu* 36 (1972) 85–87.

festival during which a rite of covenant renewal was observed.[118] The root *šb*ᶜ, which appears in this section three times (vv 14, 15), undoubtedly comes to connect the subject with the Feast of Weeks (*šwb*ᶜ*wt*) and thereby receives a double meaning: the weeks (*šwb*ᶜ*wt*) of wheat harvest and the oaths (*šbw*ᶜ*wt*) of the covenant. This ambiguity of *šbw*ᶜ*wt* is found also in *Jub.* 6:21; this feast is twofold and of a double nature.[119] It is also reflected in the Temple Scroll, which refers to this festival: "It is the Feast of Weeks and the Feast of Firstfruits for an eternal memorial" (col. 19, line 9).[120] It seems that the scroll's addition of 'for an eternal memorial' (*lzkrwn* ᶜ*wlm*) testifies to the special importance of this festival.

As I have already mentioned, the sounding of the Shofar in the rite of 2 Chronicles 15 accompanies the oath; and according to my view (see above), the sounding of the Shofar mentioned in Ps 81:3[4] is also connected with the Feast of Weeks.[121]

[118] Joy and willingness come to express the full readiness of those who enter the covenant and indicate that the commitment was not made out of pressure or coercion. Similar clarifications are to be found in legal documents in the ancient world, cf. Y. Muffs, "Joy and Love as Metaphorical Expressions of Willingness and Spontaneity in Cuneiform, Ancient Hebrew, and Related Literatures," *Christianian, Judaism and other Greco-Roman Cults, for Morton Smith at Sixty* (ed. J. Neusner; Leiden: Brill, 1976), 3:1ff. Concerning the Sinai covenant, see "Mekhilta of Rabbi Ishmael" (tractate *Ba-Ḥodesh* §2; Horovitz and Rabin [see n. 28], 209): "They all agreed singleheartedly to accept the yoke of the kingdom of heaven with joy [*beśimḥah*]." See also Muffs, "Love and Joy as Metaphors of Volition in Hebrew and Related Literatures, Part II: The Joy of Giving," *Journal of the Ancient Near Eastern Society of Columbia University* 11 (1979) 110. Compare also the Benediction after *Shema*ᶜ that is an acceptance of the yoke of the kingdom of heaven, as discussed above and in my "The Loyalty Oath in the Ancient Near East," 406ff.: "And his kingdom they took upon themselves willingly [*brṣwn*] . . . with great joy." For a similar phrasing in connection with the loyalty oath to the Roman emperor, cf. ibid., 393 n. 137. On the joy at the Pentecost festival, see Deut 16:11 and compare in relation to the covenant of Sinai in the Aramaic Targums of Exod 24:11: "and they were joyous with their sacrifices."

[119] For the tendentiousness of the double name-derivation in the book of Chronicles, see Y. Zakovitch, "*Kpl mdršy hšm*" (M.A. thesis, Hebrew University, Jerusalem, 1971) 166ff. See the commentary of R. Charles, *The Book of Jubilees* (London: Black, 1902) 53 n. 21, where he wondered about the meaning of "double nature" in *Jub.* 6:21. In my opinion, the double nature originated from the ambiguity of *šᵉbu*ᶜ*wt* here. It should be added that the Festival of Shabuoth in Jubilees is bound up with the covenants that God made with the Patriarchs (see below) and thus the duplicity is expressed also in the fact that God made an oath to the patriarchs and the children of Israel made an oath to God on this day.

[120] See the comments of Yadin, *The Temple Scroll,* 2:82.

[121] According to Philo (*On the Special Laws* 2:188) the sounding of the Shofar on Rosh Hashanah recalls the giving of the Torah. The same idea is reflected in the liturgy that opens the order of Shofaroth in the prayers of Rosh Hashanah: "You did reveal yourself in a cloud of glory to the holy people in order to speak to them. Out of heaven

The Feast of the Giving of the Law is most clearly portrayed in the Book of Jubilees, where the idea that "the Feast of Weeks be observed in the month of Sivan, in order to renew the Covenant each year" (6:17) is stated to be determined in the heavenly tablets. The Covenant with Noah was established in the month of Sivan, and Noah was the first to observe the Feast of Weeks (6:18). The "Covenant between the Pieces" was also made in the middle of the month of Sivan: "And on the day we made a covenant with Abram, according as we have covenanted with Noah . . . and Abram renewed the festival . . . forever" (*Jub.* 14:20). On the 15th of the month of Sivan, which is the Feast of Weeks according to the Book of Jubilees and the calendar of the Qumran Sect,[122] God reveals himself to Abram and makes a covenantal promise to give him offspring, whereupon he is given the ordinance of circumcision, which he immediately performs (*Jubilees* 15). Isaac was born on the Feast of Weeks (in the middle of the third month) and was circumcised five days later (16:13). God reveals himself to Jacob also in the middle of the third month (*Jubilees* 44). The covenants with Noah and with Abraham were made with a sacrifice (6:3, 14:19), as was the Sinai covenant (Exod 24:3ff., cf. Ps 50:5), and also the covenant in the days of Asa, mentioned above, in 2 Chr 15:11.

The Qumran Sect renewed the covenant every year (Manual of Discipline [1QS 1:16–17]), and according to an unpublished text from Cave 4, this rite also took place on the Feast of Weeks.[123]

The therapeutae in Egypt described by Philo in *De Vita Contemplativa* (65), who are especially close in character to the Qumran Sect, considered the Feast of Weeks "the greatest festival [*megistē*

---

you made them hear your voice . . . amidst thunders and lightnings you did manifest yourself to them and while the Shofar sounded you did appear to them." However, the sounding of the Shofar indicates the enthronement of God (see above), as Mowinckel already pointed out (cf. Ps 47:6ff., a psalm which today is indeed read at Rosh Hashanah before the sounding of the Shofar). The mention of the Shofar blowing at the revelation at Mount Sinai in the liturgy of Rosh Hashanah is no different from other references to Shofar blowing in this liturgy, which are not necessarily related to Rosh Hashanah.

[122] That 15th Sivan = Feast of Weeks in *Jubilees*, see Charles, *The Book of Jubilees*, 52; in Qumran, see S. Talmon, "The Calendar Reckoning of the Sect from the Judean Desert," *Aspects of the Dead Sea Scrolls* (ed. C. Rabin and Y. Yadin; Scripta Hierosolymitana 4; Jerusalem: Magnes, 1961) 77–106.

[123] See J. T. Milik, *Ten Years of Discovery in the Wilderness of Judea* (Studies in Biblical Theology 26; London: SCM, 1959) 113ff.; and M. Delcor, "Pentecôte," *Dictionnaire de la Bible, Supplément*, ed. H. Cazelles and A. Feuillet (Paris: Letouzey, 1966), 7:858–79.

heortē]."[124] They observed a vigil on the eve of this festival, during which hymns of thanksgiving were sung. As I will show below, this tradition exists in later Judaism. It is not said what was done on the festival day itself, but it would not be too much to assume that they observed a covenant renewal ceremony, as did the members of the Qumran Sect.

Understanding the Feast of Weeks as a celebration of the Giving of the Law provides background to the account in Acts 2 and the establishment of the first Christian community. When the Festival of Weeks came, everyone assembled together with one accord and there was suddenly a great rushing sound from heaven, as of a stormy wind, which filled the house, whereupon tongues of fire materialized, separating and alighting upon the heads of each one. After this everyone was filled with the Holy Spirit and began to speak in diverse languages, as the Spirit so led them (vv 1-4). The basic elements of this account are taken from the tradition of the Law-giving at Sinai.

The rushing sound from heaven and tongues of fire are rooted in the descriptions of the revelation at Sinai, as reflected in legends from Second Temple times. Midrashic literature, the Aramaic Targums, and Philo describe the words that came from the mouth of God as flames of fire, a notion based on the verse "all the people witnessed the thunder and lightning" (Exod 19:16). On the words "all the people witnessed," Rabbi Akiva comments: "A Word of fire was seen coming from the mouth of the Almighty and engraved itself into the tablets, as it is written: 'the voice of the Lord kindles flame of fire'."[125]

Philo speaks similarly of a flame that became "an articulate speech in the language familiar to the audience" (*On the Decalogue* 46). Similar descriptions are found in Targum Pseudo-Jonathan, in Targum fragments from the Cairo Genizah, and in Targum Neofiti I:

> A Word . . . as if going out from the mouth of the Holy One, blessed be his name, like sparks and flashes and flames and fiery torches, a torch from the right and a torch that came out of the left, flew in the air and went forth and showed itself on the camps of Israel and came back and returned and engraved itself on the tablets of the Covenant.[126]

[124] Though it is not said that "the fiftieth day" is the fiftieth day from the beginning of the waving of the Omer, the expression 'after seven weeks' (*di᾽ hepta hebdomadōn*) as well as the expression 'greatest festival' support the assumption that the festival of Shabuoth is meant.

[125] Ps 29:7; see "Mekhilta of Rabbi Ishmael" (tractate *Ba-Ḥodesh* §9; Horovitz and Rabin, 235).

[126] On the various translations, see J. Potin, *La Fête Juive de la Pentecôte: Étude des textes liturgiques* (Paris: Cerf, 1971), 2:37ff.

This description derives from Deut 33:2: "Lightning flashing at them from his right," concerning Sifrei to Deuteronomy states:

> When a Word went out from the mouth of the Holy One blessed be he, it went out from his right side . . . to Israel's left side and encompasses the camp of Israel . . . and the Holy One retrieves it . . . and engraves it on the tablet . . . as it is written: "the voice of the Lord kindles flames of fire."[127]

The second element, a fire that divides into tongues of flame, whereupon everyone begins to speak in various languages, has its source in a midrash, according to which the Word was divided into seventy tongues, that is, the tongues or languages of all the nations.[128] Thus Rabbi Yohanan says: "Every word that came out of the mouth of the Holy one, blessed be his name, was divided into seventy tongues."[129] The Midrash continues: "A student of R. Ishmael taught: 'like a hammer that shatters rock [Jer 23:29]'. Just as a sledgehammer (when shattered by the harder rock) is divided into many slivers, so every word which was uttered by the Holy One was divided into seventy tongues." Most important to this discussion is the congruence between the language of the midrash—a word (as fire) *divided* into seventy tongues—and the language of Acts 2:3, "tongues *divided* like flames of fire."

In rabbinic tradition, the Word is divided into seventy in order to enable its diffusion among the nations. In *m. Soṭa* 7:5 all the words of the Law were written on the stones of the altar on Mount Ebal in seventy languages.[130] The Christian tradition similarly speaks of tongues of fire that divided and alighted upon the people present at the revelatory event and bestowed upon the participants the ability to

[127] "Sifrei to Deuteronomy" 33:2, §343. See *Sifrei on Deuteronomy,* ed. L. Finkelstein (Berlin: Jüdischer Kulturebund in Deutschland E.V., 1939; repr. New York: Jewish Theological Seminary of America, 1969) 399.

[128] On the seventy nations of the world, see Genesis 10 and my short commentary on *Genesis* (Jerusalem: Massada, 1975); on the rabbinic legends about this matter see L. Ginzberg, *The Legends of the Jews* (Philadelphia: Jewish Publication Society), 3:350-51.

[129] *T. Šabb.* 88b. See "Midrash Tehillim" 92:3 (*Midrasch Tehillim,* ed. S. Buber [Vilna: Wittue and Gebrüder Romm, 1891; repr. Hildesheim: Georg Olms, 1967] 22), and the sources cited by Ginzberg, *Legends of the Jews,* 3:439.

[130] See also *t. Soṭa* 8:6-7, and the Mekhilta on Deuteronomy discovered by S. Schechter, "Mekilta le-Dĕbarim Parashat Rĕsch," *Festschrift zu Israel Lewy's Siebzigsten Geburtstag* (ed. M. Braun and J. Elbogen; Breslau: Marcus, 1911) 189. An extensive discussion of the subject was made by S. Liebermann, *Tosefta ki-Fshuṭah,* part 8: "Order Nashim" (New York: Jewish Theological Seminary, 1973) 699-701.

spread the new word in all the world's languages, as described in the continuation of the account.[131]

It should be added that "Sifrei to Deuteronomy" 33:2, where *a Word likened to fire* is mentioned as an interpretation of *mymynw* ᶜ*š dt lmw*, also deals with a word given in various languages: "When the Holy One revealed himself to give the Law to Israel, he did not speak then in one language but in four, as it is written: 'from Sinai'—this is Hebrew; 'from Seir'—this is Latin; 'from Mount Paran'—this is Arabic; '*mrbbt qdš*'—this is Aramaic."[132]

The last element is the tongues of fire that rested upon each one of the participants, calling to mind the crowns the Israelites received at the revelation at Sinai; the 'crowns' ᶜ*ṭrwt* are none other than a radiance of the divine presence around their heads.[133] I have elsewhere pointed out that the tradition discussed here (of men upon which tongues of fire alighted and who were thus filled with the Holy Spirit)[134] derives from Numbers 11, which speaks of the elders upon whom the Spirit fell and made them the leaders of the congregation.[135] The institution of the seventy elders corresponds to the seventy members of the Sanhedrin who had to know seventy languages (*t. Sanh.* 8:1; *y. Šeqal.* 5:1:48d; *b. Sanh.* 17a; and *b. Menaḥ.* 65a). This tradition was transferred to the founding meeting of the Christian community. According to Christian tradition, the Holy Spirit fell

[131] See also Potin, *La Fête Juive de la Pentecôte*, 2:310ff.

[132] "Sifrei to Deuteronomy" 33:2, §343 (*Sifrei on Deuteronomy*, ed. Finkelstein, 399, 395).

[133] Rested = *ekathisen.* The verb *kathizō* is used in LXX Gen 8:4 as "came to rest." On the Israelites' crowns, see *Peskita de Rav Kahana*, ed. B. Mandelbaum (New York: Jewish Theological Seminary of America, 1962), 1:266, and the parallels mentioned there, and also *t. Šabb.* (see also the discussion by Urbach, *The Sages*, 148–49). Compare "and you adorned him with glory and majesty" in Ps 8:5[6], meaning the divine radiance around his head (cf. *melammu* in Akkadian), and see also Job 19:9: "He has stripped me of my glory, removed the crown from my head." The 'diadem of glory' (*klyl tp*ᵓ*rt*) bestowed upon Moses according to Sir 45:8, which is paralleled there with glory and might (cf. the morning prayer on the Sabbath), is the radiance around his face (Exod 34:29ff.) and in the scrolls of the Judean desert is called 'diadem of glory', *klyl kbwd* in 1QS 4:8 and the Thanksgiving scroll 9, line 25. In Hellenistic literature this aureole is called *diadēma tēs doxēs*; see R. Reitzenstein, *Die hellenistischen Mysterienreligionen* (3d ed.; Leipzig: Teubner, 1927) 359–60. It is this aureole that is put on the pious ones in the world to come "who enjoy the radiance of the divine presence" (*b. Ber.* 17a). For glory as an aureole in the Bible and in the ancient Near East, see my article *kābôd*, *Theologisches Wörterbuch zum Alten Testament* (ed. G. J. Botterweck and H. Ringgren; Stuttgart: Kohlhammer, 1970–), 4:23–40.

[134] It is not clear whether Acts 2:4 refers to the 120 men mentioned in 1:15 or to the twelve apostles.

[135] "Pentecost as a Festival of the Giving of the Law," *Immanuel* 8 (1978) 15ff.

upon the leaders of the Christian community as well; and like the Sanhedrin, they also were able to speak in diverse languages by virtue of the tongues of fire that alighted upon them.

The first revelation to the people of Israel served then as a point of origin for the crystallization of various traditions concerning prophetic-mystical experiences that took place, as it were, on the Feast of Weeks. Josephus relates that on the eve of the Feast of Weeks before the war, the priests heard a voice of declaration: "We are leaving" (*Ant.* 6:299; cf. Tacitus, *Historia* 5:13).

The mystical experience of Rabbi Joseph Caro (1488–1575) is also connected with the festival of Shabuoth. On the eve of the Feast of Shabuoth during the all-night vigil, a voice came out from his mouth, the men about him heard the voice, fell on their faces, and fainted.[136]

The second experience is related to Sabbetai Tsevi's messianic declaration. On the eve of the Feast of Shabuoth, the Holy Spirit came upon Nathan from Gaza; he fainted, and out of his faint he was heard to utter various voices that were afterwards interpreted to mean that Sabbetai Tsevi was worthy to be king over Israel.[137]

A relic of the ancient celebration of the Feast of Weeks has been preserved up to the present day in the different customs attached to the observance of this festival in Jewish worship. Thus the all-night vigil on the eve of the festival (*tqwn lyl šbᶜwt*) recalls a kind of vigil on the eve of the giving of the Law. Indeed, the Samaritans preserved a tradition of reading the Torah on the eve of the revelation at Mount Sinai, from the middle of the night until the following evening, while ascending Mount Garizim and praying.[138]

The recital of the Decalogue during Pentecost is accompanied in the Jewish tradition by festive liturgies of ancient origin. Various introductory poems (*rešuyôt*) in the Aramaic language (preserved in

[136] For this evidence see R. J. Z. Werblowsky, *Joseph Karo: Lawyer and Mystic* (Scripta Judaica 6; London: Oxford University, 1962) 19–21.

[137] G. Shalom, *Shabetai Tsevi and his Movement* (Tel Aviv: ᶜAm ᶜObed, 1975), 1:178 [Hebrew]. In my opinion the swooning on the night of Shabuoth originated from the revelation at the giving of the Torah, when according to tradition all those present there fainted or fell down in a swoon. Cf. *b. Šabb.* 88b: "With every word coming out of the Holy One . . . the souls of the Israelites fled as it says: 'My soul departs when he spoke' [Cant 5:6]." Compare the Rosh Hashanah liturgy in the Geniza version (Order of Shofaroth) concerning the Sinai revelation: "they all fainted and fell on their faces and their souls departed because of the voice of the words [of God]" (J. Mann, "Genizah Fragments," *Hebrew Union College Annual* 2 [1925] 330).

[138] Cf. D. J. H. Boys, "The Creed and Hymns of the Samaritan Liturgy," *London Quarterly and Holborn Review* 186 (1961) 32–37; B. Tsedaka, "Shabuoth and the Samaritans," *Ba-Maᶜarakhah* 98 (June 1969) 10–11.

the Aramaic Targums to the Pentateuch) were composed for reciting before the reading of the Ten Commandments on the day of Shabuoth.[139] Of a similar nature is a category of liturgical poems (*ʾazhārôt*) for the Feast of Weeks in which all of the 613 Torah commandments are enumerated and classified according to the Ten Commandments.[140] All this seems to indicate that the revelation and giving of the Law was dramatized in Israel from ancient times.

[139] Cf. M. L. Klein, *The Fragment-Targums of the Pentateuch* (Analecta Biblica 76; Rome: Biblical Institute, 1980), 1:117-25.

[140] Cf. Elbogen, *Der Jüdische Gottesdienst,* 217-18.

Bernard G. Weiss

Covenant and Law in Islam

IN THIS ESSAY WEISS explores the development of the idea of covenant within the context of Islam. He shows that, as in the Judaeo-Christian tradition, so also in Islam a covenant between God and human beings is the basis of the underlying obligation to conform to the divinely revealed Law. The first part of the essay summarizes the Qur'ānic development of the covenant idea, while the remainder describes its development within later Islamic theology. Weiss argues that in Islam the covenant with God is understood along lines that are both more universalistic and individualistic than in the Judaeo-Christian tradition.

Bernard G. Weiss is Associate Professor of Arabic and Islamic Studies at the University of Utah. Prior to this appointment he taught at the American University in Cairo, the University of Toronto, and McGill University. He received his Ph.D. from Princeton University and his B.D. from Princeton Theological Seminary. His published works deal with various aspects of Arabic philology and Islamic religious and legal thought.

In Islam the notion of a divine law occupies a place no less central than in the Judaeo-Christian tradition. In the latter tradition the divine law is understood to be rooted in a covenant between God and his people, the covenant established at Mount Sinai. This rooting of the law in a covenant may not at first glance appear to be so prominent a feature of Islamic thought: one finds rather infrequent mention of the covenant theme in works of Islamic theology and jurisprudence. However, if one looks in the right places one can find a richly developed conception of covenant and of the rootedness of law in it.

The place to begin is, for obvious reasons, the Qurʾān. Since the covenant theme appears not infrequently in the Qurʾān, the commentators on that scripture were obliged to deal with it, and their writings therefore constitute a second important source for this subject. The other sacred corpus of Islam, the *ḥadīth*-cum-*sīra,* adds little of substance to what is found in the Qurʾān and therefore need not be consulted in great depth. It does in certain respects, however, provide a valuable supplement to the Qurʾānic material.

In the following pages I shall explore two subjects: first, the Qurʾānic understanding of covenant and law and, second, subsequent Muslim thinking concerning covenant and law, that is to say, the thinking of Muslims who lived in a period when Muslim religious thought, especially theology, had reached its fully developed form. The first subject has fallen within the purview of a number of Western scholars, among whom Robert C. Darnell, Jr., has provided the most comprehensive treatment known to me.[1] Later Muslim thinking about covenant and law has not received comparable attention. Since the primary source material for this subject, namely the *tafsīr* (Qurʾānic commentary) literature, is vast, I shall not undertake a comprehensive study but will confine myself to one of the major commentaries, the multi-volumed *al-Tafsīr al-Kabīr* of Fakhr al-Dīn al-Rāzī (d. 1209 C.E.).[2] Since the particular interpretation of the covenant theme that I shall be focusing upon as the most recurrent one in Rāzī's commentary and the one that in all probability reflects Rāzī's own thinking centers upon a fundamental notion of orthodox (Ashʿarite) Muslim theology, namely that of *dalīl* (to be explained

[1] Robert Carter Darnell, Jr., "The Idea of Divine Covenant in the Qurʾān." Ph.D. diss., University of Michigan, 1970. Professor George E. Mendenhall kindly called my attention to this dissertation.

[2] Fakhr al-Dīn al-Rāzī, *Al-Tafsīr al-Kabīr* (Cairo: al-Maṭbaʿa al-Bahīya, n.d.). References to this work in the following pages will consist of three Arabic numerals (each separated by a colon) indicating the number of the *juzʾ* (section or volume)/page number/line number. The symbols *t* or *b* following the line number indicate whether numbering is from the top or bottom of page (numbering from the top does not take into account lines of the Qurʾānic text). Rāzī's commentary presents a rather vast amount of discussion on the subject of covenant; however, there is no single comprehensive or systematic treatment of the subject in the commentary. Covenant was not a subject on which Muslim authors deemed it necessary to write comprehensive and systematic treatises. Had they done so, my task would of course be much easier. As

later), I shall claim to represent only the viewpoint of theologians, not that of the larger body of Muslim thinkers, which includes traditionalists (Ḥanbalī and others), mystical thinkers (Ṣūfī and Shīʿī), and the "peripatetic" philosophers, not to mention the wide spectrum of modern and contemporary Muslim thinkers.

Covenant and Law in the Qurʾān

In his study of the Qurʾānic material, Darnell takes Sūra 5 (*al-Māʾida*) as a starting point. In this sūra three covenants are mentioned: one with the believers, that is to say, the Muslims (5:7); one with the Children of Israel (5:12–13); and one with the Christians (5:14). Darnell offers a description of the *Sitz im Leben* of these references based on a section-by-section analysis of the sūra as a whole.[3] The situation reflected in the Sūra has its setting in Medina at a time when the challenge of the Jews (who had persisted in rejecting his mission since the Prophet's arrival in Medina) was calling for an ever more vigorous assertion of the spiritual autonomy of Islam vis-a-vis the older scriptural religions. God accordingly declares: "Today I have brought to completion for you your religion . . . I have ordained for you Islam as a religion" (Sūra 5:3).[4] This statement occurs in the midst of a series of legislative decrees having to do mostly with ritual and dietary matters. Following these decrees, the believers are exhorted to "remember God's favor toward you and his covenant whereby he bound you when you said: We hear and we obey" (Sūra 5:7). Thereafter follows a reference to God's covenants with the Jews and Christians. The import of this passage seems to be that the believers need not fret over the challenges directed by the adherents of the older scriptural religions toward the new religious movement led by Muḥammad. Just as God had made covenants with the older communities, so he had made a covenant with those who had chosen to follow Muḥammad. They could boast of a relationship to God no less direct than that which the older communities claimed for themselves. Thus the believers were not only, like the Jews and

---

things stand, one is obliged to plow through a considerable maze of commentary, the primary concern of which is not to expound a general topic but rather to explore the particular meanings carried by words in particular contexts within the Qurʾānic text.

[3] Darnell, "Divine Covenant," 12–62.

[4] All quotations from the Qurʾān in the following pages will consist of adaptations of the Pickthall translation. Modifications of the Pickthall version will reflect my own preference for "God" over "Allah" and for contemporary English over the Elizabethan as well as my own understanding of the Arabic text where it differs from Pickthall's.

Christians, in possession of a scripture; so too they were, like them, in possession of a covenant. Therefore, if the legislation vouchsafed to them did not conform in every respect to the legislation known to the Jews, there was no need for concern: the legislation had a fresh source. Furthermore, the older communities had broken their covenants or forgotten or distorted part of the obligations contained therein. They were thus not in a position to expound God's will to the believers.

Within Sūra 5 it is, however, the covenant with the Children of Israel that is described in greatest detail:

> God made a covenant of old with the Children of Israel and we raised among them twelve chieftains, and God said: Lo! I am with you. If you perform the *Ṣalāt*-prayer and pay the alms-tax [*al-Zakāt*], and believe in my messengers and support them, and lend unto God a goodly loan, surely I will forgive your sins, and surely I will bring you into gardens underneath which rivers flow. Whoever among you disbelieves after this will go astray from a plain road.
>
> And because of their breaking of their covenant, we have cursed them and made hard their hearts. They change words from their contexts and forget a part of that whereof they were admonished. You will not cease to discover treachery from all save a few of them. But bear with them and pardon them. Lo! God loves the kindly (Sūra 5:12–13).

Darnell has combined this passage with various other references to the covenant with Israel to form a complete account of the Qurʾānic understanding of that covenant, one which brings it close to the biblical conception.[5] The covenant is accompanied, in the Qurʾānic depiction, by a display of divine power, the elevation of Mount Sinai above the heads of the people (an idea familiar to rabbinic lore; compare the thunder, lightning, and similar phenomena in the biblical version). It furthermore embraces three basic elements: (1) a reminder of God's favor (compare "I am the Lord your God who brought you out of the land of Egypt, out of the house of bondage"); (2) a set of conditions that the people must fulfill, that is, commandments constituting a holy law (compare the Decalogue); and (3) a promise of reward for fulfillment of the conditions and a threat of punishment for nonfulfillment (compare the blessings and curses associated with the biblical covenant). In contrast to the biblical account, the rewards and punishments mentioned in the Qurʾān are primarily otherworldly. Darnell has juxtaposed the various com-

[5] Darnell, "Divine Covenant," 64–112.

mandment lists that appear in connection with the Israelite covenant in six Qurʾānic passages and formed a synthesized list.[6]

Explicit Qurʾānic references to the divine covenants with Christians and Muslims are fewer than the references to the Israelite covenant. There is only one clear reference to the covenant with Christians;

> And with those who say: Lo! we are Christians, we made a covenant, but they forgot a part of that whereof they were admonished. Therefore, we have stirred up enmity and hatred among them until the Day of Resurrection, when God will inform them of their handiwork (Sūra 5:14).

Among those passages that describe the covenant with Muslims, Sūra 13 (*al-Raʿd*) is especially instructive: here is a sequence consisting of (1) a recital of signs of God's favor (vv 1–17) followed by (2) a commandment list, which takes the form of a description of the conduct of those who fulfill God's covenant, together with (3) a specification of their reward, after which comes (4) a brief description of the conduct of those who break the covenant and of the punishment that awaits them. This same sequence of signs of God's favor, a commandment list (expressed as a description of the conduct of God's servants), and a mention of reward and punishment—which for convenience I shall call the signs/commandments/promise cluster—is detectable also in Sūra 25:45–77. Darnell attempts a synthesis of the commandment lists in these two passages with similar lists found in Sūra 23 and 70 to give a complete account of the commandments embodied in the divine covenant with Muslims.[7]

Sūra 5:7 speaks of the covenant with the believers as something that has already transpired. The question therefore arises: with what specific event or events, if any, is this covenant to be identified? According to one Muslim exegetical tradition, 5:7 is referring to two things: the pact concluded between the Prophet and the people of Medina, and the pact concluded later between the Prophet and the entire Muslim community "under the tree," that is, at Ḥudaybīya.[8] In fact, two pacts were concluded between the Prophet and the people of Medina, both at ʿAqaba prior to the Prophet's migration to Medina.

[6] Ibid., 93–94.

[7] Ibid., 180–211 (esp. 192–93).

[8] Rāzī 11:179:12–19t. These pacts are described in Rāzī as a pledging of the people to the effect that they would listen to and obey the Prophet in respect to what was preferable (*muḥbūb*) or reprehensible (*makrūh*), these being two of the five legal qualifications recognized in Islamic jurisprudence.

Of these, the earlier one reflects more clearly the structure of a divine covenant. According to an account of one of the parties to this pact recorded by Ibn Saᶜd,

> We gave allegiance to the apostle that we would associate nothing with God, not steal, not commit fornication, not kill our offspring, not slander our neighbor, nor disobey him in what was right; if we fulfilled this, paradise would be ours; and if we committed any of those sins we should be punished in this world and this would serve as expiation; if the sin was concealed until the Day of Resurrection, then it would be for God to decide whether to punish or to forgive.[9]

The first pact of ᶜAqaba thus embodied a set of commandments resembling the "thou-shalt-not" of the Decalogue and a promise of reward for obeying the commandments and a threat of punishment for disobeying them; in other words, two of the three elements in the signs/commandments/promise cluster. The second pact of ᶜAqaba as well as the later pact "under the tree" were, in contrast, concerned primarily to elicit a commitment to support the Prophet in armed conflict with his enemies, the Quraysh of Mecca and their allies.

As tempting as it may be to try to link Sūra 5:7 or any other passage in which a covenant with believers is alluded to with these pacts, particularly the first pact of ᶜAqaba, it is clear from Rāzī's commentary that the Muslim exegetes did not themselves unanimously do so, and no such linkage is unambiguously indicated in the Qurʾān itself. Indeed, there is much within the Qurʾān that would lead us to disassociate the idea of a covenant with believers from any particular historical event and to see it rather as a theme implicit within the message delivered by the Prophet from the very beginning, one having to do with a certain kind of relationship between God and human beings that was realized whenever and wherever the Divine Word was proclaimed and people heeded it. If the covenant theme is to be deemed present wherever the signs/commandments/promise cluster appears, however clearly or obliquely, then it must be regarded as nothing less than the very essence of what the Prophet was called to proclaim, even if Arabic words meaning 'covenant' (*mīthāq*, *ᶜahd*, etc.) were heard somewhat infrequently upon his lips, and perhaps not at all during the earliest days of his prophet career.

Looking broadly at the covenant theme as developed in the Qurʾān, whether explicitly by way of actual mention of a covenant or

[9] Alfred Guillaume, *The Life of Muhammad: A Translation of Ishaq's Sirat Rasul Allah* (Lahore: Oxford University, 1955) 199.

implicitly through its employment of the signs/commandments/promise cluster, I note several important points.

1. While the mention of a covenant with the believers in Sūra 5 seems designed to undergird the spiritual autonomy of Islam and the Muslim community vis-a-vis the older scriptural religious and communities, that covenant appears to be no different, in regard to essentials, from the covenants with the older communities. There is not much specific information about the covenant with Christians, but comparative examination of the Qur'ānic data pertaining to the other two covenants shows that they both entail the same signs/commandments/promise cluster but also that the three ingredients in this cluster are much the same. While the signs sometimes relate to divine favors unique to the experience of the Children of Israel or the Muslim believers, they often relate to favors of a more general nature, favors that embrace both communities as well as the rest of humankind. This is particularly true of those signs that have to do with the beneficent workings of the natural order. These signs, together with the signs of God's power (which are not necessarily different), elicit gratitude and reverence toward the Creator and prepare for the reception the divine commandments. As for the commandments themselves, those directed to the Israelites are remarkably similar to those directed to the Muslims, with the result that the covenant with Israel has a strikingly Islamic character. The cardinal commandment is: believe God's messengers, including Muḥammad, and support them.[10] This is much more emphasized in exhortations to Israel than in exhortations to the Muslims, since the former have disbelieved Muḥammad and need to be reminded that in doing so they have broken God's covenant with them. The Muslims have obeyed this commandment and therefore need to have their attention focused upon other commandments. However, the duty of believing Muḥammad is clearly implicit in God's covenant with them, and in discharging that duty they have distinguished themselves from the other communities.

Closely allied with the commandment to believe the prophets is the commandment to hold fast to that which God has given, that is, scripture, and not to conceal it, corrupt it, or forget it (Sūra 2:63 [cf. 7:144-45, 171], 3:187). Again, this commandment is more concerned with the Israelites than with the Muslims, since the latter are presumed to have complied with it. Prominent among the remaining

[10] This commandment is expressly mentioned in Sūra 5:12 in connection with the covenant. In Sūra 4:155 the phrase "breaking their covenant" is juxtaposed with the phrase "disbelieving the revelations of God" (see also 2:40-41).

commandments, given both to Israel and the Muslims, are the commandments to perform the *Ṣalāt*-prayer and to pay the alms-tax (*al-Zakāt*) (Sūra 2:43, 83; 5:12). These duties constitute two of the five ritual duties of Islam and, if the duty of belief is associated with that of public profession of faith (*shahāda*), then three of the five duties are represented in both covenants. What remains as common ground between the two covenants are commandments having to do with the proper demeanor toward God (fear, humility, etc.) and right conduct toward parents, relatives, and the needy. One commandment alone, mentioned in connection with the covenant with Israel, is distinctive of that covenant: the commandment not to violate the Sabbath (Sūra 4:154). Finally, the primary reward and punishment connected with the two covenants are one and the same: paradise for those who adhere to the commandments, ultimate ruin for those who do not. Any rewards or punishments cited that pertain to this life seem incidental to these.[11]

2. Assuming that the covenant with the Christians follows the same general lines as the covenants with Israel and the Muslims, the three covenants mentioned in Sūra 5 may be viewed, not as three significantly different covenants, but as a single covenant that God established with each of the scriptural communities in succession. While the legislation granted to the several communities may differ with respect to many details of worship and daily life, all divine legislation, it seems, flows from a covenant that embraces a number of fundamental commandments, compliance with which makes the difference between those who fulfill the covenant and those who break it. Since the divine covenant has been established with all three scriptural communities, that covenant cannot in itself be the thing that distinguishes these communities from each other. God does not elect one community or people to be the sole recipients of his covenant, thus distinguishing them forever from all other peoples. What distinguishes the Muslims is not the covenant as such but their fulfillment of it: all others, as unbelievers, have broken the covenant. Here is an important respect in which the Qurʾānic view of covenant differs from the biblical view. In the latter, the giving of the covenant is an integral part of the process of divine election: by the covenant one people is marked off from "the nations" to be the instrument of God's purposes throughout history. Even the New Testament, with its reinterpretation of the covenant and the idea of election, does not depart from this point of view. The Christian scripture frequently juxtaposes the elect people

[11] For a more comprehensive study of the Qurʾānic accounts of the contents of the covenants with Israel and with Muslims see Darnell, "Divine Covenant," 80–94, 180–211.

(*ekklēsia*) and 'the nations' (*ethnē*): those gentiles who enter into the salvation experience do so by being grafted onto an ancient trunk.

3. The fundamental commandments embodied in the divine covenant call for both belief and right conduct (toward God in worship and toward parents, relatives, and the needy) in a kind of balance that does not seem to give priority to one over the other. Muslim theology would subsequently raise the issue of the relationship between faith (*imān* 'belief') and works (*ʿamal*), and orthodox opinion would favor faith as the ground of ultimate (if not immediate, following directly upon resurrection) admission into Paradise, thus appearing to give priority to faith. It is not within the scope of this article to consider to what degree, if at all, this represented a departure from the Qurʾānic view. To the extent that entrance into Paradise is connected with the divine covenant, it would appear that both faith and works are required.

4. The Qurʾān regards the divine covenant as established with peoples who have some sort of identity prior to their reception of the covenant. Since there is by virtue of the all-important commandment to believe prophets a link between the covenant and prophecy, I assume that the peoples with whom the covenant is established are identical with the peoples to whom prophets are sent. This assumption greatly increases the number of peoples who have been recipients of the divine covenant. However, to extend the covenant explicitly to any people other than the three communities thus far under discussion is to go beyond the letter of the Qurʾān.[12] In the case of the covenant associated with Islam, however, it seems necessary to draw a distinction between the people (*qawm*) to whom the covenant is directed (being the same as the people to whom the Prophet Muḥammad is sent) and the community that is constituted through belief and fulfillment of the covenant, namely the Muslim community. It is beyond the scope of this paper to explore the identity of the former, whether they be the Quraysh or the Arabs in general or some intermediate entity. Historically, the latter was of course to far transcend the limits of an Arab identity, however conceived, and to open its doors to all humankind.

5. Since many of the signs of God's favor and power mentioned in the Qurʾān are visible to all human beings and not just members of particular communities and since the prophetic mission of Muḥammad and the fundamental commandments embodied in the covenant which that mission entailed—particularly the commandment to

[12] There is in Sūra 7:102 a possible reference to divine covenants with certain peoples, the *ahl al-qurā*, to whom prophets peculiar to Qurʾānic history has been sent and upon whom divine judgment had fallen.

believe—are in principle directed to all human beings, whatever the ethnic identity of the original audience may have been, the Qurʾān seems to point in the direction of a covenant with the whole of humankind, a universal covenant. This being the case, not only does the divine covenant not distinguish any one community from other communities, it does not ultimately distinguish any group of communities, namely the scriptural communities, from the rest of humankind.

6. The Qurʾān is devoid of any focusing of its thought upon a great covenant-making event in the life of the Muslim community. There is no counterpart in the Muslim experience, as reflected in the Qurʾān, to the Sinai event. The Muslims are never made to gather before a place of meeting between God and their prophet and to wait expectantly as the divine law is handed down to them. Any references to particular moments of covenant-making that may seem to exist in the Qurʾān are oblique and incidental. And no such moment—even the undeniably important establishment of the first pact of ʿAqaba—has in any case an aura that comes even close to the aura of the Sinai event. Clearly the covenant theme as developed in the Qurʾān owes little to any such event. The pacts of ʿAqaba are, it is true, components in the grand event of the Hijra, the migration of Medina, and play a crucial role in the establishment of a Muslim polity, a politically autonomous community through which the religion of Islam is to become more fully realized as a divinely ordained way of life. But that way of life, or rather the divine law upon which it is based, flows from ongoing revelation that is entirely detached from the ʿAqaba (or Hijra) event. While the divine law is, in Islam, clearly rooted in a covenant, neither the law nor the covenant is linked to a single concrete event on the order of the Sinai event. Both are linked, rather, to the prophetic mission in the broadest sense of the term, a historical phenomenon far too complex to be considered as in itself an event—one which rather unfolds in a great chain of events (*asbāb al-nuzūl*) stretching over a twenty-year period and beyond.

7. Of the various passages in the Qurʾan that explicitly mention a divine covenant, only three indicate a human response. In Sūra 2:84 and 3:81 this response takes the form of the declaration *aqrarnā* ('We agree, acknowledge'), while in Sūra 5:7 it takes the form of the declaration *samiʿnā wa-aṭaʿnā* ('We hear and obey'). In the first two of these passages a witness to the human declaration of agreement or acknowledgement is also mentioned, the witness being human beings themselves (2:84), or both human beings and God together (3:81). The paucity of mention of a human response in direct connection with references to the covenant should not be taken to mean that the

Qur᾿ān is in any degree disinterested in human responses. To the contrary, the Qur᾿ānic treatment of the different components of the signs/commandments/promise cluster, considered broadly, attaches immense importance to the human response as a factor in the "covenantal" relationship. The signs of God's power and favors in particular are cited continually for the primary purpose of eliciting a human response.

Covenant and Law in Muslim Theology: The Dalīl-Centered Interpretation

I turn now to the later interpretation of the covenant theme by Muslim theologians (*mutakallimūn*), among whom Fakhr al-Dīn al-Rāzī, the author of the major source for this study, was himself a leading figure. As indicated earlier, this theological approach to the subject of covenant centers around the notion of *dalīl*, one of the most characteristic concepts of Muslim theology. However, before exploring this concept and its relevance to the covenant theme, it will be helpful first to consider how Muslim theologians understood the basic nature of covenants. Rāzī himself provides a statement that is most instructive: "A covenant [*mīthāq*] occurs through the doing of those things which render obedience obligatory [*iʿlam anna al-mīthāqa innamā yakūn bi-fiʿl al-umūr allatī tūjib al-inqiyād wa-al-tāʿa*]."[13] A covenant thus appears to be a state of affairs in which one of two parties is under an obligation to obey—that is, conform to the wishes of—the other party, and the making of a covenant is the *doing* of whatever is required to establish the obligation to obey. A covenant thus has to do primarily with obligation.

The question that Muslim interpreters of the covenant theme must deal with, therefore, is the following: what is it that God *does* that places human beings under an obligation to obey him? The answer that Muslim theology, as reflected in Rāzī's commentary, gives to this question is: God implants in human intellects indicators of his existence as sole deity and of the truthfulness of his prophets.[14] Just how God's doing this gives rise to obligation will be considered presently. The point to be noted here is that the concept of *dalīl*—which I have rendered as 'indicator' but which may also be rendered

[13] Rāzī 3:106:3b. Cf. 11:179:9t where the *mīthāq* is described as *min al-asbāb allatī tūjib ʿalayhim kawnuhum munqādan li-takālīf allāh.*

[14] I am using the word "implant" to cover the sense of four different Arabic verbs used in Rāzī's commentary in connection with these indicators (*adilla* or *dalā᾿il*), namely: *awdaʿa* 'deposit', *rakkaba* 'set up', *naṣaba* 'erect', and *khalaqa* 'create'. See Rāzī 3:106:2b, 15:50:4t, 29:216:2b, 12:55:2t.

as 'sign, proof, or evidence'—plays a crucial role in the understanding of this divine action. A *dalīl* is a rational argument that indicates, points to, provides evidence for, a truth—in this case the truths in question being the two central truths of Islam expressed in the confession of faith (*shahāda*): *tawḥīd* ("There is no god but God") and *risāla* ("Muḥammad is the Apostle of God", that is, Muḥammad is truthful in what he says about himself, namely that he is the Apostle of God and that what he delivers as the Word of God is indeed God's Word). The concept of indicators reflects the essentially rationalist stance of Muslim theology: the two cardinal truths of Islam are demonstrable through rational argument. This implies that neither truth is axiomatic; that is, neither God's existence as sole deity nor the truthfulness of his prophets is self-evident. Self-evident truths are present in human intellects as innate givens; they do not require demonstration but rather constitute the starting point for the demonstration of other truths. The two cardinal truths of Islam belong among those other truths. Neither the existence of the one God nor the veracity of prophets may therefore be regarded as givens.

This is not the place to discuss in detail the rational arguments that Muslim theology constructed in support of the two cardinal truths. I note in passing, however, that a variety of arguments were used for both tenets and that among the arguments for God's existence the ones most favored were those that modern philosophers would classify as the argument from design and the argument from the contingency of the world, while arguments for the truthfulness of prophets all centered around the concept of the miraculous sign. It may also be noted that Muslim theology sought to demonstrate on rational grounds not only God's existence but also his attributes. Muslim thinkers have, of course, debated the degree of proof-value of strictly rational arguments as avenues to certainty with respect to religious realities. For Ghazālī, for example, rational arguments were satisfying only for certain minds. Some people—and Ghazālī included himself among them—were so constituted as to not be able to find certainty through rational argument alone: for them a higher level of apprehension of the cardinal truths, one grounded in a mystical experience that transcended rational categories and norms, was necessary. Among modern students of the Qurʾān one occasionally hears comments to the effect that the Qurʾān itself does not set about to prove God's existence but rather assumes it. On the other hand, one of the most recurrent themes in the Qurʾān, one which, as has been already pointed out in this study, forms an integral part of the Qurʾānic understanding of covenant, is that of the signs (*āyāt*, a word akin to *dalīl* in meaning) of God's favor and power, many of which could be construed by a mind predisposed to do so as signs of God's existence, the raw material for the construction of rational arguments. Whatever may be the case with the Qurʾān itself and whatever may be the attitude of different Muslim thinkers toward the rational arguments for the cardinal truths, such arguments are undeniably central to the Muslim theological enterprise.

The indicators (*adilla* or *dalāʾil,* plural of *dalīl*) are said to be implanted in human intellects, which therefore constitute the proper locus of these indicators. Although rational arguments for the two cardinal tenets make use of the raw material of personal experience of the world, in which the *āyāt* of the Qurʾān are surely to be located, rational arguments as such can exist only in intellects, and according to the creation theory developed in Muslim theology they can exist in intellects only because God *put* them there, that is to say, created them there.[15]

The implanting of the *adilla* is associated with the establishment of the divine covenant in Rāzī's discussions of seven Qurʾānic passages. In these discussions other interpretations of the divine covenant are mentioned that do not employ the notion of *dalīl,* indicating that the approach of the theologians was not universally adopted among Muslim thinkers, even though it alone sought to construct a truly comprehensive and systematic theory of covenant. Of the seven Qurʾānic passages, two (Sūra 2:63 and 5:70) are concerned with the covenant with the Israelites. It is in his discussion of 2:63 that Rāzī makes his only mention anywhere throughout his commentary of a name in connection with the *dalīl*-centered interpretation: al-Aṣamm, no doubt Abū Bakr ʿAbd al-Raḥmān al-Aṣamm, the Muʿtazilī theologian.[16] It is not clear whether al-Aṣamm is to be credited with first developing the *dalīl*-centered interpretation of the divine covenant as such or just with applying it to this particular verse. Elsewhere Rāzī simply mentions this interpretation as one that existed among Muslim exegetes, without mentioning names. Certain clues indicate clearly that he himself espoused this interpretation, something we would expect him, as a Muslim theologian, to do.[17] Thus, for the

[15] Rāzī speaks of God as having 'created' (*khalaqa*) *dalāʾil* in his discussion of Sūra 5:70 (12:55:2t).

[16] Rāzī 3:107:1t.

[17] Twice in presenting the *dalīl*-centered interpretation alongside other interpretations Rāzī indicates his own preference for it (2:147:5b–148:2t, 4:50:12t). Furthermore, in explaining "We made a covenant with the Children of Israel" (5:70) Rāzī states that the phrase means "We created indicators and we created the intellect which guides people [i.e., the Children of Israel] in the methods of argument" (12:55:2–3t). He does not mention other interpretations in this passage, nor does he attribute this interpretation to anyone. I gather, therefore, that he is stating his own view.

theologians, God even at Sinai established his covenant by implanting in human intellects indicators of his existence as sole deity and of the truthfulness of his prophets.

Of the five remaining passages to which the *dalīl*-centered interpretation is applied, two (Sūra 2:27, 3:77) are concerned with a covenant that has been broken or traded off for worldly gain without specifying precisely what people are involved:[18] in the case of 2:27 that people could be the Israelites, though it is more likely to have been those in Medina who believed and then subsequently abandoned their belief; in the case of 3:77 it appears to be the "People of the book" in general (inclusive of both Jews and Christians) that are involved. Another passage (Sūra 57:7–8), on the other hand, is clearly concerned with God's covenant with the Muslim believers ("He has already made a covenant with you, if you are believers"), which it seems to cite in order to encourage people not to give in to pressures to abandon belief. Still another passage (Sūra 7:102) appears to be dealing with covenants with the various vanished communities (*qurā*) to whom prophets (Hūd, Ṣāliḥ, Lot, Shu^{c}ayb) had been sent. The last of the seven passages (Sūra 7:172) is a special case that I shall turn to shortly.

I now turn to the question: In what sense are the *adilla* instruments of divine covenant-making? How can it be said that in implanting them in human intellects God places human beings under an obligation to obey him? The answer that emerges from Rāzī's commentary can, I think, be best stated as follows: by implanting the *adilla* in human intellects God ushers human beings into an encounter with himself and with his prophet. Apart from the *adilla*, human beings cannot truly be said to be in a situation of encounter with either God or his prophet since they are cognizant of neither. True encounter requires mutual awareness. In the case of a prophet, one may be in the presence of the prophet without being aware that the prophet is indeed a prophet. Even if one is cognizant of the prophet's claim to be a prophet, one is not truly aware that he is a prophet unless one knows the claim to be true, and without this awareness there is no genuine encounter with the prophet *qua* prophet. The knowledge of the truthfulness of a prophet's claim to be a prophet occurs through *adilla*.

To be ushered into an encounter with God and his prophet is to be ushered into a covenantal moment, a moment of receiving divine commandments through which one becomes aware of an obligation

[18] It may be noted that the term employed in the discussion of Sūra 2:27 is *ḥujja dālla*, rather than *dalīl* (Rāzī 2:147:11b; cf. 19:40:14t).

to obey God. A prophet is, above all other things, a bearer of commandments (*awāmir, nawāhī*). When one encounters a prophet with full awareness of who the prophet is, namely a prophet *of God*, one necessarily in the same moment becomes aware that the commandments that the prophet bears are commandments *of God*. An encounter with God *and his prophet* is thus tantamount to an encounter with divine commandments. Only in such a dual encounter—the true essence of the covenant in its totality—can one become aware of obligation. Orthodox Sunnī theology was especially uncompromising on the issue of whether moral obligation can be known through rational intuition or demonstration on the one hand or only from divine revelation on the other. It came down decidedly on the side of divine revelation: obligation can emerge only in a revelational—which is another way of saying covenantal—situation, and revelation requires a prophet. Thus orthodox Sunnī theologians, in contrast to the Muᶜtazilī theologians and some Shīᶜī thinkers, reject altogether the possibility of a rationalist, or natural law, ethic. On the other hand, rational demonstration plays a crucial role in bringing human beings *into* a situation they are able to recognize as covenantal, or revelational. That is to say, rational demonstration brings human beings to the point where they acknowledge God's existence as sole deity and are able to identify words that come forth from the mouths of prophets as a revelation from him. Once they have been brought into confrontation with the revealed word, they then learn from it that they are under an obligation to obey God.[19] This obligation cannot be inferred logically from the sheer existence of God, since

[19] It is appropriate to note at this point that Muslim theology classifies the contents of revelation as *dalāʾil samᶜīya* (indicators handed down by word of mouth from the Prophet, that is, transmitted indicators) in contradistinction to *dalāʾil ᶜaqlīya* (rational indicators). The former exist outside the human intellect; they are found only within the corpus of sacred scripture or tradition. The latter, on the other hand, have their locus within the human intellect. It is with these that I have been concerned thus far in this study. One can say that the *dalāʾil ᶜaqlīya* lead to the point where one is constrained to accept the *dalāʾil samᶜīya*, from which knowledge of obligation is in turn derived (see Rāzī 19:40:11–17t, 20:107:5t, 29:217:1t). It is the *dalāʾil samᶜīya* that Rāzī has in mind when he says of prophets that they "bring indicators of duties of all kinds" (9:124:5b).

It may also be noted that while the truthfulness of prophets is grounded ultimately in *dalāʾil ᶜaqlīya* having to do with miracles, in the case of Muḥammad it is grounded also in *dalāʾil samᶜīya*, namely the scriptures of Jews and Christians, which according to the Qurʾān, speak of the coming of Muḥammad. Thus Rāzī states that in both the Torah and the Gospel, God imposed upon Jews and Christians (*ummat mūsā wa-ᶜīsā*) the duty of making known what was in those two scriptures in the way of indications (*dalāʾil*) of the validity of his prophecy, but they instead concealed or distorted these indicators or gave false interpretations to them (Rāzī 9:124:4–11t). In so doing they have

God may or may not elect to impose obligations upon his creatures. As ultimate Sovereign, it is of course his prerogative to do so if he so wills, but that he in fact *does* so will is something that must be learned from revelation. The all-embracing commandment that serves as the capstone of God's covenant with humankind is: "Obey God and his messenger [*atīʿū allāh wa-al-rasūl*]." This commandment is the well-spring of all obligation, the source of the holy law that is to govern all aspects of human life.[20]

---

broken the covenant (Rāzī 11:186:8–7b, 188:8–4b). These indicators in Jewish and Christian scriptures of Muḥammad's prophethood and of the duty to believe him are themselves sometimes regarded by the commentators as the instruments of a covenant with Jews and Christians related specifically to the mission of Muḥammad (Rāzī 8:114:8–5b; cf. 3:34:2–1b and Qurʾān 7:157). Thus God has made a covenant with the scriptural communities to the effect that they must believe and obey Muḥammad: *qad akhadha ʿalayhim al-ʿahd waʾl-mīthāq bi-taṣdīq muḥammad* (Rāzī 2:148:2–3t; cf. 8:103:8–9t, 11:179:9–7b, 19:41:4–6t). Thus the notion of a divine covenant is given a special application to the problem of Jewish and Christian rejection of Muḥammad's mission and becomes a key factor in their indictment.

[20] The insistence of orthodox thinkers on the revelational basis of all obligation did raise a dilemma that had to be dealt with in Muslim theology. The dilemma was this: if the existence of God and the prophethood of prophets are not self-evident but must be established through rational demonstration, then if it so happens that I am devoid of a knowledge of these truths and have no special desire to engage in the requisite reasoning, how can I be *obliged* to do so? If all obligation proceeds from revelation, then the obligation to engage in reasoning that will lead to a knowledge of God's existence and of the prophethood of the prophets can proceed only from revelation. But since my ability to recognize divine revelation is itself dependent upon my knowledge of God's existence and of the prophethood of prophets, there is no way I can know of the obligation to engage in reasoning prior to my actual engaging in reasoning. Therefore, I am not culpable if I simply choose not to engage in the reasoning that will lead to the knowledge of the two cardinal truths. This dilemma was particularly serious when applied to the mission of the prophets, for it is one of the tasks of prophets, according to Muslim theology, to call upon people to consider the arguments (*adilla*) for God's existence and for prophecy. How is a prophet to answer his audience if they say, "We know of no obligation to ponder the *adilla*; therefore, we shall ignore you and continue in our heedlessness of the existence of the one God and of the truthfulness of your claims"?

Rāzī does not, to my knowledge, discuss this problem in his commentary, although there is an allusion to it in his discussion of 57:8 (see 29:217:3–5t). The theologian and jurist Sayf al-Dīn al-Āmidī, a contemporary of Rāzī, gives an idea of the position taken by orthodox Muslim theologians on this issue. In his major work on jurisprudence Āmidī states that once human beings have been exposed to the *possibility* that the Prophet's claims are true they may be said to be under an obligation to engage in the reasoning enjoined upon them (see Sayf al-Dīn al-Āmidī, *Al-Iḥkām fī uṣūl al-aḥkām* [Cairo: Dār al-Kutub, 1914], 1:127, 129–30). The obligation, in other words, arises from the mere possibility that the commandment to engage in reasoning is an expression of the will of a divine sovereign; it is not necessary that the commandment be definitely *known* to be an expression of that will. Once this first of all obligations is fulfilled,

The *dalīl*-centered interpretation of the divine covenant clearly reinforces the tendency toward universalism that I have already observed in Qurʾānic thinking about covenant. The *adilla* are implanted in the human intellect, which is the possession of all human beings. A covenant effected through the *adilla* can never, therefore, distinguish one people or community from another. The distinctiveness of any community must arise out of something other than the divine covenant as such.[21] As I have noted, faithfulness to the covenant would appear to be, in Qurʾānic thinking, a chief distinguishing mark of the Muslim community.[22] The other communities appear to be distinguished from each other by different patterns of unfaithfulness, different forms of heresy, although precovenantal natural solidarities may be a factor in some cases. Communities are also distinguished from each other in more fundamental ways that do not have to do with their behavior in history in response to the covenant: they are distinguished at the very outset by virtue of the identity of the prophets sent directly to them, by the special character or style of their scriptures, by the unique features of their sacred sagas, and by certain distinctive aspects of the divine law given to them. With respect to the last of these factors, it should be kept in mind that variation in the

---

knowledge of the existence of the one God and of the truthfulness of prophets will arise so that all further obligation will rest upon the firmer ground of knowledge.

This initial obligation to ponder the *adilla* that undergird God's existence and the truthfulness of the prophets may be said to flow from the *adilla* themselves in the sense that it flows from the possibility that the *adilla* will, on consequence of reflection upon them, lead human beings to a knowledge of the two fundamental verities and thus to a confirmation of the initial obligation. The *adilla* are thus crucial to the very rise of obligation: if there were no *adilla*, the obligation would not arise. Perhaps a distinction should be drawn between the initial, pre-speculative impact of the *adilla* on human awareness and the final, post-speculative impact. Initially—that is, the moment a prophet draws the attention of human beings to the *adilla*—these *adilla* function as possible avenues to the truth by virtue of which the obligation to reflect further arises; subsequently, after the reflection has taken place, the *adilla* engender knowledge.

[21] Rāzī observes that the purpose of the reference to the covenant with Israel in Sūra 5:12 is to show that God's covenant with the Muslims does not distinguish them from other peoples, that he had imposed obligations on pre-Islamic peoples just as he was now imposing obligations on the Muslims, that the divine 'custom' (*ʿāda*) was to impose obligation upon (ergo: establish his covenant with) all of his creatures (Rāzī 11:184:4–6t).

[22] Thus in commenting on 16:95 Rāzī equates remaining Muslim (*al-baqāʾ ʿalā al-islām*) with fulfilling the divine covenant and abandoning Islam with the breaking of the covenant (Rāzī 20:111:1–5t). In this passage he furthermore refers to the divine covenant as *ʿahd al-islām*. Thus a Muslim is by definition one who fulfills the covenant, and Islam is by definition the act of abiding by the covenant (or of covenanting to abide by the divine covenant; see the discussion that follows on the relationship between divine and human covenanting).

divine law given to the different communities relates apparently to matters of detail or ritual style, not to matters of great substance: the most fundamental postures required of human beings in the law seem to constitute a constant. Furthermore, it may be argued that such variation as is to be found in the divine law from one community to another is on the same order as the variation that may take place within one and the same community from one moment to another during a prophetic era. Variation arises, not out of a divine wish to distinguish communities from each other, but largely out of the differences in circumstances in which communities find themselves from one place to another and from one time to another, differences in what the Muslim theologians and exegetes would have called *asbāb al-nuzūl*, circumstances occasioning revelation.

The universalism of the thinking of the Muslim theologians about covenant is most strikingly evident in their interpretation of Sūra 7:172:

> And [remember] when your Lord brought forth from the Children of Adam, from their loins, their seed, and made them testify against themselves [saying]: Am I not your Lord? They said: Yes, verily. We testify. [This was] lest you should say at the Day of Resurrection: Lo! of this we were unaware.

Although this verse does not employ an Arabic word meaning "covenant," Muslim exegetes are generally agreed that it is depicting a covenant between God and the entire human family. Rāzī at least once refers to this covenant as 'the Covenant of Sovereignty and Subordination' (*ᶜahd al-rubūbīya waᵓl-ᶜubūdīya*), a convenient designation that I shall adopt.[23] The verse seems to depict an exchange between God and the entire human family in which God addresses the human family with a question that appears to have a somewhat Socratic purpose, namely that of quickening in the human mind an awareness of something the truth of which cannot, on reflection, be denied. God is, in other words, impressing his sovereignty upon the human consciousness, thus leaving to human beings no recourse but to acknowledge that sovereignty.

Before exploring the theological interpretation of this verse, it is worth noting that even among those exegetes who did not embrace this interpretation (in most cases because they predated the rise of Muslim theology) there was a tendency to interpret certain other Qurᵓānic references to covenant in its light. Thus the covenant with

[23] Rāzī 19:41:4t.

believers is thrice identified with the covenant of Sūra 7:172; the covenant with the People of the Book (or perhaps the Israelites in particular) and the covenant with the vanished communities are similarly identified.[24] Thus even apart from the theological interpretation of covenant, there is a trend toward universalizing and dehistoricizing God's covenants with particular communities by identifying those covenants with the primordial covenant with all the descendants of Adam.

In the theological interpretation of 7:172, once again, the theme of *adilla* occupies a central position. Reacting to a literalist interpretation that insisted—using *ḥadīth* material as evidence—that God verbally addressed all of Adam's descendants in a single moment just as they all verbally replied in that same moment and that in order for this encounter to take place God made all of Adam's descendants emerge momentarily from his loins, the Muslim theologians argued that the description of the encounter is metaphorical and that the all-important covenantal moment thus described occurs in the life of each human individual at the point where full humanity is reached.[25] In their view, the Qurʾān was saying that God caused human beings to emerge, not from the loins of Adam in a preexistent or primordial moment, but from the loins of fathers down through the generations through normal conception and gestation. As soon as each human being reaches the point of full maturity as a human being God then elicits from him or her, by means of the indicators of his existence as the sole deity implanted in the human intellect, a witness to his sovereignty such as may be used against him or her on the Day of Resurrection in the event of a plea of ignorance.[26] The indicators of God's existence are thus the means whereby a covenantal moment is brought about within the experience of every member of the human family, one in which he or she is made aware of the divine sovereignty and of his or her status as a subordinate or subject of the Divine Sovereign. It is this awareness that constitutes the basis of human accountability vis-à-vis the Divine Judge.

It is important to bear in mind that the Covenant of Sovereignty and Subordination involves the working only of indicators of God's existence as sole deity and that there is no mention, in connection with this covenant, of the indicators of the truthfulness of prophets.

[24] Rāzī 11:179:7-5b; 19:40:9-11t, 41:4t; 29:217:5-6t; 2:148:4-6t; 14:188:5-3b.

[25] Rāzī 15:46:11b-47:11t. The theologians argued that if such an encounter took place it is beyond the memory of human beings and it makes no sense therefore to affirm (as the Qurʾān does) that on the Day of Resurrection this covenant will be used as evidence against human beings (Rāzī 2:148:6-8t).

[26] Rāzī 15:50:1-5t.

The Covenant of Sovereignty and Subordination thus appears not to present the entire covenantal process or experience. A comment found in Rāzī's discussion of Sūra 2:63 is particularly helpful at this juncture. According to Rāzī, there was a belief among Muslim exegetes that there were two divine covenants: one consisted of God's "extracting them [i.e., human beings] from the loins of Adam and making them witness against themselves," a clear reference to the Covenant of Sovereignty and Subordination; the other consisted of God's "imposing on people the obligation to obey prophets [*alzama al-nās mutabāᶜat al-anbiyāʾ*]."[27] Interpreted along the lines laid down by Muslim theology, the second covenant clearly entails the functioning of the indicators of the truthfulness of prophets.

It is, I think, not inconsistent with the thinking of the Muslim theologians to view these two covenants, not as separate entities, but as successive phases of a larger single covenantal process. In the first phase, that which bears the name "Covenant of Sovereignty and Subordination," God quickens in human beings an awareness of his existence as sole deity; in the second, an awareness that certain individuals claiming to be prophets are indeed his prophets and that the commandments they bear place the human beings under an obligation to obey his will as expressed therein. This two-fold structure of the covenantal process clearly reflects the two-fold structure of the central Muslim creed, composed as it is of two cardinal tenets, *tawḥīd* and *risāla*. If this construction of the covenantal process be correct, then it would seem that when prophets appear, accompanied by miraculous signs, either (1) the second phase only of the covenantal process is effected, the first having already been affected at the moment of attainment of maturity, or (2) both phases are effected, the first phase for the second time in the individual's experience and the second phase for the first time. The first view appears to be that attributed to Ibn ᶜAbbās, in connection with Sūra 2:63.[28] The second view would seem to be the one necessarily held by those interpreters who saw both of the two categories of proof at work on occasions where prophets appear accompanied by miraculous signs, as at Sinai. If such interpreters accepted the notion of a universal Covenant of Sovereignty and Subordination effected at the moment of attainment of maturity, then they would have been compelled, one would think, to regard this first phase of the covenantal process as repeated with the appearance of prophets. Prophets do, after all, call upon human beings to reflect on the signs of God's existence in nature, which also

[27] Rāzī 3:107:11t.
[28] Rāzī 3:107:11t.

constitute signs of his power and beneficence. It may be apropos to recall here the often mentioned Islamic dictum to the effect that every individual is born a Muslim and is only subsequently corrupted by his environment.[29] If prophets are addressing persons whose native sense of God's existence has been suppressed through the corrupting influences of their environment, then it would stand to reason that the first phase of the covenantal process would have to be repeated.

The reader may be wondering at this point how the *dalīl*-centered interpretation of the divine covenant relates to the signs/commandments/promise cluster discussed earlier in connection with examination of Qurʾānic thinking about covenant. The commandments are obviously a central element in the *dalīl*-centered interpretation. The *adilla* have as their ultimate *raison d'être* the function of ushering human beings into a situation in which they may receive commandments from God and thus know themselves to be under obligation to obey him. However, the accounts of the *dalil*-centered interpretation in Rāzī's commentary display no interest in a particular body of commandments as fundamental. Whatever tendency toward the formulation of a decalogue-like corpus may be discerned in the Qurʾān, no such tendency is to be found in the thinking of the Muslim theologians about covenant. The commandments that human beings receive in the covenantal moment constitute the whole of the divine law, not a set of fundamentals. Muslim scholars may spend a lifetime trying to give precise articulation to those commandments, but the reception of them, no matter how imperfectly they may in some cases be understood, takes place within the covenantal moment. So strongly does Muslim theology link the whole of the divine law to the divine covenant that there is in certain passages in Rāzī's commentary a tendency simply to identify the entire body of commandments with the covenant, to make "law" and "covenant" coextensive.[30]

[29] An early Muslim creed, the Fiqh Akbar II, linked this idea directly to the covenant with the Children of Adam. See A. J. Wensinck, *The Muslim Creed* (Cambridge: Cambridge University, 1932) 94.

[30] Thus *ʿahd* in Sūra 2:40 is said to be a reference to all that God commands, not just to certain commandments, an obvious contrast to the decalogue-centered conception of covenant (Rāzī 3:34:17–18t, cf. 8:104:4b, 9:124:6–5b, 19:40:11t, 20:107:4–5t). In his commentary on 2:83 Rāzī says, "*Mīthāq* [in this verse] refers to the totality of what is required in religion, for the command to worship God presupposes a knowledge of his essence and of what is necessary, possible or impossible with respect to him and of his unity and freedom from contradiction and from partners and children and of the way in which that (true) worship is established, viz. through revelation and prophecy. Thus 'worship no (god) save God' embraces everything which is included in theology [*kalām*] and jurisprudence [*fiqh*], since there is no true worship apart form these two

The 'signs' (*āyāt, bayyināt*) that figure so prominently in Qurʾānic thinking about covenant have their correlates in the *adilla* themselves. As was noted earlier, 'signs' is a possible translation of *adilla.*[31] I have suggested, however, that the Qurʾānic signs should be located within the phenomenal world in contrast to the *adilla,* which have their locus within human intellects, and that the former constitute the raw material out of which the latter, as rational arguments, are constructed. There is, furthermore, yet another contrast to be made. The Qurʾānic signs, insofar as they relate to God, display his favor and his power. The *adilla* may have something to do with God's power (as one of the seven divine attributes), but they are primarily focused on God's existence as sole deity and sovereign, and they seem quite definitely to have nothing to do with God's favors as such. The *adilla* of Muslim theology do not seem to have proof of God's favors as a primary object. From the point of view of Ashᶜarite theology, divine favors have no bearing on the covenantal moment. Even though Rāzī occasionally mentions divine favors as a factor in the emergency of obligation, one would think that as an Ashᶜarite he would not seriously entertain the notion that the divine favors could function in this manner.[32] It is a hallmark of Ashᶜarite theology that divine favor as exhibited in the beneficent workings of the natural order does not *engender* obligation,[33] although one may suppose that even for an Ashᶜarite once obligation has arisen in consequence of the prophet Word contemplation on the divine favors may enhance one's subjective appreciation of personal obligations. Thus it would appear that only insofar as the Qurʾānic signs relate to God's power and (indirectly) to his existence—such that they may be correlated with the *adilla* of Muslim theology—may they be said to enter into the thinking of the theologians about covenant. Insofar as the signs relate to God's favors they do not seem to enter in at all, at least not in any significant way.

As for the divine promise, this is seldom mentioned in discussion of covenant in Rāzī's commentary. However, the two places in which

---

things" (Rāzī 3:164:6–1b). Thus the cultivation of the Islamic sciences of *kalām* and *fiqh* become, for Rāzī, a duty contained within the covenant with Israel.

It may be noted that the association of the term *ᶜahd* with divine commands is due in large part to the fact that *ᶜahd* may function as a *maṣdar* for *ᶜahida,* which in combination with *ilā* takes on the sense of 'to charge, to impose (as a duty)', an expression that appears in the Qurʾān (2:125, 3:183, 20:115, 36:60). With respect to 20:115 Rāzī says, "There is no doubt that *ᶜahd* means a command from God" (22:124:2t).

[31] Rāzī in fact juxtaposes *dalāʾil* and *bayyināt* in one passage, (viz. 29:217:9t).

[32] See, for example, Rāzī 11:178:8b–179:8t.

[33] See, for example, Āmidī, *Al-Iḥkam,* 1:124–30.

it is mentioned are sufficient to show that it entered into Muslim thinking about covenant. Quite apart from these instances where the divine promise is mentioned in connection with the covenant, there are untold instances throughout the religious literature of Islam where it is mentioned as a subject in its own right. It is in fact a major theme in Islam. The two passages in question in Rāzī's commentary are his discussions of Sūra 2:40 and 2:80. He mentions that the majority of the commentators, including Ibn ᶜAbbās, have interpreted God's words, "I will fulfill (my) covenant with you [*ūfi bi-ᶜahdikum*]," to mean that God will fulfill his promise in the sense that he will be pleased with those who obey his commandments and will admit them to Paradise.[34] In connection with Sūra 2:80, where again the word 'covenant' (*ᶜahd,* which appears in the phrase "Truly God will not break his covenant") is taken by interpreters to be a reference to his promise, Rāzī takes pains to show that the divine promise in no sense places an obligation upon God. In this he reflects mainline Sunnī thinking, which affirms that God cannot be under any obligation, that status being limited entirely to the creature. The term "promise," as applied to God, can therefore signify nothing more than a divine statement of what will be, of what will obtain for human beings if they obey the divine commandments. To say that God always fulfills his promise or that he never breaks his promise is thus tantamount to saying that he is always truthful with respect to what he says about the future. To speak of God as breaking his promise would be tantamount to speaking of him as lying, and to speak of God as lying is to blaspheme.[35]

The Divine Covenant and Human Oath-Taking

It may now be asked, What role, if any, does the *dalīl*-centered interpretation of the divine covenant assign to human beings in the making of that covenant? It may be recalled that the divine-human encounter described in Sūra 7:172 culminates in a human response to the divine initiative. If God does indeed employ *adilla* to awaken in the minds of the Children of Adam an awareness of his existence as their sovereign, as the theological interpretation would have it, it would appear that he is not satisfied to let matters rest once that awareness has emerged. Rather, he expects the Children of Adam to *do* something in response to the reality of which they have become aware: they must—and in fact do—say 'Yes' (*balā*) to that reality.

[34] Rāzī 3:34:6–4b.
[35] Rāzī 3:142:6b, 143:2t.

This saying 'Yes' to the divine sovereignty is called in Rāzī's commentary *Al-iqrār biʾl-rubūbīya*.[36] *Iqrār* may be translated in a variety of ways: the Children of Adam may be said to 'acknowledge, concede, confess, or agree to' the divine sovereignty. This Arabic expression brings to mind those Qurʾānic verses (Sūra 2:84, 3:81) where the cognate form *aqrarnā* ("we acknowledge, agree to, etc.") is used to indicate the human response to the divine initiative in covenant-making. Elsewhere (Sūra 5:7), the phrase "We hear and we obey" is used.

How is this human response to be understood? Obviously neither the Covenant of Sovereignty and Subordination nor the larger divine covenant of which it is a part is contractual in nature such that divine sovereignty, prophecy, and human obligation may be said to be contingent upon the consent of human beings as one of parties to a bilateral agreement. To translate *aqrarnā* as 'we agree to' does not mean that this human agreement is determinative of anything essential to the covenantal relationship and terms. It is perhaps best to see the human *iqrār* as something apart from which the divine covenant cannot become operative as a positive force in human life but as essentially distinct from the covenant per se. The divine covenant should, I think, be identified solely with God's covenanting with human beings exclusive of any response they may make. He is their sovereign, certain people are his prophets. The commandments enunciated by those prophets are therefore his commandments such that human beings are under an obligation to obey them, and if they do obey them he will reward them according to his promise, otherwise punishment will befall them. This constitutes the whole of the divine covenant, and human beings play no role in its making: it is entirely unilateral. But once made, it is to be either accepted—the only reasonable course for human beings—or disregarded. The term *aqrarnā* betokens acceptance.

Occasionally the commentators describe the human response to the divine covenant as a swearing or vowing (i.e., taking an oath) to abide by it. This human swearing can be referred to by the same Arabic terms that are used to refer to the divine covenant, especially *mīthāq* and *ʿahd* (or *muʿāhada*). Swearing is, in fact, a kind of covenanting. However, the divine covenant cannot be described as a swearing, for God by definition cannot swear to anything. Swearing is an act of binding one's self to something, of placing one's self under a limit; that is why one swears *by* something (someone) other than one's self. But God cannot, as I noted in discussing the divine

[36] Rāzī 2:148:9t.

promise, be bound or limited by anything, and by the same token he cannot swear to anything. Thus divine covenanting may be distinguished from human covenanting by virtue of its not constituting or involving an oath.

In several passages in his commentary (referred to below) Rāzī mentions a view of the divine covenant according to which God imposes obligations on human beings by exacting from them an oath. This view, which sees obligation as consequent upon human oath-taking, seems to have some support in the phrase *akhadha al-mīthāq*, which appears several times in the Qurʾān with God as the subject of *akhadha*.[37] While the translations tend to render it as "He [God] made a covenant," a more literal rendering would be: "He took a covenant." 'Took' can in turn be taken to mean either 'accepted' or 'extracted'. Although *mīthāq* typically, in the Qurʾān, is in construct with a noun naming the human party to the covenant, it is followed by the preposition 'from' in Sūra 33:7: "And when we took [accepted or extracted] a covenant from the prophets." Commenting on another passage (Sūra 3:81) that speaks of a covenant with prophets (to be considered later), Rāzī records the observation that the *mīthāq* entails two parties: one who 'takes' it (*ākhidh*) and those from whom it is 'taken' (*maʾkhūdh minhum*), the former being God and the latter the human beings.[38] I infer from this that where the word *mīthāq* appears in construct with the name of a person (or people) that person (or people) is the *maʾkhūdh minhu* (*minhum*). Those from whom a covenant is taken may likewise be described as "givers" of the covenant; accordingly, several passages in Rāzī show a complementarity between the taking (by God) of a covenant and the giving (by human beings) of that same covenant, between *akhdh al-mīthāq* and *iʿṭāʾ al-mīthāq*.[39]

The *Tāj al-ʿarūs* confirms these observations concerning the phrase *akhadha al-mīthāq*: it states explicitly that the phrase means

[37] The phrase *akhadha al-ʿahd* is also possible in Arabic, though it never appears in the Qurʾān (see Rāzī 3:34:9b, 2:148:2–3t).

[38] Rāzī 8:115:11–12t. It may be noted that *akhadha al-mīthāq* sometimes is followed, in Rāzī's commentary, by *ʿalā* rather than *min* such that the two parties become *ākhidh* and *maʾkhūdh ʿalayhi*. This seems consonant with the Arabic phrase *akhadha ʿalayhi*, which expresses an imposition of obligation even without employing the word *mīthāq* (or *ʿahd*) (Rāzī 8:103:13b). It may also be noted that the *ākhidh*, in respect to his being the one with whom (or on account of whom) the covenant is made, may also be called *maʾkhūdh lahu*.

[39] This complementarity is evident, for example, in Rāzī 15:47:6–4b. However, wherever *aʿṭū al-mīthāq* appears in Rāzī's commentary it entails a complementarity with *akhadha al-mīthāq*.

'to elicit an oath' (*istaḥlafa*).[40] It is no wonder, therefore, that some exegetes were inclined to see human oath-taking as the crucial factor in the making of the covenant between God and human beings—as the linchpin in the rise of obligation. On this interpretation, the human beings were the real *makers* of the covenant: God was merely an eliciter, an *ākhidh*, and the covenant was divine only with reference to its *ākhidh*. As *ākhidh*, God of course decides what he will take or not take from human beings. In fact, he stipulates the terms that he wants human beings to swear to and the rewards that will follow fulfillment: God may thus be said to set up the covenant he wants human beings to give to him. But it is the givers of the covenant who are the true covenanters (*muᶜāhidūn*), and the very existence of the covenant stands or falls on their action.

This oath-centered understanding of covenant is reflected, for example, in one of the interpretations of Sūra 2:63 recorded by Rāzī. According to that interpretation, God's causing Mount Sinai to tower over the heads of the Israelites was designed to so dazzle their minds and arouse awe in them that they would 'give a covenant' (*aᶜṭū al-ᶜahd wa-al-mīthāq*: note the conjoining of *ᶜahd* with *mīthāq*) to the effect that they would not return to the worship of the calf but would abide by the Torah: "And this was a covenant which they imposed upon themselves towards God [*kāna hādhā ᶜahdan wa mawthiqan jaᶜalūhu lillāh ᶜalā anfusihim*]."[41] The real covenant-makers at Sinai are thus the Children of Israel. That the covenant thus made constitutes an oath is made clear in the commentary on Sūra 2:27 (*alladhīna yanquḍūna ᶜahd allāh min baᶜd mīthāqihi*) in which Rāzī speaks of interpreters who hold that *mīthāq* in this verse refers to an oath of the sort mentioned in Sūra 35:42: "And they swore by God their most binding oath that if a warner came unto them they would be more tractable than any of the nations." On this view, "since they did not do what they had sworn (to do) he describes them as having broken this *ᶜahd* and *mīthāq*."[42]

The tendency to view human covenant-making or oath-taking as the crucial factor in the emergency of obligation was patently unacceptable to those who adhered to the *dalīl*-centered interpretation of covenant. They did not hesitate to regard the working of the *adilla* as a covenant-making process with God as its subject and with human beings in the entirely passive role of audience. Even the phrase *akhadha al-mīthāq* did not deter them from this understanding.

[40] Al-Murtada al-Zabidi, *Tāj al-ᶜarūs* (Benghazi: Dar Libya, 1966), 7:83.

[41] Rāzī 3:107:1–9t.

[42] Rāzī 2:147:8–6b.

When the Qurʾān spoke of God as 'taking' a covenant from human beings, it meant to them that he had implanted *adilla* in human intellects through which alone obligation would arise. As implanter of the *adilla* and true determinant of obligation, God was the real maker of the covenant, notwithstanding the verb *akhadha*. Thus even at Sinai God makes the covenant through the operation of the *adilla*.[43] He does not merely induce the Children of Israel to make a covenant by performing a miracle in front of their eyes. God imposes obligation to them; they do not impose it upon themselves.

This is not to say that self-imposed oaths and vows are without consequence in the Muslim theological view, or that God does not call upon human beings to swear loyalty to his covenant. Rāzī records an interpretation of Sūra 13:20 that takes into account both a divine covenanting with human beings and a human covenanting with God and seeks to establish a relationship of complementarity between them. Sūra 13:20 reads: "But only men of understanding heed, such as keep the covenant [*ʿahd*] of God and break not the covenant [*mīthāq*]." The interpretation argues that "a *mīthāq* is something which the one upon whom God has [previously] imposed obligations [*mukallaf*] makes binding upon himself [*inna al-mīthāq mā wath-thaqa al-mukallaf ʿalā nafsihi*]."[44] Accordingly, the term *ʿahd* in this passage must be referring to what God initially imposes on his human subject in the way of duties, thus making her or him a *mukallaf*, and the term *mīthāq* must refer to what the human subject by a free choice imposes upon herself or himself in the way of a commitment to obey, as for example when one swears to obey and do good works.[45] Just as human beings may covenant with God to

[43] Rāzī 3:106:2-1b.

[44] Rāzī 19:41:1-3t.

[45] Ibid. It should not be supposed from this interpretation of Sūra 13:20 that the terms *ʿahd* and *mīthāq* lend themselves to this interpretation by virtue of their lexical meanings. Lexically, they are neutral: either of them can refer either to a divine or a human covenanting. *ʿAhd* is a verbal noun, or *maṣdar* (Rāzī 8:103:5t), and *mīthāq* also, though possessing the form of a noun of instrument, is treated in Rāzī's commentary as a verbal noun (8:115:5t). Rāzī quotes Zamakhsharī to the effect that *mīthāq* may have the sense of *tawthīq* 'to make binding', just as *mīʿād* may have the sense of *waʿd*, and *mīlād* the sense of *wilāda* (2:148:13-14t). Thus where God is the subject of a *mīthāq*, he is the one who binds (*muwaththiq*) and the human party acquires the status of being bound (*muwaththaq ʿalayhim*) (cf. Rāzī 8:115:14-15t, where God is also called *muwaththaq lahu*).

It may be noted that when either *ʿahd* or *mīthāq* is in construct with a noun the person or persons designated by the noun may be either subject/agent (*fāʿil*) or object/patient (*mafʿūl*) of the *ʿahd/mithāq* (Rāzī 8:102:5t, 115:5t). Qurʾān 2:40 is an instance where *ʿahd* is used twice in a single statement, once with God as subject/agent and humans as object/patient and once with the opposite arrangement. This Qurʾānic

remain loyal to the covenant that he makes with them, so they may covenant with God with more particular actions in mind, as I will note presently; and they may of course covenant with each other to do certain things, in all these cases taking oaths in God's name. All these types of human covenanting are perfectly compatible with the divine covenant.

What the *dalīl*-centered interpretation insists on, therefore, is (1) that there is a divinely undertaken covenant distinct from and prior to all humanly undertaken covenants and (2) that the former is the ultimate source of all obligation such that any obligation that may arise from the latter is strictly derivative. Muslim theology is adamant in its insistence upon the superiority of divinely imposed obligation over all humanly self-imposed obligation. Divinely imposed obligation stands by itself: in no sense does it require human action to constitute obligation. Humanly self-imposed obligation, in contrast, has validity only insofar as it is grounded in a divinely imposed obligation. If God chooses to command human beings to fulfill the obligations they impose upon themselves, then they must do so. In that case, a higher level of obligation undergirds and accords validity to a lower level of obligation. On the other hand, if a self-imposed obligation runs counter to a divinely imposed obligation, or if circumstances change, so that what was originally grounded in a divinely imposed obligation comes into conflict with the divine will, the self-imposed obligation must be set aside. Thus no oath can in and of itself be permanently binding.[46]

After recording two conflicting interpretations of the covenant mentioned in Sūra 2:27, one *dalīl*-centered and the other oath-

---

verse in fact is suggestive of the complementarity between divine and human covenanting that the interpretation of 13:20 emphasizes.

The neutrality of *ᶜahd* with respect to subject-agent is brought home in Rāzī's discussion of Sūra 23:8. An *ᶜahd,* he says, may be something that one makes binding upon one's self (*ma ᶜaqadahu ᶜalā nafsihi*) for the purpose of gaining favor with God, or it may be something that God commands (*ma amara allāh bihi*). The latter usage is related to the verbal phrase *ᶜahida ila,* which appears in the Qurᵓān (2:125, 3:183, 20:115, 36:60) and clearly signifies a unilateral imposition of obligation (hence the common translation "God charged so-and-so"), whereas the former is related to the verb *ᶜahada* (Rāzī 23:81:11–12t). As a *maṣdar, ᶜahd* in this former sense is more or less synonymous with *muᶜāhada.* The phrase *ma ᶜaqadahu ᶜalā nafsihi* is reminiscent of *ma waththaqahu ᶜalā nafsihi* used to define *mīthāq* in one passage in Rāzī's commentary (19:41:1t). Thus both *ᶜahd* and *mīthāq* may signify an imposition of obligation by human beings upon themselves; and they may likewise signify God's imposition of obligation upon human beings.

[46] Rāzī in fact affirms that one may be duty-bound to break an oath, the duty being divinely imposed (19:40:14–15t). For further discussion of the relationship between human oaths and the divine covenant see Roy P. Mottahedeh, *Loyalty and Leadership in an Early Islamic Society* (Princeton: Princeton University, 1980) 42–50.

centered, Rāzī gives his reasons for preferring the *dalīl*-centered interpretation: "The first [i.e., *dalīl*-centered] interpretation permits inclusion [among the breakers of the covenant mentioned in the verse] of all those who go astray and disbelieve, whereas the second [i.e., oath-centered] interpretation restricts [the application of the verse] to those who are distinguished by having taken an oath."[47] Rāzī alludes to a rule of interpretation according to which a broader interpretation must be preferred over a narrower one unless there are specific contextual clues supporting the narrower interpretation, which in the case of this verse are nonexistence. One can detect here further evidence of the universalist tendency in the theological view of covenant: the *dalīl*-centered approach extends the covenant to all humankind, the oath-centered approach limits it to the oath-takers. Rāzī then goes on to point out that, on the *dalīl*-centered interpretation, blame (*dhamm*, a corollary of obligation) arises from the fact that people broke a covenant God had 'made firm' (*aḥkama*) through *adilla* "which he made clear and raised above doubt," whereas on the oath-centered interpretation blame rests upon the fact that people neglected to do something they had taken upon themselves entirely on their own (*shayʾan hum bi-anfusihim iltazamūhu*). "Obviously," says Rāzī, "it is more proper to establish blame according to the first of these methods." In another passage Rāzī states clearly that the *adilla* are more sure as a basis of obligation than oaths (*awkad min al-ḥilf waʾl-yamīn*); this is why, he says, they are called *mīthāq*.[48]

Although the *dalīl*-centered interpretation of the divine covenant takes pains to distinguish that covenant from any human covenanting done in response to it, it provides grounds for viewing the human response with the utmost seriousness. Here is a case where a lower level of obligation is clearly rooted in a higher level of obligation: in the very act of swearing to abide by the covenant one is obeying a divine commandment, for it can be argued that the commandment to obey God and his Prophet (*atīʿū allāh wa-rasūlahu*), which appears throughout the Qurʾān and which I described earlier as the capstone of the covenant, calls, not for a particular act, but for a commitment to perform all acts God may require of us. To obey this all-embracing general commandment is tantamount to swearing to obey all particular commandments; there is no other way to understand obedience to this commandment *per se* in contradistinction to obedience to particular commandments. And to swear to obey all particular commandments is to swear loyalty to the covenant. Furthermore, there is a

[47] Rāzī 2:147:6–5b.
[48] Rāzī 2:147:6b–148:2t, 19:216:1b–217:1t.

divine commandment to fulfill all covenants made with God, so that not only is one commanded to covenant with God to abide by his covenant, but one is also commanded to abide by this covenant.[49]

While covenanting to abide by the divine covenant has undeniable validity, this is not necessarily true of all human covenanting with God. In covenanting to abide by the divine covenant, one is covenanting to do something that God clearly wishes humans to do, not something they propose to do. Human covenants with God that are built upon human proposals may or may not be valid, depending on whether they are in harmony with the divine will. Thus the Pharaoh and his people covenant with God that if he removes the terror from them they will trust him and let the Israelites go free (Sūra 7:134–35). This covenant was apparently acceptable to God since he responds by removing the terror and then castigates the Pharaoh's people for breaking their covenant.[50] But Sūra 2:80 gives the impression that Israel had substituted for the divine covenant a covenant of their own making that was not acceptable to God. The case of the Pharaoh's covenant shows that one need not be a believer in order to make a covenant with God.[51]

When believers swear to a particular course of action (in contrast to swearing in a general way to remain loyal to the divine covenant), this covenanting will naturally be in harmony with the divine will. Thus the believers may covenant to fight to the finish in a particular battle in which the Prophet is being attacked by his enemies (Sūra 33:15). Those who die in battle are seen as having fulfilled such a covenant (33:23). This covenanting with God on the part of believers embraces all the pacts that believers make with the Prophet, including the two pacts concluded at ᶜAqaba, to which reference was made earlier in this discussion. Any pact made with a prophet is by definition a covenant with God himself, fulfillment of which is a divinely imposed duty.[52]

I noted earlier at some length the universalism in the thinking of the Muslim theologians about the divine covenant as reflected in

[49] The specific command to fulfill the covenant made with God is most clearly stated in Qurʾān 16:91 (cf. 6:153, 17:34). The Qurʾān in several passages commends those who fulfill their covenant (see 3:76, 13:19–20, 23:8, 33:23). It also describes human covenants as something that will have to be answered for (*masʾūl*) (17:34; 33:15).

[50] Compare Sūra 9:75–76: "And of them is he who made a covenant with God (saying): If he give us of his bounty we will give alms and become of the righteous. Yet when he gave them of his bounty, they hoarded it and turned away, averse."

[51] The notion of unbelievers making a covenant with God raises some problems, which Rāzī deals with in 16:139:13–20t.

[52] On the relationship between these pacts and certain Qurʾānic references to covenant, see Rāzī 11:179–12–19t, 20:106:3–2b (cf. Qurʾān 48:10).

Rāzī's commentary. There is yet another main feature to be noted, one which is, however, much less obvious. It, too, is most strikingly evident in the interpretation of Sūra 7:172, the *locus classicus* for the idea of the Covenant of Sovereignty and Subordination. It will be recalled from my account of the thinking of the Muslim theologians about this covenant that they viewed it as something that takes place, almost imperceptibly, in the experience of each individual, not in the collective experience of an assembled group. I see here a tendency toward an individualistic understanding of covenant. Human beings seem to be ushered into a covenantal moment in which they stand *alone* before God. This individualism clearly runs counter to the Qur'ānic language in 7:172, which employs plural forms and is powerfully suggestive of a collective experience, but then the theological interpretation of that verse does not claim to be adhering to the literal sense. If the Covenant of Sovereignty and Subordination is a covenant between God and individuals, then one can only gather that the same must be true of the second phase of the larger covenantal process, the one that relates to prophecy. However important membership in a community may be in the total experience of living out belief in a prophet and obedience to the divine commandments, one must initially be ushered as an individual into an encounter with the prophet. A prophet need not be physically present in an individual's experience in order for this encounter to take place, for after prophets die their prophetic mission continues to be effective through the preservation of the words that issued from their mouths while they were living. The rational indicators that are the instrument of this ushering into the covenantal encounter are themselves by definition catalysts in the inner working of individual human minds. The covenantal moment is thus one that is continually recapitulated in the experience of countless individuals down through the generations. Muslim theology in effect places the divine covenant outside history, outside the strictly collective experience of any people or nation. It is perhaps in this connection that the absence of a truly collective grand covenantal moment or ceremony in the history of the early Muslim community proves most telling. Also telling is a comment of al-Qaffāl on 2:63, recorded by Rāzī. Addressing himself to the question of why this verse speaks of God's making *a* covenant (*mīthāq*) with the children of Israel rather than covenant*s* (*mawāthīq*), considering that the Children of Israel are, after all, a plurality of individuals, al-Qaffāl suggests two solutions: (1) The pronominal suffix *-kum* may be taken to mean "each one of you," so that the verse would be saying in effect, "[Remember] when we made a covenant with each one of you"; or (2) the Qur'ān may be seeking to emphasize the point that the covenants God made severally with the various children of Israel were all alike, thus avoiding the implication that he made different sorts of covenants with different individuals.[53] Clearly al-Qaffāl's remarks presupposes that at Sinai God entered into a covenant, not with a people as such, but with individuals. The tendency to individualism latent in al-Qaffāl's thinking and in the interpretation of Sūra 7:172 by the Muslim theologians is no doubt not to be attributed to Muslim thinkers in a general way, much less to the Qurʾān, which displays an undeniable interest in the affairs and destinies of peoples. Nonetheless, the tendency is clearly there and can no doubt be linked with the individualism implicit in the notion of divine judgment in the Day of Resurrection.

One last matter requires brief comment before this study may be considered complete: Rāzī's mention of covenants with certain categories of people, namely prophets and the *ʿulamāʾ* (religious scholars).[54] The notion of a covenant with prophets has a clear basis in the Qurʾān (3:81, 33:7), whereas that of a covenant with *ʿulamāʾ*, though believed by certain exegetes to have a basis in 3:187, is not explicitly mentioned in any Qurʾānic passage. The rationale behind the positing of these two covenants seems to be that where substantive duties are laid upon a certain category of people (and not upon the rest of humanity) a special covenant with those people must be presumed. Thus, alongside the fundamental divine covenant that arises through the working of the *adilla*, there are at least two divine covenants of a more specialized nature. These do not, however, receive the same degree of attention in Rāzī's commentary as the fundamental covenant. The duties peculiar to prophets are clear enough: they all relate to the implementation of the prophetic mission (*risāla*), a subject whose special features are much discussed in Muslim religious literature. The duties peculiar to *ʿulamāʾ* relate to their special role as preservers and expounders of the sacred scriptures and of the divine law embodied therein. However, to the extent that these duties may be subsumed under the category of duties to be discharged on behalf of the entire community by a *sufficient number* of people (*farḍ al-kifāya*), the notion of a special covenant would seem open to question. In any case, the notion was not at all widespread. The important point to be noted with respect to the special covenants is that while a

[53] Rāzī 3:107:11–15t.

[54] Both of the covenants are mentioned in Rāzī 2:148:9–11t. The covenant with prophets is discussed at greater length in Rāzī 25:196:7b–197:7b. The exegetes differed as to whether Sūra 3:81 had to do with a covenant with prophets (see Rāzī 8:114ff; cf. 8:104:3b). The idea of a covenant with the *ʿulamāʾ* appears in the discussion of 2:84 in which reference is made to the view that God was in this verse addressing the Jewish *ʿulamāʾ* (3:170:10b; cf. 9:124:2–1b).

divine covenant never distinguishes communities from one another such a covenant may, it appears, distinguish certain categories of people—certainly prophets—*within* a community from other people.

Conclusions

There does exist within the Islamic tradition the concept of a covenant that God establishes with human beings. This covenant defines the basic relationship between God and human beings: he is their sovereign, and they as his subjects are under an obligation to obey the commandments he has revealed through his prophets. The covenant also entails a promise to those who keep it: they shall inherit the joys of Paradise. According to those who sought to understand the covenant within the framework of concepts drawn from Muslim theology (*kalām*), the divine covenant is actualized through the instrumentality of indicators (*adilla*) of God's existence as sole deity and sovereign and of the prophethood of prophets that God has implanted within the human intellect. Human beings play no part in the actual making of the divine covenant, which is wholly unilateral; but they are expected to respond to it with an attitude of acceptance and a commitment to abide by divine commandments. Since these commandments constitute the only law that is ultimately binding on human beings, law may be said to be firmly rooted in the divine covenant.

Though there are undeniable similarities between the Islamic and Judaeo-Christian conceptions of covenant, there are striking differences. In Islam, God establishes his covenant with a variety of peoples or communities, and this covenant is, in regard to essentials, the same from one community to another such that it can never distinguish one people from all others. Since one component of the divine covenant—that which in Rāzī's commentary bears the name "Covenant of Sovereignty and Subordination"—clearly embraces all the descendants of Adam and since the covenant as a whole is established with a plurality of peoples, the Muslim conception of a covenant is inherently universalistic. There is furthermore a tendency among at least some Muslim theologians to see the covenant as established ultimately, not with communities *qua* communities, but with individuals. The covenant acknowledged in Islam is thus a universal covenant in which individuals from a variety of peoples making up the human family are equally involved. It occurs, not within history as a datable and essentially nonrepeatable (even if renewable or reinterpretable) event, but beyond history in the ongoing experience of countless individuals. Its promise relates, primarily, not to the destiny of a people within history, but to individual salvation in the hereafter. In these respects, the Muslim conception of covenant stands in clear contrast to the Judaeo-Christian conception, which links the covenant idea inextricably to the idea of divine election and which places the divine covenant solidly within history as a datum within the collective experience and memory of a single people through which that people's destiny within the drama of "the nations" is to be realized.[55]

Looking broadly over the long history of the idea of covenant, one is constrained to conclude that the idea in its distinctly biblical form, though rooted in the lifeways of the ancient Middle East, was eventually to find its true home outside the region of its origin, in Europe (inclusive of Spain) where the Judaeo-Christian tradition became the dominant religious heritage. One cannot fail to acknowledge that since the advent of Islam the thought-world contained in the Bible ceased to have a major impact on the general intellectual milieu of the Middle East. Islam refused to appropriate, except with very strict limits, the scriptures of Jews and Christians and thus quite deliberately extricated itself from that heritage. The notion of covenant was accordingly to be worked out along the new lines found with the Qurʾān and developed by Muslim theology.

Despite the rather pervasive differences between them, Muslim and Judaeo-Christian thinking about the covenant were to share an important insight, and that is that all law worthy of the name must be an expression of the divine will and must emerge out of an encounter between the Divine Being and his human subjects. Christianity would, of course, confine this idea to the Kingdom of God, a realm distinct from the temporal world of principalities and powers, in which a strictly positive law was recognized to be in force. However, Judaism and Islam insisted more strongly on the relevance of God's law to the details of everyday life in this world and only grudgingly, if at all, conceded validity to positive law.

Given the theistic-covenantal basis of the law, the concept of obligation—that bugbear of Western legal and ethical philosophy—poses no problem. A divine being has given commandments, and

[55] Gen 9:9-17 does, of course, speak of a universal covenant that God establishes with Noah and his descendents (the entire human race), but this covenant is hardly the centerpiece of Judaeo-Christian thinking about covenant. Furthermore, it does not exhibit the more elaborate structure of the Sinai covenant, nor is it the basis of a body of law. The single law given to Noah and his descendents, namely the prohibition of blood (discussed by Jacob Milgrom in another chapter of this book), stands at best in an ambiguous relationship to the Noachide covenant. That covenant, in contrast to the Sinai covenant, assumes the character of an unconditional promise.

human beings are under obligation to obey them. It's as simple as that. If there is a moot point, it is that of God's existence and the prophethood of prophets: these surely must be discussed and demonstrated. But once demonstrated, the concept of obligation disappears from the agenda of philosophical problems. The divine command explains all. Since obligation has its source in the divine command, there is no possibility of relativizing or pluralizing the law: there can be only one law and only one bar of justice for humanity. And there can furthermore be no ultimate separation between law and morality. The whole race is subject to a single body of norms of conduct. Humanly instituted sanctions or customs play no determinative role in their shaping. All human cultures stand judged by these wholly transcendant norms, the institutions of government being no exception: the instruments of coercion, far from having a determinative role, are subject to uses dictated from above.

George E. Mendenhall

The Suzerainty Treaty Structure: Thirty Years Later

IN THE PAGES THAT FOLLOW, a noted authority on the subject of the development of the covenant idea in ancient Israel gives a highly reflective personal statement about the significance of the covenant idea within the broad sweep of human history from prehistoric times to the present. When the Israelites applied concepts drawn from the ancient Near Eastern suzerainty treaty to their relationship with God, they created a legacy that has had profound implications for the human situation ever since. This legacy has placed deity above all political systems, and by attaching supreme value to an event of the past—the giving of the covenant—has embued history with meaning. It has furthermore provided a transcendent ground for ethics. The modern age has for the most part, in Mendenhall's view, lost touch with this legacy. While this has been true of past generations as well—the Bible itself records times of neglect of the legacy and times of remembrance—it can have especially dire consequences for the modern age, equipped as it is with the instruments for self-annihilation.

George E. Mendenhall is now Professor Emeritus of Ancient and Biblical Studies at the University of Michigan. He received his Ph.D. from Johns Hopkins University and was an ordained Lutheran minister from 1943 to 1953. He has led archaeological expeditions to the Middle East and has published numerous important works on law and covenant and other biblical topics, including *Law and Covenant in Israel and the Ancient Near East* and *The Tenth Generation: The Origins of the Biblical Tradition.*

It was just over thirty years ago that "Covenant Forms in Israelite Tradition" appeared in *The Biblical Archaeologist,* and it seems appropriate on this occasion to reassess the thesis that the foundation of biblical Israel was the Sinai Covenant.[1] In addition, with a modicum of historical perspective, it is obvious that many basic themes of that complex instrument of international relations furnished many important motifs of subsequent religious, legal, and cultural developments in Western civilization. At the present time, the religious tradition that constituted the only unique aspect of biblical Israel's existence is not appreciated, or so it seems, in our civilization. The result of this failure to appreciate the message of the Sinai covenant is a horrendous escalation of politically organized terror that with modern technology is fully capable not only of ending civilization, but also of reducing all life on this planet to the level of microbes and insects.

Timing is increasingly recognized as an important factor in the success of many cultural as well as religious innovations and breaks with the past. Even those who emphasize this factor fail to recognize that it was already understood by the biblical writers. In the Abraham story there is the motif that "the iniquity of the Amorites is not yet complete" (Gen 15:16), particularly interesting since the process of completing that iniquity took more than 400 years. In the New Testament there is a similar recognition of the importance of the "fulness of time" involved in the sending of the ruler (= "Son") over the Kingdom of God (Gal 4:4). I would suggest that this is also true of the Sinai covenant. That covenant was widely accepted and successful because it met a greatly felt need at the time. Coming as it did at the close of half a century of destruction and uprooting of all kinds of social and institutional structures, it furnished the foundations for a new building. Above all, it furnished the ideological structure for a new society and a new set of working assumptions and norms that were both simple and functional. At the same time, the Sinai covenant structure could easily be comprehended and become operational simply because it corresponded to ways of thinking and decision making that were potentially universal throughout the West Semitic linguistic region, and were probably a thousand years old by the time of Moses.

In all theological systems, both language and patterns of thought must exist before any specific theological or religious formulation can

[1] G. E. Mendenhall, "Covenant Forms in Israelite Tradition," *Biblical Archaeologist* 17 (1954) 50–76. Reprinted with corrections in *The Biblical Archaeology Reader* (ed. E. F. Campbell, Jr., and D. N. Freedman; Garden City, NY: Doubleday, 1970), 3:25–53. (Also excerpted in *Biblical Archaeologist* 42 [1979] 189–90.)

be produced, and the Sinai covenant is a prime example. It transferred patterns of thought already known and to some extent operative in social life from the realm of the sacred/political to the sacred/religious and ethical sphere of human experience. Yahweh thus represented the common religiously sanctioned value system that (in an economically simple Early Iron Age village society) necessarily governed the functions previously controlled by kings and emperors, those functions in which it was clear that they were incompetent: war, law, and economic well-being. It is most probable that deities were associated with those functions in village society from prehistoric times. Not until the middle of the Early Bronze Age were those functions successfully transferred to a centralized and bureaucratically organized monopoly of force—not much more than a mere thousand years before the time of Moses. The first evidence of this kind of bureaucratically organized state comes from Mesopotamia and Syria in the second half of the third millennium B.C. A couple of centuries later, all of those political entities were gone, together with the language of their bureaucrats. The Tower of Babel story in Genesis 11 is very sound historical linguistics, if one grants that the "one language" was only that of the political power structure. (Someone once observed that a "language" is merely a dialect with an army and a navy.)

In the transition from the Late Bronze to the Early Iron Age the process was repeated. The old city-state and empire structures were either totally destroyed or so weakened that they could not expand their imperial control for nearly a century. At the same transition period, many languages of the Late Bronze Age either died out entirely, or were so radically changed during the Early Iron "Dark Age" that only recently has it been possible to show that here was actually some continuity. These facts are extremely important, for the simple reason that language is that aspect of culture that is most continuous, difficult to acquire, and societally dependent. When the social structure breaks down or is radically changed, so also does the language.

A major thesis of this paper is that political organization reigned supreme as god until Moses, when a radically different outlook on life and humanity began to have a continuity that still exists, though it is powerfully challenged at the present day. As always, it is not likely possible to prove that the picture presented here is correct historically, and certainly it cannot tell all of the historically real or relevant data. Yet, it would go further than any other thesis in its ability to place into a real life context the dramatic events covering not much more than one generation of people at the southeast corner of the Mediterranean region, which resulted in the formation of a religious tradition that in various forms furnished the ideological and ethical foundations for the entire Western hemisphere and a goodly portion of the Eastern as well. It would also help to make comprehensible many aspects of ancient tradition that otherwise seem to be treatable today only as "literature." Materials written in ancient times that had to do with the very foundations of society, security, and well-being are treated by the modern scholarly world as though they were mere individual expressions of aesthetic taste—and as Northrup Frye has observed, very often bad taste to boot.[2] What the Sinai covenant was instrumental in creating, however, was a society based upon a value system quite divergent from that which was normal in ancient political organizations as well as modern ones.

Quite a bit more is known today about the context of the Sinai Covenant period than was available thirty years ago. At that time W. F. Albright's thesis as developed by G. E. Wright was virtually unchallenged except by the inevitable German literary critics. Albright's thesis was that the destruction levels of the cities of Palestine could be correlated with the Israelite "conquest." I cannot now recall the process by which I began to reject that thesis; at any rate it was complete by 1962 when the article on the "Israelite conquest" was published.[3] It should be clear now that the Israelite federation of tribes did not come into existence until a generation or two after the destruction that attended and probably brought about the transition that archaeologists have labelled Late Bronze II and Iron Age I. The absolute dating of these periods is irrelevant: It is the sequence of historical events and cultural changes that is of importance. It is the course of events that brought into existence the "biblical tradition" that sheds light upon the nature of that tradition. I would hope that an understanding of that ancient historical process may aid in the modern process of sorting out our own value system—before modern technology, in concert with modern politics, renders the entire human endeavor irrelevant to the physical universe. It takes a peculiar sort of genius to make the Bible irrelevant to the modern predicament.

There is no reason to believe that the nature of the historical process is any different today from what can be observed in the fragmentary records of the remote past. There is no reason to think that human psychological processes today differ in any but culturally conditioned ways from those that held true more than three thousand years ago. The connection between historical events recorded in the

[2] N. Frye, *The Great Code* (London: Routledge and Kegan Paul, 1982) xviii; cf. his reference to ". . . this huge, sprawling, tactless book. . . ."

[3] Mendenhall, "The Hebrew Conquest of Palestine," *Biblical Archaeologist* 25 (1962) 66–87. Reprinted in *Biblical Archaeology Reader*, 3:100–120.

archaeological ash layers and the pitifully little that can be learned about the value systems that determined political choices in 1200 B.C. is virtually inaccessible to us in the modern world. For that remote period there are simply insufficient facts. The inevitable secrecy involved in the clandestine operations of political and military complexes have the same effect today as historical distance in obscuring the past; the entire archaeological record of the long range consequences is not yet available, although Beirut now gives us a representative sample. The ancient Hebrew prophets did a good job of predicting the result. There is no evidence, however, that political power structures paid any more attention to them than they do in the present world. In fact, the profession of prophet in a political theocracy always entails an understandably high insurance risk.

The Near Eastern legacy to the Western world is thus not merely the biblical tradition. It is also the tradition of Baal-worship, which is itself even less understood than is the monotheistic Sinaitic tradition. Both are quite obscured to the modern Western world by the culture gap, and by the inevitable tendency to interpret the past within the framework of what is contemporary and to exploit the ancient for modern political purposes by identifying it with formal characteristics of the modern. It is precisely this process that constitutes the Orwellian rewriting of history to make it fit modern political ideology and policy, and therefore to make it impossible for modern societies to learn anything from the past experience of humanity or to evaluate their own experience in the light of some historical perspective. Indeed, if anything is true of the Bible in the modern world, it is the fact that virtually no one believes that anything important is to be learned from the Bible—it is useful only for nice sounding liturgical snippets in the ritual (after appropriate censorship of course), or for furnishing "authority" for modern ultra-rightwing political and religious organizations. This aspect of modern life makes it very difficult for Western culture to understand the Bible, especially at a time when the combination of politics and aesthetics is the sacred operating religion of the vast majority of the educated elite, in this country at least.

I turn now to the nature and function of the Sinai covenant. It is clear to me at least that this was the only unique feature of ancient Israelite society, culture, and religion. It is difficult to identify any other trait that was not at least potentially common to many if not most extra-biblical cultures of the ancient Near Eastern world. On the other hand, where ancient biblical society radically differed from what we know of ancient pagan polytheism, those features are derived from or at least closely associated with the structure of Sinaitic covenant thought, and many became main themes and problems in theology to the present day.

The Nature of God

Two thousand years of theological and metaphysical speculation and polemics have so obscured this problem that it is very difficult to describe the Yahweh/Baal contrast in modern English. Following the *via negativa* adopted by the scholastics of the Middle Ages, it is easier to say what Yahweh was *not* for the ancient Israelites, than what Yahweh was. Yahweh was not merely the personified projection of the existing political system, for the simple reason that before Moses and Sinai the political system and the ensuing social contrast did not exist (in spite of the Abraham-Isaac-Jacob genealogy). In other words, Yahweh was not simply a Baal—the metaphysical, mythical symbolization of the existing body politic. Exactly as it was Yahweh who offered the covenant relationship in the prologue to the Sinai covenant: "I am Yahweh your God . . . ," so also it was Yahweh who created the society according to its own premonarchic sources: "is not he your Father, your Creator? He made you and established you" (Deut 32:6b).

The almost exclusive identification of religion with social organization and its concomitant ritual that is characteristic of what is called "religion" in Western cultures has obscured also the nature of the worship of Baal, which has likewise been inherited in the political tradition of the West. The most extreme expression of Baal-worship comes from Germany of the 1930s: "If the German race did not exist, God would not exist." It goes without saying that the "German race" was identical to the Nazi state and its "Blut und Boden" mentality, but the statement is a tautology. The god that the Nazi spokesman was referring to was simply the ideological projection of the political state itself, and obviously that god ceased to exist with the destruction of the Nazi regime, except perhaps for a few crackpot diehards. This is the process by which the ancient Baals also disappeared, with the destruction of the various nation-states that they symbolized. But we of the older generation know firsthand the consequences of that sort of ideology, and therefore should have some insight into the historical process that brought "civilization" temporarily to an end at the close of the Late Bronze Age. At that time, virtually all large social organizations were destroyed. The Sinai Covenant furnished the ideological foundations for a new society rising from the ash heaps of destroyed cities and empires. It should be understandable, then, why biblical Israel was so bitterly hostile to the *bĕʿālîm*. The worship of political states is not only an anachronism in the 20th century: in the form of nationalism, racism, militarism, imperialism and state-socialism, it may well prove to be incompatible with the continued existence of humanity.

It seems to have been widely accepted that there was a theophany experience at Sinai, but this historical assessment merely dismisses a most significant event by giving it a label. A "theophany" that does nothing of further significance may be nothing but superstition and, according to all extant sources, this position is the exact opposite to the truth. The event cannot be dismissed as one that merely resulted in the change of name of a tribal deity, as some have attempted to argue. There was such a change in the concept of the nature of God (as well as society), that modern scholars have to write monographs to explain modern nonbiblical concepts of deity that still exist in many parts of the world. Similarly, concepts of social relationships also changed so radically that no definition or description of the biblical Israelite society has been able to win acceptance beyond the circle of the sociologist's school, for the community did not "consider itself among the nations" (Num 23:9). The fact of discontinuity from the preceding political paganism, with its inevitable social stratification, has been a central element in almost all religious traditions that stem from that event, and constitutes a major crossroad in which history and theology meet: the problem of revelation and inspiration, which is the problem of trying to understand how something so radically different could not only come into existence, but also find wider public acceptance than any other ideological system. The emphasis on inspiration seems hopelessly old-fashioned these days, possibly because modern people do not want discontinuities in the modes of thought and value judgments that might upset the delicate balance of conflicting interests, and don't really have any confidence in anything but socially organized coercive force, which *is* Baal.

It is at this point that the "timeliness" of the Sinai covenant is of primary importance: it came at a time when the delicate balance had already broken down and resulted in universal destruction of civilization as it had been known. Therefore the way was clear—free of vested, socially entrenched interests and power structures other than pathetic remnants—for something that would avoid the consequences of social fragmentation into an endless power struggle. Though the Sinai experience was a theophany of impressive magnitude, it was far more than a theophany. Those values that were essential to the nature of Yahweh himself, and therefore upon which depended the life or death of the society (individually as well as corporately), were described in the text of the covenant. To put it into more recent patterns of thought, the covenant substance described what was to be the "Ultimate Concern" of the new community, to use Paul Tillich's terminology, or perhaps even better, "your God is that which you fear most to lose," to use an expression of Martin Luther. In its own context, then, the Decalogue described in typically pragmatic ancient Near Eastern fashion those standards of individual behavior that were necessary to any social tranquillity and cultural well-being. At the same time it furnished a definition of individual integrity ("You [2d person singular!] will not . . .") that was made feasible and possible by the coming into existence of the community of God. The importance of community to the creation and maintenance of ethical and moral standards has often been pointed out, and, conversely, the degradation of morality following the destruction of community.

To sum up, from the parable of Jotham to the predictions of destruction levied against the political state by all of the preexilic prophets, the mainstream of ancient Israelite religion was a rejection of the common ancient (and modern) paganism that deified the monopoly of force that I call the body politic. The many studies of "divine kingship" produced in the thirties and forties of this century largely missed the point: gods in the ancient world were personifications of value convictions, of value judgments that determined the behavior and choices of human beings both individually and corporately. The deification of the state meant then that any opposition to that state was treason and blasphemy combined, as poor Naboth found out, and as many people in Eastern Europe and many other places on this globe know to their sorrow.

The Lord of History

Perhaps the one aspect of human experience upon which nearly all can agree is the fact that history over the long range is not predictable. It seems in the modern world that to most people history is "bunk," to use Henry Ford's brief summation of the past experience of the human race. He probably illustrates the dominant attitude today that is particularly characteristic of high school sophomores to whom only the present is of importance, because the future is so uncertain. That being the case, the past consists of mere random and meaningless events of no further significance. In contrast, the emphasis of the Hebrew scripture is upon the course of history. This emphasis upon the meaningfulness of history is the most important contrast also between biblical thought and the ancient Near Eastern paganisms. The nature and origin of historical narrative in the Hebrew Bible is a problem that has not yet been solved, and in my judgment has hardly been seriously faced by the scholarly world. At the present time, it seems that it is deliberately being obscured by the trend toward mere literary analysis, and the separation of narrative in the Bible from the concrete facts of nonlinguistic ancient reality. Furthermore, the differences between the journalistic annals of ancient kings and the long-range historical narratives of the Bible have ideological implications that seem to be ignored, a contrast that is the most significant since the Judean kings at least also kept annals. A significant part of the problem is the fact that biblical scholarship itself has been so little historically oriented that to the present day it cannot distinguish between texts of the tenth century and those of the sixth century B.C., and therefore the history of historical narrative cannot be written.

In contrast to the universal human tendency to regard the past as mere prologue of no further significance, the entire biblical faith had profound foundations in the identification of Yahweh as that factor in human experience that governed the course of history. Since the definition of Yahweh was inseparable from values that were necessary to harmonious social and individual existence, the result was inevitably a moral interpretation of history that reached a climax of sorts with the Deuteronomic history; but it foundered on the reef of the destruction of Jerusalem and the consequent suffering of the innocent (represented by Job) as well as the guilty. One result of the destruction of Jerusalem was the withdrawal from historical interpretation in favor of "apocalyptic," and historical narrative ceased in the mainstream of the religious tradition after the production of the Chronicler only to experience a brief revival in the first generations of the Christian community. It is interesting to see the same process at work in the modern scholarly world, where serious dealing with the course of history is being denigrated in favor of mere "storytelling" and a pseudoaesthetic, neo-gnostic devaluation of concrete, material reality.

The Sinai covenant actually had a two-fold connection with real history, or, to avoid the ambiguity of this much misused term, a connection with the actual course of human experience. The first is of course the description of divine grace in the historical prologue to the Decalogue. This is itself astonishing in view of the exploitation of "history" so characteristic of the modern world. The contrast between the biblical emphasis upon benefits received in the past (characteristic of ancient covenants before the Iron Age) and the constant politically or economically motivated, modern complaints about past injustices that some corporate *we* has suffered, is so striking as to make almost impossible any understanding of the ancient covenant to modern, ambitious politicians. There was no corporate *we* before Sinai, where the community was formed.

The foundation in gratitude that was described already by Aesop as a characteristic of a noble soul is highly unfashionable in modern political society, where even dogs "deserve" Alpo. It is precisely for this reason, however, that the gratitude in the Sinai covenant is not directed to a human leader or politician, but to a deity who is above and beyond politics. Not only among the Hittites, but also in Canaan of the Amarna period, ambitious politicians were claiming to have conferred benefits, or promising them in the future, if the masses would only fall in line behind the "great man."

A significant further illustration comes from the Syllabic Texts from Byblos, which probably reflect the language and thought patterns of the coastal region toward the end of the Early Bronze Age. A certain Ḫuru-Baᶜil claims that the tribes of Byblos and vicinity had bound themselves by covenant (*yatuhaᶜhidu*) because of his "mighty deeds" (*bi* + *haᶜlali* + *ni*). In the biblical tradition, on the other hand, *ᶜălilôt* 'deeds' are unmitigated disasters except when they are performed by Yahweh, and then they are closely parallel to *niplāᵓôt* 'miracles'. The text proves beyond doubt what I have maintained for decades, that the Hittites simply took over and adapted traditions having to do with covenant structures from their southern neighbors.

The basic covenant pattern is already in this text: the identification of the giver of covenant (*hawatu ḫuru-baᶜilu*), the claim of prior beneficial 'mighty deeds', the generalized description of obligations, and the curses and blessings. The curses are carried out by the *liᵓimu* + *hu*: the deified ancestors of anyone who "murmurs [*yalānu*!], acts violently, or is an evil-doer" against his dominion. Now it is clear that that covenant structure was deeply ingrained into cultural traditions of the proto-Canaanite region already in the Early Bronze Age. It proves also beyond reasonable doubt that the population of Palestine who constituted the tribes of early Israel was a religiously distinctive segment of the larger population of the coastal and inland region, and even the language was a local realization of a larger *lingua franca* that characterized the entire eastern Mediterranean region during the earlier phases of the Iron Age. The language itself originated from the colloquial language of the streets of Late Bronze II cities and villages, as illustrated by the two Ugaritic tablets that distinguished only 22 consonants, virtually identical to the later Phoenician and Hebrew system. I have little doubt that the brash young scribe who dared to write those tablets reflecting how people actually spoke underwent some sort of experience designed to guarantee that no more of them survived. Fifty years later there wasn't any other orthography, except where the authentic old grammatical and phonetic system continued its integrity along the desert fringe region.

In addition to the "historical prologue" that was constitutive and, it seems, constantly "updated" until the Monarchy (cf. Deuteronomy 32), an even more powerful and pervasive connection between Yahweh and history was furnished by the blessings and curses formula. This was the means by which the acts of Yahweh both good and evil were applied to the human experience as an interpretation of the past (as in Deuteronomy 32 and often in the prophets), and also the means by which the value system was sanctioned, not so much by socially organized force (which existed certainly, but was minimal and decentralized), but by understanding of the process of historical cause and effect over a long period of time: " . . . visiting the iniquities of the fathers upon the children to the third and fourth generation . . ." (Exod 20:5). This historical process was an integral and transcendent aspect of the divine governance of Yahweh, and was applied equally to the religious community itself, as well as to the non-Yahwist polytheists, though in an appropriately different manner.

In this respect, the Yahwist religious tradition contrasts sharply to almost all political organizations, for politicians characteristically cannot be concerned about anything beyond the necessity of winning the next election. The ancient formula, "visiting the iniquities of the fathers upon the children of the third and fourth generation of those who hate [= sever relationship with] me" is a description of the historical cause-and-effect relationship that is no cosmic myth, but the understanding of Yahweh's governance of the historical process. It was simple yet sophisticated beyond belief, compared with the calloused indifference to the future exhibited by modern power politics and corporate behavior in general. The constant temptation of power holders is to believe that they are in secure control of all factors that might affect the well-being of the social organization under their control, and therefore they suffer under the delusion that they are in control of history. As a result, historians are hard put to try to explain how politicians could be so obtuse.

The return to Bronze Age political organization and ideology that came certainly by the time of Solomon, if not already by King David, meant that the Sinai covenant tradition and theology was overlaid by the prestige of the political system with its affluence, court and temple ritual, and international connections. The Sinai tradition largely went underground for several hundred years, but was represented eloquently by the prophetic movement from the villages beginning with Amos and Hosea. Again, the implications for this aspect of ancient cultural history have been unnoticed by a majority of scholars, including those who have been forced to admit that the book of Deuteronomy certainly does reflect the old suzerainty treaty structure. Unfortunately, these scholars have such negligible historical orientation that they do not even see the historical problem of explaining the sudden resurrection of a structure that had been dead for half a millennium.

The fact is that the book of Deuteronomy came into existence in association with the "reform" movement of King Josiah, which, of necessity, like all reform movements, was based upon a new valuation and understanding of the remote past. The unknown writers of Deuteronomy had nothing to do with creating *ex nihilo* that old treaty structure: they returned to the remote past for traditions that had been contemptuously ignored for centuries by the secure politicians of the monarchy. Josiah's powerful reaction to the recognition that there was a different and authentic tradition of covenant is guarantee enough that earlier court circles, especially that of Manasseh, knew little and certainly cared less about the authentic traditions of the Yahwist community. It is not the first time, and certainly not the last, that modern scholars have been unable to distinguish between the origin of the important cultural motif and its much later rediscovery and political exploitation.

The simplistic, deuteronomistic orthodoxy and the associated royal inquisition of Josiah foundered upon the destruction of Jerusalem. (The curses and blessings elaborated in Deuteronomy became the basis for a wooden, mechanical concept of history that is masterfully presented to Job by his super-orthodox deuteronomic "comforters"—Job's ill fortunes were proof enough of his disobedience!) The fate of Josiah and the failure of the simplistic retribution theology of history with the destruction of Jerusalem then prepared the way for the apocalyptic movement. History became too painful and unpredictable, so the new movement removed the arena of divine curse and blessing from the realm of history to the "world to come." Thus the divine justice could be protected and affirmed, but at the expense of the understanding of historical processes and, eventually, a complete unconcern with real history—(for which literary storytelling was substituted). Modern scholars often do not see that there is a difference, thus preparing the way for the Orwellian school of ancient history.

The curses and blessings motif has an importance beyond the aborted attempt to make it a rigid principle for the interpretation of history simply because it was not intended for that purpose in the first place. It was, rather, a means by which the value system was internalized, a means by which the decision-making process of persons was closely linked to the understanding that violations of voluntarily accepted obligations might have serious consequences for future generations. It takes for granted, of course, that people did have some concern for the well-being of their descendants, but that also cannot be taken for granted in the modern world. It has been estimated that the basic needs of food, clothing, and shelter could be provided for the entire population of the world for about $17 billion per year—and that is approximately what the world spends on armaments every two weeks.

The Biblical Ethic

The transcendent ground of ethic in the Sinai covenant is perhaps one of the most important aspects of the biblical heritage to Western cultures that is emphatically rejected at the present time. Since the 1930s, the idea that morality has some necessary connection with foreign policy has been contemptuously rejected by the mainstream of political science in favor of the shortsighted and often enough hypocritical concept of "national self-interest." On the other hand, the "relativism" of morality has become virtually a sacred dogma of some anthropologists that often seems to have the effect of neutralizing all moral norms. Rather than being a great scientific discovery, I maintain that the foundations of the biblical communities, both of the Old Testament and of the New as well, rested upon the full recognition of the fact that forms of behavior inevitably and probably necessarily vary from context to context. Nevertheless, the covenant ethic is one that excludes behavior that works to the detriment of others—and it is difficult to think of a society that is unaware of the fact that certain types of activity are detrimental to persons and are therefore wrong. What happens in a politically tribalized society is the concept that standards of right or wrong are a function of the political boundary line (precisely the dogma of anthropologists who deal with primitive societies). The same phenomenon can usually be observed when soldiers come into contact with foreign civilian populations—outside the social and political boundary line anything goes. In this sense, ancient Israel's ethic exhibits the process of "detribalization"—exactly the opposite of N. K. Gottwald's propaganda party line thesis of "retribalization."

This tribal mentality is of course the opposite of what is meant by the transcendent basis of the covenant ethic: it precedes the society and makes the society possible by the simple fact that all members are bound by the same obligations and thus their behavior becomes predictable. Always, of course, there are unscrupulous and criminal individuals who commit *nĕbālāh be-yiśrāʾēl,* but such events do not call into question the validity of the ethic. The ethic is tied to the individual by covenant, and is therefore valid no matter where and in what context that individual acts. It is within this context that the age-old principle, "Where shall I flee from your presence" had its operational validity, since it was already a kind of rhetorical affirmation of loyal subservience to the king of Egypt in the Amarna Period—and therefore also a guarantee of beneficial concern for the vassal on the part of the king. This is another example of the process by which a host of concepts that were operative within the realm of imperial politics were transferred in early Israel to Yahweh. It is also an excellent example of the ridiculous consequences when a biblical motif is taken out of its context by philosophers and theologians and relegated to the realm of metaphysics.

The larger implications of the biblical ethic are obscured to a very great extent simply by the failure to take into account the radically different social and historical context of the early biblical morality and what happened to it with the enormous changes introduced with the monarchy. Those implications are equally significant for the present day.

The first observation to be made is that the biblical ethic by its very nature belonged to the private realm of social existence, not to the public. Indeed the *res publica* did not exist in any normal sense of the term. This privately grounded ethic implies that adherence to the biblical norms of morality was a voluntary one—exactly as the acceptance of the covenant relationship was a deliberate, conscious choice on the part of large segments of the ancient Palestinian society simultaneously. This voluntary community ethic was then the basis for a part of the legal system of the monarchy, but the prophetic indictments demonstrate that the component of the political law that stemmed from the old religious community customary law must have been minimal by the time of Amos and Hosea. It is only to be expected, for with the enforced incorporation of the rest of Palestine and parts of Transjordan into the Davidic Empire, it was the non-Yahwist urban paganism that became dominant in the political state. Thus the distinction between religion and politics became hopelessly blurred because the state *was* the religion for four hundred years thereafter; the results of such a mixture are often horrendous, and at best highly divisive in a complex society.

Worst of all from my point of view is that this modern attempt to impose the norms of a religious community's customary ethic upon either a heathen secular population or upon a variant religious ethic seriously calls into question that religious ethic itself. The mere assumption that the religious ethic has to be upheld by political power structures demonstrates its weakness; if it is not thus enforced the ethic has no validity. In addition, those who engage in this misguided attempt to get their idea of morality and ethic enforced by the public secular institutions cannot see that they are reducing their own religious ideology to the status of a pawn in the struggle for power. In other words, religion is simply something to be used for the purpose of winning battles against opponents, and to assert domination by force over persons of diverse mores. It is precisely this motif of the divine delegation of power and authority over persons that characterizes the old Bronze Age paganism—the worship of Baal, who was the personification of the ancient political power structures. The value system is founded upon the worship of coercive force as represented through the political institutions of war and law. It is no accident that fundamentalists from Los Angeles to Tel Aviv and Teheran demonstrate their adherence to a theology of power by supporting the arms race.

Probably the most important aspect of the biblical heritage to the West was its recognition that it is the private ethic that furnishes the foundations for the public administration of law and justice, but the latter cannot create justice—it can only maintain a "delicate balance between conflicting interests" to quote Benjamin Nathan Cardozo. It is the erosion of private ethic and the discrediting of the ethic of religious communities that constitutes the most serious problem of the modern West.

The second aspect of the biblical ethic that contrasts most sharply to modern social and political conventions is that it is centered on voluntarily accepted obligations instead of "rights" possessed by virtue of political status. This concept of obligation is evidently one that makes modern humanity extremely nervous. It probably did in ancient times as well, and it is specifically for that reason that the covenant ethic embedded in the Decalogue is mostly the prohibition of those acts that are deleterious to the social harmony and security of all.

The Sinai Covenant, coming as it did after nearly a century of civilization-wide destruction of cities, of social chaos, of radical and rapid linguistic changes and the creation of new languages out of the wreckage of the old, must have been received as a real liberation from the universal insecurity of those horrendous decades. It entailed the discovery of the fact that ambitious politicians and warlords do not represent the apex of human evolutionary processes, and the thirty-one petty kings of Palestine listed in Joshua 12 are themselves expendable in favor of the realization of the fruits of peace and justice. Since Lipit-Ishtar, at least, the function of the political state has been the same: the exercise of divinely delegated force through war externally and through law internally—from the point of view of ancient thought war and law are the same thing—and the control of the national economy. It is absurd to think that political states make or create peace: it is war not peace that is the job of political systems, and the weightier matters of love, justice, and compassion are irrelevant to political institutions. As an anonymous source in an American law school campus newspaper observed some years ago, "Justice is a subject for meditation in a monastery."

Conclusion

It is a curious fact that a period of unparalleled affluence and educational levels in this country seems to coincide with a crescendo of human misery, crime, and insecurity, both here and abroad. The wide range of experience of many persons through education, travel, and communications seems to have produced a community of cosmopolitans who, as someone has quipped, "are capable of being miserable anywhere." Two centuries of rapid growth in the United States were based upon extremely lavish natural resources, but even more upon the fact that a common value system operated well enough to avoid the usual fragmentation of society into units too small to be economically viable while supporting an increasing population. In other words, the value system was held well enough to avoid the constant process of application of force to maintain the social, political, and economic unity after the horrors of the Civil War.

It is an open question whether the process of religious fusion represented by the Sinai Covenant, and on a much larger scale by early Christianity, can resist the normal processes of social fission in a time of rising population and competition for diminishing resources. In the past, such fusion movements have taken place either after or just preceding wide-scale disasters and the death of institutions and cultures. I would hope that such disasters can be avoided; but if they are, it will not be through the usual political machination, intrigue, and scheming so beloved by politicians. Anthropologists may have no use for historical events that disrupt their nice, neat categories, but the facts seem to indicate that it requires a traumatic and unpredicted event to destroy all the culturally conditioned knee-jerk reactions, pathological adherence to vicious and irrational ideologies, and the rigid forms of irrational behavior that constitute such great dangers to all of life on this planet, in order to make way for a new social bonding that is concerned for the future well-being of human beings rather than merely for the preservation of power structures increasingly incompetent for any task other than destruction of life and property.

Moshe Greenberg

Biblical Attitudes toward Power: Ideal and Reality in Law and Prophets

GREENBERG'S ESSAY BEGINS a series of eleven essays (chapters 4–14) that seek to explore the meaning and value of religiously based law. Greenberg describes the holy law of Israel, the Torah, as a *social program*, the implementation of which is Israel's primary vocation. This social program has a clear religious basis: all power belongs to God; power is therefore not to be exercised by humans except in accordance with divine dictates. The pattern that the law devises for the exercise of power calls for the dispersal of power among the people and provides mechanisms for preventing concentrations of power in the hands of the few. Thus the inseparability of religion and law in the life of ancient Israel takes the form of grounding Israel's social ideals in the will of God. These social ideals, which lie at the heart of Israel's vocation under God, are often in conflict with existing realities, as Greenberg shows in his final pages. There is a strong suggestion in Greenberg's presentation that biblical thinking about the holy law is at variance with modern positivist conceptions of law: Israel's law does not depend, in the final analysis, upon the coercive actions of the state (the role of which is in any case severely underplayed in the Torah); it depends rather upon the voluntary adherence of a citizenry made knowledgeable in the law through constant public proclamation.

Moshe Greenberg is Professor of Bible at the Hebrew University of Jerusalem. He received his Ph.D. from the University of Pennsylvania and attended rabbinical school at the Jewish Theological

Seminary of America. Professor Greenberg is a fellow of the American Academy for Jewish Research and the American Academy of Arts and Sciences. He has served on the translation committee for the new Jewish Publication Society Bible translation (*Kethuvim: The Writings*). The first volume of his edition of Ezekiel in the Anchor Bible appeared in 1983.

Throughout the Torah ("the Law") and the Prophets the relation between God and humanity is bedeviled by the issue of power.[1] Tension inheres in the conception that while God has dominion in heaven and earth he has made man in his image and given him dominion over the earth and its resources.

> YHWH our Lord,
> How majestic is your name throughout the earth,
> You who have covered the heavens with your splendor!
> When I behold your heavens, the work of your fingers,
> the moon and stars that you set in place,
> what is man that you have been mindful of him,
> mortal man that you have taken note of him,
> that you have made little less than divine,
> and adorned him with glory and majesty;

[1] In this essay the terms *Torah* and *Prophets* are literary concepts that define biblical writings by their function. Torah is mainly legislating, constitutional literature, laying down in God's name rules and standards of individual and corporate behavior, aimed at fashioning Israel into a holy people. Although this literature came into being—according to the judgment of modern critics—over generations, it is a unity as regards its estimate of political power, as will emerge in the sequel.

Prophets comprises "Former Prophets" (the books of Joshua, Judges, Samuel, and Kings), which narrate the history of Israel from its settlement of the land of Canaan until the destruction of the First Temple. Composed of heterogeneous elements, this corpus views some six centuries of Israelite history as a disastrous failure: Israel failed to fulfill the conditions of its covenant with God, on which its well-being depended. The corpus of "Latter Prophets" comprises the oracles of named prophets proclaimed from the middle of the monarchic period (mid-eighth century B.C.E.) to the Restoration after the Babylonian Exile (end of the sixth century B.C.E.). These oracles expound a consistent interpretation of the events that befell Israel from the viewpoint of God, with warnings and consolations related to this interpretation. From the Prophets the conflict between the religious ideal and the political reality can be observed. The evidence gathered from these various sources is consistent with respect to the theme of this essay.

For a survey of the nature and composition of this literature, see M. Weinfeld, "Literary Creativity," *The Age of the Monarchies: Culture and Society* (ed. A. Malamat; World History of the Jewish People 4b; Jerusalem: Massada, 1979) 27–58.

> You have made him master over your handiwork,
> laying the world at his feet. (Ps 8:1, 3-6).

Competition between the two dominions pervades the opening stories of the book of Genesis. Adam and Eve transgressed God's ban in the hope that they would become "like divine beings." A later generation planned to build a tower whose top would reach heaven. The Pharaoh of the Exodus, when commanded by God to let the Israelites worship, retorts insolently, "Who is YHWH that I should obey him? I do not recognize YHWH nor shall I let Israel go!" (Exod 5:2). The stories show a keen awareness of the pitfalls along the way of a humanity ambitious for power. So humans are in a quandary: they must dispose of power in order to fulfil their commission of dominating the earth, yet the exercise of power induces delusions of grandeur that lead to destruction.

The Ideal of Power in the Law

In the biblical view, power belongs properly to God, and he puts it to two purposes: (1) the creation and sustenance of the world, and (2) the maintenance of the moral order. To promote the second purpose, God advises people—first Adam and Eve, then Noah and his family—of the conditions of their happiness in the form of a few prohibitions: in exchange for accepting limitations on the exercise of their power (thus acknowledging God's sovereignty), they will attain happiness. God demands, and has trouble in obtaining, human acquiescence to God's supremacy and human acceptance of the order he would impose, for human nature inclines to assert autonomy and thwarts God by refusing to recognize limits to the exercise of human power. But as the generation of the Flood proved, rebellion against God's order inflicts harm only on them: "The earth was filled with violence" (Gen 6:11). Human aggression had expanded beyond the domain of its proper object—the earth—to impinge upon fellow humans. The race thus became monstrous and was wiped out in the Flood.

God then sought an alternative means to establish his order on earth; out of all the families of the earth he chose that of Abraham, Isaac, and Jacob as the human arena of his self-revelation. Among them he would reign: their descendants he would draw near to him, consecrating them as his kingdom of priests, his holy nation. By his deeds in this modest arena his Godhood would be manifest, and all people would come to see the blessing he conferred on those who acknowledged him.

In Israel, God embodied his order in a legal and moral program—the collections of law comprising the bulk of the Torah. It is formulated in a variety of styles: rulings for hypothetical cases, positive and negative commandments, and rhetorical elements designed to move the recipients to obedience. What distinguishes the style of the Torah from that of all the other treaties and law collections of the ancient East with which it has been compared is the profusion of motive clauses in all its law corpora. Here are some examples from the "Covenant Code" of Exodus:

> You must not wrong the alien or oppress him, for you were aliens in the land of Egypt (Exod 22:20).
> If you take the garment of your fellow as a pledge, by sunset you must return it to him; for it is his only clothing, the sole cover of his skin; wherein shall he lie down? (Exod 22:25).
> Six days you shall do your work but on the seventh you must cease, so that your ox and your ass may rest, and the son of your maidservant and the alien may be refreshed (Exod 23:12).

Here is an example from the priestly laws:

> Do not make yourselves detestable by eating any swarming creature. Do not defile yourselves with them so as to become unclean, for I am YHWH your God; so sanctify yourselves and be holy, for I am holy (Lev 11:43-44).

The rhetorical element in the book of Deuteronomy is so prominent that one scholar has said of its legal corpus, "It is law preached."[2] Two examples will suffice to convey an impression:

> [Three cities of refuge must be appointed for the accidental slayer] lest the redeemer of blood pursue the slayer, for his mind will be inflamed, and, catching up with him, he will kill him though he is not liable to the death penalty for he was not his [victim's] enemy previously (Deut 19:6).
> But if the man came upon the betrothed girl in open country and took her by force and lay with her, only the man must die, you must not do anything to the girl; she has not committed any mortal offence. Her case is like that of one attacked by another with intent to murder: he came upon her in open country; the girl [is presumed to have] cried out but there was no one to save her (Deut 22:25-27).

[2] G. von Rad, *Studies in Deuteronomy* (Studies in Biblical Theology 9; Chicago: H. Regnery, 1953) 16.

The endeavor to persuade goes with the published character of the legislation. According to the narrative framework, the bodies of law were from the first promulgated and done so in a manner accessible to all—by proclamation. To be sure, the laws were written down as a testimony for later times, but first Moses proclaimed them in the hearing of all Israel. God introduces the "Covenant Code" with this charge to Moses: "These are the rulings you must set out before them" (Exod 21:1). Individual laws are regularly preceded by the formula: YHWH spoke to Moses saying, "Speak to the Israelites and say to them" such and such a law. The dissemination of the laws is of their essence: unlike other ancient systems of law (or modern ones for that matter), the biblical one is designed to educate the public, to mold the national character. Having undertaken to become a holy nation, Israel must be trained to a holy life. The laws of the Torah constitute the regimen and rule of the people conceived as a priestly order. Since the success of God's venture depends on each individual Israelite both knowing the rule and willingly obeying it, it is not only published but suffused with rhetoric calculated to move the individual to assent to its exacting demands.[3]

In the divinely ordained polity provided for Israel, power is dispersed among the members of society and many devices prevent its accumulation and concentration.[4] The society envisaged in the Torah lacks a strong, prestigious focus of power; on the contrary, dignity and authority are distributed. The prestige of parents is guaranteed in the Decalogue; a child who injures them or rebels against them is liable to the death penalty (Exod 20:12, 21:15, 17; Deut 21:18-21). Every town ("gate") in Israel has its tribunal of elders, authorized to judge and punish and even to inflict the death penalty (Deut 16:18, 22:15ff.). Insult to tribal chiefs is paired with insult to God: "You must not revile God or lay a curse upon a chief among your people" (Exod 22:27). No central government is recognized in the laws, except for an isolated paragraph in Deuteronomy that treats the monarchy;

[3] On motive clauses, see the pioneering study of B. Gemser, "The Importance of The Motive Clause in Old Testament Law," *Congress Volume: Copenhagen 1953* (*Vetus Testamentum* supplement 1; Leiden: Brill, 1953) 50-66; R. Sonsino, *Motive Clauses in Hebrew Law: Biblical Forms and Near Eastern Parallels* (Society of Biblical Literature Dissertation Series 45; Chico, CA: Scholars Press, 1980).

[4] In the following paragraphs my observations on power have been shaped by these analyses: H. Heller, "Power, Political," *Encyclopedia of the Social Sciences* (New York: Macmillan, 1934), 13:300-305; B. Russell, *Power: A New Social Analysis* (London: George Allen and Unwin, 1938); F. W. Frey, "Political Power, *Encyclopedia Britannica* (15th ed., 1974), 14:697-702; and G. Tinder, *Political Thinking* (Boston: Little, Brown, 1979).

the purpose of that paragraph is to curb the king's appetite for power and prestige.

> He must not have many horses, so as not to return the people to Egypt in order to add to his horses; he must not have many wives so that his mind not be diverted; nor may he have much silver and gold. When he ascends his royal throne he must have a copy of this teaching written for him under the aegis of the Levite priests; it shall be with him and he must read it all his life in order that he may learn to fear YHWH his God . . . that his heart not grow haughty toward his brothers and that he not deviate from the commandments to the right or to the left (Deut 17:16–20).

Such a conception of a humble king seems paradoxical, if not quixotic. It is unparalleled in antiquity, and remained in Israel too an unrealizable attempt to break human pride for the good of society and the greater glory of God.

Accumulation of economic power is also severely impeded by the laws of the Torah. The foundation of ancient economy being ownership of land, God grants the Israelites a land for their possession, but he conditions their continued tenancy on obedience to his laws. If in the future the people boastfully take the credit for their prosperity, saying, "My power and the might of my hand got me this wealth"; if, forgetting that "It is YHWH your God who has given you the power to get wealth," they are disloyal to him, then they are told "you shall perish as did those nations that YHWH caused to perish before you" (Deut 8:17–20).

The correlate of God's ownership of the land is the duty of the Israelites to reflect his benevolence in their tenancy of it. The weekly sabbath rest, for instance, instituted "so that your ox and your ass may rest and the son of your maidservant and the alien may be refreshed," is in force even during the critical, busy seasons of plowing and harvest (Exod 23:12). Material considerations, which presumably are foremost in the mind of an enterprising farmer, may not prevail against God's benign provision for the needy.[5]

Furthermore, the Israelite must share the wealth gained from the land with unfortunate fellowcitizens. The farmer is obliged to let the land lie fallow once in seven years, "so that the needy of your people may eat [its crop]; thus the sabbath [-yield] of the land shall serve to feed you and your manservant and your maidservant, your hireling, and the alien resident among you" (Lev 25:6; cf. Exod 23:11). The

[5] Cf. the humanitarian motive of the sabbath commandment in the Decalogue of Deut 5:14, "so that your manservant and maidservant may rest as you do."

fullest realization of the idea that God owns the land—and a serious curb on economic initiative—is the jubilee, every fiftieth year, in which all sales of land (occasioned in ancient Israel by bankruptcy) are annulled and all real estate reverts to its original owner (who received it in accord with the divine allocation of the land of Canaan among the tribes of Israel at the time of the conquest): "The land shall not be sold permanently, for the land is mine and you are aliens resident with me" (Lev 25:23). Who will want to buy land when all one actually gets from the purchase is crop years to the next jubilee? Who will invest in a plot of purchased ground when any improvement will in the end redound to its original owner? Such a constraint prevents the accumulation of real property (the basis of economic power); its effect is to keep the economic strength of all families roughly equal (or at least static).

Similar dampening of economic enterprise and growth must result from the ban on interest, by which all loans are converted into charity; that is, money cannot be used to make money (Exod 22:24, Lev 25:35ff.). The rule that slaves must be emancipated after seven years or at the jubilee (Exod 21:2-6, Lev 25:25-28, Deut 15:12-18) prevents the accumulation of human capital, "for the Israelites are my slaves," says God, "mine, whom I liberated from the land of Egypt" (Lev 25:55).

Add to these such provisions as the poor tithe (Deut 14:28-29), the septennial cancellation of debts (Deut 15:1-6), the injunction to lend money generously to the needy at no interest (Deut 15:7-11), and it emerges that the sometimes explicit purpose of the laws to assert God's sovereignty and their implicit reflection of his attributes eventuate in measures that distribute material resources among the people with a clear tendency toward equalization. A focus of human power to rival that of God is precluded.[6]

Finally, such accumulation of power as flows from control of information is counteracted by the regime of the Torah. I have already documented the concern of the legislator to disseminate knowledge of the laws among all the people. The fruit of this concern is Deuteronomy's imposition on parents of a duty to teach the divine commandments to their children (Deut 6:7, 11:19) and its institution of a septennial public recitation of the Torah ("assemble the people, men, women and children and the alien resident in your towns")—a reenactment of the lawgiving at Mount Horeb (Deut 31:10-13). That this institution is entrusted to the Levite priests together with the care

[6] See the illuminating study of N. W. Soss, "Old Testament Law and Economic Society," *Journal of the History of Ideas* 34 (1973) 323-44.

of the written Torah strikingly contravenes their partisan interest to monopolize sacred lore.

The published laws include the regulation of human authorities and their subjection to divine authority. All Israel knows of God's admonition to judges not to take bribes or pervert justice or ignore the claim of the helpless (Exod 23:6–8); the ground is thus laid for public supervision and criticism of the judiciary. King Hammurabi of Babylon invited

> any oppressed man who has a cause [to] come into the presence of the statue of me, king of justice, and then read carefully my inscribed stela [of laws], and give heed to my precious words, and may my stela make the case clear to him; may he understand his cause: may he set his mind at ease.[7]

But since the stela stood inside a temple, well out of public view, and was written in the esoteric cuneiform script that necessitated long schooling to read, this invitation amounts to little more than a (boastful) rhetorical gesture. The Torah's regulations concerning the judiciary (to take one example) are calculated to work an entirely different effect. Their oral publication reaches everyone, and empowers whomever feels himself or herself a victim of judicial malfeasance to claim redress, armed with a publicly known divine sanction.

In like manner, broadcasting the king's subjection to God's Torah and the opprobrium attached to his accumulating symbols of prestige and power cannot but undercut his absolute sway over the people. And the publication of the priestly perquisites (e.g., Deut 18:1–5) and the cause of disqualification from divine service (Lev 21:13–23) must set limits to priestly authority and prestige in the eyes of the populace.

The promulgation of the Torah serves, in the first instance, the ideal of making Israel a kingdom of priests; it is also the basis of the common responsibility of each for all (e.g., the collective penalty imposed on the community that failed to prosecute a notorious idolater, Lev 20:4–5). But at the same time it implicitly heightens the worth and weight of the individual: by imparting information to her or him, both individual accountability and individual power are increased. Duties toward others are matched by the rights she or he may claim from others. Knowing the boundaries set by God to human

[7] Epilogue to the Laws of Hammurabi (trans. T. J. Meek, *Ancient Near Eastern Texts Relating to the Old Testament* [ed. J. B. Pritchard; 3d ed.; Princeton: Princeton University, 1969] 178).

authorities makes it impossible for the ruler to assert an absolute sway over the individual. Both are ultimately subject to the same divine sovereign whose laws are designed to keep all humans conscious of their creaturehood.

In its aversion to the concentration of power and its tendency to equalize resources among the citizenry, the system of biblical law resembles democracy. It resembles it, too, in the aspiration to create a society united voluntarily around shared values, in whose achievement all are called on to participate and share responsibility. It resembles it, finally, in its regard for the individual, whose freedom, person, and property it protects with a solicitude unparalleled in ancient societies. On the other hand, since sovereignty and the authority to legislate belong only to God, the biblical person is ideally heteronomous, not autonomous. Moreover, the collective responsibility of members of the covenant community invites mutual surveillance and pressure to conform to divine norms, as oppressive to the individual as any tyranny.

Material benefits, including victory in war, are held out in the Torah not as the purpose for which society is organized and regulated, but as the divine reward for Israel's attaining its spiritual goal of becoming a holy nation (Exod 23:27-33, Lev 26:3-13, Deut 28:1-14). God granted the land of Canaan to the patriarchs and their descendants as a gift; under Joshua, the people, loyal to God, succeeded in conquering most of the land aided by constant miracles. Completion of the conquest was contingent on the continued devotion of Israel to its holy calling, as Joshua expresses it in his farewell speech:

> Now you have seen all that YHWH your God did to all these nations on your behalf—for it is YHWH your God who has fought for you. See I have allotted these nations to you as possessions of your tribes. . . . YHWH your God will drive them away and dispossess them on your behalf, and you will take possession of your land as YHWH your God promised you. Now be strong and carefully observe all that is written in the Torah of Moses, without deviating to the right or left. Do not mingle with these nations that remain with you; do not invoke the names of their gods . . . and do not serve or worship them; but cleave to YHWH your God as you have done to this day—and God has dispossessed great and numerous nations on your behalf. . . . A single man of you put a thousand of them to flight, for it is YHWH your God who has fought for you. . . . So take good care to love YHWH your God, for if you turn away and cleave to these remaining nations . . . know well that YHWH your God will not continue to dispossess these nations on your behalf (Joshua 23).

This doctrine applies the lesson learned under Moses to the future: victory is not achieved through clever strategy or effective organization (witness Pharaoh's defeat at the Sea of Reeds, or the rout of Amalek, which had more to do with the rise and fall of Moses' arms than with Joshua's generalship). And similarly the sustenance of Israel in the wilderness owed nothing to social organization, but was the direct provision of God, "in order to make you know that it is not on bread alone that mankind may live, but on whatever God may wish to decree" (Deut 8:3).[8] The goal of Israel's existence is spiritual; polity and institutions are to be dedicated to attaining it; material blessings are God's reward for its attainment.

The Reality of Power in the Prophets

Thus far I have described the program of the Torah and the story of its realization in the Torah and the book of Joshua—both program and story being idealized constructions. What was the reality as described in the Prophets?

Israel's polity during the period to which most of the books of the prophets belong was a monarchy, which arose in the tenth century B.C.E. to free Israel from the control of the well-organized league of Philistine towns. Its goals were to save Israel from its enemies and to preserve a just social order: "Give us a king," the people demand of the prophet Samuel, "who will judge us and lead us forth and fight our battles" (1 Sam 8:20). The attempt to reconcile the kingship of God, of whom the prophet was the spokesman, with the kingship of a human, by subjecting the latter to the dictate of the former, produced intolerable tension. Where did royal freedom to initiate and decide end, and where did royal obligation to obey God's word conveyed through the prophet begin? Saul's kingship foundered

[8] "In order to make you know the power and greatness of God, who can sustain his creatures by all sorts of things apart from bread" (Commentary to Deuteronomy of Meyuhas bar Elijah, Greece, 12 century C.E. [ed. J. M. Katz; Jerusalem: Kook, 1968] 32). This correct sense of the verse in its original context has been overshadowed by its application in the New Testament, e.g. Matt 4:4, where Jesus responds to Satan's challenge to turn stones into bread by citing this verse. Jesus' meaning is given thus by J. L. McKenzie: "The answer of Jesus (Deut 8:3) does not deny that ordinary needs should be met by ordinary means, but subordinates even basic physical necessities to the revealed word of God. Jesus does not fulfill his mission by providing for basic physical necessities, but by proclaiming the word that is life" ("The Gospel according to Matthew," *The Jerome Biblical Commentary*, [ed. R. E. Brown, J. A. Fitzmyer, and R. E. Murphy; Englewood Cliffs, NJ: Prentice-Hall, 1968], 2: 69). From this comes the common use of the expression in the sense of: "Supplying man's physical needs does not answer all of an individual's needs; there is also a spiritual side that needs spiritual sustenance."

on rigorous tests set by Samuel: would the king obey God's orders when the king judged them to be in conflict with the interests of state? There was no personal clash between the two men, only a quarrel over ill-defined functions: Samuel is depicted as fond of Saul until the day he died; even afterward it was to Samuel's ghost that Saul applied in his last crisis.

The monarchy could attain its goals only by becoming a national focus of power. That entailed mobilization of public resources, including confiscation of private property and levies on workers for the army and public works. A class of royal officials developed, entitled to make exactions from the people and use them as they saw fit. Some confused the public good with their personal gain. The concentration of resources led to social inequality, and as the prestige of the court and of the officialdom grew, so did their insolence and insouciance toward the mass of the people. The people became estranged from their leaders, who in the northern kingdom eventually degenerated into soldiers of fortune. All the impositions that Samuel said would be necessitated by "the rule of the king" came to pass:

> He will seize your sons and appoint them over his chariots and horses, and they will run before his chariot. He will make them his captains of thousands and fifties, to do his plowing and harvesting, and to make his weapons and chariots. He will take your daughters for perfumers, cooks, and bakers. He will take your best fields and give them to his courtiers. He will tithe your seed and your orchards and give it to his officers and courtiers. Your male and female servants, your best youths, and your asses he will take and use for his works. He will tithe your flocks; and you will be his slaves (1 Sam 8:11–17).

The policy of the monarchy subordinated the ideal of becoming a holy nation to the achievement of national prestige and security. It was concerned with building up the military and establishing alliances with powerful neighbors. In the end it subverted the institutions of religion into instruments of royal policy. The story of the nonconforming prophet Micaiah ben Imlah (1 Kings 22) shows how northern kings coopted prophecy for state purposes—in that instance to support a military campaign into territory disputed between Aram and Israel. "Don't you know," says the Israelite king to his staff, "that Ramot Gilead belongs to us?" (1 Kings 22:3). For hundred prophets—evidently his pensioners—cry their approval and thus conscript God into the army of Israel.[9]

[9] The degeneration of institutionalized prophecy is described by W. Eichrodt, *Theology of the Old Testament* (2 vols.; Philadelphia: Westminster, 1961), 1:332–37.

Against these social, political, and spiritual abuses, classical prophecy, beginning with Amos (mid-eighth century), directed its critique. The prophets saw themselves as the spokesmen of Israel's ancient values; since they were not interested in adjusting those values to changed circumstances, they may be called regressive rather than progressive. They denounced the insolent, exploitative, tyrannical use of royal power and prerogative. They denounced the enlisting of God and religion to serve state ends. Hosea was "the first man in history to condemn militarism as a religious-moral sin" (Hos 8:14, 10:13–14, 14:3).[10] Isaiah put power politics on the same footing as idolatry; he denounced reliance on arms, fortresses, and alliances with great powers. He urged trust in God and quietism that waits on God's salvation. He foresaw universal peace as the goal toward which history moves—an age in which nations would give up their trust in power and idols, and seek the instruction of God at Zion, the mountain of his holy temple (Isaiah 2). Jeremiah and Ezekiel gave voice to God's terrible decision that the present Israel was so degenerate that he could realize his original purpose for the people only by wiping the slate clean and starting over again with renovated survivors.[11]

In the Torah and Prophets, I see an attitude toward power torn between ideal and reality. The conflict could be reconciled only by a creative interpretation of the legislation, applying the old ideal to changed circumstances. Israel's prophets mercilessly exposed the gap between ideal and reality, but did not offer a reconciliation.

The unresolved conflict, along with other issues left open in the canon of Hebrew Scripture, was bequeathed to the Jews of the Second Temple period. The various parties of early Judaism, from the Hasmonean dynasts, through the Pharisaic quietists, to the Messianic-apocalypticists, all took distinct positions on the pursuit of power and held consequent attitudes toward the Torah that sought to tame it.

[10] Y. Kaufmann, *The Religion of Israel* (trans. M. Greenberg; Chicago: University of Chicago, 1960) 375.

[11] Morris Silver, *Prophets and Markets: The Political Economy of Ancient Israel* (Boston: Kluwer-Nijhoff, 1983), vigorously indicts Israel's prophets for having demoralized the people, thereby contributing substantially to their collapse. The weak link in his intriguing argument is his assumption that the prophets' messages were effective.

John W. Welch

Reflections on Postulates: Power and Ancient Laws— A Response to Moshe Greenberg

WELCH REVIEWS THE MAIN POINTS of Greenberg's essay in the context of a similar essay written by Greenberg in 1960 and in light of the criticisms of that essay by Bernard Jackson. Welch shows that Greenberg is in the present essay expanding upon a central contention of the earlier essay, namely that legal systems, such as that contained in the Bible, can be adequately understood only when their underlying distinctive postulates have been grasped. In the earlier essay, Greenberg had spelled out three such postulates; Welch sees Greenberg as adding further ones in the present essay, ones having to do with the limitation and dispersement of power. The criticisms of Jackson relate in general to the question of how (by what method) one ascertains the underlying postulates of biblical law and the distinctiveness of these postulates. Welch, like Jackson, shows doubt concerning the distinctiveness of certain features of biblical law mentioned by Greenberg. Since Greenberg was given opportunity to reply to Welch's queries, his reply has been included at the end of this chapter.

John W. Welch, J.D. (Duke University), M.A., B.A. (Brigham Young University), is Professor of Law at the J. Reuben Clark Law School of Brigham Young University. He has edited *Chiasmus in Antiquity* and *The Collected Works of Hugh Nibley* and serves as the president of the Foundation for Ancient Research and Mormon Studies.

In 1960 Professor Greenberg published a seminal paper in the *Kaufmann Jubilee Volume* entitled "Some Postulates of Biblical Criminal Law."[1] The previous paper is an extension of that paper into the area of ancient Israelite government and politics. I shall respond to this paper in three ways: first, I will briefly summarize Professor Greenberg's 1960 paper and compare it with his present presentation; second, I then suggest that Professor Greenberg should respond to some of the technical criticisms raised by Bernard Jackson with respect to the 1960 paper; and third, because I basically concur with Professor Greenberg, I will offer a few comments about the importance of perceiving underlying postulates of legal systems, whether ancient or modern.

In 1960 Professor Greenberg rightly argued that biblical law should be "studied for itself . . . as an autonomous discipline," not merely so as to gather clues about ancient Near Eastern society or history. Then, after pointing out that biblical law can and should be studied as a single coherent whole, Greenberg advanced a bold point: namely, that "until the *values that* [a legal system] *embodies* are understood, it is questionable whether *any individual* law can be properly appreciated." He then went on to propose and discuss three such "postulates" or basic underlying distinctive values belonging to biblical law. Those three postulates were:

1. In biblical law, God is "the fountainhead of the law" and "the law is a statement of his will," whereas, by contrast, in Mesopotamia the law was conceived as the embodiment of great impersonal cosmic truths of which a god like Shamash was merely "the divine custodian." Violation of law in the biblical sense, therefore, amounted to a sin or rebellion against God personally, not just an infraction of a law.

2. In biblical law, a "sense of the *invaluableness* of human life" underlies its treatment of homicide, as distinguished from the laws of Babylonia, which were more concerned "with safeguarding rights in property and making losses good." This is, according to Greenberg, "a basic difference in judgments of value."

3. In biblical law, "vicarious punishment" (as for example punishing a son if his father injured another man's son) was eschewed, but not in other ancient Near Eastern codes. What traces of vicarious punishment *can* be found in the Bible are reserved as powers of divine prerogative.

In his present paper, Greenberg has added to the foregoing list a cluster of other postulates regarding the biblical attitudes toward power. He has articulated here the idea that underlying biblical law

[1] M. Greenberg, "Some Postulates of Biblical Criminal Law," *Yehezkel Kaufmann Jubilee Volume* (ed. M. Haran; Jerusalem: Magnes, 1960) 5-28.

and society were certain value-claims about power: namely, that power belongs to God; that power should only be used to sustain the world or to maintain the moral order; that power, delegated by God to humans, tends to be abused; that biblical law is formulated in its "motive-clause manner" in order to elicit obedience to God; that political power should be diffuse and limited; that the concentration of economic power should be impeded; that legal information should be widely disseminated. These ideals, as he has shown, left much lacking in the actual experience of ancient Israel. Notwithstanding, Greenberg suggests that it was Israel's contribution to legal history "unlike other ancient systems of law" and "unparalleled in antiquity" at least to have recognized these postulates.

The methodology here is strongly reminiscent of his 1960 approach. In both cases he is striving to identify underlying values, particularly those distinctive of or unique to ancient Israel. In both instances he works basically conservatively, harmonizing and reconciling apparent inconsistencies, in this case explaining the tension between biblical ideologies and historical realities.

That methodology, however, has been criticized by Bernard Jackson.[2] One necessarily recalls some of Jackson's arguments when considering Greenberg's latter article, and thereby hopes to stimulate dialogue on these important issues.

Jackson raised several concerns. The first asked to what extent biblical and ancient Near Eastern law codes were drafted for the specific purpose of aiding *judges* in law case decision making, as opposed to articulating general ideals. Here, Greenberg has treated statements in the Bible about power more as "ideals." One is curious whether this reflects in his mind a slight shift to see more "the *non-statutory* nature of Israel's chief religious document."

Second was the concern whether there is any reliable method of ascertaining these "inner postulates" of biblical law. In the context of the present paper, this concern is still very relevant and left largely unexplored. How can one really know what the ancients thought about power? Can the range of these value postulates be determined within reasonable limits? One must be especially cautious when drawing inferences from statements that are not express or unequivocal. Yet that is mostly what I see: the passage from Psalm 8 extolling the sublimity of God and man's dominion could have been written by people having a variety of views about power; the observance of the

[2] B. Jackson, "Reflections on Biblical Criminal Law," *Journal of Jewish Studies* 24 (1973) 8–38; revised and reprinted as chap. 2 in his *Essays in Jewish and Comparative Legal History* (Leiden: Brill, 1975) 25–63.

Sabbath and providing for the needy could have been motivated by a penchant against the concentration of economic power, but these practices also could reflect other things, like cultic or symbolic modeling of one's behavior after God's in the case of resting on the seventh day, or like mollifying the poor to prevent social disturbances. Furthermore, one wonders whether a given postulate or attitude about power remained constant over the course of many centuries or was subject to change as the history unfolded. For example, is it possible that the difference that Greenberg has discussed between the ideals and the reality of power evince a shift over time in the acceptance of or the very existence of these postulates about power? These are issues that invite further investigation and clarification.

Next, as Jackson also pointed out, the evidence with respect to the biblical uniqueness and succinctness of any proposed postulate is not quite so black-and-white on either count: Statements like "in Israel alone life and property are incommensurable" have proved not quite so crisp as one might have thought on first examination, for sometimes in the Bible, life and property may be commensurable. Witness, as Jackson offers, the mixed evidence in Exod 21:30 and Num 35:31 about the acceptability of *kofer* or ransom money. Neither the religious domination of biblical laws nor the socio-political domination of ancient Near Eastern laws holds total control. Reuven Yaron adds similar observations with respect to what he calls the phenomenon of "diminishing" and "disappearing biblical uniqueness."[3]

With regard to the present paper, similar caveats come to mind. It is true that the laws of Israel were published widely, particularly at an annual renewal ceremony. But how certain can one be that the reading of the law reached *everyone* because they were oral, or even that they reached most everyone in Israel, and not elsewhere? There is some evidence that laws were quite widely published at least in some other legal systems. The laws of Gortyn and the Roman Twelve Tables were publicly displayed in the market place, and not just in the temple out of public view. Similarly, Babylonian oaths were renewed annually, as were Greek treaties mentioned in Thucydides, as Moshe Weinfeld has pointed out.[4] Thus, this may be more a difference of degree than of kind.

Or again, if the jubilee laws and practices reflect an ethical postulate favoring a diversification of power in Israel, is not a some-

[3] R. Yaron, "Biblical Law: Prolegomena," in B. Jackson, *Jewish Law in Legal History and the Modern World* (Leiden: Brill, 1980) 32-33.

[4] M. Weinfeld, "The Origin of the Apodictic Law: An Overlooked Source," *Vetus Testamentum* 23 (1973) 72.

what similar thing reflected—at least to some extent—in the Babylonian *mišarum* practice of releasing debts, as found for example in the Edict of Ammi-saduqa, the tenth ruler in the Hammurabi dynasty?

Similarly, one can readily concur that the tendencies of biblical law promoted something like "democracy," but at the same time there remain issues about what that democracy consisted of. Baruch Halpern describes well what little can be safely concluded about the separate functions of the tribes, judges, assemblies, people, and early monarchy in ancient Israel.[5] There were democratic tendencies, but not all people participated to an equal extent. And on the other side of the coin, Thorkid Jacobsen has argued that a similar type of primitive democracy existed in ancient Mesopotamia.[6] Again, are these differences of kind or of degree?

This is not to say there are no differences. The limited powers of the monarchs of Israel, especially the requirement that they be "one from among the brethren" (Deut 17:15), surely stands in sharp contrast to other ancient kingship concepts in which the king was viewed as the near-divine provider of all to his people, including life itself.

Finally, with respect to Greenberg's significant observations about the "profusion of motive clauses" in the Torah, a motive clause is one supplied at the end of a law, not adding further legal requirements, but giving the motive or rationale behind the law.[7] Greenberg sees these motive clauses as evidence, "unlike other ancient systems of law," that biblical law is "designed to educate the public, to mold the national character." While this is surely generally the case—especially true is the comparative profusion of motive clauses in the legal texts of the Bible—a few qualifications are in order: first, it is *not* clear that motive clauses are either *totally unique* to biblical law, nor are they *ubiquitous* in the Bible. A motive clause appears in the Hittite administrative regulations: "for him who has a suit, judge it and set him right."[8] The works of Rifat Sonsino and R. W. Uitti confirm the existence of motive clauses in other ancient Near Eastern law codes,

[5] B. Halpern, *The Constitution of the Monarchy in Israel* (Chico, CA: Scholars Press, 1981) 175–249.

[6] T. Jacobsen, *Toward the Image of Tammuz* (Cambridge: Harvard University, 1970).

[7] For example, the law reads: If you take a person's coat as security for a loan, you must return it before the sun goes down, "for it is his only covering, and wherein shall he sleep?" (Exod 22:26). The last phrase is a motive clause.

[8] E. von Schuler, *Hethitische Dienstanweisungen für höhere Hof- und Staatsbeamte* (Graz: privately printed, 1957; repr. Osnabrück: Biblio-Verlag, 1967) 47, col. 3a, lines 21–37.

although not as frequent as in the biblical codes.[9] (It appears that only 5-6% of those laws were motivated, while around half of the biblical laws are—depending on how one counts them.) Moreover, the motive clauses in the Babylonian laws are routine explanations rather than hortatory admonitions. This is not to say, however, that the Babylonians were not interested in educating their people about the law: As Weinfeld has pointed out, an Assyrian inscription of Sargon reads: "In order to teach them the teaching of serving God and King, I sent overseers and officers."[10] And it can also be pointed out that motive clauses do not always appear in the Bible, even where they seem sorely needed: how nice it would be to have a motive clauses after the prohibition against seething a kid in his mother's milk! (Exod 23:19). So again, to some extent, this is a difference of degree and not of kind.

Nor should it be thought, of course, that all motive clauses serve the same purpose. It is true that some educate the public and some shape a national character. As Sonsino concludes: biblical motive clauses "ultimately . . . seem to point to a teaching function," while the Babylonian motive clauses seem more designed to "curry the favors of the gods by underscoring the lawmaker's true concern for justice."[11] Still, not all biblical motive clauses are the same, and we would do well to notice the differences. Considering just the motive clauses in Exodus 20-23, note that some explain the *aetiology* behind a law: as regarding the Sabbath, "for in six days the Lord made heaven and earth" (20:11), and regarding the feast of unleavened bread in Abib, "for in that month you came out from Egypt" (23:14). Others are *promisory*: "that your days may be long upon the land" (20:12); or as in the command to be obedient, "for my Angel shall go before thee" (23:23), and "for I will deliver the inhabitants of the land into your hand" (23:31). Others are merely *explanatory*, as in the prohibition against walking up to an altar on steps, "that your nakedness be not discovered thereon" (20:26 [23]), or in the explanation that on the Sabbath all shall rest, "that your ox and your ass may rest" (23:12). A few do shape character, either by evoking *sympathy* or by holding out *threats*. Sympathy is aroused by motive clauses like "for you know the heart of a stranger" (23:9), and "for ye were strangers in the land of Egypt" (22:21 [20]). Threats are communicated by clauses like "for I

[9] R. Sonsino, *Motive Clauses in Hebrew Law: Biblical Forms and Near Eastern Parallels* (Chico, CA: Scholars Press, 1980), to which Greenberg refers; R. W. Uitti, "The Motive Clause in Old Testament Law" (Ph.D. diss., Chicago Lutheran School of Theology, 1973).

[10] Weinfeld, "The Origin of the Apodictic Law," 70.

[11] Sonsino, *Motive Clauses in Hebrew Law*, 175.

will not justify the wicked" (23:7), and "I will hear [the cries of the poor], for I am gracious" (22:27 [26]). The point is, motive clauses are undoubtedly important in many ways to the character of biblical law. Greenberg does well to point us in the direction of investigating these clauses for sources of value-postulates in biblical law.

Finally, I acknowledge briefly the importance of basic ethical postulates to any legal system. It makes sense to talk of such postulates or premises or collective values, despite our great inability to document or define them precisely. In our own Anglo-American legal world, such ideas often unconsciously shape the course of legal analysis and dictate the direction of legal practice. For example, one will never find a law stating that every person is entitled to a "day in court," but the idea has a good ethical ring to Western legal ears. It seems that "for every wrong there should be a remedy," but that too supposes something about our postulated expectations about the domain and remedial abilities of the law. The study of such expectations yields important insights into any legal system, including that of biblical law.

Modern society would do well to learn from the value postulates of the biblical legal system. For example, we could learn much from their attitudes toward limiting the concentration of political power, from their respect for and protection of human life and property, from their immense devotion to the authority of and changeless stability of the law, from their broad commitment to the equality of mankind, from their love of God and of the law (treating law not as something in which to find loopholes but as the essential fabric without which life and society could not survive). We could benefit from recalling the way in which all members of biblical society were responsible to know and teach and participate in the enforcement of the law, and by remembering their unqualified concern for protecting the weak, the poor, the widow, and the orphan, and their unequivocal honesty under oath and unwillingness to abuse or misuse the judicial process. All these are lessons that need to be learned and relearned. The influence of such postulates on the West has been and should continue to be great.

Reply to the Comments of John Welch by Moshe Greenberg

In this reply I clarify some of my arguments, particularly as John Welch invites me to respond to Bernard Jackson's strictures.[1]

The issue raised by Jackson's critique of "Postulates," my earlier paper—which criticism Welch implies is pertinent to the present one—is whether principles may be inferred from cases. When the cases range across various areas and show a consistent pattern of evaluation, or tend to the same result, I opined and still opine that at least tacit principles underlie the pattern or tendency. And Jackson in a recent paper allows that authors of laws can have "tacit philosophical assumptions."[2] My argument can be undermined by adducing biblical evidence counter to my theses that I ignored or misinterpreted. Evidence outside of Israel (e.g., among the Hittites) that some offenses against property were not capital, and some homicides were not compoundable is irrelevant. I do not argue that cuneiform law is consistent in these matters, but that biblical law is; yet Jackson troubles himself and the reader with (too often, inconclusive) arguments on the cuneiform side.

I cannot take up here all of Jackson's strictures, some of which are very subtle if not indeed sophistical; I shall instead reply to the allegation that I have ignored uncongenial evidence.[3] Jackson alleges that I have overlooked "aspects of Biblical law" that show some property offenses to have been capital. One such aspect is "brigandage," which Jackson—referring the reader to his book *Theft*—claims to find in the early narratives, penalized with death. In "Postulates" I am concerned with the *legislation* of the Bible (and with such nonlegislative matter as illuminates it)—not with every passage that may have a bearing on legal ideas. It is not known what the relation of the legal portions of the Bible was to the narrative or the relation

[1] The following works are hereinafter referred to by short titled in the text and footnotes: M. Greenberg, "Some Postulates of Biblical Criminal Law," in *Yehezkel Kaufmann Jubilee Volume* (ed. M. Haran; Jerusalem: Magnes, 1960) 5-28, referred to as "Postulates"; B. Jackson, "Reflections on Biblical Criminal Law," *Journal of Jewish Studies* 24 (1973) 8-28, reprinted and revised in Jackson, *Essays in Jewish and Comparative Legal History* (Leiden: Brill, 1975) 25-63, referred to as "Reflections" (pagination as in *Essays*); B. Jackson, *Theft in Early Jewish Law* (Oxford: Clarendon, 1972), referred to as *Theft*.

[2] B. Jackson, "The Ceremonial and the Judicial: Biblical Law as Sign and Symbol," *Journal for the Study of the Old Testament* 30 (1984) 38.

[3] A fuller response appears in my "More Reflections on Biblical Criminal Law," *Studies in Bible* (ed. S. Japhet; Scripta Hierosolymitana 31; Jerusalem: Magnes, 1986) 1-18.

of laws to life; nor can it be simply assumed that this or that narrative statement of a threat (or self-threat) made under duress has legal significance[4] (e.g., Joseph's brothers' threat of death to the one who stole Joseph's cup, Gen 44:9). Since Jackson admits that the term *gzl*, which he takes to mean brigandage in the early narratives, has only the meaning 'rob(bery)' by an individual in the legal texts and entails only a cultic penalty, I cannot be charged, in omitting discussion of *gzl* cases, with overlooking evidence bearing on my thesis.[5]

Another aspect I failed to mention was kidnapping—a capital offense. Jackson is aware that in biblical law kidnapping (expressed by the phrase *gnb npš* 'steal a person') is an offense against person not property; but he advances as a "positive reason" for regarding it nonetheless as stealing property that the same verb *gnb* serves for stealing property and persons. But *gnb* is also used with *lb* 'mind' to mean 'deceive, mislead'; does that make misleading an offense against property? What defines the offense is the object stolen: if a piece of property, then it is an offense against property; if a person, then an offense against person. That the penalties for stealing property and kidnapping are so different must reflect a differing evaluation of person and property (even if Jackson is right that the same penalty for different offenses doesn't "necessarily imply the same value judgment of those offenses").[6]

Another aspect I failed to mention is Achan's theft (*gnb*) of *ḥerem*—loot of Jericho dedicated to God; for this he was put to death. I could dismiss this as irrelevant, since I deal with laws not narrative, yet I cannot forbear pointing out that the gist of Achan's offense was not theft but appropriation of tabooed goods (*ḥerem*) with the result that the whole camp of Israel entered *ḥerem*-status and became condemned by God. That Achan's appropriation was furtive is immaterial to the offense; it would have been a capital crime had it been open: note the terms of the ban in Josh 6:18 not to 'take' (*lqḥ*) of the *ḥerem* lest the entire camp incur *ḥerem*-status and be liable to destruction (The furtiveness of Achan is only material to the bewilderment of Joshua over the subsequent defeat of his army at Ai;

[4] Jackson, "Reflections," 38. Extensive deduction of law from narrative is a hallmark of scholars influenced, as is Jackson, by the work of D. Daube.

[5] Jackson's argument for historical development of the terms *gzl* and *gnb* ('rob', 'steal') has been well criticized by J. Milgrom (*Cult and Conscience* [Leiden: Brill, 1975] 90ff.) as Jackson acknowledges in "Legal Drafting in the Ancient Near East . . . ," *Mélanges a la mémoire de Marcel-Henri Prévost* (Paris: Presses Universitaires de France, 1982) 61 n. 80.

[6] Jackson, "Reflections," 36. I never said the same penalty implied the same value judgment.

that is why it is mentioned.) Note too the language of Deut 7:25-26: by taking (*lqḥ*) and bringing (*hby*ʾ) *ḥerem* into one's home one becomes *ḥerem*—hence liable to destruction. Achan's case is not an offense against property but violation of a taboo, a crime against God.[7]

The aspects that Jackson charges me with overlooking turn out to be irrelevant to my thesis that biblical law recognized no offense against property as capital.

Welch has been persuaded by Jackson's argument that the allowance of ransom in the case of the goring ox of Exod 21:30 contradicts my thesis of the incommensurability of life and property in biblical law. I regarded this case as the exception that defined the rule, "You may not accept a ransom for the life of a murderer who is guilty of a capital crime; he must be put to death" (Num 35:31). The criminally negligent owner of a vicious ox whose animal killed a human being is punished by alternative penalties—death (Exod 21:29) or, "if a ransom is laid on him," ransom. Such alternative possibilities here are exceptional and suggested to me vacillation due to its being a borderline case. Why does this man "who is guilty of capital crime" enjoy a privilege denied to the murderer of Num 35:31—namely ransom? A simple difference sets the ox-owner apart from the murderer: unlike the latter, the former did not personally commit the homicide (his ox did), nor did he intend or premeditate it. Num 35:31 is thereby explicated to mean: the murderer guilty of a capital crime who may not ransom himself is one who killed personally and with intent;[8] accordingly there is no contradiction between it and Exod 22:30.

Jackson seeks to rebut my argument with the remark that David's indirect causation of Uriah's death did not prevent Nathan (God) from charging him with the slaying. To this I protest once again that law cannot be derived from narrative, much less humanly-administered law from God's judgments.[9] Jackson disallows "criminal negligence" as an appropriate description of the ox-owner's

[7] So I defined it in "Postulates," 23-24, and in "Crimes and Punishments," *Interpreter's Dictionary of the Bible* (ed. G. A. Buttrick; Nashville: Abingdon, 1962), 1:737b. In *Theft*, Jackson associates me wrongly with the notion that Achan's case illustrates collective guilt; Jackson proceeds to deprecate the notion in the very terms by which I in fact explain Achan's case in the above cited publications.

[8] Jackson (*Essays*, 91ff.) prefers "with premeditation"—a dubious interpretation. His claim that Num 35:22-23 provides asylum for intentional homicides is not supported by the final hypothetical circumstance: "or without seeing [him] dropped on him any deadly stone object."

[9] See "Postulates," 25ff., which Jackson does not challenge.

guilt.[10] But is not that precisely what the law means when it says that "he failed to guard it"—that is, he was slack in his responsibility, negligent; and when it penalizes him by death does that not mean his offense is criminal? Jackson argues that the ransom clause does not sound like a remedy to an exceptional situation—but everything about the case is unusual: the situation (an ox known to gore whose owner was warned); the owner's negligence resulting in the ox killing someone; and the remedy (an allowance of alternative penalties).

Jackson's last argument is Prov 6:34–35: as he understands it, it contemplates the use of ransom in the case of adultery, "normally a premeditated offense"; hence my argument that ransom is available to the ox-owner only because of the exceptional case of unpremeditated killing fails. Since Loewenstamm before Jackson also invoked this passage to confute my position, I pause to give my understanding of it, though Welch made no reference to this issue.[11] Here is the Proverbs passage: The man who commits adultery with another's wife is a fool, because

> The fury of the husband will be passionate;
> He will show no pity on his day of vengeance.
> He will not have regard for any ransom;
> He will refuse your bribe, however great.

W. McKane explains: "However much money he may have, he will find that an outraged husband, mad with jealousy, will prefer his pound of flesh to the most handsome financial reparation and will exact his revenge in violence and in stamping the offender with an indelible stain of disgrace."[12] If the victim of other delicts might be satisfied by a payment of money, a wronged husband will disdain money and will vent his outrage in private revenge. How can any inference be drawn from this passage about the *law* of adultery? Warning is given of the unassuageable rage of the husband: not even

[10] *Essays*, 123ff. Jackson prefers the Septuagint reading "he did not destroy it," on which basis he defines the offense and the motive for the punishment differently from me. But at least since Z. Frankel (*Über den Einfluss der palästinischen Exegese auf die alexandrinische Hermeneutik* [Leipzig: Barth, 1851] 93), this reading has been suspected of distorting the Hebrew under a tendentious halakic influence; so too L. Prijs, *Jüdische Tradition in der Septuaginta* (Leiden: Brill, 1948) 57f.

[11] S. E. Loewenstamm, "Adultery and Homicide in the Laws of Mesopotamia and the Bible," *Bet Miqra* 7 (1962) 55–59 [Hebrew]. Loewenstamm used this verse to deny that adultery was uncompoundable in biblical law, as I had contended in "Postulates," 12.

[12] W. McKane, *Proverbs* (Old Testament Library; Philadelphia: Westminster, 1970) 331.

a million shekels will pacify him. Does such a statement imply that a legal arrangement existed allowing a paramour to evade the legally prescribed death penalty by paying a ransom? I think not.[13]

Replying, now, to some of Welch's strictures: I intended in this paper to describe the *tendency* of the laws of the Torah relating to political power (the concept analyzed in categories drawn from political science). To be sure, the laws hardly ever address the topic of power directly, but when diverse enactments all tend to trench severely on the accumulation of power, it does not seem implausible to suppose them to express an implicit "philosophy" that I have tried to articulate. As with the laws discussed in "Postulates," here too it is not known to what extent these rulings were ever realized in practice; I do suppose, however, that the prophets relied on some popular knowledge of the laws and tendency of the Torah literature on which they based their harangues.[14]

Many items of biblical law and religion are paralleled in the cultures of the ancient Near East; nonetheless it remains true that the accumulation of factors and rulings tending so markedly to whittle down the power of central authority is without analogy. Parallels must be examined carefully: Mesopotamian kings vaunted themselves "kings of *mišarum* (justice/equity)" and from time to time—especially at the start of their reign—they issued *mišarum*-edicts easing the plight of insolvents and debtors. This is somewhat analogous to the biblical jubilee and cancellation of debts, but the biblical easements (regular, not occasional) do not redound to the credit and enhance the glory of the earthly king; they are an expression of God's solicitude for his human subjects.[15] Comparing the educative purpose of the

[13] My objection to Loewenstamm's argument is thus not that he compared sapiential with legal literature—a procedure considered inadmissible by M. Weinfeld ("On the Conception of Law in the Bible and Outside It," *Bet Miqra* 9 [1964] 63-68 [Hebrew]), with whose principle I agree, although I deny its relevance here since in my estimate Prov 6:35 has nothing to do with law. Loewenstamm replied to Weinfeld in *Bet Miqra* 9 (1964) 77f.

[14] The relation of the prophets to the Torah literature is complicated by the paucity and equivocality of the evidence; for a summary and survey of opinion see S. Leiman, *The Canonization of Hebrew Scripture: The Talmudic and Midrashic Evidence* (Hamden, CT: Archon, 1975) 16ff. (with extensive notes). I address the more general question of the knowledge and effect of the Torah literature in biblical times in "Religion: Stability and Ferment," *The Age of the Monarchies: Culture and Society* (ed. A. Malamat; World History of the Jewish People 4b; Jerusalem: Massada, 1979) 102ff.

[15] Weinfeld has thoroughly illuminated this subject in his erudite monograph, *Justice and Righteousness in Israel and the Nations: Equality and Freedom in Ancient Israel in Light of Social Justice in the Ancient Near East* (Jerusalem; Magnes, 1985)

Torah's publication to Sargon's policy of Assyrianizing *Gleichschaltung* is far off the mark. Here is the Assyrian passage cited by Welch from Weinfeld's article in its full context:

> Peoples of the four regions (of the world), or foreign tongue and divergent speech, dwellers of mountain and lowland . . . I carried off at the command of [the god] Assur, my lord, by the might of my scepter. I unified them and settled them therein [= in the new capital Dur Sharrukin—"Sargonsburg"]. Assyrians, fully competent to teach them how to fear god and the king, I despatched to them as scribes and sheriffs (superintendents).[16]

Students of the Bible in its setting find many of its legal and ethical ideas paralleled in the writings of Israel's neighbors. Inasmuch as all people, in the biblical view, are descended from Adam, and like their ancestor are "the image of God," the basic similarity of all members of the human race is a concept congenial to biblical authors. What they insist on is the radical shift in the evaluation of the elements of civilization that resulted from Israel's covenant with its God. The same building blocks are arranged in new configurations forming an unprecedented hierarchy of values. In the two papers under discussion I have tried to do justice to some features of this revolutionary change.

[Hebrew]. Jackson taxes me with "seek[ing] to destroy the significance of the common ancient Near Eastern and Biblical tradition against oppression of the weak by the strong" ("Reflections," 52) when I describe the purpose of the Mesopotamian royal legislators as the conferring of "political benefits" (in contrast to the stated purpose of the biblical legislator to sanctify Israel through the covenant laws). That I had no such motive should be clear from my comparing the phraseology of the preamble to the Constitution of the United States.

[16] D. Luckenbill, *Ancient Records of Assyria and Babylonia* (Chicago: University of Chicago, 1927; repr. New York: Greenwood, 1968), 2:44 (§86). On the translation of the pertinent line, see the discussion of S. Paul, "Sargon's Administrative Diction in II Kings 17:27," *Journal of Biblical Literature* 88 (1969) 73f.

Ze'ev W. Falk

Spirituality and Jewish Law

Falk shows in the following essay that Judaism, far from endorsing a legalism that is at odds with genuine spirituality, regards the holy law (Torah) as the indispensable means through which spirituality is cultivated. Falk identifies spirituality with holiness, which is an undeniable concern of the law, and he notes, among other things, the importance that the terms *heart* and *spirit* have in reference to adherence to the law. He also notes, in closing, the important contribution that Jewish mysticism has made to the interiorization of the law.

Ze'ev W. Falk is the Berman Professor of Family Law and Succession Law at the Hebrew University of Jerusalem, where he also received his Ph.D. in Jewish history. He has been legal adviser to the Israeli Ministry of Social Welfare and the Ministry of the Interior. Professor Falk is the honorary president of the International Society of Family Law and the author of many works dealing with Jewish law, family law, history, religion, and philosophy. He is also a member of the Board of the Israel Interfaith Association.

Spirituality may be defined as a sensitivity for or an attachment to matters of the spirit, of the sacred sphere, or of religious values. Traditional Christian theology saw this as a gift of the Holy Spirit manifesting the grace of God, while psychology and comparative religion regard spirituality as one aspect of the human spirit.[1]

A spiritual person is less interested in law, institution, dogma, structure, and rite than in the *spirit* of religion. Since the polemics of the apostle Paul, the spirit has been taken as an alternative to law and as a charismatic gift. Paul appealed to the spirit in order to justify the abolition of the law and he referred to the grace of God rather than to the effort of man. A spiritual person (*pneumatikos*) is one who has the Holy Spirit as the determining principle of her or his life and who leads a holy and loving life. In his encounter with Judaizing teachers of the Church, the apostle rejected their commitment to the strict adherence to the law.[2] From his point of view, spirituality and Jewish law are therefore alternative ways of which the former is preferable, since he believes that the end of time is near.

My question, from the point of view of Judaism and almost 2,000 years later, is the following: Does the law have a positive function in the promotion of spirituality, and does spirituality include a sensitivity for and an attachment to the legal and social aspects of religion?

Spirituality in Jewish Philosophy

Rabbi Judah Halevi (c. 1085–1141) uses the term *ruḥani*, which is derived from *rûaḥ* 'spirit' and should therefore be translated as spiritual, metaphysical, or pneumatic,' to describe spirituality. Speaking of the pious person who controls body and life by dedicating time to contemplation, he says of prayer:

> This moment forms the heart and fruit of his time, whilst the other hours represent the way which leads to it. He looks forward to its approach because while it lasts he resembles the *spiritual* beings and is removed from merely animal existence. Those three times of daily prayer are the fruit of his day and night, and the Sabbath is the fruit of the week because it has been appointed to establish the connection with the Divine.[3]

[1] See P. Tillich, *Theology of Culture* (Oxford: Oxford University, 1959) 3–9; R. K. Bultmann, *Primitive Christianity in its Contemporary Setting* (New York: Meridian, 1957) 203 ff.

[2] See D. Fyffe, "Spirituality," *Encyclopaedia of Religion and Ethics* (ed. J. Hastings; Edinburgh: Clark, 1908–26), 11:808–10.

[3] Judah Halevi, *The Kuzari: An Argument for the Faith of Israel* (trans. H. Hirschfeld; New York: Schocken, 1964) 139.

Prayer and Sabbath observance are means of spirituality and of drawing near to God. Both are linked with the law, which provides the regular occasions for contemplation. Spirituality and cleaving to the Divine are not presented as alternatives to worldly life but as its highlight and goal. Nobody is supposed to pray the whole day or to live her or his whole life in Sabbath-like form, but these rules of Jewish law are meant to direct the rest of a Jew's time and raise its quality. Regular breaks from mundane activities are as necessary for the soul as are the meals for the body.

Both prayer and Sabbath observance should be practiced together with the congregation and the family. The pious person need not isolate herself or himself from society but draws inspiration from it and reciprocates by being available to others. Social and individual experience complement each other, so that the spiritual endeavor need not be reserved to the elite. Even less creative persons will thereby be able to join in the spirituality of the pious person and share the collective experience.

Already during the eleventh century Rabbi Baḥya ibn Paquda had described the human soul as the organ of spirituality. Relying on reason and on Scripture, he calls for regular periods of contemplation:

> You will observe that [the] body is composed of various elements with dissimilar qualities. These the creator put together by his almighty power combined by his wisdom and formed out of them a stable organism which in appearance has the character of unity but with natural qualities and functions that are diverse. To this human body God has joined a *spiritual* and ethereal entity akin to the *spirituality* of the higher beings. This entity is his soul.[4]

Baḥya makes use of the platonic idea that every individual should know himself or herself, transforming it into one of the *duties of the heart*. A person should contemplate on the correlation between body and soul. The latter is seen as the link between the body and the spiritual world. Spirituality is the awareness of and attachment to metaphysical reality, and the search for spirituality is presented by the law of religion.

Jewish philosophers called for contemplation and renewal within the framework of obedience to Jewish law. As formulated by Maimonides (1135–1205):

[4] Baḥya ben Joseph ibn Paquda, *Duties of the Heart* (trans. M. Hyamson; Jerusalem: Feldheim, 1970) 153.

> We should contemplate and meditate on his commandments, sayings and acts, until we can perceive him and enjoy fully his perception, which is the commandment of loving God.[5]

Thus the commandments are meant not only as norms of behavior but also as objects of contemplation, to lead toward the perception and the love of God. A major topic of contemplation is the disregard of reward and punishment in relation to the commandments. Love of God means performance of the rules and study of the law without ulterior motives.[6] The law is therefore a medium to demonstrate one's total dedication to the Divine and a way to express spirituality.

But the link between spirituality and law preceded medieval philosophy. Already the prophet Ezekiel had connected the *new heart* and the *new spirit* with the observance of the law. He describes the righteous person by listing the various commandments:

> He does not eat upon the mountains or lift up his eyes to the idols of the house of Israel, does not defile his neighbor's wife or approach a woman in her time of impurity, does not oppress anyone but restores to the debtor his pledge, commits no robbery, gives his bread to the hungry and covers the naked with a garment, does not lend at interest or take any increase, withholds his hand from iniquity, executes true justice between man and man, walks in my statutes and is careful to observe my ordinances (Ezek 18:6–9).

Regarding this form of righteousness the prophet then calls upon his listeners:

> Repent and turn from all your transgressions, lest iniquity be your ruin. Cast away from you all the transgressions which you have committed against me, and get yourself a new heart and a new spirit (Ezek 18:30–31).

Here the change of heart and of spirit is understood as the result of repentance and as the outcome of a strict observance of the commandments. If the new spirit is a concept similar to spirituality, then this prophecy is a way of experiencing spirituality through law. The same can be said of the other version, where God himself is described as changing man's heart and spirit:

[5] Maimonides, *Sefer ha-Mitzvot,* 3d commandment. (For a recent translation, see Maimonides, *The Commandments* [trans. C. B. Chavel; London: Soncino, 1967], 1:3.)

[6] Maimonides, *Mishneh Torah,* 1:5:10.

> I will gather you from the peoples and assemble you out of the countries where you have been scattered, and I will give you the land of Israel. And when they come there, they will remove from it all its detestable things and all its abominations. And I will give them one heart and put a new spirit within them. I will take the stony heart out of their flesh and give them a heart of flesh that they may walk in my statutes, and keep my ordinances and obey them (Ezek 11:17–20; cf. 36:24–28).

The change of spirit is again linked with obedience to the law and to morals. Spiritual life is not described as an achievement of itself but as the results of discipline and service. The righteous are not shown withdrawing from society and the world but playing an active role in both.

Similar to the concept of the new heart and spirit is that of sanctification, which again describes both the result of human action and of divine grace. Speaking of the Exodus from Egypt, Ezekial links sanctification with the commandments:

> I gave them my statutes and showed them my ordinance, by whose observance man shall live. Moreover I gave them my sabbaths, as a sign between me and them, that they might know that I the Lord sanctify them. But the house of Israel rebelled against me in the wilderness, they did not walk in my statutes but rejected my ordinances, by whose observance man shall live; and my sabbaths they greatly profaned (Ezek 20:11–13; cf. vv 19–20).

The Sabbath is described as a sign that God sanctified the people; the people are accused of having profaned the Sabbath instead of sanctifying it. The sanctity of the Sabbath and of Israel are two aspects of spirituality that are linked with obedience to the law. By sanctifying the Sabbath one becomes saintly and attached to the spirit.

There are two forms of sanctification: refraining from creative work (Exod 20:8–11, 31:12–17, 34:21, 35:2–3, Neh 13:15–19, *m. Šabb.* 7:2), which represents the creation of the world, and rejoicing in the kingdom of God and in being able to fulfill His will (Isa 58:13). In postexilic times the sanctification of the Sabbath included the recital of a thanksgiving at the beginning and at the end of the day, which was meant to create the appropriate mood for the day.[7]

[7] Cf. tractate *Ba-Hodesh* (7:71ff.) of "Mekhilta of Rabbi Ishmael" (see *Mekilta de-Rabbi Ishmael* [trans. J. Z. Lauterbach; Philadelphia: Jewish Publication Society, 1933], 2:253); Maimonides, *Mishneh Torah,* 3:29:1 (see *The Code of Maimonides, Book Three: "The Book of Seasons"* [trans. S. Gandz and H. Klein; Yale Judaica Series 14; New Haven: Yale University, 1961] 186); "zekhirat shabbat," *Encyclopedia Talmudica* (ed. S. J. Zevin; Jerusalem: Talmudic Encyclopedia Institute, 1969–), 12:223.

The observance of the Sabbath is one of a series of commandments leading towards human holiness or saintliness (Lev 19:3). The model for this concept is the special rule of the priests (Lev 21:1-9) and the Nazirites (Num 16:1-21). Both categories represent a special relationship to God that demands a standard of behavior. Likewise, the whole people of Israel was called to be a kingdom of priests and a holy nation (Exod 19:6), which implied a special standard of behavior. There were ethical requirements (e.g., love of neighbor), ritual requirements (refraining from mixture of species, Lev 19:2, 19), and especially sexual restrictions (Lev 20:7, 26).

The same explanation is given for the commandment of making tassels on the four corners of the garments:

> And it shall be to you a tassel to look upon and remember all the commandments of the Lord, to do them, not to follow after your own heart and your own eyes, which you are inclined to go after wantonly. So you shall remember and do all my commandments, and be holy to your God (Num 15:39-40).

This is a rule of law with the object of leading to a spiritual quality, that is, holiness, together with observance of all the other rules of law. The tassels are thus symbols serving as objects of contemplation on the law and on holiness. Again, the generality of this practice allowed everybody to take part in spirituality, not only the elite.

A spiritual person may be called "holy" or "saintly." Thus, the Shunammite woman called Elisha "the holy man of God" (2 Kgs 4:9) and the psalmist addressed his listeners:

> O taste and see that the Lord is good!
> Happy is the man who takes refuge in him!
> O fear the Lord, you his saints,
> for those who fear him have no want! (Ps 34:9-10).

The saints addressed seem to be still in need of this admonition, which means that they are human beings. Their saintliness seems to consist in their behavior, which separates them from any evil and transgression. Nevertheless, the fear of God, or rather the reverence of God, has no limit and is an ideal even to the saints. Likewise, in a speech of Eliphaz to Job, doubt is expressed as to human saintliness:

> What is man, that he can be clean?
> Or he that is born of a woman, that he can be righteous?
> Behold, God puts no trust in his holy ones,

> and the heavens are not clean in his sight;
> how much less one who is abominable and corrupt (Job 15:14-17).

Any moment the saintly person can change to commit evil, and the wrongdoer can repent and become saintly. By separating oneself from sin, a person can become holy.[8] Likewise, there is always the possibility of the other direction.[9]

After the destruction of the temple, holiness was internalized, as shows a rabbinic interpretation of Ps 20:3: "May he send you help from the sanctuary—from the sanctification of your deeds".[10] By sanctifying one's deeds, a person becomes a sanctuary and a source of salvation. It means first of all that one observes the commandments, but then also that one acts in the optional sphere with the intention of serving God or loving human beings. An example of the first category would be the sanctification of the Sabbath, one of the second, washing oneself as an act of worship.[11]

The idea of salvation being brought about by the sanctification of deeds found its realization in the teaching of Rabbi Israel Baʾal Shem Tov (1699-1760), the founder of the Hassidic movement. It is that of a saint who becomes the leader of the community and who teaches every individual to sanctify his or her deeds. The sanctification of deeds is indeed shown to be the central goal of Jewish law. This is expressed in the wording of the standard benediction formulated in postexilic times:

> Blessed be you God, our God King of the Universe, who has sanctified us by his commandments . . . (*t. Ber.* 6[7]:9).[12]

The presence of the Holy Spirit or the Divine Presence depends upon the sanctification of human life by observance of the law.[13] However,

[8] "Sifra to Leviticus" (tractate *Kedoshim* on 19:2). Cf. G. F. Moore, *Judaism in the First Centuries of the Christian Era* (Cambridge: Harvard University, 1927; repr. New York: Schocken, 1971), 1:61, 2:271.

[9] Moore, ibid., 1:468.

[10] "Leviticus Rabbah" 24:4 (*Midrash Wayyikra Rabbah*, ed. M. Margulies [Jerusalem: Ministry of Education and Culture and the American Academy of Jewish Research, 1953-60] 550); "Tanḥuma on Leviticus" 19:2 (*Midrash Tanḥuma ha-ḳadum veha-yashan*, ed. S. Buber [Vilna: Romm, 1885]); cf. E. E. Urbach, *The Sages: Their Concepts and Beliefs* (Jerusalem: Magnes, 1975) 482.

[11] "Avot de-Rabbi Nathan" 30 (version B) (see *Avot de-Rabi Nathan*, ed. S. Schechter [Vienna, 1887; repr. New York: Feldheim, 1945] 66).

[12] "Birkath Hamitswot," *Encyclopedia Talmudica* (ed. S. J. Zevin; Jerusalem: Talmudic Encyclopedia Institute, 1969-), 4:514.

[13] Cf. H. Cohen, *Religion der Vernunft* (Frankfurt: Kaufmann, 1929), chap. 7.

it is not only the result of the human effort but likewise that of divine grace. Therefore, the fulfilling of the law must take place with the awareness that God himself sanctifies humans through the act.

The spirituality of the law expresses itself first in the duties of the heart, as described in the book of the same title by the abovementioned Rabbi Baḥya ibn Paquda.[14] These include, *inter alia,* various divine and historical events that should be recalled into consciousness every day[15] Jewish law incorporates and refers to *derek* *᾽ereṣ* 'manners' and *middôt* 'virtues', especially the virtue of the *ḥāsîd* (the pious who goes beyond the legal duty).[16]

During the second century C.E. mention was made of a custom of the pious to keep silence for one hour in preparation for prayer (*m. Ber.* 2:1, *b. Ber.* 13a). Preparation for prayer also includes cleaning the body as a step towards purification of the spirit (*b. Ber.* 15a).

A similar rule of Jewish law demands the washing of hands before the breaking of the bread (*b. Ḥul.* 106a, *m. ᶜEd.* 5:6; cf. Matt 15:2, Mark 7:5). It was meant to elevate the meal to constitute an act of worship, to transform the table into an altar, and to ask ordinary people to feel like priests in the temple.

Prayer began with a call of the leader that the congregation join him in the benediction (*m. Tamid* 5:1; cf. 1 Chr 29:20, Ps 134:1-2). It was another technique of preparation and was called a matter of holiness.[17] Likewise, three people reciting grace after the meal are called by one of them to act together (*t. Ber.* 6:1).[18]

Ritual purification required, beside the immersion in water, the intention to create thereby the desired effect, though opinions differed during the third century C.E. whether the mental element was a *condition sine qua non* (*b. Ḥul.* 31a-b). However, the rites of the Passover were declared to be fulfilled only if the sacrifice, the unleavened bread, and the herbs had been consumed with the correct intention. During the first century C.E., Rabbi Gamaliel I introduced a formula to be spoken before the meal. This rule served to provide a mental aspect to the ritual (*m. Pesaḥ.* 10:5).[19] Likewise, intention was necessary to fulfill the commandments to listen to the sound of the horn on New Year and to the Esther Scroll on Purim (*m. Roš Haš.*

[14] See n. 4 above.

[15] Such as the Exodus or the Revelation; cf. "zekhiroth," *Encyclopedia Talmudica,* 12:198.

[16] Cf. "derekh ᾽erets," ibid., 7:672; and "hassid," ibid., 16:385.

[17] "Barekhu," ibid., 4:285.

[18] "Zimmun," ibid., 12:237.

[19] "᾽Akhilath Maẓah," *Encyclopedia Talmudica* [Eng. ed.], 2:196-204; and "᾽Akhilath Maror," ibid., 2:204-11.

3:7, *m. Meg.* 2:2). A great many rules that originally applied to the observance of a commandment were extended to the preparation for this observance. These rules show the importance of the preparation and the spirituality of the person who is engaged in optional acts to get ready for the fulfillment of the duty.

The sanctification of the Sabbath has been said to begin on Friday morning (*b. Šabb.* 117b). Thus extending the sacred to the sphere of the profane.[20] According to another opinion, the preparation for the Sabbath starts at the end of the preceding Sabbath. Shammai the Elder (1st century B.C.E.) used to save whatever he acquired during the whole week for the following Sabbath and Rabbi Judah ben Batyra used to call the weekday by the number of days that had passed since the preceding Sabbath.[21] Thus the holiness of the seventh day was felt during the whole week and the whole life was given its perspective.

Since the preparation for the observance of any commandment is essential, the law applying to this observance is also applied to the preparatory stage. For instance, in cases of conflict, certain commandments took preference over others, and even the preparation for the former took such preference over the latter. Thus, a circumcision must be performed on the eighth day after birth, even if it is a Sabbath. According to the view of Rabbi Eliezer ben Hyrcanos, one may also forge the scalpel on the Sabbath, since this was part of the preparation for the circumcision. Rabbi Aqiva, on the other hand, permitted such work only if it could not have been done before the Sabbath (*m. Šabb.* 19:1, *b. Yebam.* 6a).

Likewise, during the performance of one commandment the person is exempt from the duty to perform other commandments. For instance, collectors of charity need not eat and sleep in a booth during the Sukkot festival (*m. Sukk.* 2:4). This exemption was granted, not only for the time of collection but also for the night, since the night was needed for planning and preparation of future activities.[22]

The level of consciousness needed for the performance of a commandment was also required for the preparation, at least according to some views (*b. Yoma* 48a–b). This applied in particular to the production of phylacteries (*b. Menaḥ.* 42b), the construction of booths

[20] Cf. Z. W. Falk, *Law and Religion: The Jewish Experience* (Jerusalem: Mesharim, 1981) 49.

[21] See "Mekhilta of Rabbi Simeon ben Yoḥai" on Exod 20:8 (*Mekhilta de-Rabi Shimᶜon bar Yohai,* ed. J. N. Epstein and E. Z. Melamed [Jerusalem: Shaᶜare Rahamin]); "hakhanah," *Encyclopedia Talmudica,* 9:103.

[22] See Rashi's (Rabbi Solomon ben Isaac) commentary on *b. Sukk.* 26a.

for the Sukkot festival (*m. Sukk.* 1:1), and the baking of unleavened bread for the Passover festival (*y. Sukk.* 52b).

In conclusion, Jewish law may be said to be meant as a constant invitation to spirituality. Although a legal system tends to externalize its rites and to create a routine, it also provides a discipline and social framework, which are requirements for the continual effort at spirituality.

Spirituality and Law

Let me now treat the second problem, whether spirituality can last and be effective without law and what kind of law is the necessary complementary of spirituality. I will first study the phenomen of theophany and law as reflected in the Hebrew Bible, and then I will discuss Jewish mysticism and Jewish law.

The initial text is the promise made by God to Abraham that he would have numerous descendants, which is immediately followed by the duty of circumcision (Gen 17:1-14). The spirituality of Abraham was to be preserved by a rite to be transmitted from one to the other. Moreover, the elevation of the spirit had to be given validity by an act of the body expressing the chosenness of the people at large, not only of the elite.

The same connection between spirituality and the law appears in the description of the theophany of Mount Sinai, immediately followed by the Decalogue and a number of cultic laws (Exod 19:1-20; 22). No conflict is felt between the experience of the Divine and the daily obedience to the law. On the contrary, the experience is perpetuated through the submission in practice to the Kingdom of God.

Moses and Samuel combine the prophecy with the administration of justice (Exod 18:13, 1 Sam 7:15) and the other prophets, likewise, are concerned with the observance of the divine commandments (Amos 2:4, Hos 4:6, Isa 5:24, Mic 3:11, Zeph 3:4, Ezek 22:26, Jer 2:8, Hag 2:11, Mal 2:6-9). The prophet is not satisfied with spirituality and enlightenment, but has to deliver the divine message to the people. His own encounter with the Divine serves this purpose and continues the moral and legal tradition of the Sinaitic tradition.

However, the ordinary interpretation of the law and its application irrespectively of the moral standards was criticized by the prophets. Sacrifices, especially, and the temple cult were rejected if the moral behavior of the people did not suit these aspects of piety. Likewise, some of the rabbis around Rabbi Johanan ben Zakkai, during the first and second centuries C.E. combined this study of

Jewish law with their spirituality, as expressed in mystical speculation. The contemplation on *ma*ᶜ*ăśeh bĕrēšît* 'creation', *ma*ᶜ*ăśeh merkābāh* 'theophany', and *hêkālôt* 'temples' did not cause these teachers to withdraw from the world and from activity but was felt to be complementary to their study of Jewish law. On the contrary these speculations seem to have enriched and deepened their formal study and opened up further dimensions of understanding.

Jewish mysticism, as developed especially from the thirteenth century, was meant to find the inner meaning of legal rules, to be able to connect through their observance with the Divine. According to the formulation of a Hassidic author:

> The commandments are derived from a great light which people cannot endure in this world. It was therefore incorporated by God in the act of the commandment, so that human beings could become close to this light through the performance of the commandment. . . . The light which is in the intention to perform the commandment is but a spark of the great light concentrated in the act of the commandment.[23]

Another view even comes closer to the concept of incarnation and sacrament:

> There is a type of fear of God which is really fear of the commandments. When someone realizes that observing the commandments is a matter of divine moment, and begins to perform them with his physical limbs and other material "tools," he becomes fearful and spiritually agitated, for how can he materialize something divine? . . . Once someone has experienced this fear and spiritual agitation several times, he begins to derive strength from his faith in God, because he knows that performing the commandments is a means of establishing a connection with God. . . . He then understands that the *Shikhinah* is clothed in the commandment, because every commandment is an aspect of the *Shikhinah,* which is clothed in matter to make it possible for material, lowly beings to form a connection with God through the limbs with which they perform the commandments.[24]

Indeed, according to the teaching of Rabbi Israel Baᶜal Shem Tov, the founder of Hassidism, the performance of a commandment

[23] Rabbi Jacob ben Mordekhai Leiner, *Bet Jacob, Behuqotai* (Jerusalem: n.p., 1975) 293; M. S. Kasher, *Shevilim Bemahshevet Hahasidut* (Jerusalem: Torah Shlemah, 1978) 66.

[24] Menahem Moses of Vitebsk, *Peri* ᶜ*Ets* (Cracow, 1937); J. Dan, *The Teachings of Hasidism* (New York: Behrman, 1983) 68.

is an act of *dĕbeqût*, or communion with God.[25] A person should indeed seek this state in all his or her activities, but this goal is most important for the performance of the rules of the law and for the study of the law.

Spirituality as a lasting and communal phenomenon is in need of unified behavior as prescribed by the legal tradition. On the other hand, once law is not an end in itself but an expression of spirituality, its interpretation is bound to be anthropocentric, spiritual, and ethical.

[25] G. Scholem, "'Devekut' or Communion with God," *Review of Religion* 14 (1949–50) 115–39.

E. P. Sanders

When Is a Law a Law? The Case of Jesus and Paul

AGAINST THE VIEW OF SOME New Testament scholars that Jesus and Paul rejected a Jewish legalism that emphasized external conformity to the law in favor of a piety concerned with the fulfilling of the law through obedience of the heart, Sanders argues for an entirely different understanding of the attitude of Jesus and Paul toward holy law. Acknowledging that the determination of this attitude is made difficult by the contradictory character of statements of Jesus and Paul about the law (many of which statements are, in the case of Jesus, of doubtful authenticity), Sanders is nonetheless confident that disenchantment with legalism was not the primary motive behind their thought. Rather, what they did was, in Sanders's opinion, to introduce demands that, rather than contravening the law in a sense of setting aside its prohibitions, added further prohibitions within the sphere of what had previously been permitted. Thus the clear requirements and prohibitions of the Mosaic law continued to be for them a standard of right behavior (even in its external aspects, it appears), though it was supplemented by further requirements and prohibitions necessary for the cultivation of a behavioral perfection appropriate to the coming new age. Paul did, however, make an exception of those requirements of the Mosaic law that set Jews apart from Gentiles. Sanders argues, however, that the new demands made by Jesus and Paul did not have for them the character of law. A law was, within the Jewish context, truly a law only when it met the criteria of halakic construction, especially that of clarity as to what sort of behavior constituted obedience or disobedience. The new demands did not meet these criteria, nor was there any need, given the particular eschatological outlook of Jesus and Paul, for them to do so. In the course of his discussion, Sanders summarizes his method, developed elsewhere, of interpreting Paul's negative statements about the law while doing justice to his positive statements. The negative statements deny the validity of the law as a requirement for entry into "the body of those who will be saved," while the positive statements affirm the validity of the law as a criterion of correct behavior.

E. P. Sanders holds the Dean Ireland Professorship of Exegesis at Oxford University, in addition to a part-time appointment as Professor of Religious Studies at McMaster University in Hamilton, Ontario. Professor Sanders received a Th.D. from Union Theological Seminary in New York. His major works on Jesus, Paul, and the earliest period of Christianity in its Jewish and Hellenistic contexts have been honored with several prizes and awards, including (twice) the National Religious Book Award.

It is generally said of both Jesus and Paul that they opposed the Jewish law—or aspects of it, or ways of observing it—and that they created demands of their own, which are not, however, to be understood as law. These demands, rather, represent the pure will of God, which requires wholehearted devotion, not the legalistic and routine observance of formal commandments.[1] Into this general scheme can be fitted the diverse statements about the law that are attributed to them: (1) the law must be perfectly performed, (2) the law may be or should be transgressed or opposed, and (3) new demands must be met. These three are combined (in the common scholarly view being described here) by saying that (1) the pro-law statements refer to the perfect, eschatological law, or to the demand of God that lies behind

[1] On Jesus, see, e.g., Rudolf Bultmann, *Theology of the New Testament* (New York: Scribner's, 1954), 1:11–22; Ernst Käsemann, *Essays on New Testament Themes* (London: SCM, 1964) 38, 42; on Paul, Bultmann, *Theology of the New Testament*, 259–69, 340–45; Käsemann, *Commentary on Romans* (London: SCM, 1980) 277, 215. There is in such positions an implied distinction between Jesus and Paul on the one hand and "Judaism" on the other: they opposed Jewish legalism, externalism, and formalism, and urged instead pure, sincere, and inward obedience. On this misdescription of Judaism, see my *Paul and Palestinian Judaism* (Philadelphia: Fortress, 1977) 33–59, and Part 1 in general. On these and similar distinctions between Jesus, Paul, and their contemporaries in Judaism, see my *Jesus and Judaism* (Philadelphia: Fortress, 1985), Introduction, chap. 9; *Paul, the Law, and the Jewish People* (Philadelphia: Fortress, 1983) 144–48.

the law, (2) the anti-law statements refer either to the supposed Jewish legalistic way of doing the law, or to the "trivial" and "externalistic" parts of the law, such as purity, and (3) the further demands show that Jesus and Paul did not relax, but rather fully realized the demand of God for complete obedience.

I offer here quotations from Paul and Jesus (or, at least, attributed to him) to illustrate the three sorts of statements that are in mind:

1. The law must be perfectly performed:

   Jesus: Think not that I have come to abolish the law and the prophets; I have come not to abolish them but to fulfill them. For truly, I say to you, till heaven and earth pass away, not an iota, not a dot, will pass from the law until all is accomplished. Whoever then relaxes one of the least of these commandments and teaches men so, shall be called least in the kingdom of heaven; but he who does them and teaches them shall be called great in the kingdom of heaven. For I tell you, that unless your righteousness exceeds that of the scribes and Pharisees, you will never enter the kingdom of heaven (Matt 5:17–20).

   Paul: Owe no one anything, except to love one another; for he who loves his neighbor has fulfilled the law. The commandments, "You shall not commit adultery, You shall not kill, You shall not steal, You shall not covet," and any other commandment, are summed up in this sentence, "You shall love your neighbor as yourself." Love does no wrong to a neighbor; therefore love is the fulfilling of the law (Rom 13:8–10).

2. The law may be or should be transgressed:

   Jesus: The Son of man is lord even of the sabbath (Mark 2:28, justifying picking grain on the Sabbath).

   Paul: Now I, Paul, say to you that if you receive circumcision, Christ will be of no advantage to you. I testify again to every man who receives circumcision that he is bound to keep the whole law. You are severed from Christ, you who would be justified by the law; you have fallen away from grace (Gal 5:2–4).

3. There are new demands:

   Jesus: You have heard that it was said to the men of old, "You shall not kill" . . . But I say to you that every one who is angry with his brother shall be liable to judgment . . . (Matt 5:21–22).

   Paul: . . . that each one of you know how to take a wife for himself in holiness and honor, not in the passion of lust like heathen . . . (1 Thess 4:4–5).

The passages show immediately that both Paul and Jesus can be understood as having taken contradictory positions on the law, and that in turn makes the theological reconstruction that I first outlined attractive: neither man actually contradicted himself; the "law" that is not to be done, or need not be done, is not the "law" that is to be kept. The latter is the spiritual, true law, kept by followers of Jesus in the right spirit. Neither Paul nor Jesus actually believed in doing the law *qua law*. Sometimes one's obedience to God will coincidentally result in obeying the Torah, but not because God actually requires the specifics of legal obedience.

One who has come to doubt, as I have done, this entire theological reconstruction is faced with the problem of coping in some other way with apparent self-contradiction. I do not hope here to sort out all the problems involved in "Jesus and the law" and "Paul and the law." Further, such hard and intractable problems cannot be so quickly resolved. Thus what I propose to do instead is to sketch out why I do not find the usual theological resolution of the problems to be exegetically and historically satisfactory. This sketch rests on fuller discussions elsewhere. Then I wish to press ahead to consider examples of concrete extralegal demands made by both Paul and Jesus, and to consider whether or not these demands function as "law."

Objections to the Received View

There are several factors that count against the usual explanation of diverse statements about the law. First, with regard to the explicit permission (or requirement) to *disobey* the law, I distinguish sharply between Paul and Jesus. Paul, it is clear, did admonish his Gentile converts not to accept three parts of the Jewish law, even though they entered "the Israel of God" (Gal 6:16) of the last days: Sabbath (Gal 4:1-11, esp. 10), circumcision (Gal 5:2; cf. 1 Cor 7:19, which distinguishes circumcision from "the commandments of God"), and food (Gal 2:11-12). Sabbath and food are ruled optional by him in Romans 14, which means that they may be disobeyed and thus do not count as divine laws. As I have explained elsewhere, the three parts of the law that Paul rules out for Gentiles are those that separate Gentile from Jew socially.[2] He was apparently motivated by his view of the universal and equal lordship of Christ and his own call to be apostle to the Gentiles. He could not see his own mission as resulting in a group of second-class citizens, and he argued strenuously against the observance of the laws that would have that effect.

[2] *Paul, the Law, and the Jewish People*, 102.

Further, his rebuke to Peter indicates that he thought Jews should disobey the food laws when in a mixed church. He could maintain in theory that a Jewish Christian (for example, himself) could live like a Jew in order to win Jews and like a Gentile in order to win Gentiles (1 Cor 9:20-21), but both things could not be done at once in the same church. Gal 2:11-14 indicates that, in a mixed situation, he thought that Jews should give up those aspects of the law that separated them from Gentiles.

With regard to Jesus, however, I doubt the now frequent assertion that he explicitly recommended the ignoring of food and Sabbath laws.[3] The basic observation is simple: the disciples did not know him to have done so, since they debated them as fresh issues, and it seems that neither side (neither Paul nor his opponents) could quote Jesus directly in its favor. Thus I must doubt the authenticity of the passages in which Jesus directly opposes these laws. The explicit statements to that effect have probably been added to stories that were once more ambiguous. In a similar way I doubt the authenticity of Matt 5:17-20 (quoted above). Such a clear statement requiring detailed and complete obedience to the law of Moses would have been fatal to Paul's cause, had he and the Jerusalem apostles known it.

Thus I do not think that Paul and Jesus can be viewed together as favoring the "complete" observance of the law in the right spirit. Paul was completely against some parts of the law, while Jesus was not known to have been on record as being against the observance of any of the concrete commandments.[4] The standard theological explanation (in the right spirit) works for neither. I also note that the parts of the law that Paul opposed are not correctly labeled "cultic," "trivial," and "externalistic." I have already indicated that their actual common denominator is that they separate Gentile from Jew socially, and this is apparently what concerned Paul, not externalism. The Sabbath law is not correctly described as cultic, nor, for that matter, is circumcision. There are numerous cultic laws that Paul does not mention at all, and so he can hardly be thought to have opposed them systematically. He also appears not to have been concerned about the triviality of the purity laws. He had, as I shall show, his own version of purity requirements.

[3] See *Jesus and Judaism*, 264-67.

[4] I argue here *de facto*: Paul opposed applying the law requiring circumcision to his converts, and he thought that Jews should break the rules of *kašrût* in order to eat with Gentiles (Gal 2:11-14). He could, however, say that those who love their neighbors fulfil "the whole law" (Gal 5:14). He seems not to have brought these two points into direct relationship. See *Paul, the Law, and the Jewish People*, 96-105, 113f.

Second, when Paul criticizes the law, or argues against requiring observance of it, he never bases his argument on the mode of observance, for example, literal versus figurative observance, or technical fulfilment versus genuine intent to fulfill. It is not the case that he did not know such distinctions. At the conclusion of a long passage, all of which strongly reflects the environment of the diaspora synagogue (Rom 1:18–2:29), he offers an interpretation of the meaning of the word circumcision: keeping the rest of the law (Rom 2:25–29).[5] By using such figurative devices he could, one would think, have conducted the argument that surfaces in Galatians to better effect: *they* (the unnamed opponents) would have you be *actually* circumcised, but I tell you that those of you who do x, y, and z are *really* circumcised; *their* circumcision is no more than meaningless incision (cf. Phil 3:2–3); my way is *really* circumcision. He could have argued that way, but he did not. He argued that, since Christ could not have died in vain, there is no such thing as righteousness by the law (Gal 2:21) and that God never gave, nor even intended to give, a law that could produce righteousness (Gal 3:19–22). The argument, in other words, springs entirely from God's eternal purpose, which he believed to have been only recently revealed.[6] He does not argue that God gave certain laws (e.g., circumcision) that meanwhile have been misunderstood by being taken literally, but rather that God gave the law for a purpose other than pointing the way to obedience: he gave it to enslave to sin, so that he himself could later liberate its victims (Gal 3:22, 24).

Even though in Romans 2 he shows knowledge of the "literal" versus "real" argument, he does not use it even in Romans in the main argument against the law. The purpose of Romans 2 is quite limited: to "prove" that everyone is under sin (conclusion stated in 3:9; cf. 3:19). It is not yet the full argument that righteousness is not by the law. When that comes (chaps. 4–7), Paul turns again to the biblical story of Abraham (which he had used in Galatians 3) to argue that God never intended that the law would be determinative for righteousness. The function of the law is "to bring wrath" from which God saves (Rom 4:15). I shall not follow this argument all the way through the twistings and turnings of Romans 7, but only observe that real observance is

[5] Peder Borgen, "Observations on the Theme 'Paul and Philo,'" *Die Paulinische Literatur und Theologie* (ed. S. Pedersen; Århus: Aros, 1980) 86–92. On parallels with Philo see Henry Chadwick, "St. Paul and Philo of Alexandria," *Bulletin of the John Rylands Library* 48 (1966) 286–307. On the passage as relatively unaltered synagogue material see *Paul, the Law, and the Jewish People*, 123–35.

[6] On "eternal purpose" note the two *pro-* verbs in Gal 3:8 and the *hina* 'in order that' clauses in 3:14, 22, 24. On "recently revealed," Gal 3:23–24; 4:2, 4.

not contrasted with literal, nor good observance with bad. This holds true throughout the rest of Romans.

Thus Paul had at his disposal an argument against literal or formal observance that would have received some credit, but he did not employ it in any of his main arguments. It is incorrect to think that he grounded his dual position on the law on the contrast between right observance and wrong observance. Rather, his pro-law and anti-law statements must be explained in some other way.

It was the position of Bultmann and Käsemann (whom, among others, I have been criticizing) that Paul (and Jesus) had a steady view of the law, judging observance to be good or bad depending on interior attitude.[7] I propose that not enough is known about possible opposition by Jesus to characterize it or its motive. For Paul, however, this explanation can be shown to be false. His argument against righteousness by the law is not simply against *self*-righteousness, since he has in view God's eternal intention, not human shortcomings. His apparently contradictory admonitions to obey the law, therefore, are not just exhortations to obey it in the right spirit. In both groups of passages he has in view the whole law, not just parts of it, and in his main arguments he does not distinguish one mode of observance (e.g., literal) from another (e.g., figurative).[8] I think, then, that this is something close to true self-contradiction.[9] My own formula, however, is "different questions, different answers." When he was asked "how can one enter the body of those who will be saved?," he answered invariably "not by doing the law," and he backed that up by attributing to God a completely different purpose in giving it. When he was asked, "what is correct behavior?," he answered (among other things), "observance of the obvious and self-evident commandments." (They were obvious and self-evident to him.)[10]

I add almost parenthetically that there is no reason to attribute to the Jews of Jesus' and Paul's time the legalistic view that they are said to have had, and with which Jesus' and Paul's nobler view (obedience with the heart, not just *pro forma*) is contrasted.[11] My principal arguments here I intend to be exegetical: the sayings of Jesus are not adequately authenticated to allow discussion of the question in detail,

[7] *Paul, the Law, and the Jewish People*, 81–86.

[8] Ibid.

[9] Heikki Räisänen, *Paul and the Law* (Wissenschaftliche Untersuchungen zum Neuen Testament 29; Tübingen: Mohr, 1983).

[10] These last sentences summarize substantial parts of *Paul, the Law, and the Jewish People*.

[11] See n. 1.

while for Paul there is explicit evidence that he did not make the distinction he is said to have made.

When that distinction is seen to fail in explaining "Jesus and the law" and "Paul and the law," where shall we turn? I propose not to continue discussing pro-law and anti-law statements, but to turn to two clear "more than the law" statements, the first from Jesus, the second from Paul.

The Saying on Divorce

This passage is the best-authenticated teaching of Jesus. Like the "words of institution" at the last supper, it appears first in Paul:

> To the married I give charge, not I but the Lord, that the wife should not separate from the husband (but if she does, let her remain single or else be reconciled to her husband), and that the husband should not divorce [put away] his wife (1 Cor 7:10–11).

The prohibition appears four times in the synoptic gospels, twice in Matthew and once each in Mark and Luke. There is a long form (Matt 19:3–12 ‖ Mark 10:2–12), which contains scriptural argument, and a short form (Matt 5:31–32 ‖ Luke 16:18). There are significant variations among these passages, besides the quotation of scriptural justification. Matthew twice specifies that divorce is permitted in the case of unchastity (Matt 5:32, 19:9), which has led some to think that Jesus here entered into a rabbinic debate on the question of the justification for divorce. The other gospels and Paul, however, do not have the exceptive clause. Paul specifies that the woman should not initiate divorce, and in fact starts with the case of the woman, while Mark (apparently) tacks this prohibition on to the end of the passage (Mark 10:12). The other gospels do not mention the woman who leaves her husband. (Paul's language clearly distinguishes the action of the woman, who "separates from" her husband, from that of the man, who "puts away" his wife. Mark is ignorant of such fine points of the law, here as elsewhere.)[12]

Thus the three major variations relate to the presence of scriptural prooftexts, the clause "except for adultery," and the specific prohibition of separation initiated by the woman. This shows that, in this most secure of all passages, all is as it should be and New Testament scholars still need to explore all the possibilities.

[12] On the passage, see David Dungan, *The Sayings of Jesus in the Churches of Paul* (Philadelphia: Fortress, 1971) 102–31. Dungan proposes that the earliest form is Matt 19:3–9.

The basic authenticity of the saying, however, is not in doubt. Paul, it is to be noted, quoted the statement and then ignored it, going on to give his own quite separate rules regarding marriage and divorce, rules that he had started at the beginning of I Corinthians 7 and interrupted only to quote the saying of the Lord (which did not, however, actually address the problems that he had been asked about, 1 Cor 7:1). His further rules constitute partial contradictions to the saying of the Lord. He says, for example, that one partner may decide to separate (1 Cor 7:15), though he does not say that the person can then remarry—which would be full contradiction of the Lord. His rules are, however, independent. They neither sprang from nor did they generate the saying of the Lord. That saying is inserted as a foreign body, doubtless because he had broached the topic of divorce and had a "saying from the Lord" about it. This means that he had been told it or taught it (not, obviously, verbatim as it was taught elsewhere). This means, in turn, that it had early and wide circulation as a saying of Jesus (for without doubt the Lord here is Jesus), which is as close as possible to proving authenticity.

I prescind from further discussion of numerous aspects of this fascinating pericope, such as the prooftexts quoted, the manner of their use, and the relationship of the passage to a similar one in the Covenant of Damascus.[13] I wish, instead, to take it as a simple fact that Jesus prohibited divorce. This is the clearest case in which he laid down a requirement that goes beyond the law.

That is the clear meaning of the passage. In the long form of the pericope the formulation is explicitly set over against Moses' permission of divorce in Deuteronomy 24. Whether explicit or not, Jesus' formulation must be seen in light of that passage. New Testament scholars, with surprising unanimity and inaccuracy, say that here Jesus clearly contravenes the law of Moses.[14] But it is perfectly apparent that he does no such thing. He prohibited what Moses permitted, he did not permit what Moses prohibited. It is as if Moses permitted the mixing of Dacron and cotton, but a modern teacher forbade it. Or, as if a driver chooses to drive 5 m.p.h. below the posted speed limit, thus heeding a higher law. Actually, "as if" in these two clauses is a bit loose, for the three cases are not precisely analogous. Saying wherein they are different will help to clarify what Jesus meant by here going beyond the law of Moses.

[13] Some of the aspects are more fully treated in *Jesus and Judaism*, 256–60.

[14] Thus, for example, Joachim Jeremias, *New Testament Theology, 1: The Proclamation of Jesus* (London: SCM, 1971) 207, concludes that Jesus abolished a Mosaic regulation.

In the first analogy, I offer a matter that Moses could not have explicitly discussed. The law of Moses does prohibit certain mixtures (Deut 22:11), but it could not have referred to Dacron one way or the other. If a modern wished to discuss the use of Dacron in mixed fabrics, he might argue that the prohibition of one mixture prohibits all. A modern, however, would not in fact face the case that I proposed in the analogy: that Moses permitted the mixing of Dacron and cotton, though he (the modern) wished to prohibit it. The extension of Moses' law to cover what he had not discussed (whether one argued for or against mixing Dacron and cotton) does not have the same significance as prohibiting something that he *explicitly* permitted. The modern need not think Moses to have been an inadequate teacher, but only take into account the date of composition. Prohibiting something explicitly permitted, however (as Jesus does with regard to divorce), does imply that Moses was not strict enough, and thus potentially that his law is not adequate.

Jesus' prohibition of divorce is also not quite like observing a stricter speed limit, for the latter is only a matter of degree, not of action or nonaction. If the law says "one may drive 60 m.p.h.", and an individual teacher says "better stay at 55," the law has been implicitly criticized for not being strict enough, but not quite as severely as would be implied by an individual's proposing total prohibition of driving during rush hour.

On the one hand, then, Jesus did not actually oppose the law: observing what he said would not lead anyone ever to transgress it. On the other hand, there is the clear communication of a critical view. Here Jesus introduces a new law, one much stricter than that of Moses, since it completely prohibits something that Moses explicitly permitted. It does not just tighten the law slightly. This seems to mean that Jesus, in at least this respect, found the law of Moses to be *inadequate*.

I hold that Jesus' prohibition of divorce was part of a larger view. If he had agreed with the law in all other respects, if in no other case had he gone beyond it, then this would be a case of mere eccentricity. But an occasionally eccentric Jesus cannot be explained historically, and so I shall simply suppose that he had a larger view that included such a stance toward the law. What was it?

Matthew, particularly in the Sermon on the Mount, the first occurrence of the saying on divorce, offers a Jesus who went beyond the law in numerous ways and who did so on clear grounds: his followers, to inherit the kingdom, must be more righteous than the Pharisees. They must, in fact, be perfect (Matt 5:17–20, 48). Not only are they judged by a stricter standard, they must be different from the

Pharisees in one or two ways (they must not be seen to be fasting, but must instead anoint their heads, Matt 6:16–18); but their righteousness is basically like that of the Pharisees: it consists in concrete obedience to the statutes of a strict law. This Jesus, who dominates the Sermon on the Mount, reappears in Matthew 18, where he considers tax collectors and Gentiles to be outsiders, and Matthew 23, where he castigates the Pharisees (again) for not being righteous enough. Here is a Jesus who could truly be compared to the modern who drives slower than the legal speed limit; that is, he was *much* stricter. This is not an impossible Jesus. Such a Jesus had counterparts on the shore of the Dead Sea and doubtless elsewhere.

There is, however, another Jesus in the Gospels: one who accepted "tax collectors and sinners," including harlots; one who was criticized on this ground, whose disciples did not fast, and who talked about "the kingdom" as a coming event, not as something to be entered one-by-one by super-righteous individuals.[15]

The two settings of the sayings on divorce reveal that it is connected both to a series of super-strict regulations (Matthew 5) *and* to the conception of a new age (Matthew 19). The long form of the passage, in which appeal is made to the order of creation, almost equally clearly points to a parallel between the circumstances in which the new commandment is to be carried out and those in which nondivorce was originally observed (Matt 19:4–5‖Mark 10:6–7, quoting Gen 1:27 and 2:24): the new creation will be in part a return to Paradise.

It is not a large or difficult step to propose that, of the two settings, the appeal to the new age is more likely to represent the context in which Jesus actually prohibited divorce. I refrain from "proving" here that Jesus' ministry was set in a context of eschatological expectation, and only observe that it can be proved and is seldom doubted.[16] It is worth a few lines, however, to point out that the super-strict Jesus of much of the Sermon on the Mount (and of parts of Matthew 18 and 23) is not the real Jesus.[17] I previously pointed out that Jesus could not have said anything about the law as explicit as Matthew 5:17–20. Now I must observe that the antitheses, of which the short form of the saying on divorce is one, simply illustrate the principal statement—exceed the righteousness of the Pharisees (Matt 5:20)—and make it concrete. They end with a statement

[15] Tax collectors and sinners: e.g., Matt 11:19; prostitutes: Matt 21:32; followers did not fast: Mark 2:18–22; kingdom in future: e.g., Mark 14:25.

[16] See my *Jesus and Judaism*, Introduction and chaps. 1 and 3.

[17] Ibid., 260–64.

that puts tax collectors outside ("Do not even tax collectors do the same?", Matt 5:46). This is not the historical Jesus. The historical Jesus was "a friend of tax collectors and sinners," and he did not say that every iota and dot of the law must be observed (or this would be revealed in the history of the early church). This view of the historical Jesus leaves room for the debates on the law that convulsed parts of the early Christian movement (directly mirrored in Paul's letters and more distantly reflected in Acts).

It will be proposed, of course, that the two traditions can be harmonized, and many will see behind at least some of the antitheses original sayings of Jesus. So do I, the chief example being the saying on divorce, which shows, in part, how the Sermon was composed.[18] A saying of Jesus was removed from its original context—probably legislation for the new age—and put in a new context: a continuing movement of the super-righteous, distinguished from the Pharisees by systematically going beyond the law. One may wish to "save" other parts of the Sermon on the Mount, giving them an original meaning different from that of Matthew, but I leave such pursuits aside, and simply insist that the original meaning of the saying on divorce could not have been what it now means in its context in Matthew 5.

Now, finally, for my question: is it a law? Yes and no. I observe, first, that this saying does not constitute an instance in which Jesus seeks the pure will of God in contrast to particular legislation. If anything, he creates a law where there was none before. The Mosaic law regulates what must be done and not done if there is a divorce, but there is no law prohibiting or commanding divorce. If Jesus intended his words to be observed at all, he must be regarded here as passing legislation for his followers.

But did he intend his words to be observed in actual practice? Did he not, rather, intend by such an extreme pronouncement to score a theological point, either that one should always strive for a higher goal (though it might not be reached), or that it is pointless to seek justification by obeying the law and that the only alternative is reliance on grace?[19] These are modern attempts to harmonize the perfectionist demands of Matthew 5-7 with the "doctrine" of "Justification by

[18] On the Sermon on the Mount as a distinct and early redactional unit, see H. D. Betz, *Essays on the Sermon on the Mount* (Philadelphia: Fortress, 1985).

[19] Eduard Thurneysen, *The Sermon on the Mount* (London: SPCK, 1965) 45-64: by presenting an "unscalable wall" the Sermon on the Mount makes one rely on Christ, who has climbed it. Cf. Bultmann, *Theology of the New Testament,* 1:13, 21: the requirement is only a cipher for the absoluteness of God's claim. See my remarks in *Jesus and Judaism,* 330, 412 n. 22.

faith," forensically understood. It is better to seek the meaning of the statement in Jesus' own context.

There appear to me to be two possibilities. Perhaps Jesus was a sectarian and wished to establish a small number of those who could keep rigorous commandments and attain righteousness by a higher standard than that of the Mosaic law. These, he might well have thought, would constitute the "true Israel." I have already noted the parallel to the saying on divorce in the Covenant of Damascus, and Qumran affords numerous instances of super-strict legislation. What is against this possibility is, again, the history of the early Christian movement, most branches of which did not take this route (though that reflected in the Sermon on the Mount did).[20] But did most branches of Christianity depart here from Jesus? That is, perhaps, barely possible, though it is hard to understand how Paul could have stood up against the "false brethren" (Gal 2:4) and James the brother of Jesus if they had Jesus' own sayings explicitly on their side. "Jesus as sectarian" is rendered improbable by the same argument that eliminates Matt 5:17–20 from his authentic sayings.

The second possibility is that he actually expected a new order in which there would be no divorce. Society and perhaps even human nature would be fundamentally changed. There is rather a lot of evidence that points towards such an expectation.[21] He told the twelve that they would judge the twelve tribes of Israel (Matt 19:28), which seems to indicate that something dramatic would happen to recreate the twelve tribes. He expected a new kingdom in which he and his disciples would occupy chief places, in which outcasts and sinners would be included, and in which pride of place would be given to the meek and lowly, those who did not seek it. This is the context in which one can best understand the prohibition of divorce: he expected real change, and he here decreed for the new and better age.

Thus the saying is not really a law for an unchanged society. To have it apply to an ongoing community within the normal order whose cumulative number would eventually exceed one billion is to jerk it out of its context. Thus I conclude that it was meant to be a law, but not one that would be followed in normal human society.

I note, finally, that the saying does imply a kind of criticism of the Mosaic law. That law is held to be inadequate for the new age, and Jesus appears as an eschatological revisionist, one who thought that the coming new age required a stricter law.

[20] See Betz, *Essays on the Sermon on the Mount.*
[21] *Jesus and Judaism,* 146–48, 228–37.

The Prohibition of Lust

I shall deal more briefly with the example from Paul, part of which was quoted above. He writes this about desire for one's wife:

> For this is the will of God, your sanctification: that you abstain from immorality; that each one of you know how to take a wife for himself [*to heautou skeuos*] in holiness and honor, not in the passion of lust like heathen who do not know God; that no man transgress, and wrong his brother in this matter, because the Lord is an avenger in all these things, as we solemnly forewarned you. For God has not called us for uncleanness, but in holiness. Therefore whoever disregards this, disregards not man but God, who gives his Holy Spirit to you (1 Thess 4:3-8).[22]

[22] During discussion of this paper at the seminar, Prof. Richard Anderson quite correctly pressed me on the translation of *to heautou skeuos* [literally 'his own vessel'] as 'wife'. Whether because 'vessel' is not a pleasant metaphor for 'wife' (at least to modern ears), or for some other reason, several translators and other scholars have recently preferred another rendering. The New English Bible has "gain mastery over his body" for *to heautou skeuos ktasthai*; Jerusalem Bible reads "knows how to use the body that belongs to him," noting that 'vessel' means either 'his own body or his wife's'. J. Whitton has also recently favored 'body', arguing that Paul here proposes sexual abstinence and that his admonition is "applicable to unmarried as well as married men" ("A Neglected Meaning for *Skeuos* in 1 Thessalonians 4:4," *New Testament Studies* 28 [1982] 142-43). I think that this is grasping at straws and that the meaning 'wife' is overwhelmingly more likely: (1) The topic is *porneia*, sexual immorality. The word is common in Paul, and it refers to improper sex (especially use of prostitutes and homosexuality), not to sex as distinct from abstinence. Paul would not brand proper marital sex *porneia*; thus the context points to a condemnation of improper sex, not to a demand for the suppression of all physical desire. (2) *Ktasthai* does not naturally mean 'master', but rather 'take, acquire, or get'. One has to push very hard to make it mean 'take under control'. Thus the clause is best taken to refer to using ('taking') someone or something else, taking someone sexually (because *porneia* is the topic), or taking someone improperly when a proper manner is available (the proper manner is indicated by 'in holiness'). The last point rules out the translation ('taking one's own organ [*skeuos*] in lust." In Paul's view there could be no contrast between 'taking it in lust' and 'taking it in holiness'. These points seem to compel the translation 'taking one's own wife'. There are corroborating points: (3) The Hebrew equivalent of *skeuos* is *kělî*, sometimes used to mean "woman as an object of sexual activity or thought." See R. F. Collins, "The Unity of Paul's Paraenesis in 1 Thess 4:3-8; 1 Cor 7:1-7; a Significant Parallel," *New Testament Studies* 29 (1983) 420-29, esp. 425. (4) The admonition to avoid *porneia*, and to take one's own wife in sanctity and honor, is closely parallel to 1 Cor 7:2: on account of (the threat of) *porneia*, "let each man have his own wife [*tēn heautou gynaika echetō*]." Thus the immediate context, the broad context of Paul's ethical admonitions, and linguistic considerations all point to maintaining the traditional understanding of *skeuos* as wife.

I note first of all the degree to which this is formulated as a religious law:[23] transgression of it is said to be against God (I take "the Lord" in this instance to be God),[24] and there is retribution for the transgressor. Further, like many biblical and postbiblical laws, it is based on the holiness of God. It falls short, however, of being a full halakic statement (one precisely defined and applied). There is no definition of "in the passion of lust [*en pathei epithymias*]," with the result that an individual might well wonder whether or not he had transgressed the apostle's ruling. A certain amount of either passion or lust is required for the sex act to take place at all, and Paul had no intention of banning sex. On the contrary, elsewhere he explicitly takes into account sexual needs on the part of both men and women (1 Cor 7:3-4; only men are referred to in 1 Thessalonians 4). Once one grants that sex does and should take place and that it requires desire, one sees that earnest converts might be in a quandary as to whether or not their behavior approximated that of (nonconverted) Gentiles (*ethnē*, v 5). Thus there is doubt that this is a "law."

There are other aspects of the passage that are important: (1) There is no specified atonement for transgression (even if a man knew precisely when he had transgressed). A full statement of applied law (Halakah) should have a stated penalty or atonement. These are generally the same, since in the Judaism of Paul's day penalties were, with only a few exceptions, understood as atoning.[25] (2) The threatened punishment, "the Lord is an avenger," is vague. (3) No outside party would know whether or not the command was disobeyed. These three points, however, are not decisive against considering Paul's admonition as a law. There is precedent for omission of explicit penalty and/or atonement (a fact that cost the Rabbis a great deal of trouble, as they sought to specify what is unstated in the Bible). With regard to the privacy of the act, I note that many aspects of the purity code are not subject to external examination, but simply lie on the individual's conscience. Yet these prohibitions and requirements nevertheless function as laws, since they are defined and atonement is prescribed. Intercourse with a menstruant, for example, is prohibited by the

[23] On individual laws in Paul, see Wolfgang Schrage, *Die konkreten Einzelgebote in der paulinischen Paränese: Ein Beitrag zur neutestamentlichen Ethik* (Gütersloh: Gerd Mohn, 1961); Käsemann, "Sentences of Holy Law in the New Testament," *New Testament Questions of Today* (London: SCM, 1969) 66-81.

[24] It is not impossible that the Lord who rewards and punishes at the judgment is, in Paul's view, Christ: see 2 Cor 5:10. The present context, however, makes God more likely.

[25] *Paul and Palestinian Judaism*, see index references to Chastisements, Suffering.

Bible, and a penalty is prescribed (Lev 20:18), though the act is just as private as "the passion of lust." Further, pious groups had, by the time of Jesus and Paul, already undertaken to *redefine* the menstrual period and to extend it beyond the biblical requirement (Ps Sol 8:13 and Covenant of Damascus 5:7; cf *m. Nid.* 4:2). The privacy of the act, then, does not prevent people from passing laws about it, provided that they define what is correct and incorrect.

The three points of the previous paragraph show only that this passage is not an applicable and enforceable law. What counts in favor of its being called *admonition*, rather than *law*, is principally its initial vagueness: as I said, the most scrupulous follower could not know if he had transgressed it. Thus, here I label this directive an admonition.[26]

Did Paul avoid legal formulation because he was against reward and punishment for deeds? That is not a satisfactory explanation, since he clearly has in mind a deed, and punishment is threatened for it. Further, in his letters there are general statements in favor of reward and punishment according to works (e.g., 2 Cor 5:10). More concretely, he also threatens Apollos with posthumous scorching if his work as proclaimer of Christ is not satisfactory (1 Cor 3:5–15; cf. 4:6), and he even entertains the thought that he himself may be found guilty of some inadequacy at the judgment (1 Cor 4:4). In the case of Apollos, he also says that being singed will result in his salvation (1 Cor 3:15), which shows that he maintained the conception of atoning penalties. There are other cases of punishments that atone in 1 Corinthians: the man who was committing incest should be expelled from the community, and he should be destroyed (presumably by God), "so that his spirit may be saved in the day of the Lord Jesus" (5:3–5); those in Corinth who were sick or who had died had eaten and drunk "without discerning the body." He concludes: "But when we are judged by the Lord, we are chastened so that we may not be condemned along with the world" (11:27–32).

In these last three cases (Apollos, incest, and the Lord's supper), Paul is ready enough to prescribe punishment and to see it as atoning, though it is difficult to consider the first and third as laws. He says to Apollos, in effect, "build on my foundation with the right material or you will be punished at the judgment," but "build with the right material" is not a law. It is, rather, a metaphor that means primarily "preach the right message." "Right message" would eventually become a matter of church law, and transgression of it would be punishable, but for this to be the case one must leave the realm of

[26] Or "paraenesis," so Collins, "The Unity of Paul's Paraenesis."

metaphor and speak directly. Further, one must define the contents of right message. The implied command to "discern the body" is similarly too vague to be a law. Of these instances only incest is a specific transgression with a specific penalty. It is noteworthy that this instance, in which there is a law, is not original with Paul. The prohibition is found in the Bible, and Paul even uses the term "father's wife" in dependence on Deut 22:30 [23:1] and 27:20. Thus this is not a case, as is "passion of lust," in which he pushes beyond the biblical code and offers his own, stricter command.

On the basis of present evidence I conclude that Paul was not much of a legislator.[27] He did not avoid legal phrasing and formulation, however, because he was against reward and punishment, which is what Protestant Christians have generally thought, but for some other reason. Perhaps he simply did not know it. Perhaps he was not (despite Acts 22:3) a trained rabbi and did not know how to turn general admonition into precise law. Without ruling on where Paul was educated and by whom, I wish to propose another explanation. He did not formulate laws in the sense of *halakot* because he did not see that as part of his task. He did not even baptize (except occasionally, 1 Cor 1:15–17). Why? Because "Christ did not send me to baptize but to preach the gospel." How could such a man, with such a commission, have sat down and drafted legislation?

Does this mean that he expected someone else to draft it? I doubt it. There are three further considerations that help to understand his strict admonitions and to see why they are not formulated as laws.

The first is that the purity language in 1 Thessalonians 4 (*ho hagiasmos hymōn*, v 3; *en hagiasmǭ*, v 4; *ou . . . epi akatharsią allʾ en hagiasmǭ*, v 7; *to pneuma autou to hagion*, v 8) points to the rich deposit of purity language in Paul, most of which is used in the sense of "behavioral perfection."[28] His converts should be 'blameless' (*amemptoi*), 'innocent' (*akeraioi*), and 'without blemish' (*amōma*; Phil 2:15); their hearts should be 'blameless' (*amemptos*; 1 Thess 3:13); and they should remain "blameless [*amemptōs*] until the appearance of the Lord" (1 Thess 5:23). The admonition with which I began, not to have too much lust even toward one's wife, is part and parcel of the general line of exhortation to live blamelessly and in a "holy" manner, since the converts are "God's temple" and God

[27] See W. D. Davies, "Paul and the Law: Reflections on Pitfalls in Interpretation," *Jewish and Pauline Studies* (Philadelphia: Fortress, 1984) 91.

[28] Paul Wernle long ago stressed the perfectionism of Paul's ethics, but his sound observations have been little heeded. See *Der Christ und die Sünde bei Paulus* (Freiburg im Breisgau and Leipzig: Mohr, 1897) 126f. See also *Paul, the Law, and the Jewish People*, 106.

dwells in them (1 Cor 3:16). This is true even of the individual (1 Cor 6:19, where *to sōma hymōn* means 'each of your individual bodies'). This is the reason for the avoidance of all sin, and especially sexual sin, which affects the body itself (1 Cor 6:18). The metaphor of "temple" drives Paul's terminology in the direction of *perfect purity*. Paul's view is that his converts should be and remain completely "without blemish" since God dwells in them. In other words, his rhetoric of perfection is based on the metaphor of God dwelling in his temple. This is not practical legislation for a community, which is admittedly still made up of humans, rather than vessels of the holy spirit. Paul was not entirely unrealistic; he recognized that people may pollute the purity of "God's temple," and he urged them not to do so (1 Cor 5:1, 6:18–19, and elsewhere). But he did not sit down and work out legislation that would reduce the chances of the introduction of impurity into the ecclesial body, nor did he develop cleansing and atoning devices (except for expulsion and death in the case of incest, 1 Corinthians 5).[29] Thus, although one might think at first that he intended the admonition not to take one's wife with passionate desire to be a law, I hold that it fits in quite well with many of his nonlegal admonitions to be pure, which are based on the metaphor of the body as the temple of God, but do not lead to concrete laws.

The second observation is that Pauline theory placed Christians in "the new creation" (2 Cor 5:17). As those who had died to sin they should no longer live in it (Rom 6:2). The sharp antithesis between life in the flesh and life in the spirit (e.g., Rom 8:4–13) both led him to expect (or at least say) that Christians fulfil the law perfectly and prevented him from developing a system of atonement.[30] This, again, is perfectionism that regulates behavior in practical ways—but it is not law.

For the third observation I return to 1 Thess 5:23. Christians should remain "blameless until the appearance [*parousia*] of our Lord Jesus Christ." The time, as he says elsewhere, is short (1 Cor 7:29; cf. Rom 13:11). In this context it is reasonable to say that people should make no provision for the flesh (Rom 13:14, referring to ordinary carnal desires). What Albert Schweitzer called "interim

[29] Wernle, ibid., 69; Floyd Filson, *St. Paul's Conception of Recompense* (Untersuchungen zum Neuen Testament 21; Leipzig: Hinrichs, 1931) 16f., 84; *Paul, the Law, and the Jewish People,* 106.

[30] Wernle (ibid., 126f.) emphasized the "sharp antithesis." For the connection of ethics to the "mystical" doctrine of dying and rising with Christ, see Albert Schweitzer, *The Mysticism of Paul the Apostle* (London: Adam and Charles Black, 1931) 300f. See also Jack T. Sanders, *Ethics in the New Testament* (Philadelphia: Fortress, 1975) 56f.

ethics" in the teaching of Jesus can be seen clearly in Paul. In part he did not draft legislation because he did not think that it would be needed. Thus it is dubious that he expected it to be done by someone else, or that he taught a code of behavior prepared by the Jerusalem apostles.

Paul was not, as Jesus was not, a legal teacher. He was, if anything, less of one: Jesus initiated at least one new law (even though for a new age), but Paul, none. It has often been thought that his theology and ethics alike were determined by the contrast of grace versus works. This is generally a misleading formulation, with regard to both the nature of grace and works in the abstract and the actual issues in Paul's letters. I have just demonstrated one more instance of the nonapplicability of the contrast. Paul does not avoid legal phrasing because he is afraid that someone will attempt to fulfill the law and thus win merit. He seems not at all to have had the nervous dread of good deeds and reward that marks so much exegesis of his letters. Yet it is true that he did not decree laws; instead of new law he issued perfectionist admonitions. This, I have proposed, was based in no small part on the temple imagery. It also fits well into his view that Christians participate already in the new age, and into his expectation that the time during which perfect purity would have to be maintained was short.

Conclusion

Apocalyptic or eschatological expectation in general does not necessarily prevent people from thinking about and drafting concrete legislation. The Book of Jubilees, as it now stands, includes eschatological hope (chap. 23; cf. chap. 50), but there is much legislation. The expectation that history would come to a dramatic climax also did not hinder law-making at Qumran. Further, Qumran shows that perfectionism does not have to be reserved for the eschatological era. Concrete, detailed obedience, down to a very fine point, can be expected in the present. Jesus and Paul, however, with their eyes fixed on a future better state, seem not to have done much in the way of passing legislation for their followers. Jesus, to be sure, probably expected his disciples and other hearers to leave off divorce then, without waiting for the kingdom. It is dubious, however, if he did much more along that line (or it would be known from the early church). There is a lot of exhortation in Paul's letters, but it cannot be called new law. It seems clear that neither Jesus nor Paul had adequate halakic interest to become a legislator for a true Israel. What is missing from both is the drive to sectarianism that one sees so clearly behind the existence of the Dead Sea community. There is no isolated community, no separate code of law.

Both Jesus and Paul did share with Qumran, and doubtless other groups, a stress on perfectionism and limitless commitment. In the sayings attributed to Jesus, this is better seen in the call to follow him, than in discussions of aspects of law. I see it in both Paul's expectation that Christians would imitate Christ by suffering (e.g., Rom 8:17) and his numerous demands for blamelessness. Jesus and his movement fit well in the camp of radicalism. This is not so, however, because they went through the law and tightened its loopholes, made it stricter, and elevated the demand of obedience higher, but because they thought in terms of giving up everything in the present for the sake of the future. In the context of this future orientation they said things that might be taken as law, but in fact this is seldom the right term, and these two great figures agree in not formulating their requirements in terms of laws that may be either observed or broken, for the transgression of which there is an atoning penalty. It is a cliché that Christianity is not a religion of law, but of grace. This is a faulty contrast, since grace can be communicated through laws as well as through nonlegal admonitions and promises. It does, however, seem to be a fact that Jesus and his greatest apostle did not think in terms of new legislation, even though they were ready enough to think of new demands.

The influence of perfectionism on later church law is well known. One need do no more than refer to the continuing struggle in the Christian world over divorce laws to make clear the relevance of the topic. The *Wirkungsgeschichte* of these topics can obviously not be pursued here, but it is to be hoped that those who do pursue it might bear in mind that the originators of perfectionist admonition did not understand themselves to be giving practical laws for a church of vast diversity and size, much less for mixed cultures in other millenia. The relevance of the ancient world for understanding the present world is here as always oblique. Looking back enables one to look around with fresh perspectives, but usually not with ready-made solutions to current problems of law and ethics.

Jacob Milgrom

Ethics and Ritual: The Foundations of the Biblical Dietary Laws

THIS AND THE FOLLOWING three essays move into the realm of ritual law. Ritual law is perhaps more susceptible than other aspects of holy law to the charge of legalism since it embraces repetitive ceremonial acts whose meaning and value more easily elude the worshiper. Milgrom focuses upon a particular part of the Mosaic ritual law, namely the dietary laws and laws of animal slaughter, and argues for their meaningfulness from the perspective of ethics: life is sacred, and these laws affirm its sacredness. The principle of the sacredness of life is, in fact, not unique to the law given to Israel at Sinai but is, rather, embodied in the Noachide law, which is universally binding by virtue of a covenant with all people (Noah and his descendants). The principle applies as much to animal life as to human life. Ideally, the human race is, after the example of Adam, vegetarian. God, however, reluctantly accommodates to its carnivorous proclivities by allowing the slaughtering and eating of animals under restrictive conditions. Humans in general are allowed to eat all kinds of meat provided the blood—the repository of life—has been drained from it. Israel is placed under more severe restrictions, certain of which have the effect of limiting Israel's choice of animals that may be slaughtered and eaten. These more severe restrictions are an essential factor in Israel's holiness.

Jacob Milgrom is Professor of Biblical Studies at the University of California, Berkeley, and founder of its Jewish Studies Program.

He is a Gugenheim fellow and a fellow of the American Academy for Jewish Research. Professor Milgrom was ordained by the Jewish Theological Seminary of America and served in the active rabbinate for many years. He has written commentaries on the books of Leviticus and Numbers, *Studies in Levitical Terminology,* and *Studies in Cultic Theology and Terminology,* as well as on other biblical topics, with particular emphasis on the Levitical legal systems.

A fundamental axiom of the Bible is that law is coexistent with God, a quintessential component of the divine reality. God created the world through law. This is how the Bible describes it: God spoke and chaos became order. What is meant is that God's word or thought set law into motion, with the result that substance passed into form. Creation, then, is a manifestation of law.

According to the theologians, divine law is composed of two parts: natural law and moral law. For the Bible, however, this is not correct. A more accurate division would be natural law and human law, that is, the law as it operates in nature and in people. Furthermore, human law does not consist solely of morals. It also comprises ritual commandments, meaning all action that concerns only the individual and does not affect her or his relation with others.

The Blood Prohibition

It is obvious that ritual laws play a supreme role in biblical religion. Yet few have realized that there is one ritual that, in the Bible's view, is the very basis of ethics. To put it differently, this ritual law is higher than the Ten Commandments:

> Every creature that lives shall be yours to eat; I give them all to you as I did the green plants. You must not, however, eat flesh with its life-blood. For your life-blood, too, I will require a reckoning. . . . Whoever sheds the blood of man, for that man shall his blood be shed. For in the image of God was man created (Gen 9:3–6).

God's command to Noah and his sons takes the form of a law, the first in the Bible, the first—and only—law for humanity. It is the divine remedy for human sinfulness that hitherto polluted the earth and necessitated its purgation by flood.[1] Humankind will not change; it

[1] T. Frymer-Kensky, "The Atrahaisis Epic and Its Significance for our Understanding of Genesis 1–9," *Biblical Archaeologist* 40 (1977) 149–55.

remains sinful (Gen 8:22); but this unrighteousness need no longer pollute the earth if it will but heed one law—to abstain from blood. Human blood must not be shed and animal blood must not be ingested. The blood prohibition is, then, a bipartate law: an ethical law forbidding homicide and a ritual law forbidding the ingestion of blood. Moreover, it is incumbent upon all humanity—the only universal law in all of Scripture. And for this reason it is higher than the Ten Commandments. The Decalogue was revealed to Israel and intended solely for Israel, but this Noachide law, the blood prohibition, was imposed on all humans because it alone was deemed indispensable for a viable human society.

The position of the blood prohibition in the primeval history discloses another aspect of its significance. *ʾak* 'however' (Gen 9:4) is the language of concession. Originally, according to the Priestly account, the race was vegetarian. It ruled the animal kingdom, but not as a source of food (Gen 1:26), for God said, "See, I give you every seed-bearing plant . . . and every tree . . . ; they shall be yours for food" (Gen 1:29). After eating the forbidden fruit, however, the human race is no longer satisfied with its role as the steward of paradise. It wants to be the active agent of its own destiny.

This new race is also carnivorously inclined. No longer Adam, the ideal, but Noah, the real, it insists on bringing death to living things to gratify appetite and need. This concession is granted, reluctantly, but not without reservation: it must refrain from ingesting the blood.

The import of this prohibition is projected in even clearer relief against the backdrop of the ancient Near East. First, it must be noted that blood plays no role whatever in the cults of Israel's neighbors, with the sole exception of the pre-Islamic Arabs.[2] Second, Israel's postulate of the life force residing in the blood is found nowhere else, not even among the early Arabs.[3] Third, there is no attestation anywhere else of an absolute prohibition against ingesting blood;[4] even the Arabs, down to the age of Muḥammad, partook of blood.[5] Thus, Israel's blood prohibition cannot be passed off as an outlandish vestige of some primitive taboo; it must be viewed as the product of a

[2] J. Henninger, "Pureté et Impureté. Arabia, Animaux Impurs: Le Sang," *Dictionnaire de la Bible, Supplément,* ed. H. Cazelles and A. Feuillet (Paris: Letouzey, 1979), 9:460–70, 473–91.

[3] Ibid., 487–88.

[4] J. McCarthy, "The Symbolism of Blood Sacrifice," *Journal of Biblical Literature* 88 (1969) 166–76.

[5] W. R. Smith, *Lectures on the Religion of the Semites* (London: Black, 1927; repr. New York: KTAV, 1969) 234.

rational, deliberate opposition to the prevailing practice of its environment. Moreover, as shown above, the blood prohibition is not only intended to be absolute, but universal—it is incumbent on all humanity. Post-Noah mortals may have meat for food and may kill to get it, but they must eschew the blood. Though they are conceded animal flesh, they must abstain from its lifeblood: it must be drained, returned to its source, to God.[6]

Leviticus 17

Israel is summoned to obey an even stricter blood prohibition:

> If any individual of the house of Israel or any alien who resides among them *ingests* [lit., eats] *any blood,* I will set my face against the person who *ingests blood,* and I will cut him off from his kin. As for the life of the flesh it is in the blood. It is I who have assigned it to you upon the altar to ransom your lives; for it is the blood that ransoms for life. Therefore I say to the Israelites: No person among you shall *ingest blood,* nor shall any alien that resides among you *ingest blood.* If any individual of the house of Israel or any alien who resides among them hunts down a beast or bird that may be eaten, he shall pour out its blood and cover it with earth. "For the life of all flesh—its blood—is its life. Hence, I say to the Israelites: You shall not *ingest the blood* of any flesh, for the life of all flesh is its blood. Anyone who *ingests it* shall be cut off" (Lev 17:10-14).

This passage is especially significant because it was composed by the Priestly author of Genesis 9. Hence, I expect the same reasoning to prevail in both passages. First, it should be noted that within these five verses the blood prohibition occurs six times. Such staccato repetition is unprecedented in law; it betrays the strident alarm of the legislator lest this fundamental principle be violated. However, a new provision has been added. Whereas humanity is enjoined to abstain from animal blood by draining it, Israel is to do so only for game (vv 13-14). In contrast, the blood of sacrificial animals must be offered on the altar (v 11). Because this latter verse not only prescribes a rite but provides its own rationale, it merits a close reading on the chance it will also illumine the rationale for the blood prohibition.[7]

17:11aα,b: *kî nepeš habbāśār baddām hîˀ* [*hwˀ*] . . . *kî-haddām hûˀ bannepeš yĕkappēr*. The use of the two *beth* prepositions requires comment. The first obviously means 'with'; the second is the *beth*

[6] Henninger, "Pureté et Impureté," 489-90.

[7] Jacob Milgrom, "A Prolegomenon to Leviticus 17:11," *Journal of Biblical Literature* 90 (1971) 149-56.

pretii 'for (the price of)',[8] attested frequently in Scripture (e.g., Lev 25:37, 27:10 [both H], Gen 9:6 [P; see above], Num 17:3). The two clauses translate literally: "As for the life of the flesh it is in the blood . . . for it is the blood that ransoms for life." The clauses form an inclusion, endowing the verses with an ABA′ structure, and thereby highlighting the middle section, B.

17:11aβ: *waʾănî nĕtattîw lākem ʿal-hammizbēaḥ.* The meaning is clear except for the term *nĕtattîw*. A survey of the Priestly source shows that wherever the subject of *nātan* is God, it means 'bestow, appoint, assign' (e.g., Num 8:19 [N.B. *wāʾetĕtnâ . . . nĕtūnîm*]; 18:8, 19; cf. also Gen 1:29, 9:3, Lev 6:10, 7:34, 10:17, Num 35:6). This usage, however, is not to be confused with *nātan dām* when the subject is the priest, in which case the meaning is 'place the blood' (e.g., on a person, Exod 29:20 and Lev 14:14, 25; on doorposts, Exod 12:7 and Ezek 45:19; on the altar, Lev 4:7, 25 and Ezek 43:20). This clause is therefore rendered: "and it is I who have assigned it to you upon the altar" (with the New Jewish Publication Society translation and New English Bible; this distinction is important to prevent the association of Lev 17:11 with the *ḥaṭṭāʾt* offering, the blood of which is indeed "placed" on the horns of the altar, Lev 4:7 and passim).

17:11aγ: *lĕkappēr ʿal-napšōtêkem.* The final clause constitutes the crux of the verse and requires that each word be analyzed separately. There is general agreement about the meaning of *nepeš*. It refers to the life-essence of both human and beast, as distinct from the body. It does not disintegrate into dust but departs from the body (Gen 35:18, Jer 15:9) and enters Sheol (Ps 16:10, 30:4, Job 33:22). The translation 'life' is therefore warranted. In a legal context, moreover, *nepeš* specifically connotes capital crime or punishment (e.g., Exod 21:23, Lev 24:17, Deut 19:21), and expressions compounded with it often imply that life is at stake (e.g, Judg 5:18, 12:3, 1 Sam 19:5). Especially relevant is the condemnation of Korah and his cohorts, those who have sinned 'at the cost of their lives' (*bĕnapšōtām*, Num 17:3 [P]). Thus Lev 17:11 implies that human life is in jeopardy unless the stipulated ritual is carried out. The nature of both the crime and its atonement will follow from the explanation of the full phrase *lĕkappēr ʿal-napšōtêkem*.

First, however, a word on the meaning of *lĕkappēr ʿal.* The key to the meaning of the Piel of *kpr* is in its adjunct prepositions. It can be shown that whenever the object of *kippēr* is a person, a preposition must follow, either *ʿal* or *bĕʿad*, both signifying 'on behalf of, for'. This verse, therefore, denotes that the blood is the means of carrying

[8] Correcting my earlier proposal, ibid., 149.

out the *kippūr* rite on behalf of the persons offering the sacrifice. As for the root *kpr*, nothing less than a monograph would do it justice.[9] For the purpose of this paper, however, it will be rendered by 'ransom'.[10]

The full idiom, *kippēr ʿal-nepeš*, occurs again in only two pericopes: Exod 30:16 and Num 31:50. As noted by Rashbam (on Num 31:49), they are strikingly similar in (a) *context*, since both deal with censuses (Exod 30:12, Num 31:49); (b) *procedure*, since precious metal is brought in both to the Tent of Meeting "as a remembrance before the Lord" (Exod 30:16, Num 31:54); and (c) *purpose*, since both are intended *lĕkappēr ʿal-napšōtêkem* (Exod 30:15–16, Num 31:50).[11] More importantly, the purpose is explicated by the clause: "that no plague shall come upon them in their being counted" (Exod 30:12b). Here is an explicit statement that the purpose of the *kippūr* money is to prevent destruction at the hands of God. Implied, therefore, is that a census is a capital offense in the sight of God and that the silver half-shekel and the gold vessels are the necessary ransom for the life of the polled persons.

Moreover, the verb *kippēr* must be related to the expression found in the same pericope *kōper napšô* 'a ransom for his life' (Exod 30:12). The same combination of the idiom *kōper nepeš* and the verb *kippēr* is found in the law of homicide (Num 35:31–33). Thus, in these two cases, *kippēr* is a denominative from *kōper*, whose meaning as 'ransom' is undisputed (cf. Exod 21:30). Therefore, there exists a strong possibility that all texts that assign to *kippēr* the function of averting God's wrath have *kōper* in mind: innocent life spared by substituting for it the guilty parties or their ransom. Thus the abovementioned homicide law is elucidated as follows: though no substitute is allowed for a deliberate murderer, the accidental homicide is ransomed by the natural death of the high priest (Num 35:25). Similarly, the census money ransoms each counted soldier. A ransom function can also be assigned to the Levite guards who siphon off God's wrath upon themselves when an Israelite encroaches upon the sancta (Num 1:53, 8:19; 18:22–23) as well as to Phineas (the chief of the Levite guards, Num 3:32) who ransoms Israel from God's imminent wrath (Num 25:10).[12] Other examples of the ransom function of *kippēr* are the slaying of Saul's sons as a ransom for his

[9] See generally, B. Janowski, *Sühne als Heilsgeschehen* (Neukirchen-Vluyn: Neukirchener, 1982).

[10] Milgrom, "A Prolegomenon to Leviticus 17:11," 151 n. 15.

[11] Rashbam (Rabbi Samuel ben Meir), *Perush ha-Torah* (ed. D. Rosin; 1881).

[12] On the Levite guards, see Milgrom, *Studies in Levitical Terminology* (Berkeley: University of California, 1970) 28–31.

violation of the Gibeonite covenant (2 Sam 21:3–6), the inability of Babylon to ransom (i.e., avert its fate, Isa 47:11), and Moses' attempt to ransom Israel by his intercession (Exod 32:30–34). Thus, the meaning of *nepeš* in legal contexts and the meaning of *kippēr ʿal-nepeš* in census contexts both point to the conclusion that in Lev 17:11, Israelites have become liable to death before God and the purpose of the sacrificial blood is *lĕkappēr ʿal-napšōtêkem* 'to ransom your lives'.

The Sacrifice

The assignment of the blood to the altar makes it clear that sacrificial blood is meant. The kind of sacrifice intended, however, is unclear. Does this verse refer to all sacrifices or does it concern a particular sacrifice? The answer lies in another idiom that, by its fourfold repetition, forms a theme in the pericope in which the verse is found: *lôʾ-tōʾkal dām,* that is, the prohibition of eating blood. The notion that blood, a liquid, would be eaten rather than drunk points to the meaning. The idiom is explicable by assuming that the blood is consumed in the course of eating meat. Indeed, wherever *ʾākal dām* is met, the context invariably shows that the blood is not being drunk for its own sake but as a consequence of eating meat. Thus, Deuteronomy repeatedly warns about the danger of consuming blood as a result of allowing profane slaughter (12:15–16, 23–25) and of permitting the eating of the flesh of firstlings by the laity (15:23). So in the Priestly Code, the blood prohibition occurs exclusively in the discussion of the *šĕlāmîm,* the offering of well-being, the only sacrifice whose flesh is eaten by the lay worshiper (Lev 3:17, 7:26, 17:1–7; cf. Gen 9:4).

Furthermore, this conclusion is demanded by the content of Leviticus 17. It comprises two laws (vv 10–12 and 13–14) that together form a logical unity. Since the second deals with wild animals—obviously hunted for their meat and not for sport (*ʾăšer yēʾākēl*)—the first law undoubtedly also speaks of the flesh of edible animals; these, however, are not game but domestic animals that, according to P, must be sacrificed at the altar. Thus vv 10–14 constitute a bipartite law for disposing of the blood of all victims killed for their flesh: the blood of game must be covered, and the blood of sacrificial animals must be drained upon the altar. Moreover, it implies that just as the uncovered blood of game will cry out for vengeance, so the improperly disposed of blood of a sacrificial animal will also condemn the life of its slaughterer. For the moment I conclude that Lev 17:11 does not concern itself with all sacrifices, but refers only to the one sacrifice whose flesh is permitted to be eaten by the laity, the *šĕlāmîm.*

It is the blood of the *šĕlāmîm* that would serve as the *kippūr* agent for the lives of the Israelites.

The Contradiction

This conclusion, however, lays bare a glaring contradiction since the *šĕlāmîm* never functions as a *kippūr*! Of the four categories of animal sacrifices, three are for *kippūr*: the *ḥaṭṭāʾt* 'purification offering') and *ʾāšām* ('reparation offering') exclusively (e.g., Lev 4:20, 26, 31, 35; and Lev 5:16, 18, 26), and the *ʿōlâ* 'burnt offering' partially (e.g., Lev 1:14, 16:24). However, the *šĕlāmîm* 'offering of well-being' is the only sacrifice that never serves in a *kippūr* role. To be sure, there are two cases where *šĕlāmîm* is coupled with *kippēr*, but they do not stand up under scrutiny: (1) In Ezek 45:15, 17 the *šĕlāmîm* is the last in a series of sacrifices, and the *kippūr* function is probably that of the preceding *ʿōlâ* and *ḥaṭṭāʾt*; (2) 1 Sam 3:14 assigns a *kippūr* role to *bĕzebaḥ ûbĕminḥâ*. That specific sacrifices are not intended, but sacrifices in general, is shown in the same pericope by 1 Sam 2:17, where *minḥâ* is clearly not the cereal offering of P, but, as is correctly understood by R. Rendtorff, it stands for flesh offerings.[13] (For this generic usage of "sacrifice," see 1 Sam 2:29 and Isa 19:21.) The uses of the *šĕlāmîm* are carefully detailed in the Priestly Code and abundantly attested in the biblical literature; both law and practice unanimously testify that the offerings of well-being are joyous in character and not expiatory. The law ordains it as an expression of thanks (*tôdâ*), as the completion of a vow (*neder*), or as a freewill offering (*nĕdābâ*, Lev 7:11–12, 16). Furthermore, wherever it is found in narrative or liturgical literature, it occurs in precisely such contexts (e.g., Num 15:3, Deut 16:10–11, 27:7, 1 Sam 11:15, Ps 107:22, 116:17–19). The case of the Nazirite illustrates the point vividly. The *šĕlāmîm* is one of the sacrifices ordained at the completion of his vow. However, if he contracts severe impurity during his Nazirite period, he brings the same sacrifices, except that an *ʾāšām* is substituted for the *šĕlāmîm*. The reason is clear: his sacrifices are now for expiation, not for thanksgiving (also note the choice of verbs in Lev 7:7–9, 14; 14:18–20).

The exposed contradiction is brought into sharper relief by yet another consideration. Expiation of ordinary sin is not the subject of Lev 17:11. As noted, *lĕkappēr ʿal-nepeš* must mean that the Israelite is guilty of a capital offense against God, and unless he brings sacrificial blood to the altar, he is subject to the death penalty. However, in the

[13] R. Rendtorff, *Studien zur Geschichte des Opfers im alten Israel* (Neukirchen-Vluyn: Neukirchener, 1967).

Priestly Code, there is no sacrificial expiation for capital crime or, for that matter, for any deliberate violation. The presumptuous sinner is banned from the sanctuary because he "acts defiantly [*bĕyād rāmâ*] . . . reviles the Lord . . . has spurned the word of the Lord and violated his commandment" (Num 15:30-31; contrast vv 24-29).

Thus the contradiction is reinforced. The *šĕlāmîm* cannot be used for expiation purposes and the sin implied in Lev 17:11 cannot be expiated by any sacrifice at all. Indeed, the nonexpiatory *šĕlāmîm* is presumed to expiate that which is nonexpiable!

The Resolution

The answer to the contradiction is to be found in the opening law of the chapter (17:3-4). It ordains that any Israelite who slaughters a sacrificial animal (for its meat) without bringing it to the Tabernacle altar as an offering of well-being, 'bloodguilt shall be reckoned to that man: he has shed blood' (*dām yēḥāšēb lāʾîš hahûʾ dām šāpāk*; v 4ba). To take these two formulae as mere figures of speech is to misconstrue them. They are precise legal terms that define and categorize the guilt. The idiom *šāpak dām* is the well-attested accusation of murder (in P: Gen 9:6, Num 35:33; so in all sources: e.g., narrative: Gen 37:22, 1 Sam 25:31, 1 Kgs 2:31, 2 Kgs 21:16, 24:4; legal: Deut 19:10, 21:7; wisdom: Prov 1:16, 6:17; prophetic: Isa 59:7, Jer 22:3, 17, and esp. Ezek 16:38, 18:10, 22:3, 4, 6, 9, 12) and the Niphal of *ḥšb* 'be reckoned' is the declaratory statement in P for designating a cultic act as either acceptable or unacceptable to God (Lev 7:18 and Num 18:27, 30; cf. Ps 106:31).[14] Indeed, the coupling of these two legal formulae underscores the enormity of the crime: he who commits profane slaughter is reckoned as a murderer because he has shed blood.

The law of Lev 17:3-4, then, provides an eminently satisfactory basis for explaining the crux of v 11 (the underlying, redactional unity of Leviticus 17 is assumed). This is not to say that the materials that comprise this chapter are of a single hue, as source analysis and form-critical studies have demonstrated.

It already has been shown that v 11 and its context (vv 10-14) relate exclusively to the problem of how to eat meat without ingesting its blood, a problem that concerns only the offering of well-being. It has also been indirectly deduced from the language of the pericope that the improper disposal of the animal's blood is a capital violation. Verses 3-4 now make this explicit: animal slaughter constitutes murder except at the authorized altar. Verse 11 complements the

[14] G. von Rad, *Old Testament Theology* (New York: Harper, 1966), 1:125-30.

indictment with the remedy and its rationale: the blood must be brought to the altar to ransom the murder of the animal because "as for the life of the flesh, it is in the blood . . . for it is the blood that ransoms for life" (the inclusion: 11aα,b).

The doctrine that unauthorized animal slaughter constitutes murder is found nowhere else (another instance may be the blood of the heifer whose neck is broken, Deut 21:1-9). However, this doctrine is consistent with the general view of the animal in biblical literature, especially in the Priestly tradition. An animal also has a *nepeš* (Gen 9:10; Lev 11:10, 46; 24:18; Num 31:28). *Nepeš ḥayyâ* refers to humans in J (Gen 2:7), but only to animals in P (Gen 1:20, 21, 24, 30; 9:10, 12, 15, 16; Lev 11:10, 46; cf. Ezek 47:9; Gen 2:19 [J] is the sole exception which, however, is considered as an explanatory gloss by J).[15] Its vengeance is to be feared as much as human's; hence its blood must be covered (Lev 17:13; cf. Gen 4:10, Isa 26:21, Job 16:18, Qoh 3:18-20, and esp. Ezek 24:6-8); it is responsible under the law (Gen 9:5, Lev 20:15-16; cf. Exod 21:28-32) and is a party to God's covenant (Gen 9:9-10; Lev 26:6, 22; cf. Hos 2:20).

According to the Priestly account of creation, people initially were meant to be vegetarian. God concedes, however, to humanity's carnivorous desires: craving for meat is to be indulged, but people are to abstain from consuming the blood. Thus, P's theory of anthropogenesis reveals its reservation and, indeed, its uneasiness toward humanity's uncontrolled power over animal life. Through its law code, of which Lev 17:11 can now be seen as an integral part, it seeks to curb that power. All people must eschew the life-blood of the animal by draining it, thereby returning it to its creator (Gen 9:3-4, Lev 17:13-14). Israel, as part of its striving toward holiness (e.g., Lev 19:2, 20:26), is enjoined to observe an additional safeguard: the blood of sacrificial animals must be drained upon the authorized altar, since "it is I who have assigned it to you upon the altar to ransom your lives." Thus, the context of Lev 17:11 alone treats the *šĕlāmîm*, the only sacrifice without an expiatory function. It informs the Israelites that slaughtering a sacrificial animal for its flesh constitutes murder unless they offer the blood upon the altar to ransom its life.

On the other hand, the author/redactor of Leviticus 17 is fully cognizant that the non-Israelite is subject to a less stringent law. To be sure, the blood prohibition is imposed also on the *gēr* 'the alien' who resides in Israel (vv 10, 12). However, the prohibition against

[15] See J. Skinner, *Genesis* (International Critical Commentary; Edinburgh: Clark, 1912); E. A. Speiser, *Genesis* (Anchor Bible 1; Garden City, NY: Doubleday, 1964).

slaughtering the animal outside the authorized sanctuary is worded differently: "If any man of the house of Israel slaughters . . ." (v 3). The resident alien is missing here, and this omission is no accident. Non-Israelites are required to abstain from animal blood; otherwise, like the disobedient Israelite, they have committed a capital crime and face death by divine agency: "he will be cut off from his kin" (v 10). They are not, however, required to worship at the altar of Israel's God.[16] Genesis 9 has given instruction on what they must do: drain the meat of its blood and it becomes eligible for eating. Thus Leviticus 17 and Genesis 9 are wholly consistent with each other, a consistency to be expected since they both stem from the Priestly tradition.

In sum, the Bible decrees that human blood may not be spilled and animal blood may not be ingested. Israel is enjoined to observe an additional safeguard: blood of sacrificial animals must be drained on the authorized altar. But to complete the biblical record of the blood prohibition note must be taken of the far-reaching amendment introduced by Deuteronomy, which desacralizes the blood requirement: henceforth Israel may slaughter its meat profanely (Deut 12:15-16, 22-24). Thus, Israelite and non-Israelite are in effect equated. Jew and non-Jew are bound by a single prohibition, to abstain from blood. The rationale is now clear: The human being must never lose sight of the fundamental tenet for a viable human society—life is inviolable and may not be treated lightly. Humanity has a right to nourishment, not to life. Hence the blood—the symbol of life—must be drained, returned to the universe, to God.[17]

Ritual Slaughter

The technique for animal slaughter is nowhere prescribed in Scripture. However, it may be implied by the terminology. My investigation begins with Deuteronomy. Twice in the same pericope it concedes the right of profane slaughter: "But whenever you desire, you may slaughter [*tizbaḥ*] and eat meat . . . in all your settlements" (12:15); "you may slaughter [*wĕzābaḥtā*] any of your cattle or sheep . . . as I commanded you and you may eat in your settlements" (12:21). In

[16] Milgrom, "Religious Conversion and the Revolt Model for the Formation of Israel," *Journal of Biblical Literature* 101 (1982) 169-76.

[17] Milgrom, "The Biblical Diet Laws as an Ethical System," *Interpretation* 17 (1963) 288-301; repr. in *Studies in Cultic Theology and Terminology* (Leiden: Brill, 1983) 104-18.

both citations, the key verb 'slaughter' is rendered by *zābaḥ*. Its use here occasions surprise because elsewhere in biblical Hebrew and cognate languages it bears a sacral connotation.

Of the 129 times *zābaḥ* occurs in Scripture, it most often denotes sacrificial slaughter (e.g., Exod 23:18 [‖ *šāḥaṭ*, Exod 34:25], Isa 66:3 [‖ *šāḥaṭ*], Hos 8:13). This meaning is also the dominant meaning of all its cognates. The case of Ugaritic is most illuminating. Ugaritic *dbḥ* chiefly designates sacrificial slaughter.[18] As in Hebrew, the cultic context is corroborated by the nominal forms: *zebaḥ/dbḥ* and *mizbēaḥ/mdbḥ(t)*, that is, 'sacrificial meal' and 'altar'. Again, in both languages the verb carries with it a secondary meaning 'offer the *zebaḥ/dbḥ* sacrifice' (e.g., compare the offering of the *zebaḥ*, *lizbōaḥ lipnê yhwh* [Lev 9:4; cf. Deut 18:3, 1 Sam 2:15, Zech 14:21], with that of the *ʿōlâ* and *ḥaṭṭāʾt*: *wĕhaqrēb lipnê yhwh* [Lev 9:2; cf. 1:3, 10, 14; 4:3, 14, 23]).

Zebaḥ also describes illegitimate sacrifices to the Lord (e.g., Isa 65:3, Ezek 20:28) and worship of other gods (e.g., Exod 34:15, Deut 32:17, Judg 16:23). Its scope also includes a metaphoric usage, the *zebaḥ* of corpses that the Lord arrays for the wild beasts and birds (e.g., Isa 34:6, Jer 46:10, Ezek 39:17–19, Zeph 1:7–8), but even here the sacrificial context is evident from the use of cultic vocabulary: *hiqdîš qĕrūʾāw*, *ḥēleb wĕdām*, etc. Finally, Piel *zibbaḥ* is found twice with the iterative connotation of performing numerous sacrifices (1 Kgs 8:5 [2 Chr 5:6], 2 Chr 3:22) and in the remaining instances with regard to illegitimate or idolatrous worship (1 Kgs 3:2–3; 11:8; 12:32; 22:44; 2 Kgs 12:4; 14:4; 15:4, 35; 16:4 [2 Chr 28:4]; Hos 4:13–14; 11:2; 12:12; Hab 1:16; Ps 106:38; 2 Chr 28:23; 33:22). Thus the Piel also verifies that the root *zbḥ* is exclusively a cultic term, referring to ritual slaughter and sacrifice.

According to the lexicons, there are seven alleged exceptions. Five of them seem to deal with nonsacrificial feasts (Num 22:40, 1 Sam 28:24, 1 Kgs 19:21, Ezek 34:3, 2 Chr 18:2). However, a closer examination of their respective contexts will not support this claim. Neither Balak (Num 22:40) nor Ahab (2 Chr 18:2) would have invited Balaam or Jehoshaphat, respectively, to a profane feast whose purpose was to implore the help of the Lord against the enemy. It is hardly conceivable that Elisha would have slaughtered the team of oxen for a profane meal in celebration of his anointment as Elijah's successor (1 Kgs 19:16, 21). Nor is it likely that the witch of Endor would have

[18] See A. Herdner, *Corpus des tablettes en cunéiformes alphabétiques découvertes à Ras Shamra-Ugarit de 1929 à 1939* (2 vols.; Mission de Ras Shamra 10; Paris: Geuthner, 1963), texts 20 (col. A, line 10) and 32 (lines 24 and 32).

prepared a profane meal (1 Sam 28:24) before the very king who improvised an altar on the battlefield so that his troops would not be guilty of profane or illicit slaughter (1 Sam 14:32–35). It is possible that the last of these alleged exceptions (Ezek 34:3) deals with common slaughter—though the text is obscure—since its setting is in the Babylonian exile when sacrifice was impossible and after the deuteronomic concession had gone into effect. Indeed, according to the accepted view that common slaughter was permitted for the first time with the promulgation of Deuteronomy under Josiah;[19] a legal sanction for profane slaughter is simply out of the question for early Israel.

The two instances that remain (Deut 12:15, 21) are indeed exceptions to the rule. Their context leaves no room for doubt: Deuteronomy's demand for cult centralization has made profane slaughter imperative. Why then does it use the verb *zābaḥ*, which, as shown, never refers to profane slaughter but only to the slaughter and preparation of sacrifices?

The key to this puzzle, I submit, lies in a clause in the second citation: "you may slaughter . . . as I commanded you" [*kaʾăšer ṣiwwîtikā*] (Deut 12:21). What is the antecedent? To what command does it refer? Modern scholars, without exception, hold that this phrase in v 21 refers back to the similar instruction of v 15, that is, Israelites may now obtain meat by common slaughter (v 21) as indicated earlier in the same pericope (v 15). This interpretation cannot stand for three reasons:

1. *Ṣiwwîtikā* 'I commanded you' implies an obligation. However, the tone of the pericope—"whenever you desire" (vv 15, 20, 21), "if you have the desire" (v 20)—implies volition. Profane slaughter, just like eating meat, is a matter of choice, not a requirement.
2. Whenever Deuteronomy refers to its own statements it invariably resorts to the expression *ʾăšer ʾānōkî mĕṣawweh* 'that I command' (4:2, 40; 6:2, 6; 7:11; 8:1, 11; 10:13; 11:8, 13, 22, 27, 28; 12:14, 28 [N.B., referring to instruction in the same chapter]; 13:1, 19; 15:5; 19:9; 27:1, 4, 10; 28:1, 13, 14, 15; 30:2, 8, 11, 16). Thus when Deuteronomy cites itself it always uses the participle and never the perfect.
3. More importantly, the clause *kaʾăšer ṣiwwâ, kaʾăšer nišbaʿ*, or *kaʾăšer dibbēr* serves a specific literary function in Deuteronomy:

[19] Cf. Rabbi Ishmael in "Sifrei to Deuteronomy" 12:20; and the outside tradition (*baraita*) to *b. Ḥul.* 16b.

it is D's "cf."—its unique formula by which it indicates its sources.[20]

Thus *wĕzābaḥtā . . . kaʾăšer ṣiwwîtikā* 'you may slaughter . . . as I commanded you' (Deut 12:21) signifies that common slaughter must follow the same method practiced in sacrificial slaughter. Indeed, this is precisely how the Tannaim interpret this verse ("*Sipre* to Deut" 12:21). But it does not indicate that D relied upon a source. The plethora and minutiae of P's sacrificial laws contain not one hint concerning a proper technique for slaughtering. This glaring omission compels D. Z. Hoffmann to endorse the view of Rabbi Judah that it was an oral tradition.[21] However, I believe that there is textual evidence that has been overlooked—the verb *šāḥaṭ*.

The most significant fact about *šāḥaṭ* is that it is P's *exclusive term* for animal slaughter. *Šāḥaṭ* is found 79 times in Scripture, 40 of which are in P and 13 more in writings dependent on P, to wit: 4 times in Ezekiel 40–48 (40:39, 41, 42; 44:11) and 9 times in 2 Chronicles (29:23[22; 3x], 24; 30:15, 17; 35:1, 6, 11). Outside of P it is found 3 times in connection with the paschal sacrifice (Exod 12:21, 34:25, Ezra 6:20); 7 times in a cultic context (Gen 22:10, 1 Sam 1:25; 14:32, 34[2x]; Isa 22:13; 66:3; Hos 5:2); 3 times in regard to human sacrifice (Isa 57:5, Ezek 16:21, 23:39) and 10 times in regard to mass human slaughter (Num 14:16; Judg 12:6; 1 Kgs 18:40; 2 Kgs 10:7, 14; Jer 39:6[2x]; 41:7; 52:10[2x]). Thus, the spectrum of *šāḥaṭ* is congruent with *zābaḥ* in that both designate sacrificial slaughter and, in metaphoric usage, the mass slaughter of persons.

The lexicographical question is obvious: Why does P refrain from using *zābaḥ*, employing exclusively *šāḥaṭ*? The answer lies in the restricted application of *zābaḥ* in P. It is found only in connection with the *zebaḥ* sacrifice. Hence, it cannot denote the slaughter of *other* sacrifices. Indeed, P is reluctant to use the verb *zābaḥ* even with the *zebaḥ* (the sole exception is Lev 9:4; contrast v 18) but prefers *hiqrîb* (Lev 3:1, 3; 7:11–18, 29, 33, etc.). To be sure, the Holiness source (H), entwined with P material in Leviticus 17–26, prefers the verb *zābaḥ* (Lev 17:5[2x], 7; 19:5[2x]; 22:29). However, the specific meaning of *zābaḥ* in H is not 'slaughter' but 'offer the *zebaḥ*', that is, it refers to the entire sacrificial procedure, including slaughter (this also holds

[20] See Milgrom, "Profane Slaughter and a Formulaic Key to the Composition of Deuteronomy," *Hebrew Union College Annual* 47 (1976) 1–17.

[21] *Sipre* to Deut 12:21 and the *baraita* to *b. Ḥul.* 28a. See D. Z. Hoffman, *The Book of Deuteronomy* (Tel Aviv: Nezach, 1959), 1:183 [Hebrew], translation of *Das Buch Deuteronomium*, vol. 1 (Berlin: Poppelauer, 1913).

true for P; contrast *zābaḥ*, Lev 9:4 with *šāḥaṭ* v 18). Indeed, when H wishes to specify 'slaughter', it also resorts to *šāḥaṭ* (Lev 22:28, 29). Thus, in all of P (H included) *zābaḥ* means 'offer the *zebaḥ*' leaving *šāḥaṭ* as the exclusive term for slaughter.

Is *šāḥaṭ* capable of greater precision? I believe it means 'slit the throat'. Such is the meaning of Arabic *śaḥaṭa*. More importantly, the noun *maśḥaṭ* means 'throat'.[22] Indirect evidence is also supplied by cognate languages. Akkadian for animal slaughter is *ṭabāḫu*; but 'cut the throat' can only be expressed literally, as *nakāsu napištam*. Akkadian, then, has no single word for this concept. Ugaritic has two verbs for slaughter, *dbḥ* and *ṭbḫ*; the former, as shown above, denotes sacred slaughter and the latter, it can be shown, denotes profane slaughter.[23] Neither term, however, is limited to the meaning 'cut the throat'. In Hebrew, likewise, *zābaḥ* and *ṭābaḥ* denote, respectively, sacred and common slaughter: *zābaḥ*, as demonstrated above, and *ṭābaḥ*, by Gen 43:16, Exod 21:37, Deut 28:31, 1 Sam 25:11, Isa 53:7, Jer 11:19, 12:3, 50:17, 51:40, Ps 44:23, Prov 7:22, 9:2. Significantly, only Hebrew has a third term for slaughter, *šāḥaṭ*. Thus Hebrew would seem to contain two identical words for sacred slaughter, *zābaḥ* and *šāḥaṭ*, unless the latter had a more restricted, technical meaning, which may be slaughtering by cutting the throat.

Rabbinic evidence, also by indirect inference, points to the same conclusion. Jewish tradition has always interpreted *šāḥaṭ* in this manner.[24] Moreover, the Mishnah states anonymously and categorically "all may slaughter (ritually) at any time and with any implement" (*m. Ḥul.* 1:2), forestalling any discussion concerning the method of slaughter. Such a clear statement is evidence that the slaughtering method was already fixed by tradition and may stem from biblical times. Deut 12:21 thus adds greater force to this argument: *wĕzābaḥtā . . . kaʾăšer ṣiwwîtikā* 'you may slaughter . . . as I commanded you'. D therefore implies that there *is* a specific method of slaughtering sacrificial animals that is to be followed in profane slaughter, a method that, I suggest, may be implied by *šāḥaṭ* 'slit the throat'. (There is no proof, however, that the rabbinic technique of ritual slaughter, that is, a clean, transverse cut of both the esophagus and the trachea so that all the main blood vessels are severed [cf.

[22] N. H. Snaith, "*Zebaḥ and Šaḥaṭ*," *Vetus Testamentum* 25 (1975) 242-46.

[23] See Herdner, *Corpus des tablettes en cunéiformes alphabétiques*, texts 1 (col. 4, line 30), 4 (col. 6, line 40), 6 (col. 1, lines 18-28), 16 (col. 6, lines 17, 20), 17 (col. 2, line 29), and 22 (col. B, line 12).

[24] Cf. *b. Ḥul.* 27a and Ramban (Rabbi Moses ben Naḥman [= Naḥmanides]) on Deut 12:21, *Perushe ha-Torah* (ed. C. B. Chavel; Jerusalem: Mosad ha-Rav Ḳuḳ, 1959-60).

"*Sipre* to Deut" 12:22, *m. Ḥul.* 2:4], stems from biblical times.) The absence of *šaḥaṭ* in Deut 12:15, 21 and, indeed, in all of D is probably due to D's ignorance of its technical meaning as developed by P.

But what is the authorized slaughtering technique of the sanctuary? The Bible gives no answer, but the Talmud does, and with many details. All of these clearly demonstrate the perfection of a slaughtering technique whose purpose is to render the animal unconscious with a minimum of suffering. To be sure, these regulations are postbiblical, but they are only the refinements of the ethical impulse that generated the initial method developed by Israel's priests for the sanctuary.

For example, the law code of Joseph Karo (*Shulḥan ʿAruk*) gives meticulous details concerning the slaughtering knife.[25] It must be razor sharp and perfectly smooth with no dents or nicks, since these would tear the flesh and cause unnecessary pain. The knife must be examined before and after the slaughtering to make sure it is without blemish during the actual slaughtering. The three sides of the knife, that is, the sharp edge and its sides, must be examined (*b. Ḥul.* 17b).[26] If the slightest dent or nick is felt, the knife is invalidated. Of germane interest are the five cutting processes that invalidate the slaughter:

1. *Šĕhîyâ*, pausing or delaying. The knife must be drawn quickly across the neck of the animal, beast, or bird without a stop. The smallest delay or pause renders the slaughter defective and the animal not kosher.
2. *Dĕrāsâ*, pressing. The blade must be applied with a to-and-fro motion, not with a chopping or striking motion.
3. *Ḥălādâ*, burrowing. The blade must not be inserted under the skin and used with an upward thrust.
4. *Hagrāmâ*, cutting outside the specified zone, or deflecting.
5. *ʿĂqîrâ*, tearing out. The trachea and esophagus must be cut with the blade and not torn out or lacerated in any way.[27]

Could this concern for humaneness be the invention of the talmudic rabbis rather than their legacy from the past? Hardly so. The Rabbis themselves are ignorant of the humane rationale for their

[25] Joseph Karo, *Shulḥan ʿAruk* (see tractate *Yoreh Deʿah* 18:3, 10, 12 on the slaughtering knife).

[26] See also J. M. Epstein, *ʿAruk ha-Shulḥan* (Warsaw, 1894–98) on *Yoreh Deʿah* 18:12.

[27] The passages from *Shulḥan ʿAruk* on the five cutting processes are all from tractate *Yoreh Deʿah*: 23:2; 24:1; 24:7, 8; 24:12; and 24:15. See also I. Klein, *A Guide to Jewish Ritual Practice* (New York: Jewish Theological Seminary of America, 1979) 311.

method and resort only to Deut 12:21 as proof that the same technique was employed by the biblical priests. To be sure, they refined the technique and added safeguards. But in effect, they preserved and enhanced its original ethical motivation—that the death of the animal should be effected in such a way (by painless slaughter and the immediate drainage of the blood) that the slaughterer's sense of reverence for life will never be blunted.[28]

The Prohibited Animals

The literature on Leviticus 11 is vast and there are as many theories as theorists. The traditional view is that the list of prohibited animals is simply arbitrary: the unalterable and inscrutable will of God: "A man should not say 'I do not desire to eat the flesh of swine' . . . On the contrary, he should say 'I desire it but must abstain because my father in heaven has so ordered'."[29] This position will not be discussed since, as I shall show, there are definite and ascertainable reasons that lie behind the food taboos of Leviticus. Some other widely held theories can also be dismissed out of hand. For example, the cultic theory holds that forbidden animals either represent deities (i.e., totems) or were used in pagan worship.[30] This position, however, founders on its own premises: Canaanites sacrificed the same animals prescribed in Israel's cult and, consequently, they should have been prohibited by Scripture. A recent proposal theorizes that all the prohibited animals are life-threatening because either they are chthonic, inhabiting locations that are inimical to life, or they are predators and carcass eaters.[31] However, this theory cannot explain the exclusion of such domesticated, herbivorous animals as the camel, donkey, rabbit, or horse. Similar obvious objections springing from the biblical data can be mustered to refute many of the other proposals.[32]

There are, however, two theories that merit serious consideration. The first is the hygienic hypothesis: the forbidden animals are carriers of disease. The ancients discovered the harmful animals empirically and modern science has verified their findings: the pig is a bearer of trichinosis, the hare of tularemia, carrion eating birds harbor disease, and fish without fins and scales attract disease because they are mud burrowers. The hygienic hypothesis is an honored one. It counts

[28] See generally, Milgrom, "Profane Slaughter," 1–17.

[29] *Sipra* Kedoshim 11:22; cf. Aḥare Mot 13:10.

[30] Smith, *Lectures on the Religion of the Semites*, 269–310, 596–600.

[31] W. Kornfeld, "Reine und unreine Tiere im Alten Testament," *Kairos* 7 (1965) 134–47.

[32] Ibid., 134–36.

among its proponents Maimonides, Ramban (on 11:9), and Rashbam (on 11:3) and it is probably no accident that the former two were physicians. And more recently, W. F. Albright adopted this view in his last work.[33] Despite these proponents, there are weighty objections to this theory. For example, the camel, a prohibited animal, is a succulent delicacy for the Arabs to this day and there is no evidence that they suffer gastronomically. Also, if hygiene were the sole reason for the diet laws, why were they restricted to the animal kingdom? Why were poisonous plants not prohibited?

A different approach is taken by the symbolic theory. It avers that the behavior of animals corresponds to and informs the behavior of humans. The tabooed animals are those whose ways do not exemplify proper conduct. On the other hand, if they remind humans of virtue they are adjudged to be edible. Thus, the Letter of Aristeas, probably of the second century B.C.E., explains that cud-chewing is the sign of a permitted animal because it teaches the importance of meditation: people should have thoughts as well as food to chew on *Ep. Arist.* 153–54; cf. Philo, *On the Special Laws* 4:116–18). Nonetheless, this theory too is riddled by objections. It is highly subjective and capricious: animal behavior will mean whatever its beholder wants it to mean and no independent verification is possible.

The Anomaly View of Douglas Refined

Yet there is one modern offshoot of the symbolic theory that meets the canons of scientific method. It was advanced by the social anthropologist Mary Douglas.[34] Douglas adheres to the basic teachings of Emile Durkheim that the customs and rituals of any society are reflections of its values. So too a society's taxonomy of the animal world will mirror its value system. Douglas has applied this Durkheimian insight to Leviticus 11 by means of her theory of dirt. She defines dirt as matter out of place. Dirt, then, is a byproduct of the classification of nature found in each society: what it considers "order" is fine; whatever is "disorder" is dirt.

Douglas came to Leviticus 11 via the Lele tribe of Africa, which, she discovered to her surprise, has complex dietary regulations. What did it mean, she asked, that a primitive society could develop a sophisticated system of food taboos? Her conclusion is that it is

[33] Maimonides: *Moreh Něbukim* 3:48 (*The Guide to the Perplexed* [trans. S. Pines; Chicago: University of Chicago, 1963] 598); Ramban: *Perushe ha-Torah* (on Lev 11:3); Rashbam: *Perush ha-Torah* (on Lev 11:9); Albright: *Yahweh and the Gods of Canaan* (Garden City, NY: Doubleday, 1968; repr. Winona Lake, IN: Eisenbrauns, n.d.) 75–81.

[34] M. Douglas, *Purity and Danger* (London: Routledge and Kegan Paul, 1966).

fundamental to human nature to order and classify nature. When earliest people had to make their way through an unknown universe, they needed categories that would enable them to distinguish between what was beneficent and what was harmful. They had to know how to relate to any new phenomenon that confronted them. Therefore, criteria were created to discern whether the phenomenon was going to be helpful or prove a danger.

This taxonomic characteristic of the mind developed at the inception of humanity but it continues unabated in modern society, which also classifies, rejecting the disorderly—the "dirt." Nor are modern categories always rational or logical. For example, my wife brings several cups of tea with her as she does the household chores. Occasionally, I find a half-filled cup in the bathroom. Anything wrong hygienically? No, but I am invariably annoyed. Conversely, I recall bringing home a new pair of shoes and setting them on the kitchen table. A sweep of the hand tumbled them to the floor. "But," I protested, "they are new, never worn." "I don't care," she replied, "they don't belong in the kitchen." Indeed, the tea cups and shoes become dirty if, in Douglas's definition, they are matter out of place. This insight is the key to unlock the enigma of Leviticus 11.

First, the Durkheimian thesis that animal taxonomy is a mirror of human society is fully corroborated by the Bible, especially the Priestly source. Animals, like humans, possess a *nepeš* (Gen 9:9-10; Lev 11:10, 46; 24:18; Num 31:28). Hence, their blood must also be buried (Lev 17:13). Animals are responsible under the law: if they kill a human being they must die (Gen 9:5) and their meat may not be eaten nor may their carcasses be sold (Exod 21:28-32). Bestiality incurs the death penalty for the animal as well as for the human participant (Lev 20:15-16). Since animals were also a party to God's covenant (Gen 9:9-10) they must keep the Sabbath (Exod 20:10), and in the Messianic age they will renew their covenant with God (Hos 2:20) and they will be predators no more (Isa 11:7).

Douglas divides the animal world into three spheres. The classification is that of Genesis 1, corresponding to the three elements of creation: water, air, and earth. Each sphere has a peculiar mode of motion associated with it. For the skies, birds need two wings to fly and two legs to walk. On the land, animals have four legs and hoofs to walk on (actually split hoofs, Lev 11:3 and Deut 14:6, a crucial point overlooked by Douglas; see below). And in the seas, fish have fins and scales to swim with (in which case scales are superfluous—another point overlooked by Douglas). However, creatures that cross boundaries are anomalies. Insects that fly but have four or more legs (Lev 11:20) are an abomination, but if they have two legs to hop with

(Lev 11:21-22) they are edible. (Here Douglas confuses *šereṣ* and *remeś*, and mistakenly assumes that since frogs hop they are permitted as food. True, frogs do not defile, *m. Ṭohar.* 5:1—not being one of the eight named reptiles of Lev 11:29-30—but they may not be eaten!).[35] Birds that are carnivores (*m. Ḥul.* 3:6) are taboo because carrion contains blood (*Ep. Arist.* 146) and creepers (*remeś*) engage in an indeterminate form of locomotion. Creepers are neither fish, flesh, nor fowl; rather, they belong to the underworld—an abomination. Strikingly, Douglas reminds us, the serpent was cursed by the removal of its feet (Gen 3:14).

The parenthetical remarks, above, are a caveat to the reader of Douglas that her biblical comments, especially in her early writings, are replete with errors. A constellation of them appears in the compass of three pages of one essay,[36] where she not only cites a host of wrong or nonexistent verses but commits the following mistakes: (1) *Běhēmâ* (Lev 1:2) is a quadruped not a domestic animal (cf. Lev 11:2). (2) The sparrow may be permitted for the table but absolutely not for the altar. (3) Firstlings are eaten by their owners not by the priests, according to Deuteronomy. (4) Anomalous creatures may not be touched only when they are dead (*něbēlâ*). (5) Only bearers of impurity are banned from the Temple (Lev 12:3), not bearers of blemishes! (This last error vitiates Douglas's figure 7 and, hence, its analogy with figure 8.) (6) Priests not Levites "judge the cleanness and purify the uncleanness of Israelites." (7) Neither Levites nor priests, even unblemished ones, may enter the Holy of Holies; only the high priest may do so, under special safeguards (Leviticus 16). Besides, blemishes disqualify a priest from officiating at the altar but not from entering the sanctuary court or partaking of sacred food (Lev 21:17-23).

Furthermore, Douglas's theory of dirt as matter out of place has been trenchantly criticized by A. S. Meigs who correctly argues that though many phenomena are out of place only few are pollutants.[37] To illustrate, let me use the example I cited. Shoes on the table are polluting because they may carry feces, spit, etc., that litter the streets, but a dress laid on the table would not evoke revulsion. I objected to the cup of tea in the bathroom because I instinctively feared its contamination by bathroom odors. But had the cup been empty or had I found clothing hanging there, again, it would be matter out of place but I would not have reacted viscerally. The reason, Meigs suggests, is that things pollute only when they threaten to gain access

[35] Douglas, *Purity and Danger*, 56.

[36] Douglas, "Deciphering a Meal," *Daedalus* (1972) 73-75.

[37] Anna S. Meigs, "A Papuan Perspective on Pollution," *Man* 13 (1978) 304-18.

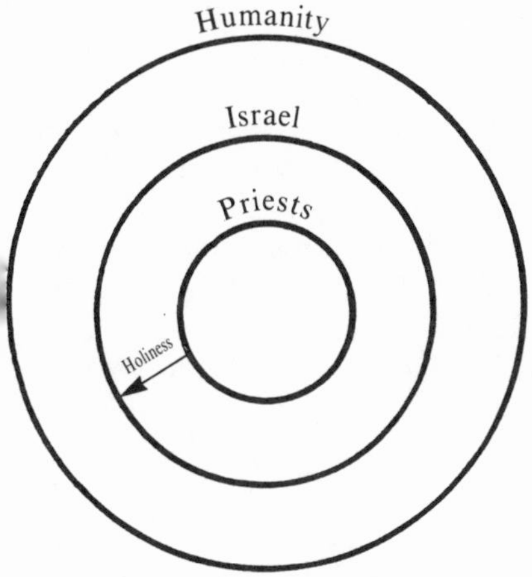

Diagram 1: Humans

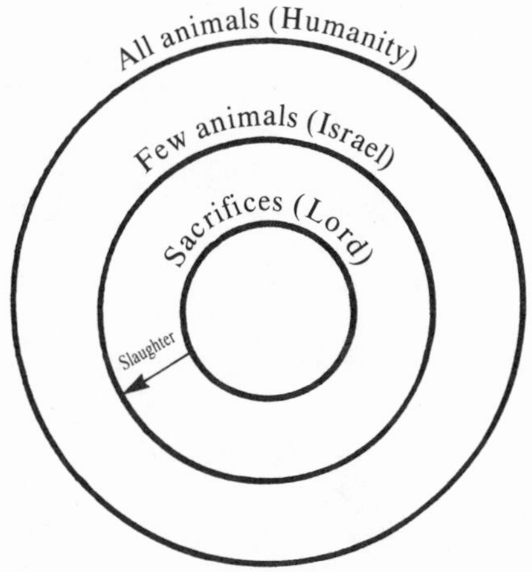

Diagram 2: Animals

to one's body: the dirt on the shoes may get into our food; the polluted tea may be ingested. In any event, Douglas's theory of dirt is proven helpful but inadequate; it throws light on the animal classification of Leviticus 11, but it does not explain it.

Far more useful, however, is Douglas's utilization of the Durkheimian hypothesis that the classification of animals reflects society's values. The correspondences between the human and animal worlds come into clearer view once it is noticed that each comprises three identical divisions that can be depicted as concentric circles, as seen by a comparison of Diagrams 1 and 2. According to P, the tripartite division of the human race corresponds with three of its covenants with God: all humanity (Gen 9:1-11, including the animals), Israel (that is, the patriarchs, Gen 12:1-3, Lev 26:42), and the priesthood (Num 25:12-13, Jer 33:17-22).[38] The three human divisions are matched by the three animal divisions: all animals are permitted to humans (except their blood, Gen 9:3-5), the edible few to Israel

[38] A word on the scriptural support for the priestly covenant is in order. Num 25:12-13 promises Phineas *bĕrît kĕhunnat ʿôlām* 'a covenant of priesthood for all time'—not the high priesthood (the prevalent interpretation) but the priesthood! Only one *Sitz im Leben* suggests itself: the banishment of Abiathar *and his entire family* from the Jerusalem Temple (1 Kgs 2:26-27; cf. 1 Sam 2:27-36), with the result that the Zadokites (the line of Phineas) became its sole officiants. To be sure, non-Zadokites continued to serve on the Temple staff but not as officiants (Ezek 40:46, 43:19, 44:15-16). Jeremiah, on the other hand, probably of the house of Ithamar, rejects the Zadokite monopoly and, hence, employs the deuteronomic term "levitical priests" (Jer 33:17-22).

(Leviticus 11), and of the edible, the domesticated and unblemished as sacrifices to the Lord (Lev 22:17-25).

The congruence of the two sets of concentric circles begs for cross-comparison. First, the innermost circles: priests-sacrifices. Both priests and sacrifices fit to serve the altar must be unblemished (Lev 21:17-21, 22:17-20). Moreover, it is no accident that two consecutive chapters of Leviticus (21-22) specify the imperfections that disqualify priests and animals for the altar—and by and large they prove identical! These are the priestly blemishes (Lev 21:18-20): *ᶜiwwēr* 'blind', *pissēaḥ* 'lame'; *ḥārum* 'split nose' or 'stunted limb',[39] *śārûaᶜ* 'overgrown limb', *šeber rāgel* 'broken leg', *šeber yād* 'broken arm', *gibbēn* 'hunchback', *daq* 'dwarf' (?), *tĕballul bĕᶜênô* 'a growth in his eye', *gārāb* 'sores', *yallepet* 'scabs', *mĕrôaḥ ʾāšek* 'crushed testes'. The disqualifying animal blemishes are (Lev 22:22-24): *ᶜawweret* 'blind', *šābûr* 'broken bones', *ḥārûṣ* 'maimed' or 'sty',[40] *yabbelet* 'wart' (?), *gārāb* 'sores', *yallepet* 'scabs', *śārûaᶜ* 'overgrown limb', *qālûṭ* 'stunted limb', *māᶜûk wĕkātût wĕnātûq wĕkārût* 'bruised, crushed, torn, cut [testes]'. Each list contains twelve items, probably to achieve parity in the totals. Certain additions were made to the originally shorter animal list, that is, the minutiae of injuries to the testes. Yet despite this artificial extension, the correspondences are manifestly clear. There are five identical items: blind, overgrown limb, broken bones (comprising two items in the priestly list), sores, and scabs. The remaining items are difficult to match because they are mainly unidentifiable. But the following are possibly semantic equivalents: *ḥārum* 'stunted limb' (?) or *pissēaḥ* 'lame'‖ *qālûṭ* 'stunted limb', *tĕballul bĕᶜênô* 'a growth in his eye'‖ *ḥārûṣ* 'sty' (?), *mĕrôaḥ ʾāšek* 'crushed testes'‖ *māᶜûk wĕkātût wĕnātûq wĕkārût* 'bruised, crushed, torn, cut [testes]'. The difference in terminology may be ascribed to the special circumstances of each species. Obviously, the exposed testes of the animal would be subject to a greater variety of injuries than those of man. A hunchback would only be considered a defect in the upright human but not in the animal. The very artificiality of the lists underscores my main point: human and animal defects are

[39] 'Split nose' according to *Sipra* Emor par. 3:7; 'stunted limb' according to Abraham Ibn Ezra (*The Commentary of Abraham Ibn Ezra on the Pentateuch* [trans. J. F. Schachter; repr. Hoboken, NJ: KTAV, 1986]).

[40] 'Maimed' according to Abraham Ibn Ezra (*Commentary of Abraham Ibn Ezra on the Pentateuch*); 'sty' according to Targum Pseudo-Jonathan and Rashi (*Pentateuch with Targum Onkelos, Haphtaroth, and Rashi's Commentary* (trans. M. Rosenbaum and A. M. Silbermann; London: Shapiro, Valentine, 1929-34; repr. New York: Hebrew Pub. Co., n.d.), 3:101).

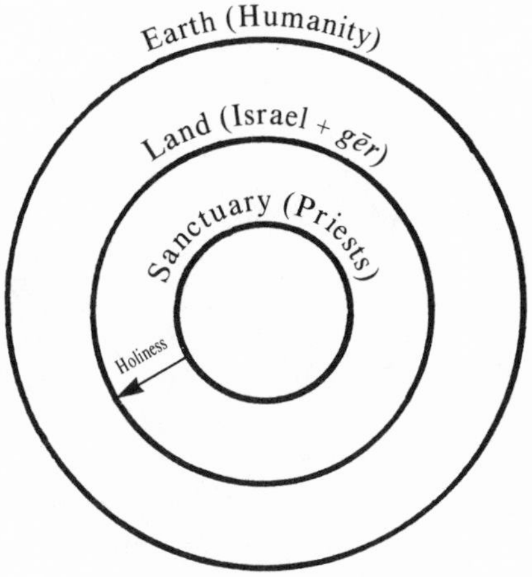

Diagram 3: Space

equated. *Mutatis mutandis*, the same blemishes that invalidate officiating priests also invalidate animal sacrifices.

Another correspondence offers greater precision: the firstborn males of both humans and animals are the Lord's property (Exod 13:2). That is why the Levites who replace the firstborn also belong to God (Num 3:11–13) and why the remaining firstborn (Num 3:44–51), and those of subsequent generations, must be redeemed from the sanctuary (Num 18:15–16).

The innermost circles, however, are not fixed and static. For both human and beast there is a centrifugal movement to the outer circles. According to the Holiness Code, although priests are inherently holy, all of Israel is enjoined to achieve holiness (e.g., Lev 19:2; see also 11:44). Israel achieves its status as a holy people not through the priestly regimen, but by scrupulously observing God's commandments, both morally and through ritual. Signs of this mobility are reflected in the animal sphere. Sacrificial animals are slaughtered by their lay owners, not by priests. Thus, it is hardly surprising that when lay people are permitted to slaughter animals at home (Deut 12:15, 21), they are enjoined to employ the same slaughtering technique practiced in the sanctuary. This dynamic quality of the innermost circle is evident in yet another realm: space. It also comprises the same tripartite divisions: humanity, Israel, and priests, as seen in Diagram 3.

The Priestly material contains an old tradition that the entire camp of Israel in the wilderness could not tolerate severe impurity

(Num 5:1-4; cf. 31:19). This tradition is echoed in D, which states explicitly that the camp must remain holy (Deut 23:10-15). It is H, however, that extends this view logically and consistently to the future residence of Israel—the Promised Land. Hence, impurities produced by Israel by violating the Lord's prohibitions—both moral and ritual—pollute not only the sanctuary but the entire land. Since God dwells in the land as well as in the sanctuary (e.g., Lev 25:23, 26:11; cf. Josh 22:19; Hos 9:3-4), the land cannot abide pollution (e.g., Lev 18:25-30; cf. Num 35:33-34). It is, therefore, no accident that H requires both the Israelite and the resident alien (*gēr*), that is, all those who live on the land, to keep the land holy by guarding against impurity and following the prescribed purificatory procedures (e.g., Num 15:27-29, 19:10b-13, in which *gēr* is an addition by H) so that the Lord will continue to reside in it and bless the land and its inhabitants with fertility and security (Lev 26:3-11).

Comparison of the two middle circles of the human and animal realms yields the following unambiguous relationship: as God has restricted his choice of the nations to Israel so must Israel restrict its choice of edible animals to the few sanctioned by God. The bond between the choice of Israel and the dietary restrictions is intimated in the deuteronomic code when it heads its list of prohibited animals with a notice concerning Israel's election: "For you are a holy [*qādōš*] people to the Lord; the Lord your God chose you from among all the peoples on earth to be his treasured people" (Deut 14:2). Furthermore, Israel's designation as "a holy [*qādōš*] people" concludes the deuteronomic diet list, thereby framing it as an inclusion (Deut 14:21).

However, what is merely implicit in D is forcefully explicit in H:

> I am the Lord your God who set you apart [*hibdaltî*] from other peoples. So you shall set apart [*wĕhibdaltem*] the pure quadrupeds from the impure, the impure birds from the pure . . . which I have set apart [*hibdaltî*] for you to treat as impure. You shall be holy [*qĕdōšîm*] to me, for I the Lord am holy [*qādōš*] and I have set you apart [*wāʾabdil*] from other peoples to be mine (Lev 20:24b-26).

What could be clearer! Israel's attainment of holiness is dependent on setting itself apart from the nations and the prohibited animal foods. The dietary system is thus a reflection and reinforcement of Israel's election.

This motif of separation in Leviticus 20 is further extended and underscored by its context (note that *hibdîl* occurs four times in these two and a half verses). It is the peroration to the pericope on forbidden sexual unions (Lev 20:7-21) that are attributed to the Canaanites, Israel's predecessors in the land, and to her Egyptian neighbor (Lev 18:3). The implied nexus between sex and food, on the one hand, and apostasy, on the other, is expressly stated elsewhere in scripture:

> You must not make a covenant with the inhabitants of the land, for they will lust after their gods and sacrifice to their gods and invite you, and you will eat of their sacrifices. And when you take wives from among their daughters for your sons, their daughters will lust after their gods and will cause your sons to lust after their gods (Exod 34:15-16).

This message was very well understood in Hellenistic times: "An additional signification [of the diet laws] is that we are *set apart* from all men, for the majority of remaining persons defile themselves by their promiscuous unions, working great unrighteousness, and whole countries and cities pride themselves on these vices. Not only do they have intercourse with males, but they even defile mothers and daughters. But we have kept apart from these things" (*Ep. Arist.* 151-52; cf. also *Jub.* 22:16). Thus, sex and food, bed and board, are intimately related. In *Marjorie Morningstar,* the Jewish heroine finally succumbs to her seducer when she tastes pork for the first time. It is no accident that the author is a learned and observant Jew who understands that a breach in the dietary system may endanger one's entire religious structure.[41]

It is also no accident that one of the first acts of Christianity was to abolish the dietary laws (but not the blood prohibition [cf. Acts 15:20]—significantly, because it is incumbent on all humanity). Historians have claimed that the purpose was to ease the process of converting the Gentiles. This explanation is, at best, a partial truth. Abolishing the dietary laws, according to Scripture, also abolishes the distinction between Gentile and Jew, and that is exactly what the founders of Christianity intended to accomplish—to end once and for all the notion that God had covenanted himself with a certain people who would keep itself apart from all the other nations. Further, it is these distinguishing criteria, the dietary laws (and circumcision), that were done away with. Christianity's intuition was correct: Israel's restrictive diet is a daily reminder to be apart from the nations (cf. Acts 10:9-16, 27-28; 11:4-12).

Which Came First: Taboo or Criteria?

To recapitulate at this juncture, the insights of the Durkheimian school, especially as exemplified in the work of Mary Douglas, have

[41] H. Wouk, *Marjorie Morningstar* (Garden City, NY: Doubleday, 1955).

led to the disclosure of the intricate connections between Israel's animal taxonomy and aspects of its value system, specifically, the requirement to separate itself from the nations by refraining from their meat and women and to separate itself to God by following his commandments along the road to holiness. In particular, Douglas has uncovered the basic postulate that underlies the criteria for permitted animals: each species must exhibit the locomotion that fits its medium. However, this postulate does not completely satisfy. Regarding the quadrupeds, Douglas writes: "Any creature which has two legs and two hands and which goes on all fours like a quadruped is unclean. . . . This feature of this list is lost in the New Revised Standard Translation which uses the word 'paws' instead of hands."[42] Douglas is wrong. The word *kap* does not mean 'hand', but its hollow, its palm. The foot, too, possesses a *kap*, that it, its sole (e.g., Gen 8:9, Deut 2:5, 28:56, Josh 3:13, 2 Kgs 19:24, Isa 1:6, 60:14). The New English Bible translation of *hōlēk ᶜal-kappāyw* as 'go on flat paws' is precise. Thus, it is erroneous to say that animals with paws are excluded because they walk on hands. Moreover, even assuming hypothetically that Douglas were correct—that the only natural way for a quadruped to walk would be on hoofed feet—why then would the hoofs have to be split? A ruminant with a solid hoof should also be permitted! Thus a new rationale for the criteria of quadrupeds must be sought. But in order to discover it, a prior question needs to be answered: which came first, the criteria or their application? Were the animals first tabooed and criteria later devised to justify the taboos? Or, the reverse: were criteria drawn up first, which then were used in classifying the animals? This takes me back to the contest between the hygienist and the anthropologist. Who is correct, Albright or Douglas? If Albright is right, criteria were devised to exclude certain animals because they were reputed disease carriers. If Douglas is right, then certain animals were excluded as a consequence of not meeting the criteria.

I submit that the four anomalous quadrupeds (Lev 11:4-8)—camel, rock badger, hare, and pig—can serve as a decisive test. Let me first set the terms. If the hygienic theory holds, then these animals were tabooed because they were injurious to health. Only much later did the categories arise to justify their exclusion: chewing the cud and having split hoofs. The fact that there were just four anomalous quadrupeds bearing one of the two qualifying criteria can only mean that ancient Israel had a negative culinary experience only with those

[42] Douglas, *Purity and Danger*, 55-56.

four anomalies. However, the chances are that Israel's environment possessed other such anomalies but they were not entered into the list because, being wild, they were either unattainable or indigestible. But if in accordance with Douglas the criteria came first, then it would have fallen upon Israelite zoologists to scour their environment to find all the anomalous creatures possessing one of the two qualifying criteria.

This then is the test: If the four anomalies were listed because they were unfit for the table (the hygienist's theory), then Israel's zoological ambience probably numbers other quadrupeds with the same anomaly. But if they are listed because, as the text states, they do not fit the criteria then the list is complete: there are no other such quadrupeds in Israel's environs. Thus, if it turns out that even one more animal known to Israel is akin to the specified four bearing one criterion, then it is a fatal blow to Douglas, for she cannot explain why the animal was omitted.

The results are in. There are six animals that bear this anomaly: the biblical four and the llama and the hippopotamus. The llama is indeed a ruminant whose hoofs are not cloven. However, it (and its relatives, the alpaca, the guanaco, etc.) are indigenous to South America and clearly were unknown to ancient Israel. The hippopotamus, on the other hand, cloven-hoofed, herbivorous, but non-ruminant, was indeed known from Egypt (and perhaps alluded to in Job 40:15ff.). However, the cleft in its hoofs is so slight that it was missed by the ancients and even omitted by Aristotle in his *History of Animals.* Thus the verdict is clear and decisive: the criteria came first and only afterwards four anomalies were found.

The Bible itself corroborates my findings. It is significant that the Deuteronomist is not satisfied merely to cite the criteria for quadrupeds; he takes pains to enumerate all the permitted animals (Deut 14:4–5): three domestic and seven wild, mostly unidentifiable. This list is then followed by the criteria *wĕkol-bĕhēmâ mapreset parsâ,* which must be rendered, 'and any other quadruped that has hoofs' (Deut 14:6). Therefore, this passage means these ten quadrupeds are permitted plus others that may fit these criteria but as yet have not been found. Thus, at least for the Deuteronomist, the criteria were before him, which impelled him to sponsor an investigation of all the fauna of the land, scouring even wild, inaccessible places in order to find all the quadrupeds that matched the criteria. That the Deuteronomist has done so is supported by the conclusion that the deuteronomic list of prohibited animals (Deut 14:4–21) is based on Leviticus 11. What, then, is true for Deuteronomy 14 holds for

Leviticus 11. The latter must be accepted at face value. The camel, rock badger, hare, and pig were excluded only for the reason stated by the text: they do not fit the criteria.

One final question remains regarding the quadruped criteria. If their intent was to confine Israel's meat diet to only the three domesticated species—cattle, sheep, and goats—why the need for criteria to begin with? Could not the priestly legislators have simply stated, *zōʾt habbĕhēmâ ʾăšer tōʾkēlû šôr śēh kĕśābîm wĕśēh ʿizzîm*: 'These are the quadrupeds that you may eat: the ox, the sheep, and the goat' (cf. Deut 14:4)?

Reference to Diagrams 1 and 2 provides the answer. These three domesticated quadrupeds are eligible for the altar; they belong to the innermost circle: the domain of God. However, Israel occupies the middle circle. It is under fewer constraints than the altar and, hence, is entitled to additional animals for its diet. These are provided by wild game, only some of which were known. Israel's privilege to hunt game is acknowledged by Leviticus (17:13-14) and confirmed by Deuteronomy, which explicitly adds seven wild quadrupeds—most of which are still unidentifiable (Deut 14:5). Thus, criteria were needed for the extension of Israel's approved diet of animals of the hunt.

The Prohibition and QDŠ

The chronological priority of the criteria implies a concomitant conclusion: they were not drawn up arbitrarily—to serve as generalizations for the already existent taboos, as erroneously maintained by the hygienists—but were formulated with a conscious purpose in mind. What was this purpose? What was the intention behind the formulation of such bizarre criteria: cud-chewing and split-hoofed ungulates?

Since outside analogies do not seem to help, I return to the biblical text. A rationale, it turns out, is not at all absent from Leviticus 11. It is found in one word, rather, in one concept—"holiness." To the casual reader of the Bible, it comes as a great surprise that this exalted concept of holiness is given as the reason in all four sources where the prohibited foods are enumerated (Exod 22:30, Lev 11:44-45, 20:22-26, Deut 14:4-21). The sound of repeated words in these verses is impressive: "make yourselves holy . . . that you be holy . . . for I am holy" (Lev 11:44). Of the six Hebrew words here, three contain the root *qdš* 'holy'; and twice more it occurs in the succeeding verse. Relatively few individual statutes of the Bible are coupled with the demand for holiness, and none of these demand with the same staccato emphasis and repetition as do the food prohibitions.

Thus, the Bible takes greater pains to offer a rationale for these laws than for any other commandment. Yet because the rationale, holiness, has been so variously interpreted, its exact meaning is difficult to determine. Since both the blood prohibition and the ritual slaughtering, as I have demonstrated, are invested with the same ethical principle, I surmise that the food prohibitions, too, as a part of the same dietary system, would be similarly rooted in ethics. Surmises and guesswork, however, are not sufficient; an investigation of the biblical concept of holiness, however brief, must be essayed. Thus, the biblical dietary laws that limit Israel's diet to only a few of the animals permitted to others constitute an experiential mnemonic. Israel was confronted daily at the dinner table with the imperative that it must be separate from the nations.

Again, I resort to the heathen environment of ancient Israel to understand both their common cultural legacy as well as the unique distinctiveness of Israel's religion. An examination of Semitic polytheism (and indeed of any primitive religion) shows that the realm of the gods was never wholly separate from and transcendent to the world of people. Natural objects, such as specific trees, rivers, or stones, was invested with supernal force. This earthbound power was independent of the gods and can be an unpredictable danger to the latter as well as to humans. "Holy" is thus aptly defined, in any context, as "that which is unapproachable except through divinely imposed restrictions," or "that which is withdrawn from common use."

In opposition to this widespread animism I note a marked distinction in the Bible, where there is no animism and where holiness is not innate. The source of holiness is assigned to God alone. Holiness is the extension of his nature; it is the agency of his will. If certain things are termed holy—such as the land (Canaan), person (priest), place (sanctuary), or time (holy day)—they are so by virtue of divine dispensation. Moreover, this designation is always subject to recall. Thus, the Bible exorcises the demonic from nature; it makes all supernatural force coextensive with God. Just as in the idolatrous religions, the sancta of the Bible can cause death to the unwary and the impure who approach them without regard for the regulations that govern their usage. Indeed, the sense of withdrawal and separation that inheres in *qādôš* is verified by the Bible. Within the pentateuchal codes, instances of where Israel is enjoined to holiness are found outside of the dietary laws in just two other connections: the priesthood and idolatry. In relation to priesthood, the root *qdš* occurs seven times in three verses (Lev 21:6–8). As shown above, the priesthood, Israel, and humanity, respectively, form three concentric circles of decreasing holiness. The biblical ideal, however, is that all Israel shall be "a royalty of priests and a holy [*qādōš*] nation" (Exod 19:6). If Israel is to move to a higher level of holiness, then, it must bind itself to a more rigid code of behavior. Just as the priest lives by severer standards than his fellow Israelite, so the Israelite is expected to follow stricter standards than citizens of other nations. Here again, holiness implies separation. As for idolatry, since the quintessence of immorality, not to speak of impurity, is imputed to the cult of idolators, it is not startling to find the third grouping of *qādôš*—words in the context of a stern admonition to Israel to separate itself from idolatry (Lev 20:6-7, Deut 7:4-6, 14:1-2).

Since for Israel the holy is the extension of God's will, it means more than that which is "unapproachable" and "withdrawn." Holiness means not only "separation from" but "separation to." It is a positive concept, an inspiration and a goal associated with God's nature and his desire for humans: "You shall be holy, for I am holy." That which humans are not—nor can ever fully be—but that which they are commanded to emulate and approximate, is what the Bible calls *qādôš* 'holy'. Holiness means *imitatio dei*—the life of godliness.

What is God, that people may imitate him? The Godhead is the ground of ethics for Israel, but the ethical is bound up with an inseparable from the ritual, and the pentateuchal codes make no distinction between them. It is surely significant, however, that wherever Israel is commanded to be holy, ethical precepts are also involved. Thus, Israel is consecrated to attain the ideal of a "holy people" when it is given the Decalogue (Exod 19:6). Again, the demand for holiness, as phrased in the text of the dietary laws, is found at the beginning of Leviticus 19; here ritual commandments are inextricably interwoven with ethical commands such as "Love your neighbor as yourself" (v 18). The book of Psalms, moreover, which contains the prayers of the Temple service, speaks of striving after God's holiness exclusively in ethical terms: "Who shall stand in his holy place? He that hath clean hands and a pure heart" (Ps 24:3-4). And as for the prophets, their main burden is to teach the supremacy of ethics as the will of God. For Isaiah, "the holy God becomes sanctified in justice" (Isa 5:16); and when he hears the heavenly adoration of God as "*qādôš, qādôš, qādôš*" (Isa 6:3), he is smitten with the awareness that he and his people are morally inadequate.

Thus, the emulation of God's holiness demands following the ethics associated with his nature. Since the demand for holiness occurs with greater frequency and emphasis in the food prohibitions than in any other commandment, I conclude that they are Torah's personal recommendation as the best way of achieving this higher ethical life.

But what could be the specific ethical teaching of the diet laws implied by the concept of holiness? The answer surfaces in realizing that this list of prohibited animals (Leviticus 11, Deuteronomy 14) forms a unified and coherent dietary system with the blood prohibition and the prescribed slaughtering technique whose clear, unambiguous purpose is to inculcate reverence for life. Once this conclusion is granted, the enigma of the criteria for quadrupeds is resolved. Their purpose is to limit the Israelite's access to the animal kingdom. The reconstruction of the process by which these criteria were formulated might go as follows: a deliberate attempt was made to limit the edible species to those quadrupeds that were bred for their flesh: cattle, sheep, and goats. Split hoofs sufficed to do the job. When, however, this criterion was found to admit the pig—an abominated creature—the criterion of chewing the cud was added.

What of the other animal categories: fish, birds, flying insects, land swarmers? Criteria for edible animals are specified only for flying insects (Lev 11:21-22) and fish (Lev 11:9). Douglas suggests that "the case of the locusts is interesting and consistent. The test of whether it is a clean and therefore edible kind is how it moves on the earth. If it crawls it is unclean. If it hops it is clean."[43] However, locusts are distinguished not from creepers (vv 29-42) but from "winged creatures that walk on all fours" (v 20). Since locusts do not exclusively hop but also "walk on all fours" their saltatory ability does not comprise their total means of locomotion. Here it would seem an exception was made because allowing locusts as food was a hallowed practice stemming back to the wilderness period when, as pastoralists, they lived off their herds and feasted on locusts, a delicacy among the Bedouin of the Sinai and Arabian peninsulas to this very day. On the other hand, the criteria for fish (fins and scales) fit my conclusion neatly. As demonstrated, ancient Israel was unacquainted with marine life for the main reason that there were few varieties of fish in its waters. In effect, these criteria effectively eliminated, with a single stroke, shell fish (mollusks do abound plentifully on the Mediterranean shores) and fish without scales, thereby reducing the eligible species to a handful. Thus, access to marine life was severely restricted just as it was with quadrupeds.

In sum, if a count is taken of the permitted animals, excluding game available only to hunters, the inventory reads as follows: cattle, sheep, goats, several kinds of fish, pigeons, turtledoves, several other birds, and locusts. The net result is self-evident: the Israelite's choice of animal food was severely circumscribed. To be sure, certain animals may have been eschewed (e.g., the pig) or sanctioned (e.g., the

[43] Douglas, *Purity and Danger*, 56.

locust) on independent grounds. But aside from these few, the animal kingdom is governed by the criteria set forth in Leviticus 11. This conclusion provides the needed piece to complete the reconstruction of the rationale of the dietary system. Its purpose is to teach the Israelite reverence for life by (1) reducing the choice of flesh to a few animals, (2) limiting the slaughter of even those few permitted animals to the most humane way, and (3) prohibiting the ingestion of blood and mandating its disposal upon the altar as acknowledgment that bringing death to living things is a concession of God's grace and not a prerogative of human whim.[44]

Two related questions arise at this point. First, since limits are placed on the animal species (variety), but not on their numbers (quantity), how can the criteria of Leviticus 11 keep the Israelites from wholesale butchery? The answer is rooted in the economic realities of biblical times. The average Israelite could not afford to deplete his livestock. Eating meat was therefore reserved for special occasions, as evidenced by the three stipulations of the *šĕlāmîm*: (1) thanksgiving, (2) spontaneous joy, and (3) fulfillment of a vow. Animal slaughter was thus an infrequent event in the Israelite household. Such a rationale fails, however, to explain the practices of the Sanctuary, which was not subject to economic constraints. The public cult (Numbers 28-29) and private offerings, both voluntary (Leviticus 1-3) and mandatory (Leviticus 4-5), assured it of an undiminishable torrent of animal blood. How then could God have circumscribed Israel's access to the animal world but permitted, indeed mandated, interminable holocausts of animals for himself? The answer to this second question resides in the postulate of priestly legislation: the supernal realm runs by different rules than the earthly realm. For example, the deity punishes collectively—the child, the family, even the tribe and nation for the sin of the individual—but only the guilty party may be punished by humans (cf. Exod 21:31, Deut 24:16, Lev 20:4-5 [contrast vv 2-3]). Moreover, in this instance, logic reinforces the postulate: what God has created he has a right to recall. A person is a criminal if she or he appropriates an animal's lifeblood; it is divine property. But when one returns it to its source either via the ground or, for Israel, via the altar, no crime is committed.

One final problem remains. Why a ritual? Could not the Bible have acted in a more ideological way by defining its concept of reverence for life and then leave each individual free to live by it without the encumbering restrictions? The answer implied by the

[44] This rationale is further elucidated in Milgrom, "The Biblical Diet Laws" (see n. 16 above).

priestly legislation is that ideals are just abstractions to which humans may pay lip service yet rarely actualize. All religions urge reverence for life, few adherents live by it. Albert Schweitzer, who made this principle the core of his life and word, wrote, "The universal effort of Reverence for Life shows the sympathy with animals, which is often represented as sentimentality, to be a duty which no thinking man can escape."[45]

But Schweitzer's influence on humanity is a result of his life commitments, not his preachments. In fact, the latter can be conveniently subverted by tendentious reasoning. Thus as noted by Joseph Wood Krutch, Schweitzer's rule—that life may be destroyed only in the service of some higher life—can justify the decimation of plumed birds in the year 1914 to gratify the millinery fancies of the ladies of London.[46] The Bible, to the contrary, takes no chances with the variables of human nature and insists on being rudely pragmatic. It allows the slaughtering of animals only for human food. A ritual, then? Yes, if it is to discipline. So frequent? Yes, if it is to sanctify the home. So tedious? Persistent rain makes holes in rocks.

The priestly legislators were so sensitive to the ethical primacy of the dietary system that they enjoined one of its tenets, the blood prohibition on all humankind. As noted at the beginning of this paper, the Ten Commandments were originally intended for Israel alone. Only one biblical statute, the blood prohibition, is enjoined upon all humanity. In the biblical view the Decalogue would fail were it not rooted in a regularly observed ritual, central to the home and table, and impinging on both senses and intellect, thus conditioning the reflexes into patterns of ethical behavior.

[45] A. Schweitzer, cited in the note below; cf. also *Reverence for Life* (New York: Pilgrim, 1979).

[46] J. W. Krutch, "The Sportsman or the Predator," *Saturday Review of Literature* (17 August 1957) 8.

David P. Wright

Observations on the Ethical Foundations of the Biblical Dietary Laws: A Response to Jacob Milgrom

WRIGHT RAISES QUESTIONS CONCERNING two points developed by Milgrom: (1) the categories of animals that were forbidden to Israel in Leviticus 11 were determined on the basis of formal criteria, not on the basis of an abhorrence of these animals that preceded the development of the criteria, and (2) the purpose behind the restriction of Israel's choice of edible animals was to inculcate in Israel a reverence for life. Concerning the first point, Wright suggests that the determination of the categories of nonedible animals should be seen as arising out of an interplay between the formal criteria and preexisting attitudes or customs. The second point he regards as lacking conclusive evidence. He concurs, however, with Milgrom's judgment that dietary and ritual regulations relating to blood entailed a reverence toward life.

David P. Wright is Assistant Professor of Hebrew and Near Eastern Languages at Brigham Young University. He received his B.A. from the University of Utah and his Ph.D. from the University of California at Berkeley. He is the author of *The Disposal of Impurity: Elimination Rites in the Bible and in Hittite and Mesopotamian Literature.*

My response to Jacob Milgrom's paper on biblical dietary laws will address two issues in his presentation that I would argue or think about differently. The first is his argument that the criteria determining abominable animals came first, before the animals were treated as abominable. The second is his argument that a main informing principle of the food prohibitions is a desire to teach Israel a reverence for life by restricting its choice of edible animals. These questions or objections are not intended to call for an abandonment of his major thesis that the blood, slaughter, and food laws teach the Israelite a reverence for animal life. Rather, it is hoped that they will lead us to a better understanding of the meaning of these regulations in ancient Israel.

Milgrom argues that the criteria for determining which animals were considered abominable came before the animals were considered abominable; this is, I think, incisive and important for understanding the nature of the food prohibitions in the Priestly writings. To recapitulate, he argued that the rules concerning the four anomalous quadrupeds in Lev 11:4-8 showed that the criteria preceded this particular listing of irregularities. The reason for this was that this listing contains the only four animals that have only one of the two required traits (i.e., chewing the cud or having split hoof)—the only animals with which the ancient Israelites could have been acquainted. That this list is exhaustive (in the context of ancient Israel) indicates that the criteria preceded and a search for animals not fitting the criteria followed. These are the only four found not fully fitting the dual requirement. This argument is made more convincing by viewing the opposite possibility, that these particular four were abominated and the criteria were made up from their particular characteristics. If this were the case, then one would expect to find any number of other animals that were anomalous in similar ways. But since this is not the case, it seems that the criteria came first and the list was made after applying the criteria to faunal reality.

I believe that this observation is valid. But I question what seems to be a rejection of the idea that certain culinary customs in operation before the criteria were established did not have an influence on the formulation of the criteria. In all fairness to Milgrom, I note that toward the end of his paper he does suggest that the pig was already considered an abominable creature; hence the criterion of chewing the cud was enumerated to exclude that particular animal. Moreover, he says that locusts, though seemingly anomalous (according to Mary Douglas's principle), were allowed because eating such "was a hallowed practice stemming back to the wilderness period when, as pastoralists, they lived off their herds and feasted on locusts. . . ." But in general, his conclusion is that "the criteria came first and only afterwards four anomalies were found."

I feel that this conclusion needs to be modified. That is to say, I think that a compromise must be made between the view that the food prohibitions (in particular, the four anomalous animals of Lev 11:4–8) represent what was already considered taboo in Israel and the view that the criteria were more abstractly developed without custom in mind. It seems that the then current culinary custom and tradition provided a certain impetus to the development of criteria. These criteria were then used in a search of animal life and further animals were specifically prohibited (on the basis of the criteria, and not on the basis of preexistent tradition).

When I say that preexistent custom had something to do with the determination of the criteria, I do not intend to say that these preexistent taboos were based on hygiene. *Some* aversions probably had something to do with the fact that certain meats were injurious, but it certainly does not explain all aversions. Preexistent taboos probably had multiple reasons. Perhaps certain animals were rejected and considered unclean since it was just not the custom to eat them (here I note many people's aversion to eating things like brains, kidney, horse meat, etc.). Perhaps some were rejected because they were dirty and smelly or connected with dirty things like carcasses (birds of prey, pigs, etc.) Maybe some were rejected since they were economically detrimental. (Here I am thinking about Marvin Harris's argument that pigs competed with humans for the same food, while bovines, sheep, and goats did not.)[1] Some animals might have been rejected on nationalistic grounds ("we do not eat this animal since those other people do"). What I emphasize here is that in the stage before the criteria were determined there were probably several animals that were considered abominable, and they were considered such for several diverse reasons.

I would argue further that the criteria were not solely developed out of preexistent abominations, but were developed out of an interplay between these abominations and those animals that were customarily eaten. For example, it seems rather clear that bovines, sheep, and goats were allowed in the precriteria stage (otherwise I doubt they would have been allowed). On the other hand, the pig (which does not chew the cud) and perhaps one or two other animals (which did

[1] *Cows, Pigs, Wars, and Witches* (New York: Random, 1978) 28–50, esp. 34–37.

not have split hoofs) probably were abominated in the precriteria stage. The features of these various animals were analyzed and criteria were developed.

It is at this point that Milgrom's argument that the criteria came first is relevant. The criteria deduced from tradition were then practically applied. Other animals besides the pig and perhaps some other animals were found to be quasi-anomalous, having only one of the two criteria. These newly-found, marginal cases were particularly specified in Leviticus 11 to leave no room for question.

Milgrom's argument about the development and application of the criteria helps to resolve the problem of Douglas's purely synchronic theory of the food laws, which does not diachronically explain where the Priestly legislators' perception of regularity or order came from. Milgrom's argument of the precedence of the criteria, with my added emphasis on the influence of preexisting tradition, has the virtue of explaining, in a general way, the diachronic development of the prohibition.

Though, in my view, the criteria had a foundation in traditional aversions, they reoriented these traditional taboos and consequently included new animals among those considered abominations. The change from the traditional approach of designating particular animals as impure, to using criteria served to abstract and unify the perceptions about abominable animals. This abstraction, unification, or systematization of determination of such animals was accompanied by a new unified rationale for avoiding such animals (as Milgrom says): so that Israel might be a holy people. In the stage before the criteria were determined, various animals were avoided for all sorts of reasons: economic competition, hygiene, simple aversions, nationalism, or tradition among other people, but the Priestly legislator ignored, perhaps entirely rejected, these traditional reasons and gave to the prohibitions the unified rationale of maintaining holiness. Thus, in the formulation of criteria and the formulation of the rationale of holiness I see a significant abstraction of—even a revolution against—traditional customs.

I quite agree with Milgrom that there appears to be an ethical basis to the prohibition against consuming blood and requiring that it be brought to the altar. The prescriptions teach that one must be careful not to misuse the life essence of animals, that is, their blood. There appears also to be an ethical basis to slaughtering; it is done in a way to prevent undue suffering of the animal. But I note that the perception that this manner of slaughtering is chosen because it is the most humane is nowhere explicitly attested to in the Bible. (I also note that the best way to collect blood for use in the various blood application rituals of the priests would be to cut the main blood vessels leading to and from the head and let it drain into a bowl, thus corroborating Milgrom's argument that the verb *šḥṭ* indicates slaughter by slitting the throat.)

But if the ethical intent in the blood prohibitions and slaughtering prescriptions is relatively clear, it is not as clear in the food laws of Leviticus 11 (or Deuteronomy 14). First of all, besides the lack of testimony regarding this idea in the text (as Milgrom recognizes) there seems to be a symbolic contradiction between the wording and orientation of the food laws and any ethical basis they may have. The laws talk about inedible animals (in particular, their carcasses) in very negative terms. Besides calling them "unclean," some species are called *šeqeṣ* 'abomination' (Lev 11:10, 11, 12, 13, 20, 23, 41). The Israelite is to hold the animals' carcasses in abomination (*šiqqēṣ*; Lev 11:11, 13). In Deuteronomy, the word *tôᶜēbâ* 'abomination' is used to describe these animals (14:3). The negative character of unclean animals would be further impressed upon the Israelite in the rules that such animals are not acceptable as sacrifices to God. This negative characterization of nonpermitted animals seems to me not to support a desire to inculcate a reverence for animal life. A different motivating ideology lies at the base of the food prohibitions in Leviticus 11: a desire that the people remain holy. The ethical intent, therefore, seems only peripheral or incidental.

A second difficulty I see is that the meat prohibitions do limit the choice (and Milgrom is careful to use this particular word) of animal food, but do not limit the amount of meat consumed or the number of animals killed. The natural reaction of not being allowed to eat a large number of different animals is not to decrease one's intake of meat, but to breed a larger number of permitted animals to make up the difference. This sort of thing is already seen in the flood story. Noah is commanded to take with him seven pairs of each species of clean animals, but only one pair of each species of impure animals (Gen 7:2). Whether this passage be attributed to the Yahwist or to Priestly influence, the same idea appears: a greater number of pure animals are kept alive since they can provide food. (I note that if there is a law calculated to limit the consumption of meat it would be the requirement to bring animals to the sanctuary for slaughter.)

In view of the foregoing reasons, it seems difficult to understand the ethical notion of reverence for life as the main informing notion of the Priestly food laws; rather, the main reason for their formulation is to provide a means of making and maintaining Israel as a holy people, setting them apart from other nations. The notion of reverence for life through a limitation of the choice of the number of animal species available for human consumption seems to be a peripheral intent that gains its significance only in connection with the prohibition of the consumption of blood and the procedure of slaughtering.

In closing, let me say that despite this questioning of certain of Milgrom's premises and conclusions (which is always proper to any scholarly endeavor), he has provided a well thought out, penetrating study of the biblical food regulations that will do much to advance our understanding of not only biblical cultic prescriptions, but of biblical ethics as well.

Frederick M. Denny

Ethical Dimensions of Islamic Ritual Law

In contrast to Jacob Milgrom's essay on "Ethics and Ritual," which focuses primarily upon dietary laws and laws of animal slaughter and upon the ethic of reverence for life that undergirds these laws, the following essay treats under the heading of ritual the whole range of duties connected with worship as set forth in Islam. Since outsiders to the Islamic tradition have often regarded Islamic worship as legalistic, consisting mainly of "rote repetition," Denny's primary concern is to show that the various components of Islamic worship have an ethical dimension that makes them meaningful and fulfilling for the ordinary Muslim. As he makes clear, "ethics" in the Islamic context can have reference to at least two different things: it can refer to the cultivation of a moral and upright character (for which the usual word in Arabic is *akhlāq*), or it can refer to the scale of five categories of human acts: obligatory, meritorious, indifferent, reprehensible, and forbidden. It is this latter concern that generally predominates in discussions of ritual acts, although these acts are frequently discussed in terms of the former (for example, by al-Ghazali). The ethics of the five categories is, from the human standpoint, deontic rather than teleological: Islam does not attempt to provide a full rational justification for its ethics but bases that ethics upon divine revelation. Nonetheless, it is not indifferent to the inner state of mind that lies behind human acts, as the concern with "intention" in the acts of worship shows.

Frederick M. Denny is Professor of Islam and the History of Religions in the Department of Religious Studies at the University of

Colorado, Boulder. He received his Ph.D. in Islamic studies from the University of Chicago. His published works deal with the Qurʾān, Islam, and the history of religions. In addition, he has done extensive field work on Islamic ritual in Egypt and Indonesia.

++++++

Ethics has never been a dominant intellectual discipline in the Islamic religious sciences in the sense of an autonomous field independent of the study of theology and jurisprudence. This is especially true of Sunni Islam after a traditional pattern of orthodox and orthoprax principles was established in it.[1] Theoretical ethics have been pursued brilliantly by Muslim thinkers—Miskawaih is a case in point—but their work, however sophisticated and subtle, came to have secondary status to the *sharīʿa*. The relative lack of prominence of ethics, in the formal sense, does not in any way indicate lack of concern for practical moral and ethical convictions and guidelines. It simply testifies to the overwhelming prestige and authority of the religious law, whose essence and core details are believed to be the product of divine revelation. It is not humankind's place, so a strict Sunni theological viewpoint would suggest, to speculate on the good or to seek it in the world of concepts and forms; rather, humans are commanded to obey the ground and source of all that is good: Allah, the exalted, who does not will what is good, if good be conceived as an independent entity,[2] but whose willing is the only criterion for what is right: "His command, when he desires a thing, is to say to it 'Be,' and it is" (e.g., Qurʾān 36:82).[3]

Islamic devotion and everyday life are permeated with a concern not only for knowing the right way in all things, but especially for

[1] See George Makdisi, "Ethics in Islamic Traditionalist Doctrine," *Ethics in Islam* (ed. Richard G. Hovannisian; Malibu, CA: Undena, 1985) 47–63. Makdisi demonstrates that traditionalist thinkers did concern themselves with ethical theory, but that in the final analysis obedience to revelation predominated.

[2] I refer here, of course to Muʿtazilite "rationalist" ethics, which were developed in a quite thorough and sophisticated manner, to be generally rejected by Sunni orthodoxy of the dominant Ashʿarite variety. For a brilliant survey of Muʿtazilite ethics, see George Hourani, *Islamic Rationalism: The Ethics of ʿAbd al-Jabbār* (New York: Oxford University, 1971). For an accessible brief treatment, see the same author's "Divine Justice and Human Reason in Muʿtazilite Ethical Theology," *Ethics in Islam,* 73–83.

[3] See Frederick M. Denny, "Ethics and the Qurʾān: Community and World View," *Ethics in Islam,* 103–21, for a discussion of basic ethical assumptions in the Qurʾān, which are closely linked with ideas of community.

following it. Moreover, authority to prescribe conduct is an essential criterion of Islamic moral thought. That authority is never, in the first place, derived from reason. It is based either on the revelation of God in the Qurʾān or on a trusted teaching of the Prophet Muḥammad, derived either from word or example as contained in his Sunna ("custom"). Reason does have an important place, however, in the use of analogy and in the forging of consensus among qualified scholars of the law.[4] The imposing edifice of Islamic legal precedents, systematizations, and procedures is very much a product of human reason, even to the ordering and application of the sources, which themselves are believed to be supernatural in origin.[5]

Islamic ritual law is not exhaustive of religious law, if by "ritual" one intends the more restricted field of *ʿibādāt* 'acts of worship'. The *sharīʿa* is all-encompassing and "religious" in the sense that it derives from divine and not human legislation; but it is not wholly concerned with ritual matters, at least directly, although certain aspects of such topics as marriage, divorce, contracts, wills, the waging of war, and the punishment of apostasy display attitudes and prescribe procedures that are rooted in ritual orientations and values.[6]

The Vocabulary of Islamic Ethics

It is usually the case that Islamic legal discussions begin with acts of worship (*ʿibādāt*). The threshold of worship is purification (*ṭahāra*), and therefore this concept is the necessary first order of business. The Prophet Muḥammad is credited with two correlative pronouncements pertaining to worship and purification; the first is the key to Paradise and the second the key to worship, or the "key" to the "key."[7] Purification, according to this simple formula, is thus a necessary, though not a sufficient, condition for salvation. Worship entails purification, without which it is invalid.

Worship itself may be understood in two different, though interrelated, ways. The first is in the restricted, formal sense of specific attitudes and actions collected under the main headings of *ʿibādāt*,

[4] I am referring, here to the 'foundations of jurisprudence', *uṣūl al-fiqh*.

[5] See Fazlur Rahman's masterful appreciation of this development in his article, "Law and Ethics in Islam," *Ethics in Islam*, 3-15.

[6] For example, Islamic law does not require any religious ritual of marriage, but when there is such—and there almost always is, no matter how simple—then it must be performed correctly within a fairly well delimited range of acceptable forms.

[7] For the precise texts, see M. Muhammad Ali, *A Manual of Hadith* (Lahore: Ahmadiyya Anjuman, 1951) 41-42.

and often referred to as the five "pillars" of Islam: (1) *shahāda,* or 'witness' to the Divine Unity and the Apostlehood of Muḥammad, (2) the *ṣalāt* prayer service, (3) giving of legal alms (*zakāt*), (4) fasting (*ṣawm*) during daylight hours in the holy month of Ramaḍān (and at other times), and (5) pilgrimage (*ḥajj*) to Mecca during the prescribed season. As was observed, at the beginning of all discussions of worship (*ʿibādāt*) is a treatment of purification, which entails a substantial, highly ramified subject matter. The Pillars constitute a sort of minimal requirement for the religious life, so that it would be a basic error simply to equate Islam with conduct prescribed by them. Beyond the pillars are many more topics covered by the *sharīʿa,* all of which are definitively influenced by *ʿibādāt.* Every believing Muslim is an *ʿabd,* a 'slave' of God, whether engaged in formal acts of worship or simply going about the business of making a living, eating, sleeping, playing, raising a family, and so forth.

The proper Muslim life is continuously informed and enlivened by the spirit of worship, especially at the level of ethics and values. To conclude from superficial, outside observation that Muslims divide their lives with cartesian sharpness between periods of (more or less) rote ritual, on the one hand, and mundane or profane tasks and pastimes, on the other, is to miss the essence of Islam, which is *tawḥìd,* or 'unification' of all life in the service of the one God.

Muslims have always acknowledged a complementary duality between the outer (*ẓāhir*) and the inner (*bāṭin*) dimensions of things. Sometimes this distinction has been symbolized with reference to the *sharīʿa,* the holy law, being the outer guide for human belief and conduct, while the *ṭarīqa,* the mystical 'path,' is regarded as the interior discipline of gnosis and union. Another duality is created by the distinction between "ethics" and "etiquette." The two words derive from the same Greek root, *ēthikē,* but have different specific meanings. Ethics is the science of morals and values, delving deeply into the very nature of reality in its metaphysical forms; whereas etiquette is the conventional code of proper behavior in any human community. For example, good people may lack etiquette while evil folk sometimes exhibit exquisite etiquette.

A similar distinction exists in Arabic-Islamic terminology as well as in social usage. But the root words are different and more precise. *Adab* mean 'refinement, good manners, morals, decorum, decency, humaneness' or related concepts.[8] To be *muʾaddab* is to be 'well-mannered, civil, urbane'. The root indicates that its meanings arise

[8] *Adab* also means 'literature', especially *belles lettres,* in Arabic. An excellent collection of articles on *adab* and related matters is Barbara Daly Metcalf, ed., *Moral*

from the sense that *culture* produces proper behavior. Thus a person who lives in an Arab-Islamic context must exhibit *adab* if he or she wishes to be regarded as cultured and polite. But there is another word that derives from a different root, *kh-l-q*. This root occurs frequently in the Qurʾān, where it most often refers to God's creation of things and dispositions (e.g., 3:191, 6:102, 82:7). The word *khulq/khuluq* means 'natural disposition, innate peculiarity, or original nature', in the singular, and 'ethics [personal], morality, or character' in the plural (*akhlāq*). True morality, then, is not a matter of *adab* but of *akhlāq*, not of *culture* (which is a *human* product), but of *nature* (which is *God's* creation). *Fiṭra,* humankind's God-given, sound, original nature is a closely related Qurʾānic idea (e.g., 30:30).

So, although ethics as an intellectual discipline is not very prominent in Islamic scholarship, the key word for ethical behavior is deeply rooted in the Qurʾānic view of reality. It is significant, for this discussion at least, that the root for *adab* does not occur in the Qurʾān. This absence should not be misinterpreted as an early Islamic aversion to good breeding or cultural refinement, nor should it be treated anachronistically. *Adab* did not arise as a regulative principle until the Arabic language and an international Islamic civilization had spread from the Nile to the Oxus under the Caliphates of the Umayyads and ʿAbbasids. Of course, the *adab* concept has often been prominent in civilizations, under other names, and informed by other absolutes.[9]

To return to Islamic ritual law and practices, it is instructive to note that neither *adab* nor *akhlāq* is dominant in the vocabulary of the legal manuals. Instead, one finds terms such as *sharṭ* (pl. *shurūṭ*) 'condition, proviso, stipulation'; *ḥukm* (pl. *aḥkām*) 'judgment, jurisdiction, opinion, rule, ordinance, command, principle, or precept', depending on context; and *aṣl* (pl *uṣūl*) 'principle, fundamental, axiom', and in the phrase *uṣūl al-fiqh* 'foundations of jurisprudence'. Nor do the simple correlative terms "good" and "bad" adequately characterize most legal discussions;[10] rather, a graded hierarchy of five values or principles evaluates, prescribes, and regulates behavior.

Conduct and Authority: The Place of Adab in South Asian Islam (Berkeley: University of California, 1984), especially the articles in part 1, "Classical *Adab*," by Peter Brown, Ira Lapidus, and Gerhard Böwering.

[9] See Peter Brown's comparison of *adab* and the Greek *paideia* in his article, "Late Antiquity and Islam: Parallels and Contrasts," *Moral Conduct and Authority*, 23–37.

[10] But the 'determination of good and evil' (*al-taḥsīn waʾl-taqbīḥ*) was an important task of traditional legal discussions. See Makdisi, "Ethics in Islamic Traditionalist Doctrine," 50.

It is important to note that the Qurʾān itself frequently speaks of a duality between the good and the bad, or perhaps more precisely, between that which is right and that which is wrong. The Qurʾānic stereotyped phrase *taʾmurūna bi ʾl-maʿrūfi wa tanhawna ʿan al-munkari* is translated variously as, for example, "enjoining good and forbidding evil" (Muhammad Zafrulla Khan) or "bidding to honour, and forbidding dishonour" (A. J. Arberry).[11] This phrase is very often encountered in discussions of Islam's mission on earth, particularly inasmuch as the Muslims believe that they are called to strive in God's way in bringing about a just order under his *sharīʿa*. But it should not be imagined that the notions of good or honor, on the one hand, and of evil or dishonor, on the other, can be discerned primarily by means of philosophical and, therefore, human theories of value and ethics. The good and the bad of which the Qurʾānic phrase speaks is known only in the context of obedience to God in a covenant relationship that requires continuing, regularized worship, whose Arabic term (*ʿibāda*) includes, like the Hebrew *ʿăbōdāh* and the Latin Christian *opus Dei*, a strong sense of "service," even "work."

An Islamic Scale of Values

All possible acts that a person can perform or neglect to perform (or refuse to perform) are classified under five values or principles (*al-aḥkām l-khamsa*) of action that have developed in Islamic jurisprudence. Islamic ritual is fully governed by the *aḥkām*, just as are all other human acts.[12] Before proceeding to list them, it will be helpful to observe that the middle principle, *mubāḥ*, means 'indifferent'—neither obligatory nor recommended, on the one side, nor reprehended nor forbidden, on the other. Most human acts are in this neutral category and are thus a matter of indifference to the *sharīʿa*, save for the fact that Islamic legal scholars have worked out the classification in the first place. Sometimes recognition of *mubāḥ* status requires considerable intellectual exertion because there can be a sharp difference of opinion between schools.

The highest and ritually most significant of the five principles is known in technical Arabic as *wājib* or *farḍ*, both of which mean

[11] E.g. 3:104; A. J. Arberry, *The Koran Interpreted* (New York: Macmillan, 1955); Muhammad Zafrulla Khan, *The Qurʾan: Arabic Text with English Translation* (London: Curzon, 1981). For an illuminating discussion of *maʿrūf* and *munkar*, see Hourani, "Ethical Presuppositions of the Qurʾān," *The Muslim World* (January 1980) 1-28, especially 14f.

[12] For background on the complex and protracted development of the principles, see Kemal Faruki, "Legal Implications for Today of *Al-Aḥkām Al-Khamsa* (The Five Values)," *Ethics in Islam*, 65-72.

'obligatory', and include the stipulations that performance will be rewarded and nonperformance will be punished by God. Furthermore, this principle contains subdivisions between acts (like the five daily prayers) that are incumbent on each qualified Muslim (*farḍ ʿayn*), and other acts (like attending funeral prayers) that are required only of a representative group of Muslims (*farḍ kifāya*).

One step removed from *wājib* is the *sunna* principle, also called *mandūb* and *mustaḥabb*. This category includes acts that are 'meritorious' and whose specific performances are rewarded, but whose nonperformances are not punished. Such meritorious acts would include supererogatory (*nāfila*, pl. *nawāfil*) prayers during or at a time different from the required *ṣalāt*. There are several subcategories of 'meritorious acts', each with its additional subcategories of legal meaning and application, because this principle contains the greatest number of ritually relevant possibilities, whose correct discernment and interpretation require a considerable knowledge of the Qurʾān and the Sunna of the Prophet.

On the other side of *mubāḥ*, the 'indifference' principle, is *makrūh*, or 'reprehensible'. Actions classified under *makrūh* are disapproved, sometimes strongly, although they are not punishable. There has often been considerable divergence of legal opinion on specific acts within the *makrūh* category, and the wide range of viewpoints on individual acts testifies to the flexibility of the Islamic legal system, particularly when viewed in different cultural regions. For example, some Indonesian Muslims consider listening to gamelan music as *makrūh*, if not forbidden altogether, while others regard gamelan as an honorable element in the Javanese cultural tradition. The fact that gamelan music is closely identified with shadow puppetry (*wayang kulit*), whose stories and characters are based largely on Hindu epic, does not make it inimical to Islam, as long as no religious significance is attached to it. In at least one instance, the gamelan orchestra has been adapted to Islamic festival forms, in the process showing a kind of benevolent condescension of the *sharīʿa* in the direction of folk customs, while at the same time coopting them for Islamic purposes.

The fifth *ḥukm*, or principle, is known as *ḥarām*, which means 'forbidden'. There are different grades of forbidden acts, but all are punishable. Another technical term for this principles is *maḥẓūr*, which also means 'forbidden' in an unequivocal sense. *Ḥarām*, like its mate *ḥaram* ('sanctuary'), has a strong religious meaning, whose specific sense depends on context and relationship to other things. For example, *al-masjid al-ḥarām* means 'the sacred mosque', and refers to the Kaʿba in Mecca. Instead of 'sacred', *ḥarām* here could as well be translated 'forbidden' or 'taboo'. In this case something is "set apart and forbidden," as Durkheim expressed it, not because it is repugnant or prohibited, like sin or foulness, but because it is *too holy* for profane use.[13] Perhaps in no language is the ambivalence of the sacred more apparent than in the Arabic root ḥ-r-m, which also gives us *ḥarīm* ('harem', meaning the inviolable females of a Muslim family), *muḥrim* (ritually pure state of a pilgrim), and *maḥram* (forbidden to marry, because of consanguinity). The use of *ḥarām* as name of the fifth principle forcibly reminds one that what has been forbidden entails ultimate answerability to God, that to trespass is not only to commit a crime but, also, to sin.

This presentation of the *al-aḥkām al-khamsa* has been very cursory. I have not attempted to place them within the context of their specifically legal significance. My purpose has been to illustrate the ethical dimension of Islamic law, as it attempts to recognize and account for gradations in a fairly broad spectrum of human acts and their consequences. In some ways, the most interesting of the principles is the central *mubāḥ* category. The other four categories act as a sort of compass or gyroscope for it, helping the devout Muslim to plot his or her course through daily life. Most of the acts that a human may perform are indifferent in the face of the *sharīʿa*, but their very indifference is a matter of permissibility. This is so in spite of the fact that there is another technical term that means 'permissible' (*jāʾiz*), which is itself still another category of acts. Something that is *jāʾiz* is *declared* so by a competent legal expert, and so it is in a distinct class from that which is merely indifferent, from the *juridical* standpoint. Most acts are *mubāḥ*, some may be *jāʾiz*; all the rest are covered in some way by the other categories and subcategories.

There really is nothing toward which the Islamic system is truly indifferent within the possible range of human actions, even though the majority are not subject to juridical authority or attention, being *mubāḥ*. It is important to ascertain just how a Muslim should proceed in life, apart from the specified rules concerning his or her relationship with God (*ʿibādāt*), or with fellow humans (*muʿāmalāt*), both of which are fraught with ethical implications and imperatives.

Teleology Versus Deontology

Ethical theories since classical times have clustered around two poles: deontology and teleology. The first takes its name from the Greek word for duty (*deonton*), whereas the second derives from the Greek *telos*, 'goal' or 'end'. Deontological ethics require absolute obedience

[13] Emile Durkheim, *The Elementary Forms of the Religious Life*, (trans. Joseph Ward Swain; New York: Free Press, 1965) 62.

to duty, whether commanded by God or discerned, as in the kantian perspective, in an abstract manner. Teleological ethics reckon morality in terms of the end to be realized and leave the details of any calculating of good and evil results to the rational abilities of humans. Teleological ethical systems always assume that the natural is inherently good, and so ethics becomes a matter of humankind's realizing its own true character and living in accordance with it. The important question is not so much whether God exists as whether *whatever* exists finally *matters*.

Now it would appear that Islamic ethics must be grounded in duty because of the belief in the sovereign and inscrutable will of God and the desire to obey his commands as known in the *sharīᶜa*.[14] Refinement of morals along the lines of etiquette and mere propriety, as in the Islamic civilizational tradition of *adab*, does not result in a profound ethic. But what of *akhlāq*, which I have observed refers to humankind's innate character as created by God? It would seem that *akhlāq* is in fact teleological and not deontological. That is, the aim of human life is to attain a saving realization of what one's inherent nature is as a creature called into fellowship with God—a type of gnosis.

There is a certain hazard in relying on the kinds of formal distinctions that the terms deontology and teleology entail. The danger inheres largely in radically separating the two streams of ethical theory, when in fact they subsist in mutual interrelation and polar tension in the real world. That is, to insist that something as nuanced as human motives and actions could be determined purely by duty or ends is to overemphasize what is chiefly an analytical distinction while ignoring human behavior. Without meaning to be flippant, I posit that, in the case of Islamic ethics, God may be a teleologist and humans deontologists. All that humans can know of God is what he has commanded in his revelation and granted as "signs", in his creation. His will is the measure of all good and right, without regard to whether he acts according to an independently grounded standard of goodness or justice as the Muᶜtazila believed.

To suggest that Islamic ethics are deontological from the standpoint of humans is simply to acknowledge the dominant place of duty and obedience, without independent speculation about or questioning of the religious system. One searches almost in vain in the literature of ritual regulations for what might be called "functional" reasons for performing the *ṣalāt*, fasting during Ramaḍān, or the

[14] Hourani has used the phrase "theistic subjectivism" for this position in his illuminating article, "Ethics in Medieval Islam: A Conspectus," *Essays on Islamic Philosophy and Science* (ed. G. Hourani; Albany: State University of New York, 1975) 128-35.

going on a pilgrimage (*ḥajj*). The reasons have to do with obedience to God's command or conformity with Muḥammad's example, without much explicit regard for such functional considerations as community enhancement (*zakāt*), hygiene (*ṭahāra*), Islamic unity (*ḥajj*), health (fasting), and the moral strengthening engendered by regular periods of daily worship (*ṣalāt*). The only pillar that is explicitly altruistic is almsgiving, but even here there is a strong prudential element. That is, property on which the *zakāt* has been calculated and the proper percentage given is thenceforth purified (purification being a key meaning of the term *zakāt*) for the legal and wholesome uses and enjoyment of the owner. Moreover, the Qurʾān declares that the givers of alms (actually *ṣadaqa*, but this term is nearly synonomous with *zakāt* in the Qurʾān) have made, as it were, a "goodly loan" unto Allah, who will multiply it and pay a generous reward (Qurʾān 57:18).

For the greater part, even *zakāt*, the most self-consciously utility-oriented of the pillars, is also centered in obedience to God and the cultivation of piety. It is possible, of course, to generate varied and highly suggestive interpretations of the acts of worship in the direction of their ethical implications as well as their inner spiritual meanings. Al-Ghazālī did precisely that, for example, in the first part of his "Revivification of the Sciences of Religion."[15] It would be difficult to say more on the subject than he did with respect to ethical implications and imperatives at the practical level. But al-Ghazālī's selection of materials and his own deeply insightful and sensitive commentary were products of his peculiar genius, which combined great rational and devotional skills in a brilliant, sustained focus on Islam as a complete way of life. The prestige and influence that al-Ghazālī's synthesis of the elements of the religious life as total commitment have had over the centuries is powerful testimony to the ethical motivations of countless Muslims who have been guided by it. Nevertheless, the actual legal discussions and the authoritative sources that underlie them do not normally focus on ethical issues, at least formally. Rather, obedience to God's commands is central, particularly in the matters which are *farḍ wājib*, that is, 'obligatory'. *Practical* ethics and law are, of course, inseparable in Islam.

Acts and Intentions

The ritual laws of Islam are not a theory of ethics in themselves, although it would be possible to generate one from them within the

[15] *Iḥyāʾ ʿulūm al-dīn*. See Nabih Faris, *The Book of Knowledge, Being a Translation with Notes of the Kitāb al-ʿIlm of al-Ghazzālī's Iḥyāʾ ʿUlūm al-Dīn* (Lahore: Sh. Muhammad Ashraf, 1962). Many other Muslim writers have also written commentaries on the benefits of ritual, both in the spiritual and pragmatic sense.

broader context of the *sharīʿa* as a whole. The best attempt in this direction so far is al-Ghazālī's great synthesis. At the core of Islamic law are the five principles described above, but even more fundamental to the goodness, or in the ritual context the *efficacy* of an act, is 'right intention', known by the Arabic technical term *nīya*.

All Muslims agree that *nīya* is essential before performing any *ṣalāt*, that greatest of Islamic ritual acts that, by its frequent repetition and intensity of focus, serves as both compass and rudder of the Ummah.[16] Without *nīya* before the performance of worship, the act, however technically correct otherwise, is invalid (*bāṭil*). It is noteworthy that *nīya*, whenever and in whatever context it is uttered, must immediately precede the act. If it does not, its status is reduced to mere 'decision' (*ʿazm*), which would be no more than what precedes ritual *nīya*. *Nīya* is believed to emanate from the worshiper's innermost being. It safeguards the sincerity (*ikhlāṣ*) of the ritual performance. I think that there is a close connection here between the notion of *akhlāq*—especially as characterized earlier in this paper—and *nīya*. Only by a sort of descent into the self's core before resurfacing with correct intention in the presence of one's creator may the Muslim truly commune with God. There is thus an ethical relationship between worshiper and Lord. Because of the intrinsic value of this relationship, it must be protected by means of ritual purification (*ṭahāra*) and other disciplined procedures, such as correct orientation (*qibla*) and proper covering of the body (*sitr*), among other things. The *nīya* must be kept in mind throughout the ritual performance. Like *kawwānā*, its close functional parallel in Jewish worship, *nīya* ensures spiritual spontaneity as well as integrity in worship. *Nīya* is itself a ritual act, of course, and as such it is defined and explicated in the *fiqh* books.

'Works are in the intentions' (*Innamā ʾl-aʿmāl bi ʾl-nīyāt*) is a frequently cited *ḥadīth*. This saying is encountered in many contexts—ritual, legal, and others—and serves as a universal ethical principle among Muslims. In the case of ritual, there is a kind of dialectic between *nīya* and the performance of the various acts of worship, whether obligatory or recommended, reprehended or forbidden. Individual and personal moral responsibility are required for *nīya* and without it the act would be devoid of ethical meaning.

It appears that ritual acts are at the heart of Islamic ethics, and in fact are their source and ground to the extent that they function as a means of drawing near to God in a predictable pattern. This supremely valuable relationship must, then, be hedged about with the

[16] There is difference of opinion about whether *nīya* is required before other ritual acts.

protection and minute regulation of law. *Nīya* is the basic moral act involved in ritual. The *nīya* ensures the validity of the specific ritual to be performed, and the performance itself reinforces the integrity of both the individual and her or his "moral community," to adapt Durkheim's phrase.[17]

Conclusion

Christian thinkers at least since the Apostle Paul have denounced legalism in relations between humankind and God. The history of Christian liturgy, however, displays much concern for regulation and decorum, although there has never been a universally uniform cultus since the primitive church. Judaism is another matter, although even in its carefully regulated rituals there has been more latitude and variety than has been known in Islamic ritual, which itself is remarkably uniform worldwide.

When *nīya* and the core meaning of *akhlāq* are considered, along with the flexible "five principles," Islamic ritual may be understood to be anything but legalistic in its authentic form. Many western critics of Islam who have sometimes decried what they have perceived to be rote repetition in Islamic worship have known little about the inner dimensions of Muslim piety, whose patterns and habits in and outside the mosque are informed and energized by religion as a complete way of life. The legal elements are strong and determinative, not because they are the possession of a legalistic people, but because they safeguard the spiritual path of a serious people. As the West comes into ever closer relations with Muslims, we need to be sensitively aware of the intimate relationship between ritual, legal, and ethical norms in the Islamic scheme of things. This relationship derives from the common Semitic ethical monotheism that Jews, Christians, and Muslims share, and that at its most authentic always bases itself on God as sole source of value.

[17] Durkheim, *Elementary Forms of the Religious Life*, 62.

Lois A. Giffen

Another Perspective on Ethics in Islamic Law and Ritual: A Response to Frederick Denny

THE "OTHER PERSPECTIVE" ADOPTED in this essay is one that takes into account the broader historical framework within which the ethical dimensions of Islamic ritual law were developed. Giffen regards Denny's contribution as basically sound, but somewhat one-sided. By focusing on mainstream Islam, it loses sight of the diversity of the Islamic community through time. Not only does it give inadequate attention to philosophical ethics in Islam, which though outside the mainstream was richly developed, but it does not take account of the interplay *within* the mainstream between rationalist and nonrationalist approaches to ethics. In placing Islamic ethics in the nonrationalist camp, Denny has, in Giffen's view, left out an important part of the total picture. To correct this lacuna, she provides a brief survey of the development of Islamic ethical thought during the most formative centuries. At the close of her essay, Giffen also points out, by way of added information, that Islam provides an ethical basis for another part of its ritual law not dealt with by Denny, namely its dietary laws and laws of animal slaughter. This final note is reminiscent of Jacob Milgrom's essay.

Lois A. Giffen is Associate Professor of Arabic Literature and Islamic Studies at the University of Utah. She is the author of *The Theory of Profane Love among the Arabs: The Development of the Genre* and various articles in scholarly journals and other published volumes. She received her Ph.D. from Columbia University in Arabic and Islamic Studies.

++++++
++++++

Frederick Denny's analysis of an underlying ethics of ritual law is a profoundly reflective statement. Partly as a consequence of his approach, however, he does not do justice to the role of ethics as a subject matter in Islam. He pushes it into a corner, as it were, to give himself room to present the interpretation—valid for many Muslims, certainly—that says the holy law, or *sharīᶜa,* is all that the Muslim needs to know or to do about ethics. But the Islamic community is not monolithic, and vast numbers of equally devout and sincere scholars and believers have felt or still feel that this is not the sole answer. I see it as important to offer alternate interpretations of several key points he has made, as well as to offer a further point on ethics in Islamic ritual law, the law as it relates to the slaughter of animals.

There is truth in Denny's statement that ethics, as an independent, intellectual discipline, does not exist in the Islamic *religious* sciences. However, in the classical Islamic organization of the intellectual disciplines, a second group, the *rational* sciences, includes philosophy. Muslim scholars who continued the intellectual tradition of the Greek and post-classical philosophers dealt with ethics as one of the branches of practical philosophy.[1]

This brings me to Denny's assessment that ethics as an intellectual discipline is even rarely found in the corpus of philosophical literature produced by Muslims. I suppose that "rarely" needs definition. Constantine Zurayk asserts that practically every Muslim philosopher dealt with ethics, since the science of ethics formed part of the accepted Aristotelian schema of the branches of philosophy.[2] A substantial number of Muslim philosophers wrote treatises or commentaries on ethics.[3] A partial roll of authors includes the most

[1] That philosophy was regarded as one of the rational sciences (as opposed to the religious sciences) does not mean that philosophical ethics were strictly secular and untouched by Islam. To the contrary, the so-called rational sciences were constantly being studied in the light of Islamic teachings and efforts were made to harmonize the two.

[2] Aḥmad ibn Muḥammad Miskawayh, *The Refinement of Character* (Tahdhīb al-Akhlāq) (tran. Constantine K. Zurayk; Beirut: American University in Beirut, 1968) xvi.

[3] Any count of even the extant Muslim works on ethics would have to await the completion of Fuat Sezgin's *Geschichte des arabischen Schrifttums* (Leiden: Brill,

illustrious philosophers of Islam: al-Kindī, "the philosopher of the Arabs" (d. 870), al-Rāzī [Rhazes] (d. 925), al-Farābī [Alfarabius] (d. 950), al-Amīrī (d. 994), Ibn Sīnā [Avicenna] (d. 1037), Miskawayh (d. 1040)—whose *Refinement of Character* is the most influential single work, Ibn Rushd [Averroes] (d. 1198), and Naṣīr al-Dīn al-Ṭūsī (d. 1198). Ibn Ḥazm of al-Andalus (d. 1064), theologian, jurist, poet, and historian, also wrote a notable treatise on ethics.[4] Al-Ghazālī (d. 1111), who in the First Quarter of his *Revivification of the Religious Sciences* provided an inner ethics of ritual acts, as Denny has noted, also wrote on philosophical ethics in the Third Quarter of the same work. Book Two of the Third Quarter is largely based on Miskawayh's *Refinement of Character* together with insights from Ṣūfī ethics as taught by Muḥāsibī (d. 857). I count this as one of the major Muslim syntheses on ethics.

The ethical tradition in Islam had many roots other than philosophical ethics, however, and it found many different forms of literary expression.[5] More than four hundred years passed after the coming of Islam before Islamic ethics had assimilated and integrated the several different strands of ethical tradition that contributed to it. During this formative period, the various concepts of morality that found written or oral expression frequently existed side by side.

The customs, virtues, and ideals of the pre-Islamic Arabian tribes provided the first guide to ethics. Their tribal traditions and ideals of conduct (*sunna*) did not die out with their acceptance of Islam, though the preaching of Muḥammad and the message of the Qurʾān brought new ethical emphases and correctives. The Prophet's commands were sanctioned by the fear of God and the Last Judgment. A detailed semantic analysis of the language of the Qurʾān by Toshihiko Izutsu has shown on the other hand a certain continuity between the Qurʾānic outlook and the old Arab world view, particularly in the sphere of ethical qualities.[6] More precisely, the Qurʾān adopted and

---

1967–), covering the period to A.H. 430/A.D.1038–39, as well as a similar series to cover the later centuries. However, an admittedly cursory glance at the index of Carl Brockelmann, *Geschichte der arabischen Litteratur,* supplement vol. 3 (Leiden: Brill, 1942), now out of date, shows something over a score of title entries beginning with "*Akhlāq,*" "*Risāla fiʾl-akhlāq,*" and "*Tahdhīb al-Ahlāq*" alone.

[4] Ibn Ḥazm, *Épître morale* (Kitāb al-Akhlāq wa-l-Siyar), (ed. and trans. Nada Tomiche; Collection UNESCO d'Oeuvres Representatives, Serie Arabe; Beirut: Commission Internationale pour la Traduction des Chefs-d'Oeuvre, 1961).

[5] Though the scholarship is uneven, Dwight M. Donaldson's *Studies in Muslim Ethics* (London: SPCK, 1953) offers a detailed study that gives constant quotations from the rich variety of material available in the literature.

[6] Toshihiko Izutzu, *Ethico-Religious Concepts in the Qurʾān* (McGill Islamic Studies, 1; Montreal: McGill University, 1966) 74.

in some cases revived some of the virtues of paganism, giving them a new form suited to the demands of devotion and obedience to one God, Allāh.[7] The *ḥadīth,* traditions on the sayings of Muḥammad, provided another rich source of ethical material. The moral thought of the Persian courtly tradition also entered literary and political circles in the ninth century, especially in the treatises and translations of the Persian convert Ibn al-Muqaffaᶜ. In only slightly Islamicized form, Persian moral thought was taken up by the *litterateurs* and writers in the "Mirrors of Princes" tradition. One of the most significant contributions to Islamic ethics was the elaboration of ethical theory by the Muᶜtazilite theologians. The ascetic and mystical movement of Sufism produced an anti-intellectual ethics that at times nearly dominated Islam. For many, Sufism was a spiritual response to the worldly pomp, power, and corruption of the new Islamic empire. Later it was also a corrective to the dry formalism of scholastic theology and legalism in religious law.

The relationships between the meanings of *adab* and *akhlāq* and the history of their use are more complex than Denny has indicated. He makes a clear distinction between *adab* and *akhlāq* similar to the distinction that most people would see between "etiquette" and "ethics." Noting that the word *adab* does not occur in the Qurᵓan, he states that *adab* did not arise as a respectable notion until the achievement of an international Islamic civilization under the Caliphates of the Umayyads and the ᶜAbbasids. In fact, it has been shown that the word *adab* among the pre-Islamic Arabs was essentially a synonym for *sunna,* and meant '[praiseworthy] habit, hereditary norm of conduct, custom' learned from ancestors and others looked up to as models, just as, in a religious sense, was the *sunna* of Muḥammad.

The refining of Bedouin ethics and culture brought about by the influence of Islam and contact with foreign cultures in the first two centuries after the *Hegira* brought a corresponding change in the meaning of *adab,* accentuating both the ethical and practical social content. Thus it took on the meanings 'high quality of soul, good upbringing, urbanity, and courtesy'.[8] In the first meaning there is a clear overlapping of semantic fields between *adab* and the phrase *ḥusn*

[7] The Qurᵓān contains numerous passages reflecting criticism of the abandonment of the ideals and virtues of the old nomadic Arab tradition by greedy Meccan businessmen in a period of ruthless rivalry for profits and economic power at the time of Muḥammad.

[8] See Francesco Gabrieli, "Adab," *The Encyclopaedia of Islam* (new ed.; ed. H. A. R. Gibb et al.; Leiden: Brill, 1960-), 1:175–76, which outlines the history of the term. On the earliest meaning of *adab,* see Carlo Nallino, *Raccolta di Scritti editi e inediti* (Rome: Istituto per L'Oriente, 1939–48), 6:2–17.

al-khulq (or *ḥusn al-khuluq, ḥusn al-akhlāq*), 'good character, or good nature'. *Ḥusn al-akhlāq* and *makārim al-akhlāq*, on the other hand, can often cross over into the semantic field of *adab*, having to do with good behavior as well as inner qualities. Although the word *adab* does not occur in the Qurʾān, the terms *adab*, *khulq* (or *khuluq*), and *akhlāq* occur in the canonical collections of the *ḥadīth* (sayings) of the Prophet.[9] In all but one of the six canonical collections of *ḥadīth* and in at least two other authoritative collections, one finds a subject category (chapter) headed by one of these terms. It is not too much to say, with Richard Walzer and H. A. R. Gibb, that the term *adab* in this early religious context had definite ethical connotations.[10]

It may be true in a certain sense that, as Denny says, the lack of prominence of ethics is due to the overwhelming prestige and authority of the Islamic religious law. This, however, is an ahistorical diagnosis. This apparent situation is the outcome of the struggle between two ethical theories, those of the rationalists and of the traditionalists, that raged between the eighth and tenth centuries and in which the traditionalists gained the upper hand. Before and during this struggle, Islamic law was far from being the finished edifice it was to become. The principle battle on ethics in medieval Islam began in the late eighth century among the jurists, while the *sharīʿa* was in the process of development.

On one side in the historic struggle were those Islamic jurists who supported the right of *raʾy* ('opinion', or more precisely a learned judge's or lawyer's judgment of equity and public interest) in cases where neither the Qurʾān, the *ḥadīth*, or their extension by analogy, nor the then-accepted local practice or administrative law provided the answer. Naturally allied with these partisans of *raʾy* was an early school of theologians, the Muʿtazila, whose first principle was the belief that God is just. He is just in his essence, though that is beyond human understanding. The justice of God's acts, however, being of the same kind as the justice of human acts, is knowable in principle and often known in fact through human reason without the aid of revelation. For this reason, George Hourani has labeled the Muʿtazilī theory of ethics "rationalistic objectivism."[11] A consequence

[9] See these headings in A. J. Wensinck et al., *Concordance et indices de la tradition musulmane* (7 vols.; Leiden: Brill, 1936–69), and see "Adab" and the numerous cross-references in Wensinck, *A Handbook of Early Muhammadan Tradition* (Leiden: Brill, 1927).

[10] R. Walzer and H. A. R. Gibb, "Ak̲h̲lāḳ," *Encyclopaedia of Islam*, 1:325–29.

[11] Hourani, *Islamic Rationalism: The Ethics of ʿAbd al-Jabbār* (Oxford: Clarendon, 1971) 10.

of this was belief in a measure of free will for humans. Since God is just, the rewards or punishments of the hereafter must be deserved and therefore people must be free in this life to choose between right and wrong. A just God must have given enough guidance through revelation, supplementing that of reason. The Qurʾān was constantly quoted and interpreted in support of these positions.

Allied together in opposition to these supporters of *raʾy* and "the partisans of justice" were the conservative religious groups who labeled themselves "the party of tradition" (*sunna*). Their opposing theory of ethics Hourani has termed "theistic subjectivism."[12] The reader will recognize in their views Islam as described by Denny. His description of the Islamic position on ethics, which denies the right of rational speculation on good and justice, is essentially that of the theologian al-Ashʿarī (d. 935). This man fashioned the traditionalists' most influential statement of belief early in the tenth century, although another century passed before it was accepted as the orthodox position. Al-Ashʿarī emphasized God's overwhelming power and humankind's utter dependence on him. God is not limited by the necessity of conforming to any human standards, such as an "objective" justice, perhaps wrongly conceived by humans. All the believer can know with any certainty is the law prescribed by God in the Qurʾān and the other recognized sources of the law. Obeying the law is the only meaning of righteousness or justice. As to the hereafter, "the Lord of Worlds is not under a *sharīʿa*," and therefore one cannot speak of the justice or injustice of his acts in any sense intelligible to the believer.[13] This theistic subjectivism is "subjectivism" because the value of an action is defined by relation to certain attitudes or opinions of a mind in the position of judge or observer," such as approving and disapproving, willing and not willing.[14] It is also "theistic" because it is God's mind that, in the position of judge and observer, does the willing, etc., and determines whether an act is right or wrong. The *sharīʿa*, a mere product itself of his will, does not.

Although theologians were among the "people of tradition" from the beginning, the jurists al-Shāfiʿī and Aḥmad ibn Ḥanbal led the combat against *raʾy* and rationalism. Shāfiʿī's jurisprudence prepared the way for the success of theistic subjectivism among theologians. In law, he triumphed in gaining general acceptance for his

[12] Ibid., 10.

[13] Al-Ashʿarī, *Al-Ibāna ʿan Uṣūl al-Diyāna* (Cairo: Munīrīya, 1930) 50, quoted by Hourani, *Islamic Rationalism*, 12.

[14] Hourani, ibid.

thesis of the preeminent authority of *ḥadīth* in determining law.[15] He limited the sources of the law to the Qurʾān, the *ḥadīth*, analogies drawn from these, and the consensus of the Muslim community as authorized by the Qurʾān. The implication of his theory of law for ethical theory is that "either there are objective ethical values but man's reason cannot know them, or that the only ethical values derive from divine commands."[16] "Right" means commanded by God, and "wrong" means prohibited by Him—again, a stance the reader will recognize from Denny's description of the Islamic view of ethics.

But there is another way to look at the relative positions of ethics and holy law, that is, to look at its relation to forms of ethics other than philosophical ethics, for ethics were incorporated into the developing *sharīʿa* in an identifiable way through its sources. According to Denny ethical assumptions and values are implicit in the law. But how did they become implicit in the *sharīʿa*? Several of those diverse sources enumerated above as contributing to the formation of Muslim ethics are also the formally recognized sources or roots (*uṣūl al-fiqh*) of the *sharīʿa*. Thus it was that ethical considerations entered into the formation of the developing *sharīʿa* through its sources.

One of the sources was of course Qurʾānic ethics. The teachings of the Qurʾān produced many changes in moral values besides giving specific commands to moral and ethical conduct in particular circumstances. It teaches kindness, fair treatment, compassion, generosity, self-control, sincerity, and the fellowship of believers. Another of the sources of the law, the *ḥadīth*, purport to record the Prophet's sayings or behavior in particular circumstances but also include material from his companions (the *aṣḥāb*) and integrate ethical material from the cultural or religious traditions antedating Islam, particularly pre-Islamic Arab, Jewish, and Christian traditions. The *ḥadīth* determined in an important way the whole ethos and framework of the developing religious law. In a major sense, the whole body of the *ḥadīth* constitutes a vast handbook of ethics.[17] The *ḥadīth* corpus was never merely a source for the sacred law, however, for it had its own autonomous character and existence and to this day "The Six Books,"

[15] See Joseph Schacht, *The Origins of Muhammadan Jurisprudence* (Oxford: Clarendon, 1959), chap. 3.

[16] Hourani, *Islamic Rationalism*, 12.

[17] A number of them deal with the kind and ethical treatment of animals, for example. See my article, "In the Artist's Mind(?): Some Prevalent Ideas about Animals from the Qurʾān and Traditions Literature," *Studies in the Art and Literature of the Near East in Honor of Richard Ettinghausen* (ed. Peter Chelkowski; Salt Lake City: University of Utah Middle East Center/New York: New York University, 1974) 105–10.

the canonical collections, and others are a major treasure of ethical teachings for believers. A third source of the *sharīᶜa*, scholarly consensus (*ijmāᶜ*), seen in its early form in the early legal handbooks such as the *Muwaṭṭaʾ* of Mālik ibn Anas of Medina (d. 795), frequently supports judgments of ethics and equity, though not always explicitly. In spite of the victory of Shāfiᶜī's theory, ethical reasoning had already been incorporated into the law through a process of Islamicization that was largely already complete.[18]

Denny observes that the key word for ethical behavior (*akhlāq*) is deeply rooted in the Qurʾānic view of reality. On the way to this, he says that the root *kh-l-q* occurs frequently in the Qurʾān and that it refers to the creation of things and dispositions, always by God. In that connection, he sees a linkage in the meaning of the Arabic word *khulq*, a singular form, 'natural disposition, original nature' and the meaning of the plural form *akhlāq* 'ethics, morality, character'. He deduces that "true morality, then, it not a matter of *adab* but of *akhlāq*, not of *culture* (which is a *human* product), but of *nature* (which is *God's* creation)." He appears to portray Islam as denying human ability to cultivate ethical and moral character. This would be consonant with his earlier statement that in Islam "it is not humankind's place . . . to speculate on the good or to seek it in the world of concepts and forms. . . ."—again, an Ashᶜarite doctrine of the tenth century. However, in the twelfth century, al-Ghazālī, whose teachings in his *Revivification of the Religious Sciences* have found general acceptance in *sunnī* Islam, argued against this doctrine in that work:

> There are those who are somewhat inclined to be careless who have expressed the opinion that the disposition (*al-khulq*) is like the created nature (*al-khalq*), and that it is therefore incapable of change (*al-taghyīr*). They have referred to the saying, "Allāh ceased from creation (*faragha Allāhu min al-khalqi*)." Consequently they say that the desire for a change in disposition is equivalent to the desire for a change in what Allāh, the Great and Glorious, has created. Observe, however, that they have forgotten the text, "Refine your dispositions." Now if this were indeed impossible, then commandments and admonitions, encouragement and threatening, would be useless. For if actions are the results of disposition, just as a material object falls in consequence of its gravity, then is reproach to be attached to action from a disposition and to the falling of an object?[19]

[18] See Schacht, *An Introduction to Islamic Law* (Oxford: Clarendon, 1964) 46.

[19] See *Iḥyāʾ ᶜUlūm al-Dīn* (ed. Badawī Tabbāna; Cairo: Dār Iḥyāʾ al-Kutub al-ᶜArabīya, n.d.), 3:54. The English is from Donaldson, *Studies in Muslim Ethics*, 138. The forgotten text referred to is a *ḥadīth* of Abu Bakr, according to Tabbāna. It is not

Ghazālī continues at length with the discussion, at one point taking the position that an effective kind of freedom of the will is experienced as a fact of life. He also gives some theory and advice about how one can actually achieve progress in the improvement of his moral character.[20]

In choosing ritual law as his subject, Denny has in one sense taken perhaps the most difficult area in Islamic law to look for ethical considerations. It is perhaps easier to look for ethics—as it is most commonly understood—in the law of commercial transactions or family and inheritance law. He has outlined a profoundly spiritual kind of ethic pervading religious ritual, and this is especially worthy of attention because of the priority of worship in believers' lives and its frequency. But there are special ethical considerations, in the more common sense of these words, that enter into the law of ritual slaughter and related dietary laws. (Brevity requires that I not discuss the latter.) The Islamic *sharīᶜa* is at least as comprehensive in coverage as Jewish religious law, and parallels it in numerous details. Like Jewish law it details what foods are lawful (ritually clean) and what are unlawful (ritually unclean). It also prescribes the manner of slaughter of animals, whether needed for sacrifice or for food. This is where an explicit ethics of the ritual act of slaughter is seen, an ethics toward God and toward the animal. The name of God must be pronounced in gratitude over the animal as it is slain, or according to another interpretation, as a declaration of divine permission.[21] Because the blood is *ḥarām* (sacrosanct and forbidden to eat), slaughter (*dhabḥ*) must be by cutting the large blood vessels of its throat with a sharp object, usually a very sharp knife as in Judaism.[22] Other cutting

---

included in the six canonical collections or Mālik or Aḥmad ibn Ḥanbal (see Wensinck et al., *Concordance et indices de la tradition musulmane*). However, it recollects another tradition spoken to Muᶜādh ibn Jabal (Mālik, *Muwaṭṭa*ᵓ, "Kitāb Ḥusn al-Khulq" (2 vols.; ed. Muḥammad Fuᵓād ᶜAbd al-Bāqī; Cairo: Dār Iḥyāᵓ al-Kutub al-ᶜArabīya, 1951), 2:902.

[20] *Iḥyā*ᵓ *ᶜUlūm al-Dīn*, 3:55ff.; Donaldson, *Studies in Muslim Ethics*, 140–42.

[21] "How can one take control of [these creatures of Allah] and deprive them of life unless he first obtains permission from his, and their, common Creator, to Whom everything belongs? Mentioning the name of Allah is a declaration of this divine permission, as if the one who is killing the animal were saying, 'This act of mine is not an aggression against the universe nor of oppression of this creature, but in the name of Allah I slaughter, in the name of Allah I hunt, and in the name of Allah I eat.'" Yusuf al-Qaradawi, *The Lawful and the Prohibited in Islam* (Al-Ḥalāl waᵓl-Ḥarām fiᵓl-Islām) (trans. Kamal El-Helbawy, M. Moinuddin Siddiqui, and Syed Shukry; Indianapolis: American Trust Publications, [1982]) 58.

[22] The camel is properly slaughtered by *naḥr*, spearing the major vessels where they pass close together in the lower neck near the breast bone.

or trauma is considered abominable (*makrūh*). The action must be accomplished in one swift, smooth movement without throwing the animal down or otherwise causing it pain or fright beforehand. The law books and *ḥadīth* go into other detail on lawful and unlawful slaughter, including proper methods to follow in hunting. Meat not obtained by permitted (*ḥalāl*) means of slaughter is not lawful as food. The parallels between Muslim and Jewish prescribed means of slaughter and their lists of prohibited meats gave rise to the saying among medieval Muslims traveling away from home: "Eat with the Jews and sleep with the Christians."

The ethic of sacrifice in Islam is not that of expiation. The annual Feast of Sacrifice (*ᶜĪd al-Aḍḥā*) commemorates the preparation of Abraham to offer up Ismāᶜīl (Ishmael, rather than Isaac, as in the biblical account) and his being supplied a ram, instead, by God. William Graham, drawing on the typology of sociologist Mary Douglas for what she calls "ritualist" and "nonritualist" societies, has noted that the reformational bent in Islam rejects both sacramentalism and "condensed" symbols as Douglas uses these terms. This sacrifice of the 10th of the month of Dhu ᵓl-Ḥijja, just after the formal conclusion of the pilgrimage rites proper, is given an ethical interpretation that is internalized and pietistic.[23]

In summary, I have tried to demonstrate in this analysis of some of the relationships between ethics and religious law in Islam that orthodox Islam by the eleventh century accepted a theory of ethics that in its pristine form declared that all that humans needed to know or could know of good was encompassed by the *sharīᶜa* and obedience to it. However, ethical thought had already been woven into the fabric of the law during its formation. The Qurᵓān and the *ḥadīth* continued to speak directly of ethics to their readers, and literary, mystical, and philosophical works dealing with ethics continued to be written and read. In addition, specific elements of Ṣūfī and philosophical ethics returned to the mainstream of orthodox thought through al-Ghazālī, the great synthesizer.

[23] William A. Graham, "Islam in the Mirror of Ritual," *Islam's Understanding of Itself* (ed. Richard G. Hovannisian and Speros Vryonis, Jr.; Malibu, CA: Undena, 1983) 66–67. Graham refers to Douglas's *Natural Symbols* (New York: Random House, 1970) 19–39. He discusses (pp. 64–66) how her typology seems to fit or not to fit Islamic communities.

Mahmoud Ayoub

Law and Grace in Islam: Ṣūfī Attitudes toward the *Sharīʿa*

AYOUB SHOWS HOW the meaning and value of the holy law of Islam, the *sharīʿa,* is understood from a mystical, or Ṣūfī, perspective. Mysticism is, of course, closely related to ethics and spirituality, and this essay, therefore, does not move into a sphere totally different from that which informs the previous essays. Ayoub cites sayings of a number of famous Ṣūfīs to show that they regarded the *sharīʿa* as an indispensable complement to the mystical life. Mysticism consists of an inward experience of truth, called in Arabic *ḥaqīqa.* The attainment of this experience requires a method, or discipline, called *ṭarīqa,* resulting in a trinity of *sharīʿa, ḥaqīqa,* and *ṭarīqa.* For the Ṣūfī all three are indispensable components of Islam as a totality. Holy law as the regulator of human actions vis-à-vis both fellow humans and God thus produces the requisite setting within which the cultivation of the inner life becomes possible. The perspective developed by Ayoub is especially reminiscent of that reflected in Falk's essay (chapter 6).

Mahmoud Ayoub is Professor of Islamic Studies in the Department of Religion at Temple University. He was previously affiliated with the Centre for Religious Studies at the University of Toronto. He received his Ph.D. from Harvard in the History of Religions. He is a member of the Kennedy Institute Trialogue Group for Jewish-Muslim Studies and spends one month each year as Visiting Professor at the Belamont Greek Orthodox Seminary in Lebanon. His published works are concerned with the Qurʾān, Islamic law and religious thought, and Muslim-Christian relations.

I wish to begin by defining the religion of Islam, and then both the *sharīʿa* (or sacred law) and the mystical path (the Ṣūfī *ṭarīqa*), which leads to the knowledge of the *ḥaqīqa* (truth). Then I will examine some of the major Ṣūfī attitudes towards the *sharīʿa*. Finally, I will pose a question: in what way can one see the element of grace in both the *ṭarīqa* and the *ḥaqīqa*, and what does this mean for today?

Islam is the religion of divine oneness, of *tawḥīd*. It is an active submission or commitment to the divine will, and thus constitutes the primordial divine covenant between God and humanity. It is not a covenant of worldly gifts, but of a witness. Before human beings came into existence God asked them, "Am I not your Lord?" The answer was "Yes, we bear witness" (Qurʾān 7:172).

In witnessing to the divine oneness, human beings add their voices to the chorus of the entire creation. The angels and all of God's creations testify to his oneness, sovereignty, and absolute power over all things (see Qurʾān 3:18). To keep his part of the covenant, God sent prophets and apostles with laws (*sharāʾiʿ*). The notion of the *sharīʿa* in Islam, however, is not so much one simply of *law*, but rather of a highway (the literal meaning of the Arabic *sharīʿa*), or the bank of a river to which people come for refreshment and guidance. The purpose and nature of the *sharīʿa* are defined in the Qurʾān; "To each of you have we appointed a law, and a way to follow . . ." (5:48).

What is the purpose of the *sharīʿa*? The same Qurʾanic verse continues, "Vie therefore with one another in the performance of good deeds." The purpose of the *sharīʿa* is to guide humanity on the long road that begins in God, goes through history and creation, and returns to him. The *sharīʿa*, therefore, is the teacher or pedagogue of human beings. Abū Naṣr al-Sarrāj, an early Ṣūfī (d. 988), defined three categories of "knowledge" and divided "scholars" into three groups. The first category of scholars includes those who know the Qurʾān, its meaning, exegesis, and of course the text itself. The second group includes those who know the prophetic tradition and accept it as the basis of all religious knowledge. The third group, al-Sarrāj says, are the Ṣūfīs, who take a broad attitude to the *sharīʿa*. They seek consensus among the competing parties of jurists, and they are careful in performing their prayers and other duties of faith.[1] Al-Sarrāj quotes the great theologian and cofounder of the mystical path in Islam, Ḥasan al-Baṣrī: "Surely a true jurist is one who renounces the world and seeks the hereafter."[2] Is this not what a true mystic should also strive to be?

Sharīʿa is the outer shell of religious practice without which the kernel or truth of the faith of Islam cannot grow and bear fruit. Yet

[1] Abū Naṣr Sarrāj al-Ṭūsī, *Al-Lumaʿ* (Baghdad: Al-Muthannā, 1960) 21ff.
[2] Ibid., 36.

the shell is merely the necessary covering of the kernel. The threefold division in Ṣūfism of the *sharīᶜa*, the *ṭarīqa* (mystical path), and the *ḥaqīqa* (the truth) is analogous in Christianity to the threefold way to God: the way of purification, the way of contemplation, and the way of illumination. According to al-Hujwīrī (d. 1072–73), the earliest writer on Ṣūfism to write in Persian, the *sharīᶜa* and *ḥaqīqa* are separate and yet interdependent. The *sharīᶜa* is necessary for the *ḥaqīqa* as the body is necessary for the spirit. Al-Hujwīrī further asserts that to follow the *sharīᶜa* is merely an outward display, while to follow the *ḥaqīqa* alone is hypocrisy:

> Rejection of the law is heresy, and rejection of the Truth is infidelity and polytheism. Any (proper) separation between them is made, not to establish a difference of meaning, but to affirm the Truth, as when it is said, "The words 'There is no god save God' are Truth and the words 'Muḥammad is the Apostle of God' are Law."[3]

Sharīᶜa and *ḥaqīqa* can also be understood as the mutually dependent exoteric and esoteric modes of devotion and cognition. It is only through the *sharīᶜa*, al-Hujwīrī insists, that one can enter into the mystical path that will eventually lead to the knowledge of the truth.

How did the Ṣūfīs regard the obligations of the *sharīᶜa*? First, let me reiterate that in my view the *sharīᶜa* is not only 'law' in the sense that we know it. Rather, the *sharīᶜa* is a codified body of moral imperatives enshrined in the Quʾrān, embodied in the sunna of the Prophet, and comprehended by a group of scholars, known in Arabic as *fuqahāʾ*—not 'lawyers' but 'people with understanding'. Ṣūfīs, or more precisely the majority who were committed to the faith and practice of Islam, did not deny the validity of the *sharīᶜa*, they sought rather to internalize its obligations.

Among God's creatures, the Ṣūfīs insisted, only human beings are required (*mukallafūn*) to fulfill specific divine commands that ultimately earn them salvation. In this sense, Ṣūfīs have insisted that the *sharīᶜa* is an act of divine grace, because it is the way of salvation.

The *sharīᶜa* requires, among other things, five daily prayers. According to Najm al-Dīn Kubrā (d. 1220), prayers on the level of the *sharīᶜa* are worship or service (*ᶜibāda*), on the level of the *ṭarīqa* they are proximity to God, and on the level of the *ḥaqīqa* they are union with God.[4] The *sharīᶜa* is thus considered the beginning of a process of purification, of renunciation of the lower qualities of the soul. Through the *sharīᶜa* the soul may reflect the divine beauty, or, in Ṣūfī

[3] *The Kashf al-Maḥjūb* (trans. R. A. Nicholson; London: Luzac, 1967) 139–40.

[4] Annemarie Schimmel, *Mystical Dimensions of Islam* (Chapel Hill: University of North Carolina, 1975) 152–53.

terminology, the divine attributes of beauty, *al-ṣifāt al-jamālīya*. The attitudes of the Ṣūfīs towards the *sharīʿa* and its obligations may also be exemplified by a dialogue between a very well-known early Ṣūfī, al-Junayd al-Baghdādi, and a man who had just returned from the pilgrimage. Al-Junayd asked, "When you set out on your journey from home, did you journey to God and away from all sensual pleasures?" "No," the man said. Al-Junayd said, "Then you have not made the journey. When you halted for the night along the journey, did you traverse the road to God through stages [*maqāmāt*]?" The man replied again, "No." Al-Junayd said, "Then you have not trodden the road stage-by-stage. When you put on the garb of consecration [the garb of a pilgrim when he or she reaches Mecca] did you take off all the clothes of sins and attachment to this world?" "No," he said. "Then," al-Junayd said, "you have not put on the garb of consecration." Finally (referring to all the stages of the pilgrimage) al-Junayd asked, "When you threw the pebbles [symbolic pebbles, called *jamrāt*, thrown by the pilgrims in emulation of Abraham when he was about to sacrifice his son] did you throw away all attachment to the pleasures of this world and purify yourself from sin?" "No," replied the traveler. "Then," said al-Junayd, "you have not made the pilgrimage."[5] The Ṣūfīs therefore attempted to internalize the *sharīʿa* without losing its exoteric significance.

I would characterize the Ṣūfī attitude toward the *sharīʿa* as the Ṣūfīs themselves have done. To do this, it may be useful to say a word about the rise of Ṣūfism itself. Islam, as is well known, presented history with a story of unparalleled success. Within a hundred years of the Prophet Muḥammad's death, Muslims had conquered west to the foot of the Pyrenees and east to the borders of China. But worldly success brought with it worldly desires and often led Muslims to a loss of commitment to their faith. A protest movement, later called Ṣūfism, isolated itself and sought to return to the faith. These early mystics of Islam were ascetics, although if Islamic mysticism had remained an ascetic movement, it would have died, for Islam is not a religion of asceticism.

The Ṣūfīs then began to see Islamic life as consisting of three important stages. Islam is the *sharīʿa*, which provides the identity of a person that would make him or her a member of the community. Then *īmān*, or faith, is the way to God, in which the heart and the mind and the body take part. Yet higher than both these is *iḥsān*, goodness or wholesomeness. When Muhammad was asked, "What is *iḥsān*?" he said, "*Iḥsān* is to worship God as though you see him, but

[5] See R. A. Nicholson, *The Mystics of Islam* (New York: Schocken, 1975) 91-92.

if you do not see him you must know that he sees you."[6] Thus Ibn ʿArabī (d. 1240), one of the greatest mystical minds in religious history, said, "Every creature in existence worships God on the principle of concealment [al-ghayb], except the Perfect Man, the man of faith, for he worships God in accordance with the principle of divine presence [*shahāda*]. Yet a servant does not achieve perfection except through faith."[7]

The early ascetic movement of Ṣūfism led in the end to two important groups or approaches: the mystics of love (*maḥabba*) and the mystics of knowledge (*ʿirfān*). The earliest manifestation of the "mystics of love" posed something of a threat to the "orthodox" ʿulamāʾ. This may be seen clearly in the love poetry of later centuries and in the Ṣūfī practices of music, ecstatic dance, and *samāʿ*, or audition.

Both the *sharīʿa* and *ṭarīqa*, however, are rooted in the Qurʾān, which repeatedly enjoins people to pay the alms, to perform the prayers, to observe the fast, and to make the pilgrimage. The Qurʾān also says, "To God belongs the East and West, and wherever you turn, there is the Face of God" (2:115). That principle goes beyond the *sharīʿa*. The Qurʾān says further, "It is not righteousness that you turn your faces towards the East and West. True righteousness is this: to have faith in God and the last day, the angels, the scriptures and the prophets; to give of one's wealth, though it may be cherished, to next of kin, the orphans, the destitute, the wayfarer, and for the redemption of slaves. . . ." (2:177).

In their attempts to root the *sharīʿa*, the *ṭarīqa*, and the *ḥaqīqa* all in the life-example (*sunna*) of the Prophet, the Ṣūfīs placed an interesting tradition in his mouth: "*Sharīʿa* is my words [*aqwālī*], *ṭarīqa* is my actions [*aʿmālī*], and *ḥaqīqa* is my inner states [*aḥwālī*]."[8]

Let me first describe the Gnostics among the Ṣūfīs and their attitude towards the *sharīʿa*. (Because there are many such attitudes, I will treat only two examples here.) Ibn ʿArabī compares the human body to God's broad earth (*arḍ Allāh al-wāsiʿa*). This earth is illuminated by the moon, which is reason. But as the moon must also derive its light from another source, so must reason be illuminated by the lamp of the sun of *sharīʿa*.[9] Ibn ʿArabī concludes that without the

[6] For a discussion of the Ṣūfī emphasis on *iḥsān*, see Schimmel, *Mystical Dimensions of Islam*, 29.

[7] Muhyī al-Dīn Ibn ʿArabī, *al-Futūḥat al-Makkīya* (Beirut: Dār Ṣādir), 3:250–51.

[8] Schimmel, *Mystical Dimensions of Islam*, 99.

[9] Ibn ʿArabī, *al-Futūḥāt al-Makkīya*, 3:250.

sharīʿa one cannot know God. Yet he boldly asserts that the *sharīʿa* must always kneel before the *ḥaqīqa*, or the truth.

Truth, for Ibn ʿArabī, is the divine reality, or that which is truly real, as opposed to that which is contingent or merely derives its existence from another source. *Ḥaqīqa* is God, as God's name is al-Ḥaqq, the Truth. Through the *sharīʿa*, Ibn ʿArabī felt, the traveler seeking God could obtain knowledge. There are those among God's friends, however, who discover the truth at the first step along the way. This knowledge is given to only a few. A follower of Ibn ʿArabī, al-Farghānī (d. ca. 1301), elaborated this way of knowledge into a system of cycles of representatives (*khulafāʾ*) of God on earth. These representatives become representatives of the prophet or the Perfect Man. They are necessary if the world is to subsist, and the criterion of their lives is also the *sharīʿa*, which serves, according to al-Farghānī, as the *mīzān* or 'criterion' of achieving justice or balance in society.[10] This same balance or justice is referred to in the Quʾrān: "Thus have we made you a community of the middle path, that you may be witnesses over humankind and that the Apostle be a witness over you" (2:143).

The Ṣūfīs could not accept the notion that Muḥammad's life would end only after some sixty years, or that his prophetic mission would be terminated only after little more than twenty years. They insisted that, just as *ḥaqīqa* remains constant and unchanging in the world from its beginning to its end, so must God continue to send witnesses to that truth in every age. These witnesses are the "perfect men." The perfect man is the pole around which the universe must turn, just as the pole around which the millstone moves. In fact, the difference between *sharīʿa* and *ḥaqīqa* is like the difference between changing messengers and constant truth. *Sharīʿa* may be abrogated, but *ḥaqīqa* is primordial and eternal.[11]

Some theosophists, like al-Niffarī (d. 965) who denied the existence of anything other than God, began also to deny the validity or reality of divine revelation, lest some confuse it with the divine oneness. Of course, excesses such as these left al-Niffarī (and others like him) open to accusations of antinomianism.[12]

The orthodox ʿulamāʾ also had a great deal of trouble with the mystics of love, the poets. The love of God is not a notion unknown

[10] Saʿīd al-Dīn al-Faghānī, *Muntahā al-Madārik* (Cairo: Maktabat al-Ṣanāʿi, A.H. 1293), 1:76ff.

[11] According to orthodox Muslim belief, the Islamic *sharīʿa* abrogated the *sharāʾiʿ* of earlier prophets, and within the Islamic *sharīʿa* certain earlier parts were abrogated by later parts.

[12] See Nicholson, *The Mystics of Islam*, 85ff.

to the Qurʾān, but Ṣūfīs (like other mystics), began to speak of divine love in human terms, and soon also to speak of 'infatuation' (*ʿishq*) rather than love (*maḥabba*). The emphasis upon love in human terms led them as well to regard the lover and the beloved as one. Thus Bayazid Bistāmī (d. 874), who himself was committed to the *sharīʿa*, said in one of his famous ecstatic utterances (*shaṭaḥāt*), "Praise be to me, how great is my majesty!" On another occasion he declared, "Under my garment there is nothing but God!"[13] Yet Bayazid has been regarded as one of the important Ṣūfī masters of all times.

Another poet of love, al-Ḥallāj (d. 922), was more explicit in his terminology. In one of his celebrated poems, he says, "I am He whom I love, He whom I love is I, We are two spirits dwelling in one body. If you see me, you see him; if you see Him, you see us both."[14] Al-Ḥallāj was martyred for his utterance, "*Ana al-Ḥaqq* [I am the Truth (that is, God)]."

The attitudes of later Ṣūfīs toward al-Ḥallāj are interesting. Al-Ḥallāj's statement suggested adherence to the doctrine of *ḥulūl* (incarnation), a doctrine that has been condemned no more vehemently by the orthodox than by the Ṣūfīs themselves. Thus some of al-Ḥallāj's disciples argued in his defence that his only sin was that he committed a great offence against the *sharīʿa* by divulging a secret that people could not comprehend. The idea of the mystic vision as a divine secret not to be divulged is a common theme in religious history. Paul also claimed concerning his rapture to the third heaven that "he heard things that cannot be told, which man cannot be told, which man cannot utter" (2 Cor 12:4). Others said that al-Ḥallāj spoke under the influence of intoxication—the intoxication of love. Therefore he was to be excused, for his only fault was that he remained in this state of intoxication (*sukr*) and did not return to a state of sobriety (*saḥw*). Still others defended al-Ḥallāj by admitting that he had mistakenly believed that he had achieved union with a divine Essence, when in reality he had achieved only union with the divine attributes.[15] One of al-Ḥallāj's important disciples, Rūzbihān Baqlī (d. 1209), perhaps defended his master best when he explained in his commentary to al-Ḥallāj's *Ṭawāsīn* that the words "I am the Truth" were uttered by his master just as the burning bush of Moses uttered the words "I am God."[16]

[13] Schimmel, *Mystical Dimensions of Islam,* 49 and 50.

[14] Nicholson, *The Mystics of Islam,* 151–52.

[15] Schimmel, *Mystical Dimensions of Islam,* 72–77.

[16] Rūzbahān al-Bāqī, "Commentaire des Ṭawāsīn," in Ḥusayn ibn Manṣūr, *Kitāb al-Ṭawāsīn* (ed. L. Massignon; Paris: Geuthner, 1913) 81.

Both Arab and Persian poets spoke of love instead of the principles of religion, of wine instead of prayers. Arab poets like Ibn al-Fāriḍ and Persian poets like Sanāʾī, Rūmī, and Ḥāfiẓ, used such metaphors as literary conventions to express a mystical love of God (although the extent of this is difficult to determine). These metaphors are not to be regarded as theological statements!

The grace of divine law is guidance to God's people, whom Rūmī describes in these words:

> The man of God is made wise by the Truth,
> The man of God is not learned from book.
> The man of God is beyond infidelity and faith,
> To the man of God right and wrong are alike.[17]

For the man of God, then, who can see the value of the *sharīʿa* as divine guidance or divine grace and who can infuse into it piety and humanity, Ṣūfism gives that needed element to all law—humanism. Ṣūfism is the humanism of Islam. It gives Islam that tolerance which the Qurʾān often enjoins, but it goes beyond what the jurists have made of the sacred scriptures. Thus Ibn ʿArabī declares,

> My heart has become capable of every form,
> A pasture for gazelles, a cloister for monks,
> A temple for idols, the votary's Kaʿba,
> The tablets of the Torah, the scroll of the Qurʾān.
> It is the religion of love that I hold: wherever turns
> Its mounts, love shall be my creed and faith.[18]

Muslims today have ignored the value of that spiritual heritage that Ṣūfism gave to Islam—without which Islam remains a body without life. They gave up on Ṣūfism not because there were Ṣūfīs who were charlatans, who used their powers of psychological discernment to intimidate and to achieve their own glory, but because Muslims today have forgotten their heritage and become too materialistic.

Let me conclude with an interesting interpretation of the one-eyed antichrist of Islamic eschatology by Nāṣir-i Khusraw, the eleventh century poet and philosopher:

> Beware of that one-eyed man, the Antichrist; if the right eye is taken to signify the inner meaning, the left eye the outward meaning of the

[17] Nicholson, *The Mystics of Islam*, 95.

[18] Muḥyī al-Dīn ibn ʿArabī, *Tarjumān al-Ashwāq* (Beirut: Dār Ṣādir, 1966) 43-44.

> Koran and the religious law . . . then the one-eyed Antichrist has this meaning: The one-eyed Antichrist is he who directs men to the outward, i.e., the left side. This Antichrist, who is blind in the right eye, is accursed, for we have the tradition that the Prophet said: He who is blind in the right eye is assuredly cursed. By which he meant the orthodox, who annulled the inward. The other one-eyed Antichrist is he who summons men to inner understanding. . . . He is blind in the left eye, and there is a tradition that the Prophet said, He who is blind in the left eye is accursed. By which he meant the heterodox who annuls the outward sense of religious dogma. . . . Neither of these two Antichrists has religion. . . . The true religion . . . is advocated only by him who soundly perceives both outward and inward at once and through them both obeys and worships God.[19]

The problem today is that we have forgotten that equilibrium—the balance that Islam is all about—between excess and negligence, between extremism and indifference, between the body and the spirit, between asceticism and indulgence. When Muḥammad ᶜAbduh became the head of the great al-Azhar University in Egypt, he reformed the schools of law but did nothing to promote Ṣūfism. According to prophetic tradition, God will send from time to time a renewer (*mujaddid*) of religion, one who will recapture that equilibrium of Islam and restore its principles. Al-Ghazzālī (d. 1111) revived that equilibrium by restoring Ṣūfism to its rightful place. It is hoped that the *sharīᶜa* will once more be revitalized and humanized by the spiritual heritage of Islam that is Ṣūfism.

[19] Fritz Meier, "The Mystery of the Kaᶜba: Symbol and Reality in Islamic Mysticism," *The Mysteries: Papers from the Eranos Yearbooks* (ed. J. Campbell; New York: Pantheon Books, 1955), 2:151n–52n.

Leonardo P. Alishan

Beyond the Law: The Experience of Some Persian Ṣūfī Poets—A Response to Mahmoud Ayoub

ALISHAN CONSIDERS THAT Ayoub's discussion of the relationship between the Islamic holy law and Ṣūfī mysticism has presented but one side of a total, more complex picture. While many Ṣūfīs—especially those commonly known as the "masters of sobriety"—did indeed understand this relationship in the way described by Ayoub, others, particularly among those who expressed their mysticism through Persian poetry, understood the relationship differently. These were the "masters of inebriety," and among them a definite antinomian tendency is to be found: in place of the complementariness between the holy law and the inner life emphasized by Ayoub, one finds a never relenting tension between these two poles. The holy law promotes order and control; the inner life plunges people into the chaotic and unsafe depths of the unconscious. Here, as in no other essay contained in this volume, is the value and meaning of the holy law subject to serious qualification.

Leonardo Alishan is Associate Professor of Persian Literature at the University of Utah. He received his Ph.D. from the University of Texas at Austin. His published works deal with Persian and Armenian literature.

As Mahmoud Ayoub has mentioned, many of the Ṣūfīs were significant theologians themselves. Imām Qushayrī, while practicing

Ṣūfism, also conducted classes on orthodox (Ashᶜarī) theology and on jurisprudence as taught in the Shāfiᶜī school. ᶜAbdullāh Ansārī (d. 1089), well known for his ecstatic utterances and meditations, also remained to his last days a Ḥanbalī theologian with the revered title of *Shaykh al-Islām*. Bahaᵓ ad-Dīn Muḥammad ibn Muḥammad Valad (d. 1230), the father of Jalāl al-Dīn Mawlānā Rūmī (d. 1273), was a Ṣūfī and a professional orthodox preacher at the same time. However, it is in the influential figure of Imām Abū Ḥāmid Muḥammad ibn Muḥammad Ghazālī (1058–1111) that Ṣūfism and orthodox Islam are said to have found their ideal state of equilibrium.[1] These Ṣūfīs, whom I shall call *aṣḥāb-i ṣaḥw* 'masters of sobriety', have constituted the core of Ayoub's impressive presentation. My own complementary response will concentrate on the other group, referred to as *aṣḥāb-i sukr* 'masters of inebriety', whose attitude toward many aspects of the *sharīᶜa* differed considerably from the masters of sobriety.

The Ṣūfīs I wish to discuss presently are all Persian poets. For Ṣūfism, after all, finds its ideal lyrical expression in Persian poetry. I shall concentrate only on the attitude of a few of these poet-mystics toward one of the five pillars of Islam, namely the *ḥajj* (pilgrimage to Mecca and the performance of the rituals included therein), as reflected in their lyrical poems. For in didactic poetry seldom does the Ṣūfī forget the limitations of the orthodox audience, whereas in the personal lyrical poems the poet's soul dances more freely among the words.

On the religious significance of this pillar of Islam, Seyyed Hossein Nasr has the following succinct and lucid remarks:

> The pilgrimage to Mecca [*ḥajj*] is another obligatory act which may, however, be undertaken only when certain conditions are fulfilled. A man, if he has the sufficient means, should once in his lifetime make the pilgrimage to Mecca which for Islam is the centre of the world. The *ḥajj* with all the difficulties that it entailed and still entails, despite modern conveniences, is also a means of purification. Man journeys to the Centre, to the house of God, there asking pardon for his sins and being purified through his repentance and the performance of the rites. Henceforth, he should try to live a devout life and when he returns to his homeland he brings the purity and grace [*barakah*] of the house of God with him. Something of the Centre is thus disseminated in the periphery

[1] See ᶜAbdulḥusayn Zarrīnkūb, *Justijū dar Taṣawwuf-i Īrān* (Tehran: Amīr Kabīr, 1978) 240–41; and Julian Baldick, "Medieval Sufi Literature in Persian Prose," *History of Persian Literature from the Beginning of the Islamic Period to the Present Day* (ed. G. Morrison; Leiden: Brill, 1981) 88–90.

> and through this yearly act the whole of the Muslim community is purified.[2]

On the mythic and sacred dimension of such journeys, Mircea Eliade writes:

> The road is arduous, fraught with perils, because it is, in fact, a rite of the passage from the profane to the sacred, from the ephemeral and illusory to reality and eternity, from death to life, from man to the divinity. Attaining the center is equivalent to a consecration, an initiation; yesterday's profane and illusory existence gives place to a new, to a life that is real, enduring, and effective.[3]

It should be noted at this point that in Islam the *kaᶜba* is both the 'navel of the earth' and its 'highest point', lying "over against the center of heaven."[4] Hence, it is in the vicinity of the *kaᶜba*, the center and high point of the earth, that the Muslim pilgrim performs the rites and becomes renewed by virtue of integration with that sacred center of the Islamic society. For just as each neighborhood has for its sacred center a mosque, the whole of the Islamic community finds its center in the *kaᶜba*. As Nasr has noted, "The *sharīᶜa* [an important aspect of which is the *ḥajj*] is for Islam the means of integrating human society. It is the way by which man is able to give religious significance to his daily life and is able to integrate this life into a spiritual centre."[5] Just as the *sharīᶜa* is the means of integrating the Islamic society, the *ṭarīqa* (Ṣūfism, 'the path') is the means of integrating the individual. It is the individual in Ṣūfism who, after passing through internal and spiritual stages no less arduous or perilous than the road described by Eliade, ultimately becomes identical with the sacred center. This individual, whom Ṣūfīs refer to as *al-insān al-kāmil* ('the complete human being'), realizes God and the essential Islamic concept of *tawḥīd* ('unity') within. For, after all, there is nothing in the universe that does not find its constituents also in individuals.[6]

[2] Seyyed Hossein Nasr, *Ideals and Realities of Islam* (2d ed.; London: George Allen & Unwin, 1971) 116.

[3] Mircea Eliade, *The Myth of the Eternal Return* (trans. Willard R. Trask; Bollingen Series 46; Princeton: Princeton University, 1965) 18.

[4] Kisaʾi, fol. 15; cited by A. J. Wensinck, *The Ideas of the Western Semites concerning the Navel of the Earth* (Amsterdam: J. Müller, 1916) 15, and referred to by Eliade, *Myth of the Eternal Return*, 15.

[5] Nasr, *Ideas and Realities of Islam*, 97.

[6] *Al-insān al-kāmil* is often translated as 'the perfect man', but as I shall show, in a psychological sense the integration of the unconscious into the consciousness results

Since from the very beginning God dwells within individuals as their soul—as the breath of God blew into the lifeless Adam, the breath that gave life to the other four elements (earth, water, fire, air) and from which all creation, including Adam, found its material manifestation—the Ṣūfī's task becomes to die to the carnal soul (*al-nafs al-ᶜammāra*) and to the profane world so that one may be reborn to spiritual life and realize this divine essence. By going through this purification process, the Ṣūfī allows the essential Creator within to emerge through the multi-layered clouds of the carnal soul, which bind the Ṣūfī to the material creation. Once *tawḥīd* is realized and the annihilated temporal self of the Ṣūfī has made way for the truth to emerge in its full integrity, the Ṣūfīs themselves become the sacred center and the highest point of creation, hovering above the world and its laws.

This *religion* is the religion of love where the lover (the Ṣūfī) is eternally in quest of the beloved (God), and where finally the dichotomy of lover and beloved is absorbed and assimilated into perfect Love. As Sanāᶜī (d. 1141), one of the earliest Persian Ṣūfī poets, put it, love is something that "the Ḥanafī theologian cannot teach, / nor the Shafiᶜī cleric comment upon."[7] Love, by its very nature, negates rational and regulated behavior. As Abū Saᶜīd Abuᵓ l-Khayr (967-1049) says,

> Know for a fact that a lover cannot be a Moslem,
> In the religion of Love there is no belief or disbelief.
> In Love there is no room for heart or reason or body or soul,
> And know no such lover to be a fool.[8]

Abū Saᶜīd has also been credited with several quatrains that make indirect or direct references to many aspects of the *sharīᶜa*, including pilgrimage to Mecca. In the following poem (which, in a slightly difference form, has also been attributed to Awhad al-Dīn

---

in what may best be described as 'a complete individual' rather than one who is 'perfect'. Nasr's translation of the same as 'the universal man' is also very expressive but would require an explanation that the brief nature of this paper does not allow ("Ṣūfism and the Integration of Man," *Ṣūfī Essays* [New York: Schocken, 1972] 43-51).

[7] Sanāᶜī, *Dīvān* (ed. Mudarris Razavī; 2d ed.; Tehran: Ibn Sīnā, 1962). Rūmī writes, "Where love was increasing the pain / Bū Ḥanīfah and Shafiᶜī had nothing to say" (ᶜAlī Dashtī, *Sayrī dar Dīvān-i Shams* [3d ed.; Tehran: Javīdān, 1965] 31).

[8] It has not been clearly established that Abū Saᶜid wrote any verse at all, however, the Iranian scholar, Saᶜīd Nafīsī has attributed more than seven hundred quatrains to him, noting that some also appear in the *dīvāns* of other poets (*Sukhanān-i Manzum-i Abū Saᶜīd Abuᵓl Khayr* [3d ed.; Tehran: Sanāᶜī, 1971] 39, no. 268).

Kermānī), the poet expresses the concept of *tawḥīd* in a manner that would surely have aggravated the strict followers of the *sharīᶜa*:

I went to the Christian church and the Jewish temple,
All were engaged in talk of You.
With You in mind, I entered the temple of idols,
The rosary of idols were invoking Your name.[9]

Abū Saᶜīd's perception of God's beauty is of such extraordinary proportions that he fears the whole structure of Islam would crumble before a vision of such beauty:

Whoever found himself around You
Became weary of mosque, monastery, and the *kaᶜba*.
If You dishevel Your hair in the *kaᶜba*
Islam will surely fall at the feet of Christians![10]

Farīd al-Dīn ᶜAṭṭār (d. 1220), the great Ṣūfī poet and master, goes even further than Abū Saᶜīd. Sometimes he declares the *kaᶜba* of the lover to be the face of his beloved.[11] At other times he calls himself a "fire worshipper," "the man with whom the brothel's musician shares his secrets," "a drunkard," or "a sinner" in the presence of whom Satan bows and tips his hat in respect![12]

In his monumental *Tadhkirat al-Awlīyāᵓ* ᶜAṭṭār describes the lives of Ṣūfī saints. In his sections on Shiblī and Abuᵓl-Qāsim Naṣrābādī, ᶜAṭṭār says that both of these Ṣūfī masters were seen running toward the *kaᶜba* with torches in their hands. When asked of their intentions, each responded, "I wish to set fire to the *kaᶜba* so that people may return to the Lord of the *kaᶜba* [i.e., God]."[13] In his section on Bāyazīd of Bistām (d. 874?), ᶜAṭṭār says that Bāyazīd once set off on a pilgrimage but returned soon after leaving. When asked to give a reason, Bāyazīd replied that he had been stopped by a black man with a sword in hand who had told him, "How could you leave God in Bistām and come to the *kaᶜba*?"[14] But the most interesting anecdote that clearly demonstrates the idea of the ideal Ṣūfī as

[9] Ibid., 37, no. 257.

[10] Ibid., 26, no. 175.

[11] Shaykh Farīd al-Dīn Muḥammad ᶜAṭṭār, *Muntakhab-i Ashᶜār* (ed. Taqī Taffazolī; Tehran: N.P., 1966) 271.

[12] Ibid., 115, 117.

[13] ᶜAṭṭār, *Tadhkirat al-Awliyāᵓ* (The Lives of the Saints) (ed. Muḥammad Istᶜilāmī; Tehran: Zavvār, 1967) 617, 788.

[14] Ibid., 165.

the sacred center is related by Sahl ibn ᶜAbdullāh. On his way to the *kaᶜba*, Sahl sees an old man (in reality, a master Ṣūfī) to whom he offers a few coins as assistance. The master raises his hand and scatters a fistful of gold he has caught from the air. He then tells Sahl, "You get it from your pocket, I from the invisible," and disappears. When Sahl arrives at the *kaᶜba*, he sees the *kaᶜba* circumambulating the old man. Then the anonymous master says, "O Sahl, whoever takes a step to see the beauty of the *kaᶜba*, he may circumambulate the *kaᶜba*. But if one steps out of himself to see the beauty of the Truth [i.e., God], he must be circumambulated by the *kaᶜba*"[15] The master in this story, the complete and integrated individual, has attained such sanctity and has become so clear a mirror of *tawḥīd* that the very sacred center of the *sharīᶜa*, the *kaᶜba* itself, must circumambulate him![16]

In his lyrical poems, Rūmī also makes numerous references to the *kaᶜba* and the *ḥajj*. In one such *ghazal*, he says:

> O people off to pilgrimage, where are you? Where are you?
> The Beloved is right here, come back! come back!
> When your Beloved is your next door neighbor
> What's the purpose of wandering in the wilderness?
> Once you see the faceless face of the Beloved
> You'll know that you're the master, you're the house, and the *kaᶜba*. . . .[17]

In another *ghazal*, referring to sincere and anxious but totally unaware pilgrims, he writes:

> When those who ran to the *kaᶜba* on their heads
> Finally arrived at their destination,
> They entered that abode hoping to see God—
> Long they sought, but saw no God.

Finally, when the disappointed pilgrims have settled sufficiently in their sorrow, they hear a voice from the invisible world that tells them:

> "O house worshippers, why worship mud and stone?
> Worship the house that the pure ones sought!

[15] Ibid., 310–11.

[16] For more on the Ṣūfī Master see Nasr, "The Ṣūfī Master as Exemplified in Persian Ṣūfī Literature," *Ṣūfī Essays*, 57–67.

[17] Rūmī, *Kullīyāt-i Dīvān-i Shams* (ed. Badīᶜ al-Zamān Furūzānfar; 7th ed.; Tehran: Amīr Kabīr, 1979) 247, no. 648.

> That house is the heart; the heart and house of God are one!
> Happy are they who crept into that house!"

Elsewhere Rūmī writes,

> Circumambulate the *kaᶜba* of the heart, if you have a heart!
> The heart is the meaningful *kaᶜba*, or else what is mud?[18]

Rūmī's realization that God resides within the human heart ultimately leads to his becoming the sacred center himself. Thus, with total justification, referring to himself, or rather to the God within himself, he writes, "I am the *kaᶜba* of mysteries."[19] In another poem, he becomes all the communal sacred centers of Islam: "I am the *qibla* of souls, / I am the *kaᶜba* of hearts, / I am the *mosque* of heaven. . . ."[20] Since the *kaᶜba* was considered in Islam to be the highest point of the earth in proximity to heaven, Rūmī, through his ecstatic whirling dance, rises above the earth and occupies the high position allotted to the sacred center:

> If you seek your "self," exit yourself,
> Leave this shallow ditch and come towards the Oxus.
> Why pull the burden of the heavens like an ox?
> Whirl once and rise to the top of heaven.[21]

This very same Rūmī is also a prominent theologian who does not, by any means, condemn the *sharīᶜa*. The *sharīᶜa*, after all, is a set of divine laws that will guide all faithful creatures ultimately to their Creator and is essential to them to make their circle just. This is based on the exoteric meaning of the Qurʾān, and it is indispensible to the body of believers who, without the *sharīᶜa*, would not be able to achieve social integration but would live in a perpetual state of loss with no connections to sacred time or to their sacred origin. Ṣūfism, on the other hand, is based on the esoteric meaning of the Qurʾān. Commenting on this aspect, Nasr writes:

> The *Tarīqa* or spiritual path, is meant only for those who seek God here and now and who search after that immutable Truth which, although

[18] Both poems are quoted by Dashti, *Sayrī dar Dīvān-i Shams*, 254. This Ṣūfī attitude to the *ḥajj* had become so common by the late twelfth century that even Khāqānī (d. 1199), who was not a Ṣūfī, referred to "the *kaᶜba* of the Soul" (*Divan* [ed. Zīyāʾ ad-Dīn Sajjādī; Tehran: Zavvār, 1959] 88-9).

[19] Dashti, *Sayrī dar Dīvān-i Shams*, 245.

[20] Ibid., 148 (see also pp. 252-56).

[21] Rūmī, *Kullīyāt-i Dīvān-i Shams*, 1316, no. 62.

present here and now, is at the same time the transcendent and eternal source of all revelation.[22]

Rūmī, the impatient lover-dancer-poet-Ṣūfī, realizes that the *sharīᶜa* is indispensible to the people who live in this world and who seek a harmonious relationship with the Creator. However, he is also aware that "everything that exists in the world is [also] found in the human state. . . ."[23] Thus, rather than journey into the external world, Rūmī chooses to journey into the internal world. Within his true self he finds the same manifestation of *tawḥīd* that the world without bears witness to with all its multiple manifestations. The joy of perceiving the integrity of the divine within their own selves is what sets Rūmī, ᶜAṭṭār, and Abū Saᶜīd, along with a host of others, apart from the pilgrims of the *ḥajj* and on a pilgrimage into their own selves. Although, in the final analysis, both the *sharīᶜa* and the *Ṭarīqa* bear witness to *La ilāhā illā ʾllāh* ('the ultimate integrity and unity of the truth').

The Ṣūfī's main difference with the strict adherent of the *sharīᶜa* is that only the Ṣūfī "sees God everywhere."[24] If an analogy may be permitted, the orthodox believer's perception is like that of a camera filming the external reality. One sees and (by applying the *sharīᶜa*) knows how to interact with what one sees in a manner pleasing to God. The Ṣūfī's perception goes a step further. After the internal journey, the Ṣūfī becomes a *projector* that projects the truth that he has found within himself on the world without: he/she sees God everywhere.

Naturally, the realization of the divine within sometimes leads to fatal ecstatic proclamations. Language, the creation of the creature, cannot hope to express the nature of the creature's Creator, with the unique exception of the Qurʾān of course. The violent deaths of such prominent mystics as Shihāb al-Dīn Yaḥyā Suhrawardī (d. 1191) or ᶜAyn al-Quḍāt Hamadānī (d. 1131) testifies to the condemnatory attitude of the strict followers of the *sharīᶜa* toward the people of the *ṭarīqa*. Manṣūr al-Ḥallāj (d. 922) was tortured, crucified, burnt, and his ashes dispersed for having declared, "I am the Truth [i.e., God]." Unlike Ayoub, I do not believe that Ḥallāj was referring to or believed in reincarnation. As Abū Saᶜīd or Rūmī has expressed in a quatrain, "When he was saying 'I am the Truth,' / Where was Manṣur? God! It

[22] Nasr, "The Ṣūfī Master," 57.

[23] See William C. Chittick, *The Ṣūfī Doctrine of Rumi: An Introduction* (Tehran: Offset Press, 1974) 64–65 n. 4, for Rūmī's verses on this subject and Jami's commentary on these verses.

[24] Nasr, "Ṣūfism and the Integration of Man," 43.

was God!"[25] In other words, Ḥallāj had not thought that *he* was the reincarnation of God. But once he had cleansed himself of his clouded carnal soul, he—Ḥallāj—disappeared and only God, the ultimate truth, remained.

The process of attaining this metaphoric "pearl," which Ḥallāj, Rūmī, and others did, is itself an extremely dangerous journey. The *sharīᶜa,* after all, allows the human consciousness to stay in continuous control of the vessel *over* the potentially hazardous waters of the unconscious by formulating its contents and by gradually integrating it through sacred rites. The pearl of *tawḥīd,* however, lies at the *bottom* of these waters. Consequently, the Ṣūfī has no alternative but to put the safeguarding laws of the *sharīᶜa* aside, temporarily at least, and to delve into the true self. If one does so unaided by a master, chances are that he or she will never emerge from these waters but will remain lost therein, known to the outside world only as a lunatic. Thus Ṣūfism has its own laws and its own stages, according to and through which a master guides a disciple who may or may not complete the journey. Substituting what was referred to as the pearl with "Paradise," Nasr writes,

> The descent to the "inferno" is the means whereby the soul recovers its lost and hidden elements in dark and lethel depths before being able to make the ascent to "Purgatory" and "Paradise."[26]

Here lies the core of my response to Ayoub: unless the Ṣūfī discarded—temporarily at least—the protective filter of the *sharīᶜa,* the *sharīᶜa* would not have allowed the descent into this "inferno." And as ᶜAṭṭār's Shaykh Ṣanᶜān and his disciples discovered, without this nightmarish but vital descent—which for the Shaykh involved the drinking of wine, the herding of swine, and the burning of the Qurʾān—there is no access to that "Paradise."[27]

The *sharīᶜa* helps the Muslim to find his or her place in the world and gives a sense of spiritual security. The *ṭarīqa* leads its follower to an initial sense of loss and insecurity. Hence, in ᶜAṭṭār's poetic parable, for example, the Ṣūfī is depicted as a child lost in a

[25] Abū Saᶜīd, in Nafīsī, *Sukhanan-i Manzum-i Abū Saᶜīd Abuʾl Khayr,* 2, no. 135; Rūmī, *Kullīyāt-i Dīvān-i Shams,* 1317, no. 72.

[26] Nasr, "Ṣūfism and the Integration of Man," 47.

[27] Interestingly, C. G. Jung's perceptions on the collective unconscious and its archetypes, namely the shadow and the anima, offer no inconsistencies with what the Ṣūfīs had so fully realized and practised centuries ago. See, for example, Jung, "Archetypes of the Collective Unconscious," *The Collected Works of C. G. Jung,* vol. 9/1 (2d ed.; ed. G. Adler, M. Fordham, and H. Read; trans. R. F. C. Hull; Princeton: Princeton University, 1968).

crowded marketplace, seeking his "mother" but does not know her name. The child is in tears and no one can assist in locating his mother.[28] The laws of the *sharīᶜa* predetermine the Muslim's reactions to a variety of situations and clarify the path that Muslims are expected to take. The *ṭarīqa* is the way of love, where nothing is predetermined and the path is populated with unpredictable hazards. Hence, Abū Saᶜīd says,

> In the beginning, the way of Your love seemed easy to me,
> I thought I would soon arrive at my destination.
> I took a few steps and the path turned into a sea;
> One more, and a wave snatched me away![29]

In this religion of love, the traveler has no companion:

> That burning fire which we call Love
> Is like a fever in both the bodies of belief and disbelief.
> Faith is something, the Religion of Love something else,
> The prophet of Love is neither an Arab nor non-Arab.[30]

The *sharīᶜa* does not allow its follower to enter such dangerous waters, whereas the *ṭarīqa* requires it. Thus, Rūmī also alludes to such submersions and the consequent sense of loss:

> Now that I am totally immersed, how may I describe the river Jaihun?
> I used to do so when my head was out and my lips were happily at work!

In another poem also, Rūmī refers to this total sense of loss, which must precede the realization of one's true and divine identity:

> You ask me, "How are you!" How do I know?
> "Who are you and from what family?" How do I know?
> You ask me "From what wine have you drank
> To be so drunk and ecstatic?" How do I know?. . . .[31]

[28] ᶜAṭṭār, *Muntakhab-i Ashᶜār*, 352 (the poem is from ᶜAṭṭār's *Ilāhī Nāmih*). Rūmī also has verses of this nature, for example, "I am like a child lost in a street in the bazaar / For I neither know this street nor this bazaar. . . ." (cited by Dashtī, *Sayrī dar Dīvān-i Shams*, 300).

[29] Abū Saᶜīd, in Nafīsī, *Sukhānan-i Manzum-i Abū Saᶜīd Abuᵓl Khayr*, 38, no. 258.

[30] Ibid., 10, no. 62.

[31] See Dashtī, *Sayrī dar Dīvān-i Shams*, 300–301, for a selection of verses by Rūmī on the same subject.

The Ṣūfī realizes that every oasis is preceded by a desert, every pearl involves an immersion into dark and deep waters, every new order and integration must be preceded by chaos and disintegration, and every birth into a spiritual state can only follow a death to the profane plane. The following final poem, which has been attributed to Abū Saᶜīd, describes this symbolic death and rebirth:

> Till the minaret and the seminary are not destroyed,
> The work of the *qalandar* will not be done!
> Till belief does not become disbelief, and disbelief, belief,
> No one will become a true Muslim![32]

The followers of the *sharīᶜa* and the *ṭarīqa,* all Muslims, found God in different places, by different means, under different names. And he was there, within and without them, for there is nothing outside him.

[32] Abu Saᶜid, in Nafīsī, *Sukhānan-i Manzum-i Abū Saᶜīd Abuʾl Khayr,* 41, no. 281. Note that the antinomian *qalandars,* a loosely structured order of wandering mendicants, were more extreme that the Ṣūfīs, and were not considered Ṣūfīs in the strict sense of the concept. However, it should also be noted that Shams-i Tabrīzī, the man who drove Rūmī from the rhetoric of the pulpit to ecstatic poetry, was himself a *qalandar.*

Bernard S. Jackson

Legalism and Spirituality

Historical, Philosophical, and Semiotic Notes on Legislators, Adjudicators, and Subjects

IN THE FOLLOWING ESSAY legalism has to do not so much with an absence of meaning and value as with the application of rules to concrete situations. Two senses of legalism emerge in the final section of Jackson's discussion: legalism is in the broader sense simply "rule-centeredness" and in the narrower sense (drawn from Judith Shklar) an application of rules to situations that call for something more. Legalism in the former sense can be either good or bad: it is good in the context of resolution of questions of legal doctrine, bad in the context of adjudication of actual cases. Legalism in the latter sense can arise only in the context of adjudication; it is therefore always bad.

Jackson argues that judicial legalism was avoided in ancient Israelite tradition through a detachment of the judicial process from the rules expounded in the written (or statutory) law. There is no evidence in the Bible, he contends, that judges were expected to apply rules; the emphasis on the charisma and innate sense of justice of judges in fact points in the opposite direction. This freedom of the judge from the control of rules makes good sense according to Jackson, both from the standpoint of legal philosophy (especially the later views of Hans Kelsen) and from the standpoint of semiotics. Spirituality, in Jackson's view, is possible both in the judicial realm and in the realm of doctrine, but in different ways. In the judicial realm it has to do with relationships between people, in the realm of doctrine with "deep structures."

Bernard S. Jackson is Professor of Law at the University of Kent at Canterbury. In addition to professional degrees in law, he holds a

D.Phil. from Oxford and an LL.D. from the University of Edinburgh. He is editor of the *Jewish Law Annual* and has written articles and monographs dealing with various aspects of law and religion.

In this paper, I shall argue an extremely radical, highly controversial, and even "counter-intuitive" thesis; namely, the conventional view that judges exist to apply general rules laid down by higher authority—whether by the legislature or by superior courts in a system of precedents—is no more than a culturally contingent claim that has become typical of the Western conception of law. This is not merely a "skeptical" or "realist" argument based on the sentiment that the law in practice is in fact different from the law in the books. This now-common judgment is often made pessimistically, with a note of regret: one would prefer to ensure that judges applied nothing but the general rules directed to them, but alas human nature interferes. My argument goes far beyond this: that judges *ought* to see their role as the application of general rules laid down by authority is itself both culturally contingent and contestable in substance. To make this case, I shall advance three types of arguments: historical, philosophical, and semiotic. I shall adduce evidence to suggest that this was not the dominant conception of the relationship between legislator and judge in the Bible and early Judaism; I shall draw attention to the later views of Hans Kelsen, despite the barrage of criticism directed at them, in order to sketch a philosophical argument as to why there can be no conceptual connection between the act of adjudication and that of legislation; and I shall allude to some current work in structuralism and semiotics that reinforces this view and points toward alternative models. All this may appear as neither legalistic nor spiritual. I therefore conclude by indicating what values I attach to these two concepts, and what role I see them playing in an evaluation of the activities of legislator and judge. I hope to show, at that point, that the biblical conception of the role of judge, so different from that of the *official* legal ideology of our times, continues nevertheless to exert an influence.

Historical Evidence

The Old Testament on Torah and Judges

The historical record appears to show that it was only slowly that the idea grew that judges were actually supposed to apply *torah*, and even then one has to wait, probably to the postexilic period, for any indication that the judges were expected to refer to an authoritative written source, a *sefer torah*.[1] There certainly did exist written *torah* in the preexilic period. But a number of sources seem to indicate that its function was *not* the provision of statutory rules to be applied as such by the judges, in the sense of rules regarded as authoritative in their linguistic form as well as their content. When one thinks of the typical setting of judicial activity outside Jerusalem—the elders sitting at the city gate—a different impression is conveyed. Both in the norms preserved in Deuteronomy and in the historical account of the reform of Jehoshaphat, one finds clear indications that the functions of written *torah* did not include the provision of rules for application by these judges. Deuteronomy 16 prescribes the appointment of judges, and charges them in entirely general terms:

> You shall appoint for yourselves judges and officers, tribe by tribe, in every settlement which the Lord your God is giving you, and they shall dispense true justice [*mišpaṭ ṣedeq*] to the people. You shall not pervert the course of justice or show favor, nor shall you accept a bribe; for bribery makes the wise man blind and the just man give a crooked answer. Justice, and justice alone, you shall pursue [*ṣedeq ṣedeq tirdōp*], so that you may live and occupy the land which the Lord your God is giving you (Deut 16:18–20).

The judges are here told simply to act justly and avoid corruption. They are not asked to follow any particular rules. I am not, of course, suggesting that they are being given an entirely free discretion. The passage has clear wisdom connections, as seen by the proverb used as a motive clause. That seems to me to be a clue as to the kind of criteria which the judge is expected to apply: his sense of justice is to be tempered by the conventional norms of practical wisdom. Wisdom, in this context, should not be understood as the literary expression of wisdom that Moshe Weinfeld has so convincingly shown to be associated with the court;[2] rather, in this context, it is the wisdom of local tradition.

The next chapter of Deuuteronomy tells what should happen when local wisdom proves insufficient:

[1] On this theme, see also my "Ideas of Law and Legal Administration: A Semiotic Approach," *The World of Ancient Israel: Sociological, Anthropological, and Political Perspectives* (ed. R. E. Clements; Cambridge: Cambridge University, 1988). These papers form part of a wider project on the relationship between law and religion in the early Judaeo-Christian tradition, supported by a grant from the Leverhulme Trust.

[2] *Deuteronomy and the Deuteronomic School* (Oxford: Clarendon, 1972).

> When the issue in any law suit is beyond your competence, whether it be a case of blood against blood, plea against plea, or blow against blow, that is disputed in your courts [lit., in your gates], then go up without delay to the place which the Lord your God will choose. There you must go to the levitical priests or to the judge then in office; seek their guidance, and they will pronounce the sentence. You shall act on the pronouncement which they make from the place which the Lord will choose. See that you carry out their instructions. Act on the instruction which they give you,[3] and on the judgment which they tell you;[4] do not swerve from what they tell you, either to right or to left. Anyone who presumes to reject the decision either of the priest who ministers there to the Lord your God, or of the judge, shall die; thus you will rid Israel of wickedness. Then all the people will hear of it and be afraid, and will never again show such presumption (Deut 17:8–13).

The local judges thus have to consult the central, impliedly Jerusalemite, authorities: there appears to be a division between secular and cultic jurisdiction. But again, there is no reference to any authoritative set of rules that these Jerusalem authorities are required to apply. There may even be an implication, from the use of the verb *dāraš*, that an oracular consultation is used to resolve the matter.[5]

The next passage mentions a *sefer torah*, but in a quite different context. The famous deuteronomic law of the king concludes:

> When he has ascended the throne of the kingdom, he shall make a copy of this law in a book at the dictation of the levitical priests. He shall keep it by him and read from it all his life, so that he may learn to fear the Lord his God and keep all the words of this law and observe these statutes. In this way he shall not become prouder than his fellow-nor shall he turn from these commandments to right or to left; then he and his sons will reign long over his kingdom in Israel (Deut 17:18–20).

It has been suggested that this instruction to have a *sefer torah* inscribed is an interpolation in the passage, in that the motive of the avoidance of pride (v 20) more naturally follows immediately after the ban on the multiplication of wives and gold bullion reserves.[6] Regardless, the point is that the *sefer torah* is for the instruction of the king,

[3] *ᶜAl pî hattôrāh ᵓăšer yôrûkhā. Torah* here clearly refers to an *oral* instruction.

[4] *Wĕᵓal hammišpāṭ ᵓăšer yōᵓmĕrû lĕkā. BHK* suggests that this phrase may be interpolated.

[5] For example, Exod 18:15, 1 Chr 10:13–14; further B. Jackson, *Theft in Early Jewish Law* (Oxford: Clarendon, 1972) 242.

[6] Weinfeld, *Deuteronomy and the Deuteronomic School*, 5 n. 1.

a clear link between literary wisdom and the royal court. It is commonly believed that the association between law and covenant is a characteristic theme of Deuteronomy; it is therefore quite appropriate that in the deuteronomic literature, where kingship is equally given a covenantal legitimation, the writing of the *sefer torah* is for the purposes of instruction of the king.

There is a close relationship between these deuteronomic sources and the account of Jehoshaphat's reform recorded in 2 Chronicles. Once again, two quite separate matters are treated in separate literary units: the commissioning of judges on the one hand and the teaching of *torah* on the other. 2 Chronicles 19 deals with a judicial reform. Jehoshaphat appoints judges, *šôpṭîm*, in all the fortified cities. What does he ask them to do? Nothing concerned with any set of laws written in a *sefer*, nor is there even any mention of *torah*. The judges are asked to remember that they are accountable to God, but no substantive rules of divine law are commended to them. Rather, they are warned (as in Deuteronomy 16) against injustice, partiality, and bribery:

> Be careful what you do; you are there as judges, to please not man but the Lord, who is with you when you pass sentence (*wĕʿimmākem bidbar mišpāṭ*). Let the dread of the Lord be upon you, for the Lord our God will not tolerate injustice, partiality, or bribery (2 Chr 19:6–7).

Jehoshaphat's appointment of judges for Jerusalem follows a similar pattern. The charge to those judges is entirely general in character; the only reference to any authoritative source of law is oblique: they may have to deal with cases *bên dām lĕdām bên tôrāh lĕmiṣwāh lĕḥūqqîm ûlĕmišpāṭîm*, a threefold division of jurisdiction comparable in form, and also partially in substance, to that in Deut 17:8. There is an implication that the intuition of the judges—like that of Solomon—will be divinely directed. The fact that the Jerusalem judges have to report to the chief priest *lĕkōl dĕbar yhwh* 'for *every* matter concerning the LORD', suggests that these officers were the real sources of the law to be applied by the judges. But here too, as in Deuteronomy 17, there is no reference to a binding set of rules that even these ultimate authorities must apply.

The other passage taken to refer to "Jehoshaphat's reform," 2 Chronicles 17, tells a very different story. In the third year of his reign, years before the judicial reform mentioned above, the king sent some of his officers (*śarîm*) "to teach in the cities of Judah," accompanied by two of the priests:

> They taught in Judah, having with them the book of the law of the Lord (*wayĕlammĕdû bîhûdāh wĕʿimmāhem sēper tôrat yhwh*) (2 Chr 17:9).

There is an interesting terminological parallel between the passages. God himself is said to be *immākem* 'with you,' (you = the judges) in chap. 19, whereas the *sēper tôrat yhwh* is said to be with the officers (*immāhem*) in the case of the royal instructors. I see no reason to conflate these sources; they deal with separate matters. And there is corroboration from elsewhere. Weinfeld has pointed to a practice of the Assyrian kings in sending royal officers to each town to exercise a teaching function with regard to the law.[7] The object of this odd practice can hardly have been to train experts in legal doctrine. It was far more simple. Given the prevailing levels of literacy and a limited medium of communication, acts of proclamation by king's officers were clearly necessary. Equally, and for the same reasons, permanent judges in the towns outside Jerusalem were unlikely to have continuing access to authoritative written sources; notwithstanding, they were asked to adjudicate in the spirit of God's justice.

Ancient Parallels

Ancient Israel was by no means unique in this respect.[8] The Code of Hammurabi was widely disseminated, as the archaeological evidence indicates. Moreover, the evidence of thousands of records of judicial decisions from Old Babylonia shows that some of them appear to conform to the rules stated in the Code, others do not. Yet throughout this huge judicial corpus, there is but one quotation of the Code, and not even this is of a substantive legal provision. Moreover, the Code itself commends, like Deuteronomy, the ideal of justice to the judges, rather than imposing upon them a set of binding rules.

It is now a quarter of a century since F. R. Kraus wrote his seminal article on the character of the Code of Hammurabi, followed almost immediately by J. J. Finkelstein on the Edict of Ammiṣaduqa and the Babylonian "Law Codes."[9] The conclusions then reached have attracted increasing adherence. The Laws of Hammurabi are the product of scribal circles closely in touch with Babylonian wisdom

[7] Ibid., 163f.

[8] For the documentation of points made in this section, see my "From *Dharma* to Law," *American Journal of Comparative Law* 23 (1975) 490–512.

[9] Kraus, "Ein zentrales Problem des altmesopotamischen Rechtes: Was ist der Codex Hammu-rabi?" *Genava* 8 (1960) 283–96; Finkelstein, "Ammiṣaduqa's Edict and the Babylonian 'Law Codes.'" Review of *Ein Edikt des Königs Ammi-ṣaduqa von Babylon*, by F. R. Kraus. *Journal of Cuneiform Studies* 15 (1961) 91–104.

literature; the monument was intended as a glorification of the king and a dedication to the sun-god, Shamash. Hammurabi proclaims in the prologue his desire to establish *kittum u mesharum*, of which the latter refers either to equity in general or, as some take it, to the process by which equity is secured by the king. The former denoted the sum of the eternal and immutable truths upon which the cosmos was founded and which the law strove to safeguard. Hammurabi is described as *emqum*, a wise man, as well as *sar mesharum*, a king of justice (which may refer as much to the customary edictal activity, remitting debts, etc., at the beginning of the reign, as to the promulgation of the Code itself). The appellation *emqum* is that typically used of the scribe rather than the judge. The wisdom circles that were responsible for the drafting of the laws projected the king in their own image in recognition of the authority that the king was giving to the wisdom laws contained in the monument. The monumental form of the laws (ultimately reflected also in ancient Israel where, however, stone monuments were originally "mute," i.e., uninscribed)[10] tells its own story. There can be no widespread dissemination of laws in the medium of large, engraved stelae. Such stelae have a quite different purpose, they are public monuments. True, one finds in the epilogue of the Laws of Hammurabi the invitation to the oppressed man to have the words read to him, so that "his heart be set at ease." But this is far more a sacral than a judicial act: the poor man is bade to make a declaration praising Hammurabi, and indeed to pray for him. Similarly, future kings who choose to follow the inscription are to be blessed; those who choose not to follow it are to be cursed. The matter is entirely a choice for future kings. There is no notion of the automatic continuity of the law (something that H. L. A. Hart has noted as a feature of modern legal systems) to distinguish the very concept of a "rule" from that of a "command."[11]

The New Testament

I believe that the distinction between the role and functions of legislation and adjudication assists in understanding the thorny question of the relationship of Jesus to the law in the New Testament.[12]

[10] Deut 27:2-3, Josh 8:32. In the latter, it seems implied that the law was inscribed on the *altar* stones.

[11] H. L. A. Hart, *The Concept of Law* (Oxford: Clarendon, 1961) 50-64.

[12] For a detailed account of the argument in this and part of the next section, see my "Jésus et Moïse: Le statut du prophète à l'égard de la loi," *Revue historique de droit français et étranger* 59 (1981) 341-60. See also my "On the Tyranny of the Law," *Israel Law Review* 18 (1983) 327-47, esp. 344f.

On this, of course, the New Testament sources are not uniform. I here confine myself to the Synoptic Gospels, including however the parable of the woman taken in adultery, which, although attached to the Gospel of John, is generally thought on account of its form and style to come from the same milieu.

The famous introduction to the Sermon on the Mount may be taken as an affirmation of the integrity and stability of divine legislation: "Not a letter, not a stroke, will disappear from the Law" (Matt 5:18). Of course, Jesus then goes on to his famous antitheses, "You have heard . . . but I say unto you . . . ," which is put together so as to indicate a special form of authority.[13] Nevertheless this is simply an interpretative restatement, no more radical than many interpretations that are stated quite categorically in rabbinic commentaries such as the "Mehkilta of Rabbi Ishmael," which, for example, baldly asserts (only later backed up with reasoning): "An eye for an eye—that means money."[14] The reason why Jesus adopts a particularly categorical form, thereby claiming special authority even while affirming though restating the law (in the tradition of Deuteronomy), is that he associates himself with the tradition of the coming of future prophets like Moses, with a special authority in relation to the law (Deuteronomy 18). The Teacher of Righteousness at Qumran also appears to have claimed this authority, and he too provides a restatement of the rules. But the "prophet like Moses" has a dual function, not only to restate laws but also to apply them and direct the people in particular circumstances. The latter is recognized in the biblical text, and it is the principal function that the "prophet like Moses" performs in rabbinic interpretation. But here, in cases of specific application, the Rabbis themselves accept that such a prophet may—at least in biblical times—suspend the law on particular occasions. For example, Elijah authorized his followers to sacrifice on Mount Carmel, contrary to the law centralizing the cult in Jerusalem (*b. Yebam.* 90b, *Sipre* Shoftim 175). Elijah had the authority to suspend the law because of the exigencies of the particular moment—here the probability that the people would otherwise have sacrificed to foreign gods. The Talmud explicitly distinguishes between particular sus-

[13] Jesus' style of interpretation is partly based on formulae commonly found in rabbinic literature. See D. Daube, *The New Testament and Rabbinic Judaism* (London: Athlone, 1956; repr. New York: Arno, 1973) 55–62.

[14] Tractate *Nezikin* §8 on Exod 21:24; see J. Z. Lauterbach, *Mekilta de-Rabbi Ishmael* (Philadelphia: Jewish Publication Society of America, 1935), 3:67. As to the meaning of the original see my *Essays in Jewish and Comparative Legal History* (Leiden: Brill, 1975) 82–85.

pensions of the law and its abrogation. The prophet who attempts the latter is thereby proved to be a false prophet.

The Gospels provide several examples of activities of Jesus, in relation to specific events, which I have argued should be viewed as suspensions in line with this tradition. The first is the incident where Jesus is accused of having allowed his followers to pluck corn on the Sabbath (Matt 12:1-8, Mark 2:23-28, Luke 6:1-5). The accusation comes from the Pharisees, who claim that this act is not permitted. In reply, Jesus does not argue on the basis of interpretation as to what the law actually says, but rather cites as a precedent the story of David, who himself ate and allowed his followers to eat the presence bread of the Temple, even though this was permitted only to priests. This suspension of the law by David was justified by the men's hunger, and Matthew adds that the disciples of Jesus were plucking the corn for the same reason. A second example concerns the entry into Jerusalem. Jesus sends two disciples to a neighboring village to bring an unmounted ass for his use. In his instructions, Jesus anticipates the likely reaction. If challenged, the disciples are to reply "The Lord had need of it" (Luke 19:31; cf. Mark 11:3, Matt 21:3). Again, reference may be made to the anointing at Bethany (Matt 26:9, Mark 14:6, John 12:5). To the objection that the oil given by the woman would better be sold for the benefit of the poor rather than used to anoint Jesus, a reply is given in terms of the special needs of Jesus in anticipation of his funeral. Then, finally, there is the one occasion in the Gospels when Jesus formally adjudicates on a past action, as opposed to authorizing a future one: the case of the woman taken in adultery (John 7:53ff.). Although the woman admits her guilt, Jesus refused to apply the punishment that the law ordains: "Go home, and sin not again."

Early Rabbinics

This action of Jesus is not as unprecedented as may be supposed. Quite a substantial number of incidents—totalling about thirty—occur in the Babylonian Talmud, where rabbinic judges are said to have adjudicated "not in accordance with the law."[15] For example, according to Jewish law, daughters do not inherit as heirs, but have

[15] See H. Ben Menachem, "Extra-Legal Reasoning in Judicial Decisions in Talmudic Law" (Ph.D. diss., Oxford, 1978). For a partial publication in Hebrew, see "The Respective Attitudes of the Babylonian and Jerusalem Talmuds to Judicial Deviation from the Law," *Shenaton Ha-Mishpat Ha-Ivri* 8 (1981) 113-34.

a (prior) claim to maintenance out of the estate. But this claim is leveled against the deceased's immovable property only. In a particular case, one rabbinic judges sought to award maintenance out of the movable property of the estate. The account implies that his action was not disapproved of by the compilers of the Babylonian Talmud. But one contemporary objection is indeed recorded: "Said R. Simeon Eliakim: Master, I know that in your decision you are not acting on the line of the law, but on the line of mercy, but [the possibility ought to be considered that] the students might observe this ruling and fix it as an *halakah* for future generations" (*b. Ketub.* 50b, *y. Ketub.* 6:6 [30:9]). It is thus implied that what may be right for the decision in a particular case may not be appropriate to serve as a precedent, whether for the schoolhouse or for a subsequent court. Ben Menachem argues, rightly in my view, that many of these cases clearly go beyond formal discretion such as is given to the judges in a number of well-known sources. This question of maintenance, for example, is not a normal case of *lipnîm mišurat hadîn,* despite the terms in which the objection is put. In many cases, the reason that the judge himself gave for his deviant decision is recorded in the Talmud; there are several examples of what Ben Menachem calls decisions based on "individual considerations," as opposed to "social considerations." One habitual robber is punished, for example, beyond the normal sanctions, not because of a general breakdown of law and order, but in the light of his individual record (*b. B. Qam.* 96b).[16] That is the category, I would suggest, into which the adjudication of the woman taken in adultery also falls.

The Jewish sources are by no means unanimous in their approval, sometimes merely condonation, of this practice, and Ben Menachem has identified two interesting correlations in attitudes. First, the Babylonian sources are more sympathetic than the Palestinian. This in fact is part of a wider pattern, in which the Rabbis, particularly in Palestine, acted against various practices associated with Jesus, even though they had a perfectly respectable Jewish origin. Second, the early rabbinic commentaries on the Pentateuch, the "Midrashei Halakah," which were primarily concerned with the exposition of the divine text rather than with adjudicating particular cases, are hostile. But the "Midrashei Halakah" are didactic and expository; they are concerned with doctrine, with the activity of the schoolhouse. The passages to which I have referred from the Babylonian Talmud, on the other hand, purport to report actual cases of adjudication.

[16] See my *Theft in Early Jewish Law,* 202.

Max Weber would have been very interested in the analysis of this phenomenon, for there is clearly a correlation between the degree of charismatic authority and a willingness in the act of adjudication to go beyond the rules as laid down. (This holds true even when the charismatic leader, at one and the same time, lays down an interpretation of doctrine that does *not* purport to diverge from tradition.) Early rabbinic Judaism became increasingly wary of charisma (one can understand why), and sought increasingly to institutionalize the judicial process. One finds, for example, restrictions placed upon the authority of prophets concerning the law, and even a tradition that seeks to appropriate for the rabbis themselves the power to suspend the law in particular cases that had originated in the tradition of the "prophet like Moses."

I would like to relate to this theme two well-known aspects of the history of Jewish law that are not generally viewed in this light. First, a text in tractate Sanhedrin of the Mishna appears, contrary to the law, to give rabbinic courts a power to inflict the death penalty, or at least the likelihood of death, in the absence of the eyewitness testimony required by law: "[As for] the slayer of a man without witnesses, they [the court] take him to a prison-cell and feed him with 'the bread of adversity and the water of affliction'" (*m. Sanh.* 9:5).[17] I have argued that this text should not be viewed, as later rabbinic interpretation does, as restricted to cases where there are indeed two eyewitnesses, but where the testimony is disqualified on technical grounds; the text is quite simple and straightforward—"he who kills *šellōʾ bĕʿēdîm*." It may very well *include* technical defects, but there is nothing at all in the language or the context to suggest that it is restricted to them. So it seems that the rabbinic court has the power to detain such an offender indefinitely and to put him on a starvation diet. Will he survive? Is he supposed to survive? The text, as here translated in English, does not say. But the answer is revealed in the phrase "the bread of adversity and the water of affliction," which is not rabbinic Hebrew, but rather is a quotation from the prophet Isaiah (30:20). In its original context, it refers to the judgment of God. In using it here in the Mishna, the Rabbis, I believe, are aware of that connotation, and deliberately wish to incorporate it. The implication is as follows. The offender will be detained (a social benefit, no doubt, provided that he really is the killer) and put into a position where his life is in jeopardy. But the rabbinic court itself will not take the final step; it will not kill him. Whether he survives or not is in the hands of God. It is only god, in this mishnaic text, who ultimately has the

[17] See further my *Essays in Jewish and Comparative Legal History*, 187ff.

authority to determine whether this killer should lose his life, in circumstances where the rules of law do not authorize his execution.

Not only did the Rabbis increasingly hesitate to countenance judicial deviation from the law, they eventually shrank back (in criminal matters) from the application of those sanctions that they *were* authorized to apply. I have in mind here not those evidentiary and procedural restrictions that led to the virtual abolition of the death penalty, but rather the insistence that only a judge authorized by *sĕmîkhâ* was able to inflict a "penalty" going beyond mere restoration or compensation.[18] Since the chain of *sĕmîkhâ* came to be broken, the whole biblically based system of criminal law fell into desuetude. What kind of value underlies this development? There is no suggestion that the later judges were any less learned or humane. What they lacked was the manifest charisma of someone who had received the "laying on of hands" from someone who had himself received that "laying on of hands," in a chain that extended back to Moses, and impliedly to God himself. Why, one may ask, should such charisma be expected if adjudication is merely a matter of the mechanical application of rules? And we may note a further historical paradox. The full literary and substantive development of Jewish law, in the post-Talmudic period, characterized by the enormously creative codificatory and responsa literature, takes place at a time when this original *sĕmîkhâ* is merely a historical memory. Legal doctrine continued to develop; for that, one needed intellect and application.

An Argument from Legal Philosophy

One might expect to receive little support from contemporary legal philosophy for the counter-intuitive view I have been advancing. After all, the "Rule of Law," which says precisely that adjudication should be governed by laws, not by people, seems to affirm the contrary value. Nowadays, it is true, neither the judges nor the legal philosophers are particularly enamored of "mechanical jurisprudence." But at the same time, the discretion that judges are recognized to possess is regarded either as somewhat exceptional in practice (Hart's view) or as constrained by a form of systemic rationalism (as in Dworkin).[19] One might expect that any "Pure Theory of Law," such

[18] See Aaron Rothkoff and Isaac Levitats, "Semikhah," *Encyclopaedia Judaica* (Jerusalem: Keter, 1971), 14:1140–47.

[19] See my *Semiotics and Legal Theory* (London: Routledge & Kegan Paul, 1985), chap. 7 on Hart, chap. 9 on Dworkin.

as that advanced by Hans Kelsen, would insist on the interrelationship between rules and adjudication. And this is precisely what we find, at least in Kelsen's earlier views. The judge's decision is valid insofar as it falls under, is subsumed beneath, a more general norm found higher in the legal hierarchy. Thus, the typical relationship between legislation and adjudication is that the validity of the latter is derived from the former, precisely because adjudication is no more and no less than an application of the legislation. But even the classical Pure Theory does not reduce law entirely to logic. The act of the judge, even when applying a statute, creates an individual norm. This occurs because the basic unit of the legal system according to Kelsen is the "norm" (defined as the meaning attributed to an act of will). There can be no such meaning without an actual act of will. The act of will is that of the judge, and indeed that of the individual judge in the individual case.

Already in his *Pure Theory of Law*, Kelsen indicates a number of places where there is a divergence between the logical elements of this theory—represented by what has been called the "normative syllogism"—and the emphasis upon will.[20] If the legislature passes a statute that, in its content, appears to be "unconstitutional," that statute is in fact regarded as valid (as a majority of American constitutional lawyers affirm) until such time as it is declared unconstitutional. Similarly, if a court makes a manifestly "wrong" legal decision, that decision remains valid until such time as it is reversed on appeal.[21] Moreover, that "wrong" legal decision may involve a question of statutory interpretation. Even if the judge interprets the statute manifestly outside of what Kelsen calls the "frame" (of the possible meanings of its words), that interpretation remains "authentic" by virtue of the office of the judge, until such time as it is reversed by higher authority.[22] In order to account for these phenomena, Kelsen advanced the theory of "normative alternatives." Whatever the legal system may explicitly say, the fact that one recognizes these "anomalous" cases as possessing legal validity shows that legal validity may be acquired in two alternative ways. It may be desirable that the elements of the legal system, constitution and statute, statute and adjudication, should be related to each other in terms of their

[20] On this development in Kelsen, see my *Semiotics and Legal Theory*, chap. 10; and my "Kelsen between Formalism and Realism," *Liverpool Law Review* 7 (1985) 78-93.

[21] H. Kelsen, *The Pure Theory of Law* (Berkeley: University of California, 1967) 267-76.

[22] Ibid., chap. 8.

content.[23] That, indeed, may be regarded as both the normal and the desirable case. But the "anomalous" cases show that purely "formal" (as opposed to "material") authorization is in fact sufficient: the legislature or the judge may choose, in the exercise of its will, not to follow the content of the higher norm, but the decision it makes will still be valid, purely as a result of the office of the decision-maker. As Kelsen says, "determination of the organ" is the minimum necessary—and is thus sufficient—for legal validity.[24]

It seems to have been the analysis of such anomalous cases that led Kelsen ultimately, in the last decade of his life, to revise his theory more radically. Ultimately, he rejected the "normative syllogism" entirely. He decided that he had to choose between logic and will, and he opted for will. The norm was the meaning of an act of will; its validity now rested only on the authority of the person who made the decision in question, not on any logical relationship that the content of that decision might have to the content of a superior norm. Subsumption could work with legal *propositions*; it could not work with norms, for as Kelsen argued the will of one person could not be subsumed within the will of another. If the legislature decided (by its own act of will) that thieves should be subject to a maximum of ten years in prison, what it thereby made valid was the *general norm* only, namely that thieves in general may be imprisoned up to the maximum period. But the legislators do not know the identity of any future thief who may be brought before the court, nor can their act of will somehow replace the act of will of the judge who will determine the case of the future thief. Therefore the act of that future judge cannot be validated in terms of the general norm created by the legislature; it can be validated only by virtue of the office of the judge who made the decision. There can be a logical, syllogistic relationship between *propositions*; there cannot be such a logical relationship between *norms,* where the latter are strictly regarded as the meanings of actual acts of will. Hence, and rightly in my view, Kelsen ultimately opted to view legal doctrine and legal decision-making as quite separate spheres. Whether he was right to regard only legal decision-making as part of the positive law is a different question.

I believe that there is more to Kelsen's argument than a mere philosophical quibble, one apparently based upon what some may

[23] Kelsen himself suggests this, although it fits ill with the "purity" of his method. The significance of this claim is discussed in my "Kelsen between Formalism and Realism."

[24] Kelsen, *Pure Theory of Law*, 235 n. 21. See further chaps. 10–12 of H. Kelsen, *Essays in Legal and Moral Philosophy* (ed. O. Weinberger; Dordrecht: D. Reidel, 1973).

regard as a very restrictive, stipulative definition of a "norm." Kelsen does not elaborate, to my knowledge, the reasons why he so defines the norm or what values may be served by the conceptual separation for which he argues. I would hazard the following kind of reconstruction. For Kelsen, it is the coercive order contained in the apodosis that characterizes a norm as legal; unlike John Austin, for example, he did not regard "nullity" as a sufficient sanction.[25] A coercive order was understood as meaning the infliction of an evil such as deprivation of life, health, liberty, or economic assets "even against his will by the employment of physical force."[26] The exercise of force by the state thus stood, for Kelsen, as a residual consequence of the breach of *any* norm. In defining the norm as the meaning of an act of will, and in separating the individual norm (usually created by act of will by the judge) from the general norm (usually created by act of will of the legislature), Kelsen insured that every coercive order results from an act of will specifically directed toward that particular act of coercion. Such a view is certainly compatible with (and, I would like to think, may flow from) a sense of the unique moral responsibility of the individual coercive order. One cannot claim that one is engaged in a purely logical exercise (a mechanical jurisprudence where cognition excludes will). Nor can one claim that the moral responsibility resides only with the creator of the general norm that one "applies": the act of will of one person cannot be implicit in the act of will of another. For positivism allows the judge *validly* to make a "wrong" legal decision.

A Semiotic Argument

I turn now to a related argument, one that I have developed in the context of a semiotically inspired approach to legal philosophy,[27] an approach that distinguishes between questions of the following two kinds: (*a*) "what does a particular law mean?" and (*b*) "does a particular situation fall within a particular general law?" If one regards the law in question, whether in (*a*) or (*b*), as comprising a set of words whose meaning needs to be elucidated, one can distinguish the two questions as follows; the first is the question "what is the meaning of words x in the statute?" and the second is "does situation y fall within words x of the statute?"

[25] *Pure Theory of Law*, 33–58, 108–14, 276–78.
[26] Ibid., 33.
[27] *Semiotics and Legal Theory*, 156ff. and passim.

The first of these questions calls essentially for a paraphrase. As such, it invites replacement of one verbal proposition by another. When the question is posed in this form, our attention will inevitably be concentrated upon what Hart has called the "core" meaning of the words, rather than the "penumbra," for there is nothing to direct our attention to anything other than the core.[28] But to ask a question in the second form does not necessarily call for a paraphrase. It depends upon the context in which the question is asked. If it is for didactic purposes, as in common problem-solving questions posed to law students, it is, in one sense, still asking whether a particular proposition falls within the meaning of another more general proposition. Here, a penumbral question may very well arise. No doubt, law students should be encouraged to discuss it in terms of contextual (including policy) considerations, but they will still be considering it without the involvement of the two features that are crucial to Kelsen, namely the presence of a real human being whose fate is actually being determined by a real (not merely supposed) act of will of a human individual who takes responsibility for that decision. In such a situation, rational consistency—whether represented by Kelsen's (ultimately rejected) logic of subsumption, the Herculean attribution of Dworkinian rights, or even the practical reasoning of MacCormick's consequentalism[29]—is not the same as the doing of justice in the particular human situation with which the judge has to deal. General rules, of course, can and should guide the judge towards a decision. But human situations, of their very nature, cannot be fully described by general normative propositions laid down in advance. Traditional legal theory—the theory embodied in the "Rule of Law"—does claim precisely this. Or at least, it bravely adopts a closure rule that says that only those circumstances that the legislator envisages in advance shall count as legally relevant circumstances. The alleged certainty of the law is thus purchased by a terrible gamble. But this is the theory, the normative theory, that legal realists have long shown to be significantly removed from the reality of the judicial process, not least because of the capacity of the court to construct the facts in such a way as will lead to justice, even while paying lip service to the rules of the system. My argument here, however, goes beyond the conventional claim to the existence of a gap between normative theory on the

[28] *The Concept of Law*, 12, 121-32.

[29] R. M. Dworkin, *Taking Rights Seriously* (London: Duckworth, 1977), esp. chap. 4, "Hard Cases" (reprinted from *Harvard Law Review* 88 [1975] 1057-1109); D. N. MacCormick, *Legal Reasoning and Legal Theory* (Oxford: Clarendon, 1978), esp. chap. 6.

one hand, and reality on the other. What I wish to contest, in conclusion, is the *value* of the pretence to the conformity of those levels—for that very pretence is indeed held out as a value. I quote from the extra-judicial writings of a distinguished English judge, Lord Radcliffe, who argued explicitly for a policy of "dissimulation":

> If judges prefer the formula, for that is what it is, that they merely declare the law and do not make it, they do no more than show themselves wise men in practice. Their analysis may be weak, but their perception of the nature of the law is sound. Men's respect for it will be the greater, the more imperceptible its development.[30]

Legalism and Spirituality

Lord Radcliffe may be right, at the level of social psychology; then again, he may be wrong. What strikes me as significant is the power that the dissimulation has acquired, the degree to which it is popularly held to represent the truth. But there are some circles in which this truth has not proved as palatable as Lord Radcliffe would suppose. In the modern age, I suggest that this provides a diagnosis of that condition popularly known as legalism.[31] Legalism is the activity of dealing strictly through the use of rules with a situation that calls for more than the application of mere rules. That is the sense in which Judith Shklar uses the term in considering legalism as an approach to ethics.[32] But if that diagnosis is correct, then the charge of legalism *cannot* be rightly applied in a situation where rules *are* a sufficient means of the resolution of a question. It has been the argument of this paper that legal doctrine and adjudication are two quite different phenomena, in which rules *are* sufficient in the former, but are *not* sufficient in the latter. Rule-centeredness is therefore not an evil in itself; it is only an evil when applied in the wrong context.

I conclude by briefly sketching a relationship between these issues and the notion of spirituality. I believe that I can, and should, go beyond the negative conclusions of this paper (that legalism is not a bad thing in the context of doctrine but is a bad thing in the context of adjudication) and affirm that positive values exist in both these two spheres, and identify in what sense they may approach the concept of spirituality.

[30] *The Law and its Compass* (London: Faber & Faber, 1961) 96, quoted in A. Paterson, *The Law Lords* (London: Macmillan, 1982) 140f.

[31] I have discussed the premodern roots in "Legalism," *Journal of Jewish Studies* 30 (1979) 1-22, esp. 5f.

[32] J. Shklar, *Legalism* (Cambridge: Harvard University, 1964) 1.

As for adjudication, the historical material on which I have touched gives us something of a clue. Spirituality here consists in a relationship between people; in practice the law is ruled by people, people are not ruled by the law. There have, indeed, been approaches towards the identification of spiritual values in the act of adjudication in a number of nonmainstream legal theories: for example, Georg Cohn's *Existentialism and Legal Science* and even Karl Llewellyn's "Lawyer's Natural Law" peering over the shoulder of the judge as he sits on the bench.[33] The modern jurisprudential tradition of the *nature des choses* also seeks to reconstruct the values inherent in an individual, but total situation.[34]

But there is also a form of spirituality in doctrine. There are two ways in which one can look at legal systems. One, which is endorsed by a crude form of legal informatics, would see the legal system as no more than an accumulation of rules, the statute book being a reference book like a telephone directory where all one does is to look at the particular entry in which one is interested, regarding that as an isolated and self-sufficient unit. Some forms of positivism endorse this approach, even if they recognize the systemic characteristics of the law through rules of priority designed to eliminate contradictions (like the *lex posterior* rule). But there is a second approach, increasingly gaining momentum, inspired in part by structuralism. Here, one looks at the substantive interrelationships of rules, not merely at the level of their explicit statement and rationalization, but also at a deeper level, of which the authors may not necessarily be conscious. I think, for example, of André-Jean Arnaud's study of the French civil code and, in different ways, of the analyses of Mary Douglas or Claude Lévi-Strauss of ritual and kinship rules.[35] Indeed, the idea that there is more than one level of meaning to be attached to legal rules—even to the mundane rules of civil law—is a very old one, expressed very directly by Aquinas.[36] Now what has this to do with spirituality?

[33] G. Cohn, *Existentialism and Legal Science,* (Dobbs Ferry, NY: Oceana, 1967); on Cohn, see further my "On the Tyranny of the Law," 331; K. Llewellyn, *Jurisprudence: Realism in Theory and Practice* (Chicago: University of Chicago, 1962) 111-15.

[34] For example, N. A. Poulantzas, *Nature des Choses et Droit* (Paris: L.G.D.J., 1965).

[35] A.-J. Arnaud, *Essai d'analyse structurale du code civil français* (Paris: L.G.D.J., 1973); M. Douglas, *Purity and Danger* (London: Routledge & Kegan Paul, 1966); C. Lévi-Strauss, *Les structures élémentaires de la parenté* (Paris: Mouton, 1967).

[36] *Summa Theologiae* §la2ae question 104.2; see my discussion in "The Ceremonial and the Judicial: Biblical Law as Sign and Symbol," *Journal for the Study of the Old Testament* 30 (1984) 25-50, esp. 26-28.

I do not believe that one has to adopt the kind of theological, revelational basis that Aquinas would suggest. What goes into the deep structure of legal doctrine is none other than the unstated, implicit, but (by that very reason) basic, social evaluations of a particular society at a particular time. It is certainly the "spirit of the people," or at least the spirit of some group of them, an idea difficult to express in English, but commonplace in the Francophone world, when they talk, even in the legal context, of *mentalités* and *l'imaginaire*.[37]

In short, different forms of spirituality exist in both doctrine and adjudication. Legalism enters the lists only when those categories are confused.

[37] For example, Arnaud, *Critique de la raison juridique 1: Ou va la Sociologie du droit?* (Paris: L.G.D.J., 1981), esp. 326ff.

Jo Milgrom

Some Consequences of the Image Prohibition in Jewish Art

In considering how holy law influences and shapes artistic activity, one continues to ponder the relationship between law and spirituality, for art is intimately connected with spirituality and mysticism, especially the art explored in the following pages. Milgrom is, in a sense, placing before the reader a particular instance of the general proposition, advanced especially by Falk and Ayoub, that holy law promotes spirituality. She is interested in the ways in which the second commandment, which prohibits images, has shaped—and promoted—art among Jews. Taking as paradigmatic the interaction between Aaron the articulator and Moses the lisper (or between Bezalel who succeeds in image-making and Moses who fails), she sees Jewish art as caught in a tension between image-making and the avoidance of images. The former is undertaken by artists who maintain that it is not the making of images that is forbidden but rather the worshiping of them. The latter characterizes the art of the "alephbet," art that concentrates on the letters of the Hebrew alphabet. A large part of Milgrom's essay is taken up with an exploration of the kabbalistic roots of much of this latter type of art.

Jo Milgrom is Assistant Professor in Residence of Theology and the Arts at the Center for Judaic Studies of the Graduate Theological Union in Berkeley, California, as well as a consultant for the *Biblical Archaeological Review*. She received her Ph.D. from the G.T.U.

The basis for my topic—some consequences of the image prohibition—is found in the Pentateuch: "You shall not make for yourself a sculptured image, or any likeness of what is in the heavens above, or on the earth below, or in the waters under the earth. You shall not bow down to them or serve them . . ." (Exod 20:4-5a). The snarls of the image prohibition itself have been treated by other scholars, particularly Joseph Gutmann.[1] This paper deals only with a few of the consequences of that prohibition. I begin with two stories separated from each other by almost 2000 years.

The first is midrash from "Numbers Rabbah" 15:10 on Exod 25:31. Rabbi Levi bar Rabbi says:

> A pure menorah came down from the heavens, as the Holy One said to Moses: "Make a menorah of pure gold [Exod 25:31]." He answered, "How shall I make it?" "The menorah shall be made of hammered work [*miqšāh*]," the Holy One said. But Moses found it difficult [*hitqāšāh*], came down and forgot how to do it. Moses went up again, asked how to do it, and heard the same instructions: "Make it *miqšāh* [of hammered work]." Moses came down and *hitqāšāh* [found it difficult], and promptly forgot.[2]

He went up four times (because *miqšāh* appears four times in Scripture—twice in Exodus 25 and twice in Numbers 8), probably more embarrassed each time. Exod 25:40 reads: "See it and do it according to the pattern that was shown you on the mountain." So he saw it, and got the instructions four times, and came down the mountain four times and *hitqāšāh*, and forgot it four times.

The Holy One, a bit short on patience by this time, gave Moses an excellent referral. Go to Bezalel, he said, "whom I have endowed with a divine spirit of skill, ability and knowledge in every kind of craft . . . to work in gold, silver, brass, in cutting of stones for setting, in the carving of wood" (Exod 31:3). Of course Bezalel easily did it because he stood 'in the shadow of God', *bĕ-ṣēl-ʾēl*. Thus, while the "write" hand is delivering the image prohibition, the right brain is giving divine sanction to work of art.

The second story takes place in the 1960s. George Steiner, in writing about Arnold Schoenberg's opera *Moses and Aaron*, notes that in certain significant moments of the opera, Moses does not sing. Instead he speaks in a highly cadenced, loud voice, bitter against the

[1] See "The 'Second Commandment' and the Image in Judaism," *No Graven Images* (ed. Joseph Gutmann; New York: KTAV, 1971) 3-14.

[2] "Numbers Rabbah" 15:10. See *Misrash Rabah*, vol. 6: *Numbers II* (ed. H. Freedman and M. Simon; 3d ed.; London: Soncino, 1983), 650.

fluencies of the music, and in particular against Aaron's soaring tenor. Steiner defines the tragic subject of the opera:

> Moses' incapacity to give expressive form (music) to his vision, to make revelation communicable and thus translate his individual communion with God into a community of belief in Israel . . . , Aaron's contrasting eloquence, his instantaneous translation—hence traduction—of Moses' abstract, hidden meanings into sensuous form (the singing voice), dooms the two men to irreconcilable conflict. Moses cannot do without Aaron. . . . But Aaron diminishes or betrays Moses' thought, that in him which is immediate revelation, in the very act of communicating it to other men. . . . There is in *Moses and Aaron* a radical consideration of silence, an inquiry into the ultimate tragic gap between what is apprehended and that which can be said. Words distort; eloquent words distort absolutely.[3]

Even as Aaron sings, exulting in the grandeur of God, Moses cries out, "No image can give you an image of the unimaginable." This scene was ingeniously staged by Sarah Caldwell with Moses and Aaron on a circular disk that turns before the eyes of the audience. They are standing back to back, representing the irreconcilable dual aspects of a single humanity, the vision apprehended and the vision translated but mistranslated (compare fig. 1). Moses needed Aaron's words to translate the revelation into language, and Bezalel's art to translate the revelation into forms. His story is our story. Like Moses, we need both words and art. What the image prohibition really says, therefore, is not "don't make images"; it says "don't worship images." The purpose of the prohibition is clear: all images and words are only partial. To mistake the part for the whole is what idolatry is all about.

Sculptor Milton Horn perceived the shared identity of Moses and Bezalel (fig. 2). The remarkable juxtaposition of the two men, and the apparent contradiction between them, can be seen in his representational ark doors in Temple Israel, Charleston, West Virginia. Carved and perforated out of white Appalachian oak by Horn in 1960, the seven foot doors, left in their natural color, slide open in front of a pair of side panels bearing the first ten letters of the alephbet. The motif of the doors is *aggadah* and *halakah*, translated by art historian Avram Kampf not only as Legend and Law, but as Imagination and Deed.[4] The menorah that Moses could not duplicate from the divine

[3] G. Steiner, *Language and Silence* (London: Penguin, 1968) 176–77.

[4] *Contemporary Synagogue Art* (Philadelphia: Jewish Publication Society, 1966) 211ff.

Fig. 1. Twelfth-Century Winchester Bible perceives Moses and Aaron as halves of a single identity. Reprinted with permission from H. Swarzenski, *Monuments of Romanesque Art* (Chicago: University of Chicago, 1967) fig. 309.

Fig. 2. Moses and Bezalel on representational ark doors in Temple Israel, Charleston, West Virginia. Sculpted by Milton Horn in 1960. Reprinted with permission from Avram Kampf, *Contemporary Synagogue Art* (Philadelphia: Jewish Publication Society, 1966).

pattern occupies the upper right corner of the Bezalel panel, its form derived from and in harmony with the almond branches at Bezalel's feet (center left). In the Moses panel these almond branches became the burning bush where Moses receives the Torah.

Bezalel, who resembles artist Horn, is busy with chisel and mallet, having already completed the most controversial figures of sanctuary art, the cherubim, who kneel in embrace beneath the protective wings of Shekhinah, representing the love relationship between God and his people when Israel fulfills the divine will.[5]

[5] Louis I. Rabinowitz, "Cherub in the Aggadah," *Encyclopaedia Judaica* (Jerusalem: Keter, 1971), 5:399. 2 Chr 3:13 states that the faces of the cherubim were inward,

Fig. 3. Detail of Figure 2.

Because the wood for the doors is roughly hewn, light plays on the gouge strokes emphasizing a vibrating, animated surface. The ark extends itself upward, visually terminating in the eternal light glowing steadily through amber glass placed behind this upper burning bush-menorah and between its parted curtains.

Of great interest in Milton Horn's doors, is the ambidextrous God whose right hand delivers the tablets of the law, while his left hand showers blessing rays onto Bezalel's head (fig. 3). The notion of sinister left is abandoned. The right brain is welcomed, surfacing to restored left-handed recognition in 1960, and resurrected from the obscurity of late antiquity.

The right and left hands of God are also conspicuous in the Exodus and Ezekiel panels at the Dura Europos Synagogue (third century A.D.). In the Exodus panel (fig. 4), God's left hand is associated with the visionary work of the rod; in the Ezekiel panel, God's left hand knits the dry bones back together.

Horn's ark doors represent one of the more common artistic responses to the so-called image prohibition. If the art of the desert sanctuary did not violate the image prohibition, neither does the art of any subsequent sanctuary. The issue has boiled down to the representation of the human face, which is the essence of the divine image. Horn and many others feel that *worshiping* the image is the critical matter, not making the image.

---

regarded as facing away from each other, whereas Exod 25:20 states that their faces were to one another. Disparity creates place for the midrashic interpretation.

Fig. 4. The Exodus panel, Dura Europos Synagogue, Syria (third century A.D.). Reprinted with permission from E. R. Goodenough, *Jewish Symbols in the Greco-Roman Period* (Princeton: Bollingen, 1964).

The Dura Europos Synagogue confronted the same issue in the central panel over the Torah niche of the Akedah, the Binding of Isaac, in which the participants, Abraham, Isaac, and Sarah, have all turned their faces away from the viewers (fig. 5). They face the ubiquitous hand of God. It is very clear from the distinct style that a different artist executed this panel. Did a different ideology also govern the interpretation? Later manuscripts show that the face, which is the divine image, is sometimes partly concealed by a hat pulled low, or the features left incomplete, or the face literally defaced, or animal faces substituted for humans. But this was a localized phenomenon. At the same time, a few miles away in a different community, the same biblical passage might be visually interpreted with complete indifference to an image prohibition.

The Alephbet as Image

There is another approach to the image prohibition: it concerns the use of the alephbet as a visual, phonetic, and numerological symbol set. An initial hint regarding the esoteric functions of the alephbet is to be found in "Genesis Rabbah," which puzzles over how God

Fig. 5. The Binding of Isaac, Dura Europos Synagogue, Syria (third century A.D.). Reprinted with permission from E. R. Goodenough, *Jewish Symbols in the Greco-Roman Period* (Princeton: Bollingen, 1964).

created this world and concludes that God did it by means of Wisdom.[6] The clever part is how the Rabbis worked out the grammar and syntax of that creation. The linguistic problem here starts at the beginning, in the first word of the Torah—*bĕrēʾšît*—which means not 'in the beginning' as the whole world knows, but the insoluble construct 'in the beginning *of*. . . .' In the beginning of what?

Following one route, "In the beginning of" led to a different translation of v 1 of Genesis, found in the New Jewish Publication Society *Torah: The Five Books of Moses*: "When God began to create heaven and earth. . . ."[7] In terms of how God created, that grammatical route was a dead end, so the Rabbis tried a different route. Since *bĕ-* can also mean 'by means of', v 1 might have something interesting to say if one could discover a unique definition of *rēʾšît*. And Rabbinic scholars discovered an occurrence of *rēʾšît* in Prov 8:22, where Wisdom, speaking about herself with decreasing modesty,

[6] "Genesis Rabbah" 1:1. See *Midrash Rabbah*, vol. 1: *Genesis* (ed. H. Freedman and M. Simon; 3d ed.; London: Soncino, 1983), 1.

[7] This translation is justly credited to Rashi (Rabbi Solomon ben Isaac) in *Notes on the New Translation of the Torah* (ed. H. M. Orlinsky; Philadelphia: Jewish Publication Society, 1969), 49-50.

boasts, "God has created me, the *beginning* of his way." Since *rēʾšît* is "me," and me is wisdom, *rēʾšît* must be wisdom. Thus Gen 1:1 reads: "by means of wisdom God created heaven and earth." The acknowledgment that wisdom can only mean Torah leads one to begin to discover how at least one branch of Judaism expressed in art the creation of the universe by means of the letters of the Torah.

An ancient fragment from the Midrash records a conversion between the Holy One and the Torah as God prepares to embark on the work of Creation: "I request laborers." The Torah replies, "I put at your disposal 22 laborers, namely the 22 letters which are in the Torah."[8] These 22 letters (and the first 10 numbers) are established in the "Sefer Yeẓirah" (ca. third century C.E.) as the tools of creation: everything comes into being as a result of 231 combinations (some say 221) of the 22 letters.[9]

Another statement appears in the first mishnah of this Sefer Yetzirah: "God created his world by three permutations of the root *spr*, by number, by book, and by story" (*sepār, wĕsēper, wĕsippûr*). This is interpreted by R. Kiener as a numerological, a graphic, and a phonetic component of the Hebrew letters.[10] Kiener defines this system as one of two kabbalistic symbol sets that convey cosmological process (the other being the *sefirot*). I believe the visual art that emerges from these systems with its profound tendency toward abstraction is a consequence of the image prohibition and a protest against the seductive limitations of the representational image.

The first vignette comes via Gershom Scholem in a work entitled *On the Kabbalah and its Symbolism.* Scholem focuses on the revelation of Sinai as an issue of the relationship between authority and mysticism. The authority part is clear: Israel receives "a sharply defined set of doctrines, a summons to the human community," but this revelation is not "a mystical formula open to infinite interpretation."[11] The mystical aspect arises when we ask what was actually heard when Israel received the Ten Utterances. Some traditions say they heard it all; others, that they heard only the first two, and were so terrorized by the divine presence that they implored Moses to mediate the remaining eight.

[8] L. Ginzberg, *Legends of the Jews* (Philadelphia: Jewish Publication Society, 1925), 5:5 nn. 10ff.

[9] See *The Book of Formation: Sepher Yetzirah* (trans. K. Stenring; London: W. Rider, 1923; repr. New York: KTAV, 1970).

[10] "Hebrew Language as Metaphor for Emanation in 13th Century Qabbalah," delivered at the annual meeting of the American Academy of Religion, 1982; published in *The Early Kabbalah* (ed. J. Dan; New York: Paulist, 1986) 153–64.

[11] (New York: Schocken, 1969) 29.

Rabbi Mendel Torum of Rymanóv (d. 1814) believed the revelation on Sinai was both an acoustic and a linguistic challenge and concluded that Israel heard only the *ālep* of the first word, *ʾānōkî* 'I'.[12] The *ʾālep*, however, is a silent letter. Scholem explains that the *ʾālep* may be said to denote the source of all articulate sound, the "potential sound of a divine larynx, as it were, about to speak." In that way, Rabbi Mendel transformed the revelation at Sinai into a mystical revelation "pregnant with infinite meaning but without specific meaning." It remained for Moses to translate the nonverbal into the human linear language of the receivable Torah. But Rabbi Mendel's image is powerful. Scholem writes that the word of God made itself heard through the medium of human language, which is one of the most important legacies bequeathed by Judaism to the religions of the world. It means language is the connection between humans and God.[13]

The second vignette concerns what was seen at Sinai. Moses ben Naḥman (Naḥmanides = Ramban), one of the early kabbalists (thirteenth century), gives a clue in the introduction to his commentary on the Torah, although his image goes back to the Palestinian Talmud.[14] The Torah, he says, was originally written in black fire on white fire. His meaning may be understood by visualizing a page of the Torah, the same scroll that is read regularly in public Jewish prayer, with letters written in expert calligraphy in very black ink, closely placed on invisible lines, without vowel points, punctuation, or musical trops. Since there is only a hair's breadth between all the letters to begin with, dividing them up differently would lead to a totally different configuration of Torah, reflecting the midrash that Moses received two Torahs: one as we know it, and one with secret combinations of the letters representing another reality. This esoteric Torah consists of a continuous unbroken stream of letters, which can therefore be read in mysterious ways. This is black fire on white fire, a concentration of divine energy of infinite meaning. White fire is the divine utterance, heard as the *ʾālep* and seen as white fire when it is set against the black. The black fire is the word written in black ink on the white paper—the words of the Torah and the words of commentary that explain the words of the Torah. Another way of saying and imagining this Torah is to call the white fire "negative space"—

[12] Ibid., 30.

[13] Scholem, "The Name of God and the Linguistic Theory of the Kabbalah," *Diogenes* 79 (1972) 59-80.

[14] Ibid., 77-78. See *Perushe ha-Torah* (ed. C. B. Chavel; Jerusalem: Mosad ha-Rav Ḳuḳ, 1959-60).

Fig. 6. Alphabet of Creation. Reprinted with permission from Ben Shahn, *Alphabet of Creation* (New York: Schocken, 1964).

the background of the concrete images. It is also the human effort that gives reality to the Divine.

A good example in Jewish art is the *Alphabet of Creation* by Ben Shahn (fig. 6), which is based on the charming alephbet tale of Abraham Abulafia (thirteenth century meditating and wandering kabbalist), which in turn is based on the concept of God using the Torah to create the world. Starting with *tāw*, each letter stands before the Holy One, presenting a positive quality and imploring that it be the instrument of creation. Thus, *tāw* stood for Torah and *śîn* for *Šaddai,* but in each case the Holy One found the negative aspect to cancel the positive. For *tāw* it was the mark of the doomed man; for *šîn,* it was the word *šeqer,* meaning 'lie'. All letters follow until the *bêt,* which stands for the irresistible *bĕrākâ* ('blessing').

Therefore God creates with the *bêt* of *bĕrēʾšît,* and begins the *dibrôt* (the Ten Utterances) with the *ʾālep.* Ben Shahn's alephbet is a study in black fire on white fire. Because it moves toward abstraction one is increasingly conscious of the space around the letters, the negative space, the white fire.[15] Thus, two of the consequences of the image prohibition have been to move Jewish arts to the Hebrew letter—resulting in calligraphy and micrography (an extension of calligraphy)—and to abstraction, which began by scrutinizing forms that exist within and around the letters.[16]

Šîn. Scholem writes of the strange idea that there is a letter missing in the present form of the Torah.[17] Since each letter represents a concentration of divine energy, deficiency in a letter means that there is a lack of God's energy in one's life. For example, some say that the *šîn* now written with three teeth, should in its complete form have four (see fig. 7). The correct form of the letter would result in different configurations of both black and white fire—other aspects of God, of meaning—made available to us. Moreover, it may be that the four toothed *šîn* is the original form in the Ten Commandments, allowing the tablets to be read from both sides.

Nûn. Another example of black fire on white fire is the visualization by artist Mark Podwal of the letter *nûn* as *nābîʾ*, 'prophet' (fig. 8). The prophet and the Torah are black and white reflections of each other. The prophet is reflected in the Torah for which he is the instrument.

ʾĀlep. The curious phonetic, visual, and numerological qualities of the elusive *ʾālep* are recounted in the following prose-poem,

[15] Ben Shahn, *The Alphabet of Creation* (New York: Schocken, 1964).

[16] Early among the moderns to revive the art of Hebrew calligraphy outside of the sacred art of the *sōfĕrîm,* the Torah scribes, was Raymond Katz (*Prelude To a New Art For An Old Religion* [Chicago: Stein, 1945]). The intervening forty years have seen a flowering of the art, climaxing in the state of the art of Jerusalem goldsmith Janet Berg, who incorporates graphic design and talmudic lore into her crystal and gold sculpture. On micrography, see Colette Sirat, *La Lettre hébraïque et sa signification* and Leila Avrin, *Micrography as Art* (Jerusalem: Israel Museum, 1981) [bound together]); Leila Avrin, "Note on Micrography: A Jewish Art Form," *Journal of Jewish Art* 6 (1979) 112-17.

[17] Scholem, *On the Kabbalah and its Symbolism,* 80-81.

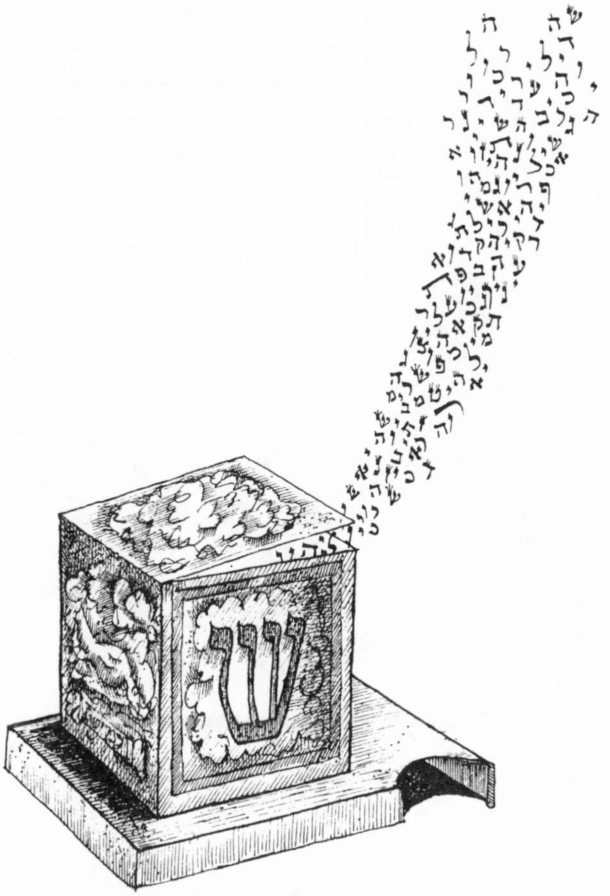

Fig. 7. *Šîn.* Reprinted with permission from Mark Podwal, *A Book of Hebrew Letters* (Philadelphia: Jewish Publication Society, 1978). Copyright © 1978 Mark Podwal.

which I have translated and edited from Yaakov ben Yaakov Ha-Kohen's medieval mystic commentary on the alephbet (thirteenth century);[18] it is followed by a commentary on the commentary, accompanied by figures that illuminate the art and theology of the *ʾālep* (see fig. 9)

[18] Gershom Scholem (ed.), *Madaʾe ha-Yahadut* II (Jerusalem: publ., 1927) 201–19 [Hebrew].

Fig. 8. The prophet (*nābîʾ*) as Torah. Reprinted with permission from Mark Podwal, *A Book of Hebrew Letters* (Philadelphia: Jewish Publication Society, 1978). Copyright © 1978 Mark Podwal.

"Perush Ha-otiot"

a.

Behold, I draw the *aleph* and speak about her form. . . .

Look at the *aleph* with your eyes
and understand her in your heart
and you will find her truth in
the shape of the (other) letters
enclosed in her.

Fig. 9. *ʾĀlep* (Dresden Mahzor, ca. fourteenth century).

b.

Why?
all the letters have a fixed place
in the mouth
but the *aleph*, chief of all remembered
by the mouth

rests in the mouth's air, powerfully at ease
like the Holy One
concealed from all eyes, deep down where tongue meets throat.

c.

Who like the skinny ethereal *aleph*
lets Herself be known only in thought
because only thought is pure and spare like air
but even thought can't hold the hiding one.

d.

You see, as all letters press into the *aleph*
the might of all creatures hides in the power of the Holy One
waiting for Will to will the time of birth.
So the *aleph* teaches us
there is no creatures without a creat-or
no form without a form-er
no image without an artist.

e.

Now understand the *aleph*'s white in side
and her black out side as well
and you will find that in side carries out (side),
that in side is *maqom* of out
to teaches us that inside is the hidden Holy One
while outside is world itself,
a cameo on the right arm of the mighty one.

As in is *maqom* of out
so the Holy One is the place of the world—
but the world is not His place.

f.

Now, as I said, the white of the *aleph* is the Holy One.
(Looking for a proof text) Our Sages asked, how was light created?
By the psalm which wrapped the Holy One in white glory
from one end of the world to the other,
and Daniel added, "Light dwells with him."
Furthermore, (kabbalistic tongue in cheek)
can you think of spelling Light (*ohr*) without an *aleph*!

g.

Now the robe of light—it's no *p'shat* simple robe.
Everyone knows the Holy One
isn't fleshed in blood, that sages speak in human tongues.
There's nothing to His face but
light
So David said, even dark cannot darken you.

h.

Now see four arms of *aleph* flowing from the center point—
they are four sides of the sky
four letters of the Name
four beasts of the chariot throne
four camps of messenger angels.

i.

As inside white reaches outside black
the right arm embraces all.

Though His forms are many, His powers protean fire,
He is One, unchanging. Malachi said it, I am God I do not change.
Like the *aleph,* from whom all forms are drawn,
yet the *aleph* is forever.

j.

Here's a gematria game. The picture of the *aleph* = God's name.
How so?
Its head it *yod*; that equals ten. Its foot another *yod.*
The torso in between is *vov,* a six.
Thus *aleph* (26) = YHVH . . . hmmm.
Y=10; v=6; 2H=5x2; a divine grand total: 26.
The picture is the name
For limbs and letters both add up
Now we know for sure the *aleph* is god's portrait.

k.

And since Adam was created in the Image,
does s/he add up too? Let's see.
The *yod*s we said are ten: Fingers and toes.
The torso-*vov* is six: front and back, right and left,
up and down, so there!

l.

Say, what about the head? We'll count up yet another clever way
The *yod* on top, now that's the head. Two eyes two ears two nostrils
and of course, four holy sections of the tefillin head
squeezing fingers and toes to a single *yod*
(squeezing a mitzvah from a kabbalistic kvetch).

m.

But Exodus 15:11 proves that all ends well.
"God is awesome of praise doing wonders."
O Wonder of wonders, phela reads backwards
aleph!

Commentary

Verse *a*: "The Kabbalists always regarded [the *ʾālep*] as the spiritual root of all other letters, encompassing in its essence the whole alphabet and hence all other elements of human discourse".[19]

Verses *b*, *c*: Yaakov haKohen demonstrates by analogy that the *ʾālep* is the phonic divine-human connection. The *ʾālep* works effortlessly like a breath of air. Just as the Creator creates without a show of power of effort, the breath of the *ʾālep* refers to the vowels, which are the breath of language that make sound possible. The *ʾālep* is the first of the *matres lectiones*, the four mother letter-vowels that antedated the pointed text (*ʾālep, hēʾ, wāw, yôd*).[20] These very letters compose two of God's name: *ʾehyeh* 'I AM', and the tetragram *yhwh*, letters whose essential meaning is 'being'. Thus, these letters, the spiritual or breath elements among the consonants, are symbolic of the divine element among the letters. In this manner, all letters, in the language of the poem, are part of the *ʾālep*. There is an easy identity between the breath/wind/spirit of God's presence hovering in Genesis 1, and the breath/wind/spirit of the vowels that makes possible the miracle of human language.

Verse *d*: Just as the strokes of all the letters emerge from the *ʾālep*, so everything emerges from God as an aspect of God's will and purpose. This verse conveys the visual connection between Creator and creature by means of component parts of the *ʾālep*, namely the *yôd* apostrophe and the *wāw* stem.

[19] Scholem, *On the Kabbalah and its Symbolism*, 30.

[20] M. Z. Segal, *Dikduk Lashon HaMishnah*, (Tel Aviv: D'vir, 1936) 32–33 [Hebrew].

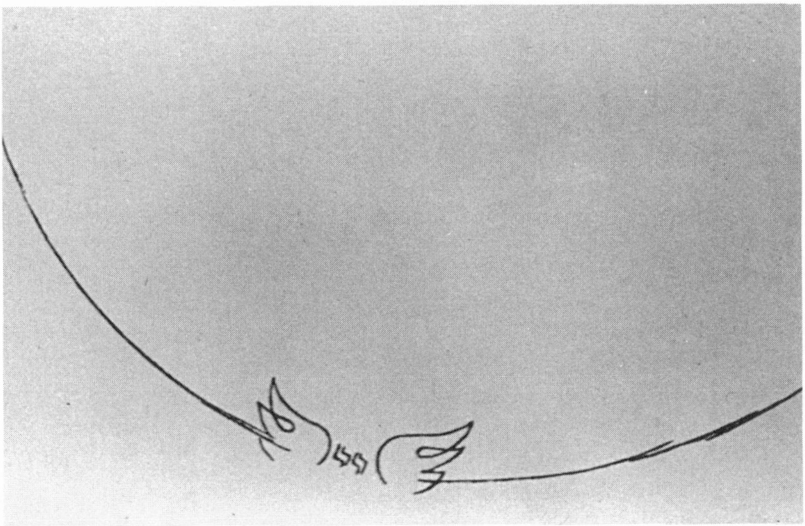

Fig. 10. *Yôd* as wings. Reprinted with permission from Benn, *Visions of the Bible* (Tel Aviv: Sinai, 1954).

Yôd. The *yôd* point is a tiny apostrophe, mostly a dot shape, the first position in the tetragram. It is the source of all visible language and a physical, spatial connection with God. All forms in space start with it. To get from ordinary space to that dot, the religious part of humans must find a way to transcend ordinary secular space to connect with the sacred space that begins at the *yôd* dot. Our ancestors knew intuitively how to bridge the gap. They would reach up and imagistically poke a hole in space and connect with the tiny *yôd*: "On the most archaic level of culture, transcendence is expressed by various images of an opening. Communication with the gods happens via an opening."[21] That is why comparative religion has a variety of terms for that tiny opening and the planting of the connection: hidden seed, divine egg, root of roots, and now in Kabbalah, the *yôd*. The *yôd* apostrophe is the opening and the visual source of linguistic movement. It can be written as two coincident right-angled apostrophes: wings that evolve from the original point and movement. This *yôd* point is the little initial upper flag stroke of the *ʾālep*. Benn has incorporated the *yôd* into the wing composition as both the signature and presence of God (fig. 10).

[21] M. Eliade, *The Sacred and the Profane* (New York: Harcourt Brace Jovanovich, 1959), chap. 1: "Sacred Space and Making the World Sacred" (p. 26).

Fig. 11. Modern *wāw*. Reprinted with permission from E. Wiesel, *The Golem* (illus. by Mark Podwal; New York: Summit, 1983). Copyright © 1983 Mark Podwal.

Wāw. If the *yôd* apostrophe is the tiny opening into space that admits the sacred "Other," the *wāw* is the vertical axis of the world, the *axis mundi* that connects one to the opening. It is the same vertical connection served by Jacob's ladder, which reaches to the gates of the heavens, another opening into the divine sphere; the same vertical served by the Tree of Life in the Garden, by Mount Sinai, and any height where theophanies usually take place.

Figures 11 and 12 represent two *wāws* separated by 500 years, both operating as an *axis mundi*. The modern *wāw* is by Mark Podwal (fig. 11), intended to double as a *yôd*—a Torah pointer and an *axis mundi*—as it reaches up to become the middle letter of the Tetragram. The second *wāw* is the trunk of the inverted kabbalistic Tree of Life (fig. 12) whose trunk also bears the Tetragram. (I will later examine this tree as part of the second symbol set of *sefirot*). Isaac the Blind, thirteenth century kabbalist in his commentary on the

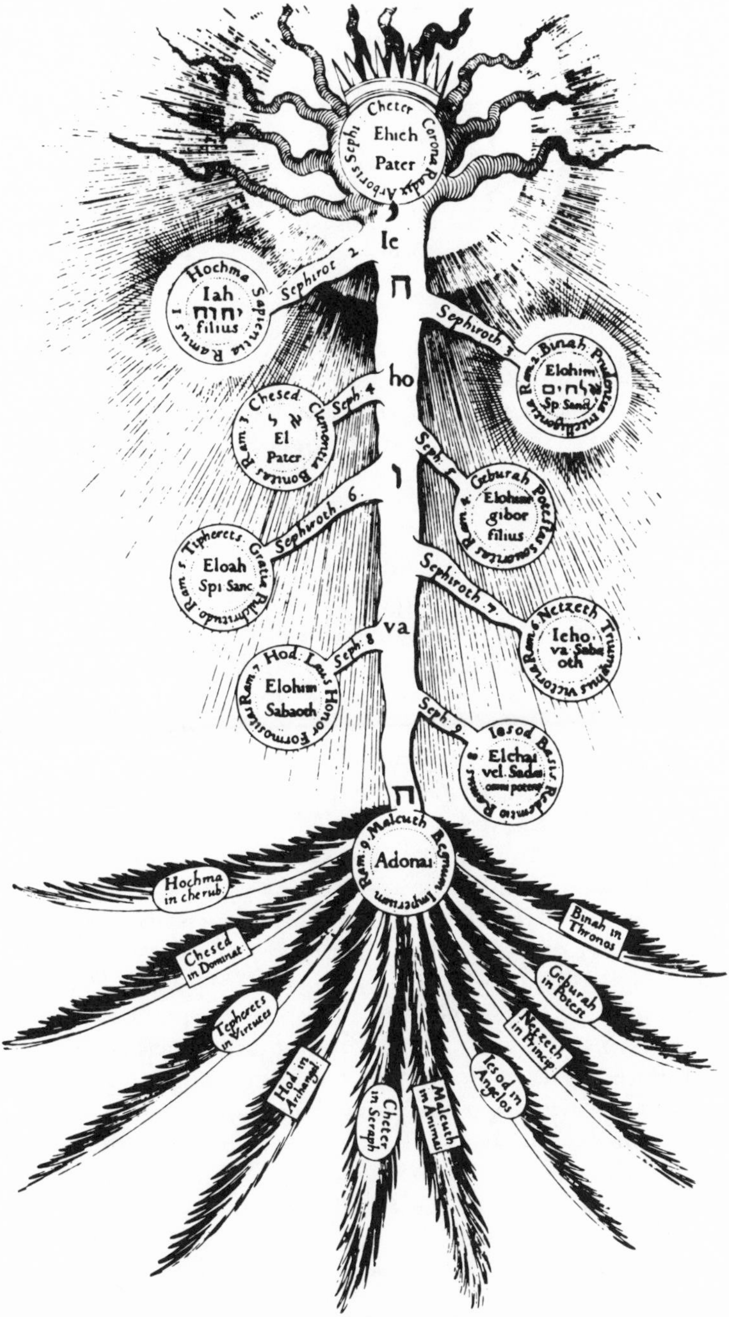

Fig. 12. Inverted kabbalistic Tree of Life. Sefirotic tree engraved by Robert Fludd, *Philosophia sacra* (1626). Reprinted with permission from Roger Cook, *The Tree of Life* (New York: Avon Books, 1974).

"Book of Creation," the oldest kabbalistic linguistic mysticism, combines the image of tree with fire and God's name:

> The root is the spoken word, the one name
> The letters are the branches, flames flickering and leaves
> All forms issue finally from the one name
> Just as the twig issues from the root.
> It follows then that everything its contained
> In the root which is the one name.[22]

Thus organic growth, the basic human experience of the world, is directly related to the sacred space of point and stroke.

Verse *e*: These ten lines play on the figure-ground relationship of positive and negative space of, as the Kabbalah expresses it, black fire on white fire. Physically one can experience a larger presence of God if she or he can focus visually on the shape of space around objects, rather than on the objects alone. The negative space, white fire, is called *māqôm*, the Place and Name of God. Thus God is both the Name and the Place of the world; in other words, the world would have no reality but for God. On the other hand, God is not limited to the world, therefore "the world is not his place."

Verses *f*, *g*: Rabbinic theology sought an organic rather than a philosophic way of demonstrating the reality of God. Verses from Scripture were therefore chosen that make the presence of God concrete. Human language and analogy are deliberately selected not because there is no alternative, but to make God more accessible to human beings. These verses are particularly successful because they make God physically real by means of God's most ordinary, yet miraculous, nonpalpable feature—light. Torah is seen as a fabric woven from the name of God (fig. 13), which merges with the psalmist's image of God wrapped in a robe of light, itself woven from the fabric of God's names (Ps 104:2).

Verse *h*: Four arms emerging from a center point is a mandala image that conveys a sense of stability and rest and, as an instrument of meditation, gives one a sense of safe grounding in a balanced eternal structure, free from disruptive dangers of change.[23]

The center point where the four arms meet is also the *omphalos* image of the sacred center made familiar by the works of Mircea Eliade. God and human meet each other at a point where humankind

[22] Scholem published Isaac the Blind's commentary on the "Book of Creation" ("Sefer Yeẓirah") as an appendix to his *Ha-Kabbalah be-Provence* (ed. R. Schatz; Jerusalem: Hebrew University, 1963).

[23] E. Edinger, *Ego and Archetype* (Baltimore: Penguin 1973) 182.

Fig. 13. Torah woven from the names of God. Reprinted with permission from Mark Podwal, *A Book of Hebrew Letters* (Philadelphia: Jewish Publication Society, 1978). Copyright © 1978 Mark Podwal.

reaches up and breaks through space to connect with the transpersonal source of nourishment via the connecting cord, the axis of the world. The primeval Tree of Life is such an image, clearly related to the four-armed *ʾālep*, as the primeval river branching into four also flows from the center of Creation. The Tree of Life in Judaism becomes Torah, and in Christianity becomes the Cross; such imagery makes the connection to the four-armed *ʾālep* even more graphic.

The four letters of the Name refer to the Tetragram, YHWH; the four beasts are the composite mythic cherubim who surmounted the holy ark and in Canaanite mythology were the "wheels" for the gods. A vestige of this metaphor remains in the psalmist's image of God riding the clouds (Ps 68:5). The four camps of angels accompanying the chariot may also allude to the winds that are God's messengers/angels (Ps 104:4). These series of fours may also allude to the four worlds of creation, a doctrine that appears in Zohar, a generation or so after Yaakov.

Verses *j*, *k*: A semi-serious game, gematria, or numerology, is employed by the kabbalists. Although there are a number of variations, the simplest form of gematria gives a sequential numerical value to the letters of the alephbet. (Thus *ʾālep*=1, *bêt*=2, etc.) With this system theological relationships can be established that expand consciousness in unexpected ways. Thus, for example, *raz* 'secret' and *ʾôr* 'light' have the same numerical value, forcing one to see connections not otherwise considered so directly without this exotic equivalence.

Verse *j*: Verse *j* depicts in graphic quantitative terms what earlier verses said with poetic analogy, namely, that *ʾālep* is a picture of God and the universe. Verse *j* says that there is a parallel energy in their element / letter construction that creates yet another identity. The *ʾālep* is a graphic equivalence of God "limb for limb" and a numerological equivalence by means of the gematria of God's name.

In a recent "Hand-made Midrash Workshop," I encouraged my graduate divinity students to experience the biblical text in other than the usual cognitive, linear, academic mode. They were instructed to make an *ʾālep* by tearing and pasting colored construction paper—but not an ordinary *ʾālep*. Their *ʾālep* was to graphically convey the concepts that (1) the *yôd* particles of the *ʾālep* are the image of God and therefore their own individual human image, and (2) the *wāw* stroke is their individual connection between themselves and God. The final purpose of the exercise was for the individual to "know" deeply how language creates the God-human connection. Paradoxically they would experience this initially in a prelinguistic way. The exercise requires no art training and is introduced in such a way as to encourage free associative play and to eliminate intimidation.

One of my students, Amy, tore out a flaming torch of yellow light for the diagonal *wāw* stroke. The *yôd* particles were two green hands, the upper somewhat larger than the lower. Underlying the center of the torch is a thin green archway, which in addition to providing a delicate compositional element, relates the hands to each other and

Fig. 14. Amy's *ʾĀlep*. Photograph by the author.

identifies them as a focal support for the torch. Both the center of the torch and the area above it have been torn away, exposing space so the *aleph* can take flight (fig. 14). Relating to the *wāw* stroke Amy cited the following passages:

1. And God said, "Let there be light" (Gen 1:2).
2. And a flaming torch passed between the pieces (Genesis 15).
3. And the angel of the Lord appeared to him in a blazing bush (Exodus 4).
4. And there appeared to them tongues of fire . . . and they were filled with the holy spirit (Acts 2).

In an authentic midrashic mode stimulated initially by the visual forms, Amy moved divine light from its first appearance in Creation, prior to human creation, to its second appearance during Abraham's trance, to its third and fourth appearances to individuals of heightened consciousness, Moses and the Apostles. The experience engendered a process of growing consciousness in Amy that was expressed in her conscious selection of biblical passages mirroring the same spiritual expansion. For the *yôd*/hand particles, she wrote: (1) In the image of God he created them, male and female he created them (Gen 1:28); (2) Mother Theresa has said we are Christ's hands.

As noted earlier, the four directional *ʾālep* (cf. fig. 15) evolved in Judaism to the image of the Tree of Life in the Garden from which flow the four rivers of the world; this Tree of Life then became Torah. In Christianity the same Tree of Life with its quaternal configuration became the cross. The basic imagery, in both its Jewish and Christian evolution, emerges from the shared synchronic reservoir of the unconscious as clearly illustrated in Amy's work.

To complete the unity, humankind must be seen as an image of God, and of the *ʾālep*, as another gematria established. Adam and YHWH have the same equivalence (45) if the Tetragram is spelled out *yôd, hēʾ, wāw, hēʾ*.

Sefirot in Jewish Mysticism

The *sefirot* (*sĕpîrôt*) presents the *ʾālep* as Adam. The mystical *ʾālep* represents the harmonic unity of the ten *sefirot* as follows (fig. 16): the upper *yôd* as head of Adam is represented by the head *sefirot—keter, bînâ,* and *ḥokmâ* ('crown', 'wisdom', and 'understanding'). The *wāw* (the torso in verse *k*) represents the arms here and the opposing *sefirot* of *gĕbûrâ* and *gĕdûlâ* or *ḥesed* ('fear' and 'compassion'), and *hôd* ('majesty') and *nēṣaḥ* ('endurance'), while the lower *yôd* is represented as the feet, by *yĕsôd* ('phallus') and *malkût* or *šĕkînâ* ('Indwelling Presence' and 'community of Israel').

The doctrine of the *sefirot* is the vocabulary of Jewish mysticism. *Sefirot* might be related to *sappîr* 'sapphire', hence an association with emanations of light; or it might be related to *sāpar* 'to count'. Kiener refers to the *sefirot* as one of two symbol sets that Jewish

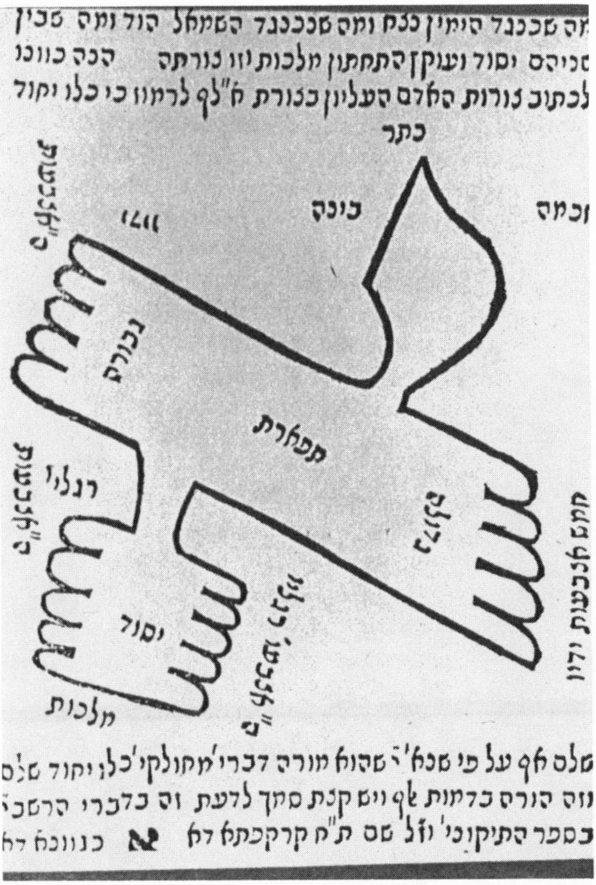

Fig. 15. The four directional *ʾālep*, representing the harmonic unity of the ten *sefirot* contained in it. Reprinted from Moses Cordovero, *Pardes Rimmonim*, 1592. Used with permission of the Jewish National and University Library, Jerusalem.

mysticism has created to convey spiritual realities, the other being the alephbet, as discussed above.

To describe this diagram of the *sefirot*, one must start at the top before there is an emanation, and call that the *ein-sof*, (*ʾên-sôp*), the Infinite one; also nothingness: no-thing-ness. The *ein-sof* may be conceptualized as a hidden spring that will become manifest by watering the tree and giving soul/life to the body. What is hidden will become manifest by means of a series of symbols that say something about the life of God.

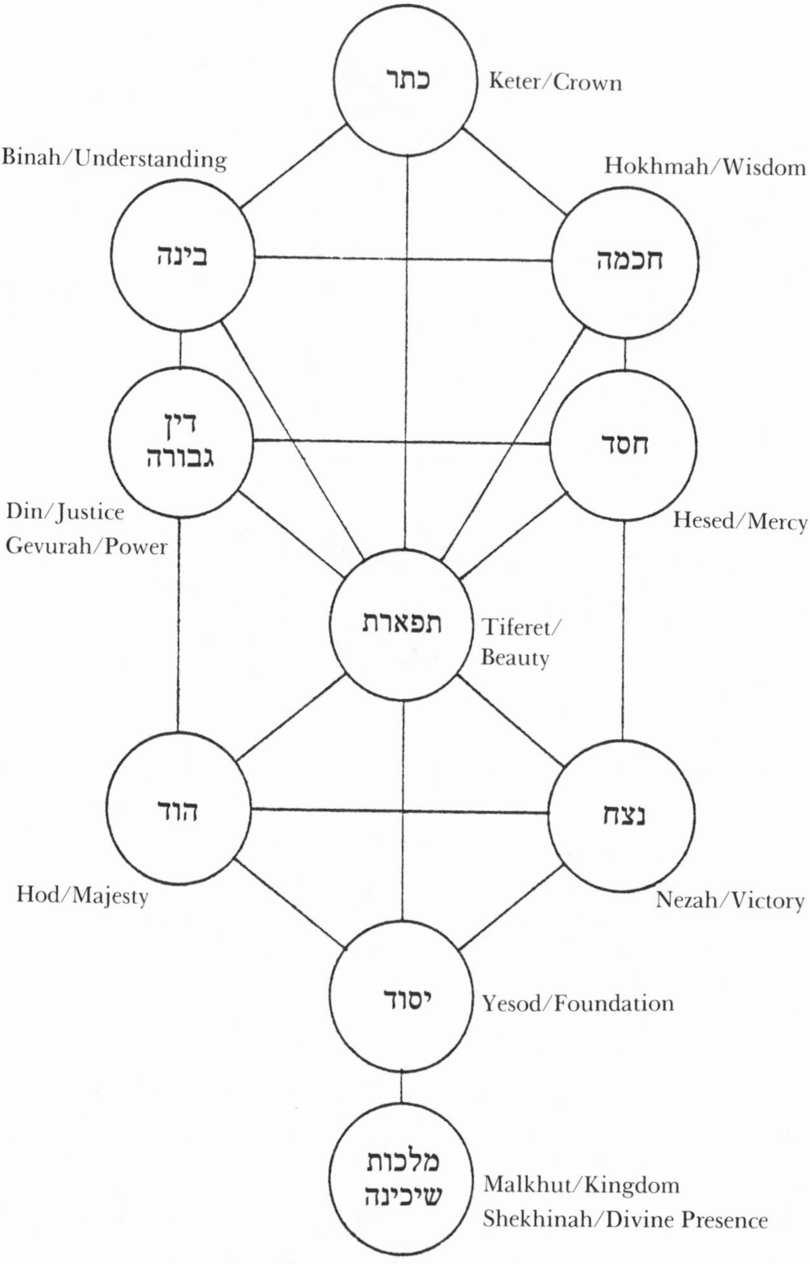

Fig. 16. The ten *sefirot*. Adapted with permission from Barry W. Holtz, ed., *Back to the Sources: Reading the Classic Jewish Texts* (New York: Summit, 1984).

The first *sefirah* is called *keter* 'crown', which is not part of either the tree or the man, but a link. The Zohar moves it a bit past *ein-sof* by calling it *ᶜayin* 'nothing'. It may also be called the "will to will." It is the beginning of the God's process of self-revelation.[24]

The next pair of *sefirot* (they work in pairs now, on the right and left) are *ḥokmâ* 'wisdom' and *bînâ* 'understanding'. These are processes of the divine. From the will to will comes the will to create. In human language, *ḥokmâ* is the idea and *bînâ* the working out of the idea. There are analogies. Thus *ḥokmâ* is the 'pinpoint' first impulse of God to create what is not God. *Bînâ* is sometimes called 'palace'. It becomes a structure because it is the working out of an idea. The potential and the actual even take on sexual connotations, as masculine and feminine, and those dualities continue throughout the diagram.

The highest three *sefirot, keter, ḥokmâ,* and *bînâ* concern divine thought. Humans can't really say very much about them. But they have engendered yet another translation of Gen 1:1: "By means of the sefira *Ḥokmâ,* the *ein-sof* created God, the sefira *bînâ.*" A summary statement would be: Through the divine will to create, the God of religion emerges from its concealment in *"ein sof."*[25]

The fourth *sefira* on the right side is called *ḥesed* 'compassion', and represents God's abundance and love and blessing. The fifth *sefira,* opposite on the left, makes clear the dualities in the life of God. This *sefira* counterbalances the love. It is called *dîn* or *gĕbûrâ* 'judgment or severity'; it is the presence of evil built into the system. Evil too is part of God: "He makes peace and creates evil [*ᶜōśeh šālôm ûbôrēᵓ rāᶜ*]" (Isa 45:7).

Ḥesed and *dîn* "express the intuition that love and strictness, flow and restraint, are dialectical principles that are part of the very nature of all existence."[26] These two extremes, in fact the whole structure, achieve equilibrium through *tipᵓeret* 'beauty', the sixth *sefira,* and center of the *sefirot.*

Nēṣaḥ and *hôd,* on the right and left, respectively, are the seventh and eighth *sefirot* and concern the nature of divine kingship. *Nēṣaḥ* 'lasting endurance' is a continuation of *ḥesed* ('loyalty, love') and represents the king's benevolence, while *hôd* 'majesty' continues the *sefira* of severity and means regal aloofness. These two *sefirot* seem to be extensions of *dîn* and *ḥesed.*

[24] Louis Jacobs, *Seeker of Unity* (New York: Basic Books, 1966) 34.

[25] Ibid., 37.

[26] L. Fine, "Kabbalistic Texts," *Back to the Sources* (ed. B. Holtz; New York: Summit, 1984) 323.

The ninth sefira is *yĕsôd* 'foundation'. *Yĕsôd* harmonizes benevolence and regal aloofness, and is represented as the phallus; it is the vehicle of divine procreativeness flowing downward.

The tenth *sefira, malkût* 'sovereignty', is visualized as a feminine receptacle and is also called *šĕkînâ* 'divine dwelling'. The *šĕkînâ* is the lower of *tipʾeret* who is the Holy One. Their union expresses the principle of both the love and tension that characterizes male-female relationships.

The *sefirot* can also be visualized in human form as *Adam Kadmon,* or primordial man (fig. 17). This is the kabbalistic way of saying androgynous humankind is created in the image of God. The *sefirot* are an abstract expression of representational androgyny in the visual arts. Thus the three top *sefirot* correspond to head and intellect. *Ḥesed* and *nēṣaḥ* are the right limbs (arm and leg), and *dîn / gĕbûrâ* and *hôd* are the left.

This is the inverted tree of the *sefirot* (see fig. 12), dating back to 1626, in an engraving from Robert Fludd, entitled *Philosophia Sacra.*[27] Its roots are in heaven and its branches grow down toward the earth in an image that is found both among primitive and the sophisticated, for example, among Australian aborigines and Jewish kabbalists. It is a symbol that shows the one transcendent root religious source of human experience. The *sefirot* of the trunk illustrate the many names and characteristics of God and are repeated in the branches below. The trunk itself carries the Tetragram. Root and trunk are primary vertical image of the axis of the world, linking humans to their sources, and centering them both above and below.

Modern Jewish Art

Thus far I have shown how traditional Jewish art has "responded" to the image prohibition by means of symbol sets, derived from language and light in the alephbet. In concluding, I ask the question, How has this response filtered into modern artistic sensibilities?

This question may be answered by examining the work of two artists who are of particular importance because their religious sensibilities are not establishment. They are important because their art is evidence that religious art and mainstream contemporary art do not have to run separate courses.

Swartz

The first is Beth Ames Swartz who went in search of her rootedness in the historical and metaphysical past of Israel. She spent two

[27] See Roger Cook, *Tree of Life* (New York: Avon, 1974) fig. 38.

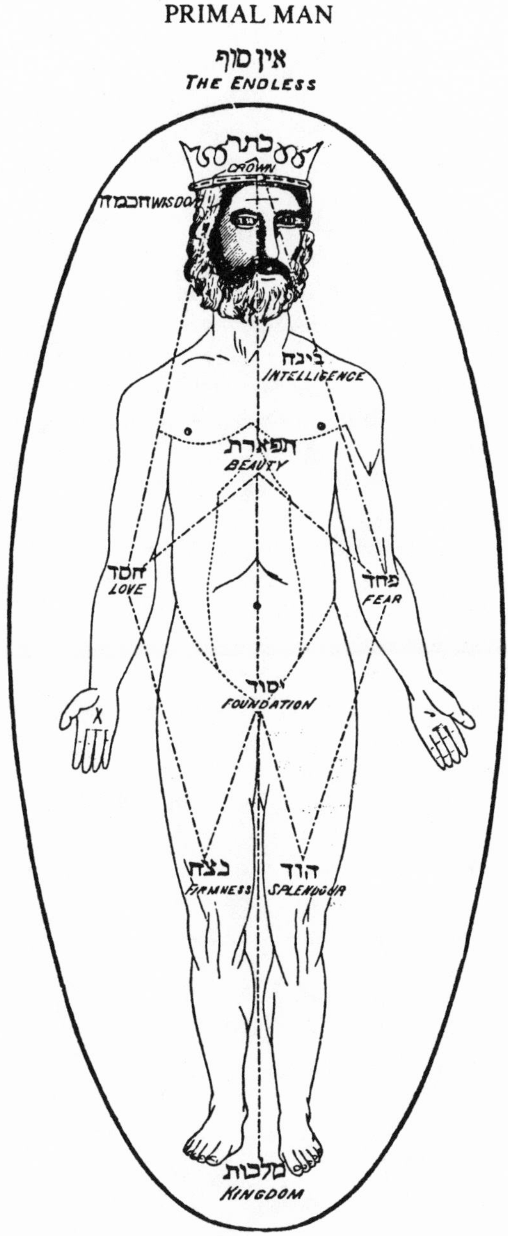

Fig. 17. *Adam Kadmon.* Reprinted with permission from *Old Jewish Manuscripts Calendars* (Tel Aviv: W. Turnowsky & Sons).

years there creating her own ten feminine *sefirot* out of its earth, air, fire, and water.[28] The land, however, was more than earth. It was *māqôm,* the sacred name and place.

Her creative process requires the initial use of chaos. She must first make the chaos, then do combat with it, and only then, create out of it. So she takes pristine handmade paper and mutilates it. She tears it, stabs it, burns it, pound and crushes it, scars it, destroying all its old limitations. Only then can she form, shape, mold, and sculpt these ravaged fragments to create the dappled, layered, painted, and gilded effects she commands—so varied that the final appearance does not even suggest they are made of paper. This ritual takes place at each of the ten sites associated with women and Jewish history. At each site she climbs mountains, speaks words, invokes the power of the past and healing of the future inherent in each of the *sefirot.*

Fine grained soil has worked itself into the surface of *Safed,* representing Safed the founding city of Lurianic kabbalah, tucked into the purple mountains and overlooking the sea of Galilee. It glowers copper and reddish cloud, a configuration of four major sections composed of many smaller parts, that open to expose the letter *ʾālep* that surfaces within the negative space of its heart, black fire on white fire again—the human search for meaning that once more gives shape to God's word.

Tiberius is golden with prismatic colors of the rainbow. Its lower section draws apart to make space for a *wāw,* the vertical link that hooks us up to the beyond (*wāw* is Hebrew for 'hook'). Appropriately the *sefira* honored here is *tipʾeret,* which is the center balancing *qāw,* the balancing line between judgment and love.

Colors are a channel for identifying individual strands. Thus the blue and silver scheme for *Solomon's Pillars* can be associated with the mountainous copper mines in the Negev desert. So too, the dedication to the *sefira* wisdom, *ḥokmâ,* in the top triad of the kabbalistic tree of life, appropriately displays a tiny *yôd,* the divine signature.

However letters are not obligatory. *The Red Sea,* hot and glowing with indistinct depths, reveals no forms in negative space. Its gnarled pear shape however is sufficiently uterine to remind one that sea is not just a place of death. While Egyptians drowned there, Israel was also born there.

Harry Rand, in the catalog essay, writes that Beth Ames Swartz's work *is* what modern art is "not supposed" to be—engaged, mystical,

[28] For the following discussion, please consult Beth Ames Swartz, *Israel Revisited*; Introduction by Harry Rand (Scottsdale, AZ: privately printed, 1981).

iconographically complex, and historical, with emotion-laden obligations. The result is that her work feels authentic, natural, strong, and mature.

Newman

In the wake of World War II, Barnet Newman felt that the ideas that had shaped earlier American art were obsolete. "Social realism, geometric abstraction, which constructed a meaningful universe were failed stems, as were all styles derived from faith in technology and the values of mass culture," writes art historian, Avram Kampf.[29] The war had shown the power of irrationality in human nature and artists were turning into themselves and their private visions for the content of their art. So after World War II Barnet Newman embarked on a religious art venture to "assert a subject matter, tragic and timeless that would transcend the here and now and evoke elemental cosmic forces that penetrate the universe."[30] Rejecting the imagery of Western art, he sought to approach the absolute by painting on his canvases a single flat color divided by one or more bands of a second color, which were called color field painting. He wanted a visual system for expressing philosophical ideas. In his religious search he saw identity between Creation in the absolute sense and the creation of a new art. He worked in the classic "no graven image" style of Judaism.

Newman designed a sanctuary that was never built. It is the tree of the *sefirot* in concrete and glass. It is a complete synthesis of the Jewish and the American. The zigzag walls, at ninety-degree angles were all glass, placed on the left and right sides of the building. What started out as an ingenious solution to the problem of how to show paintings in architecture ended up as an architectural translation of the kabbalistic tree of *sefirot*, whose interconnected branches move out from the central trunk at ninety-degree angles from each other. I concur with Thomas Hess, Newman's biographer, that the image was most likely inspired by a sixteenth century woodcut, a reproduction of which was in his library (fig. 18).[31] The woodcut illustrates the Gates of Light, the mystic's entrance to the Secret Orchard (*pardēs* = Paradise) of the Kabbalah and his ascent toward the Throne.

The basic form of the sanctuary was a rectangle, with the Torah Ark and the bleachers (women's seating) at opposite ends of the long axis. The twelve accordion-fold windows (cf. fig. 19), symbolic of

[29] A. Kampf, *Jewish Experience in the Art of the Twentieth Century* (Hadley, MA: Bergin and Garvey, 1984) 196–201.

[30] Ibid., 197.

[31] T. Hess, *Barnet Newman* (New York: Museum of Modern Art, 1971) 114.

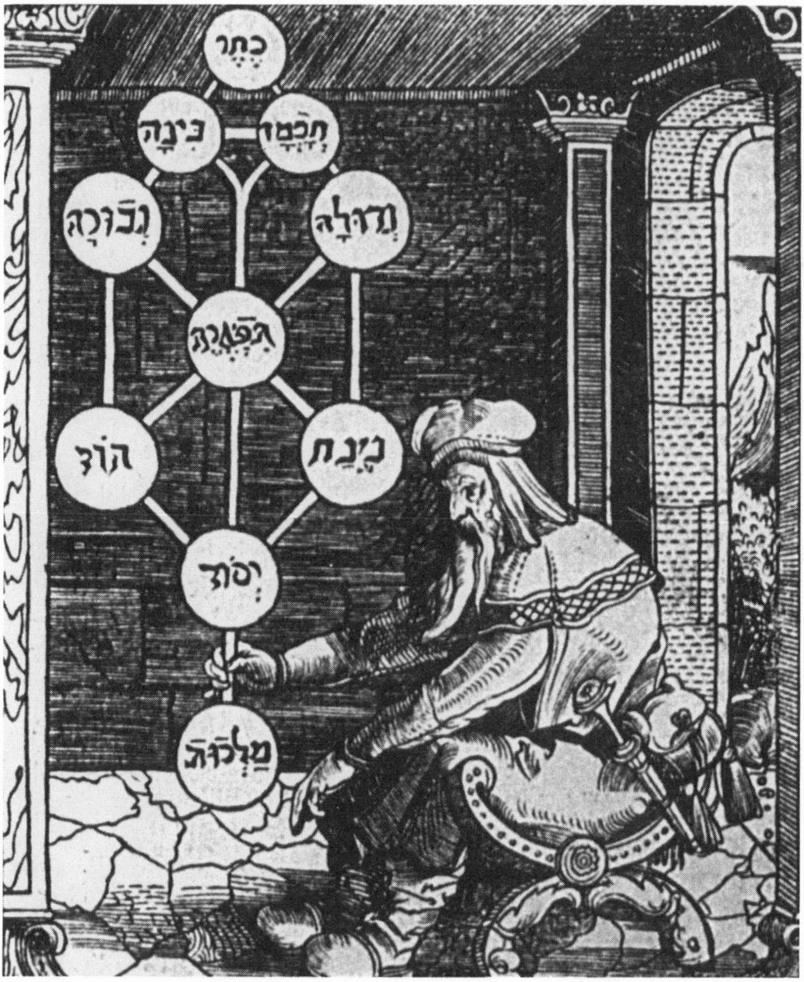

Fig. 18. A kabbalist mediating on the Tree of the *Sefirot*. Title page of *Portae Lucis* (Gates of Light), by Gikatilla (Augsburg, 1516). Wood engraving by Leonhard Beck. Used with permission of the Jewish National and University Library, Jerusalem.

the tribes of Israel, were on the sides; the men sat below them in the "dugouts." At the center is the mound, the place from which the Torah is read aloud during the service. The mound, which replaces the traditional *bāmâ* (raised stage or platform), is another creative kabbalistic application. The mound is literally the *māqôm*, the Name and the Place; it is the center point from which the *qāv*, the line of communication, goes out to the world. Newman designed separate

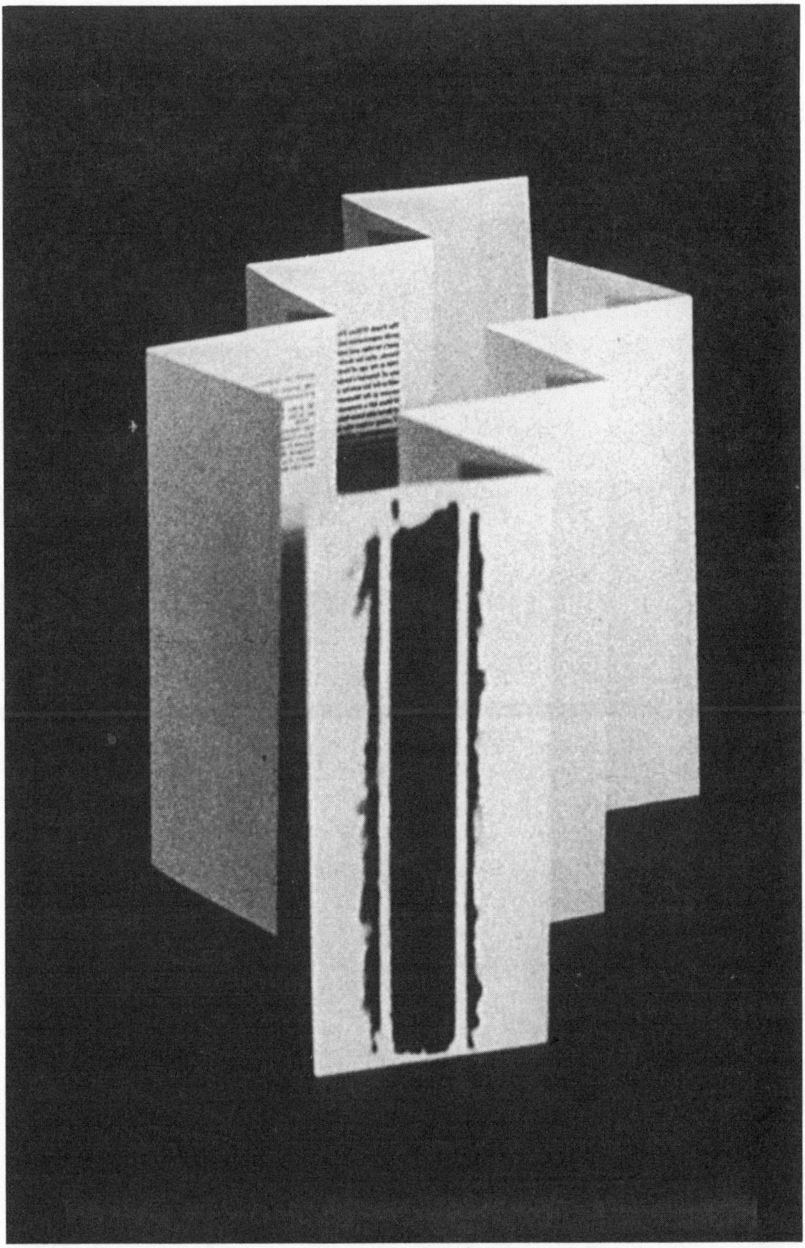

Fig. 19. Announcement of Newman's exhibition at M. Kneedler & Co., New York, 1969; used to help visualize the proportions of his sculpture, *Zim Zum I*. Photograph by Wm. D. Hess.

seating for men and women, not to sustain the second-class citizenship of women in orthodoxy, but out of respect for the distinct female and male elements in the sefirotic structure. Newman wrote eloquently of his design:

> Here in this synagogue, each man sits, private and secluded in the dugouts, waiting to be called, not to ascend a stage, but to go up to the mound where, under the tension of that *tzim-tzum* [the concept that God contracted Himself to make place for the world], that created light and the world, he can experience a total sense of his own personality before the Torah and His name.
>
> The women are also there, as persons, not as wives and mothers. Here the women are out in the open, sitting not in any abstract connection with what takes place, but as persons, distinct from their men, but in the full clear light, where they can experience their identity as women of valor.
>
> My purpose is to create a place, not an environment . . . where each person can experience the vision and feel the exaltation of "His trailing robes filling the Temple."[32]

Conclusion

I have dealt here with two of the consequences of the image prohibition in Jewish art: the ongoing affair of Jews with the alephbet—with the graphic, phonic, and numerologic aspects of letters and light—and the recurring tension with the figural image resulting in a fascination for abstract forms. Maybe the two are really one.

Perhaps both the modes and the preoccupations of Jewish art have seen their continuity in Christianity and Islam. For example, medieval manuscript illumination is a developed art and craft in both Christianity and Islam. I learned from Kiener that letter mysticism exists in both Sufi and Shiite traditions. As to fear and fascination of the image, the yes-no-maybe pendulation of Christian iconoclasm and iconolatry is well documented by history, as are the adjustments of Islam to outside contacts and changing concerns of their communities. The midrash on Moses and Bezalel, with which I began, and Sarah Caldwell's back-to-back placement of Moses and Aaron in Schoenberg's opera, an antecedent of which is seen in the twelfth century Winchester Bible, both address universal and recurring issues of the perception of the divine and communication with the divine.

The image prohibition may be a blessing in disguise. The tension around the nature of representation may also give a clue to

[32] Ibid., 111.

the elusive character of Jewish art. Surely it isn't just menorahs and magen davids, the abbreviated labels of ritual life. Like the thoughtful religious life, so the Jewish arts constantly struggle to admit, to express, and to apprehend the Presence.

The challenge of the religious image is that good art must be transparent enough to lead through it and beyond, to where it points. The paradox about Newman and Swartz, and other not included here, is that the more authentically Jewish they are, the more universal is their achievement. For when art is authentically Jewish it is not just ethnic: one is carried through it and beyond to the universal. This should trouble both the most fundamentalist (Jew) and the most assimilationist. The former, in being stereotypically limited, loses sight of the universal, while the latter, in thinking she or he is all-embracing, has sacrificed individuality.

Stanley Ira Hallet

The Role of Iconoclasm on Islamic Art and Architecture: A Response to Jo Milgrom

HALLET TO A LARGE EXTENT does for Islamic art what Jo Milgrom has in the previous essay done for Jewish art: he explores the effects of image prohibition. He notes that, even though images have existed in Islamic art, the real genius of that art has—largely on account of the general distaste for images—lain in the realm of abstract and non-representational art, including calligraphy. Hallet notes that this distaste for images, although reflected in *Ḥadīth*, was present among Arabs before Islam and reflected a sympathy with Jewish sensibilities.

Stanley Ira Hallet is presently Associate Dean and Chair, Department of Architecture and Planning, The Catholic University of America. Prior to this appointment he was Professor of Architecture at the University of Utah Graduate School of Architecture. He received his Master of Architecture degree from MIT and has been a professional architect in Salt Lake City. He served in the Peace Corps in the Middle East and subsequently coauthored a book on traditional Afghan housing. He has published articles in architectural journals.

In responding to Jo Milgrom's description of the mysterious Kabbalah and the not-so-silent *ʾālep*, the first letter of the Hebrew alphabet, I will address the issue of image-making and icon-breaking in Islam, responding as an architect, filmmaker, camera-man, taker-of-images, even Sunday painter. Yet my connection to image-breaking or image-making is my love of Islamic architecture, her gardens and tile work, her carpets, miniatures, and her incredible calligraphy. I will explore some of the imagery of Islam, searching for connections to Milgrom's silent *ʾālep* when possible.

But now I want to retell the story of Muḥammad riding victoriously into Mecca early in the seventh century. He has just made a pact with the Meccans, ironically enough with his own family tribe, the Quraysh, the keepers of the *kaʿba*. Part of the political settlement was to reestablish the *kaʿba* as the final pilgrimage site for every Muslim. But what is the *kaʿba*, this mysterious center of pious devotion? Briefly, the *kaʿba* is a squat, almost squarish building. It holds a precious black stone imbedded in one corner, the object of much pilgrimage long before Muḥammad's time. On this victorious day Muḥammad circumambulates the *kaʿba*—a movement later to become revered as the *ṭawāf*, the rite of circumambulation, reminiscent of the rotation of the heavens around the *kaʿba*'s polar axis, Milgrom's *axis mundi*. As Muḥammad circles the *kaʿba*, he smashes 360 idols that surround the sacred stone. Is Muḥammad an iconoclast at heart, an "image-breaker"? When he finally enters the *kaʿba*, then full of gifts, worshiped objects, paintings, and sculpture, he orders them obliterated, saying, "Rub out all these pictures, except these under my hands."[1] One of the objects he was protecting was a painting of Mary with Jesus seated on her lap. What is Muḥammad trying to say? Is it the same point that Milgrom makes when she proclaims, "What the image prohibition really says, therefore, is not 'don't make images'; it says 'don't worship images.' The purpose of the prohibition is clear: all images and words are only partial. To mistake the part for the whole is what idolatry is all about" (see above, p. 265).

Thus on that day a fine line was drawn in the sands of Mecca; a line blurred with time, shifting with the prevailing religio-political climate. In fact, early Islam was full of image-making. For example, the Palace of al-Baydā at Baṣra was full of images. The Caliph ʿUmar's own censer, used to perfume the mosque at Medina, was decorated with human figures, and the coins of other early caliphs were struck in their own effigies.[2]

[1] Araqi (d. A.D. 858), author of earliest extant history of Mecca, recounts Muḥammad's victorious ride into Mecca. See K. A. C. Creswell, *Early Muslim Architecture* (Oxford: Clarendon, 1969), 1:2:410.

[2] A further list of early examples of image-making is outlined by Creswell, ibid., 410–14, and discussed by Oleg Grabar, *The Formation of Islamic Art* (New Haven: Yale University, 1973).

However, these early examples are not the subject of my comments, for they will soon become, historically speaking, the exceptions. Although the Qurʾān is unquestionably silent on the subject of the prohibition of imagery, the *Ḥadīth,* the written traditions concerning the actions and sayings of Muḥammad, are emphatically not. Over a span of 150 to 200 years following the Meccan event just described, a change of heart or at least disposition is clearly taking place. Take this example from the *Ḥadīth*: "On the day of judgment, the punishment of Hell will be meted out to the painter, and he will be called upon to breathe life into the forms that he has fashioned. But he cannot breathe life into anything."[3] Words like these certainly don't promote the visual arts. Who would wish to take up painting in a climate like that?

Another example from the *Ḥadīth*: "The angels will not enter a house containing a bell, a picture, or a dog."[4] Yet according to K. A. C. Creswell, bells were unknown in Mecca during the time of Muḥammad. So what was happening? Poetic license? A question of transliteration? Still, the value of painting is diminished when placed in the company of the infamous Islamic dislike of dogs. Finally, one last example: "At the end of the world, when ᶜĪsā appears, he will break the cross and kill the pig."[5] Pigs? Before Islam, Creswell says, there was no widespread aversion for pigs (that is, except among the Jews). Could this be proof of what Creswell calls the Talmudic influence on Islam, or the Jewish connection?[6]

Yet how could such influence occur? Again, one must understand the story of the *Ḥadīth,* how it developed and how it was finally written down. Knowing that Bukhārī, one of the earliest expositors of *Ḥadīth,* accepted only 7,000 out of 600,000 sayings that he heard, raises the question who were these devout scribes making the final selections and tying down so many loose ends.[7]

One such early authority of *Ḥadīth* was Rabbi Kaᶜb, the Yemenite Jew Kaᶜb-al-Aḥbar, so-called rabbi on account of his great knowledge of the Bible and theology.[8] Many of his pupils, for example ᶜAbd Allāh ibn al-ᶜAbbās and Abū Hurayra, were also among the earliest expositors of Qurʾān and *Ḥadīth.* Thus, there were many distinguished Jewish converts to Islam, and along with them a dislike

[3] This excerpt from the *Ḥadīth* is taken from the Juynball edition of Bukhārī, 2:41 and 4:106. See Creswell, ibid., 412 n. 1.

[4] Ibid., 413.

[5] See Creswell's discussion of this portion of the *Ḥadīth,* ibid.

[6] Ibid., 411.

[7] Ibid.

[8] Kaᶜb-al-Aḥbar entered Jerusalem with the Caliph ᶜUmar and was converted to Islam in A.D. 688.

(commonly described as "Semitic") for human representation in sculpture and painting was considerably felt during this early period of Islam.

Many Arabs long before the advent of Islam, however, were sympathetic to the Jewish abhorrence of image worshiping, and Creswell describes them as "a suspicious, superstitious group who felt the maker of an image or a painting in some ways transfers parts of the personality of the subject to the image or painting, and in doing so acquires magical powers."[9] Thus I observe with interest that even though image-worship was frowned upon by the Jews, the same Jewish tradition, as seen in Milgrom's presentation, still found plenty of room for image-making, and this tradition continues today. However, among the desert nomads of early Islam this was not to be, for the strong Talmudic message (combined with the Semitic fear of image-making) found in the Arabian desert a more anxious and receptive audience.

With this introduction, let me now present the art of Islam, the poetry of shadows, and the search for meaning that lies behind the image, behind the temporal form of things. I cannot address the wonderful images illustrative of Muslim science, medicine, astronomy, and cartography, nor can I possibly explain the breathtaking religious imagery that found its home in the high plateaus of Iran (figure 1 is an example). Instead I wish to start by singling out and focusing upon the perennial life of the nomad, those early tribes that flocked to the victorious message of Islam—their art of graphic formulae, the ornamental motif, the art that can be carried and only later carved and/or painted in place.

According to Titus Burckhardt, a language only rots and decays in the city.[10] However, in the nomadic camp it is conserved, for the nomads live outside of time. They became the guardians of linguistic heritage, of the word, of the sound of that word, of the poem and the sound of the line. With the advent of Islam, the larger Muslim community zealously conserved the Qurʾān, the word of God, and when written, the art of calligraphy—Islam's most precious art form. In this way the sound of the word soon became the shape of that word. Or as Milgrom suggests, anthropomorphic language is "deliberately selected not because there is no alternative, but to make God more accessible" (p. 284, above). In order to sing, the letters of the "sacred" Arabic script blossom in the appropriately called florid Kufic script (fig. 2)—Islam's version of black fire and white fire. This is what

[9] Creswell, *Early Muslim Architecture,* 414.

[10] Titus Burckhardt, *Art of Islam* (London: World of Islam Festival, 1976) 41.

Milgrom calls "negative space": "One can experience a larger presence of God if she or he can focus visually on the shape of space around objects, rather than on the objects alone" (p. 284, above). The Islamic calligraphers not only understood negative space, but enthusiastically explored it, anxiously filling in the space between the letters, or even inside the letters with the continual praise of God (fig. 3). This celebration is not limited to just black and white fire, but rather bursts into colors that know no limitations of style or age. The colored strokes play one phrase against another, diacritical marks against letters, or explode into a bouquet of flowers dancing about the central message of God (fig. 4).

It is in its inimical sense of order, however, that this calligraphy also explores the geometry of an abstract world—a world of mathematical patterns that recombines itself in one variation after another. As Milgrom said, "the visual art that emerges from these systems [and I present these Islamic examples as further proof] with its profound tendency toward abstraction is a consequence of the image prohibition and a protest against the seductive limitations of the representational image" (p. 271, above). However, so-called abstraction can be equally seductive, melodic, and mysterious. For example, the love of the nomad for the abstract song knows no bounds, neither in the geometry of its structure and its underlying rules, nor in the patience of the artist and her precious craft.

In the case of the Arabic spirit, it is hard to tell which came first, the prohibition of images or the profound tendency toward the abstract. At an early stage in the history of Islam, the sacred words of the Qurʾān and the art of calligraphy, decoration, and building soon became intertwined, interconnected, never-ending. The geometries of decoration of formulae were extended to first decorate a platter, then protect a book, finally to cover all objects, in a heroic effort to ennoble all earthly matter (fig. 5).

One thousand years ago in Cordoba the word, the phrase, the language of Islam permeated space, covering every square inch, understanding both the grace of the flower and the precision of the square. As Ali Lawati said, "Muslim art was an epigraphical art. The word of God materialized, covering all things, based on the vegetal and the geometrical, not merely decoration, but valued for itself."[11] As the surface becomes entwined with structure, so structure becomes one with space: no edges, only a continuous dialogue (fig. 6). André

[11] Cited in André Paccard, *The Traditional Islamic Craft in Moroccan Architecture* (Saint-Jorioz, France: Ateliers, 1980), 1:25. Ali Lawati speaks to the question of Islamic art.

Paccard describes such an architectural place as being lost "in perpetual thought . . . deciphering one figure, another one will appear enigmatically."[12] No beginning, no end. Lines weave in and out ceaselessly. A continuous and infinite network. As Milgrom demonstrated, the *yôd* is the tiny opening into another space (p. 281, above). Paccard concurs when he says, "decoration [and, I add, architecture] becomes a window upon a limitless world, a world of unity in multiplicity."[13] Thus, the Islamic world of matter is eventually dematerialized; space is finally desubstantiated in an effort to become only closer to the space or place of God.

Even the organizational patterns of Muslim cities contained the same multiplicity of related form, growth, and change. Louis Massignon explains ". . . the proof of God is the changing of everything that is not God."[14] Muslim art and architecture is an art that emphasizes change. The great gate or doorway of the Shāh ᶜAbbās Mosque tells the same story. As one approaches, each layer of organization only opens up to introduce another layer of organization, related but varied. These interrelated geometries of place take one only closer and closer to that indescribable place that dwells for an instant between one tiny opening and the unavoidable window beyond (fig. 7). For Ali Lawati, "Islam claims [that the] aesthetic proof of God and all of the Moslem ornamental art is but a vast multiform song of praise which . . . attests through its multiplicity the Permanence of God as against the Plurality of the world."[15]

This song is not only sung in the celestial domes overhead (fig. 8), in Islam's organizations of the heavens, but also on the maps of the earth where each Muslim prays to the one central stone in the *kaᶜba*, the *axis mundi* of the Islamic world.

In conclusion, Islam as well as Judaism, as Jo Milgrom has demonstrated, has witnessed the continual battle between man's desire to express himself and his understanding of God through his reflection of the world, and religion's need to hold supreme and unique the act of God's creation. Finally, I must also note with admiration that whereas most often the land-based cultures absorb the nomadic ones, in the Islamic case of language, graphic formula, calligraphy, and architecture, this unique manifestation of the Arabic genius did conquer all, from Cordoba and Granada in Spain to Agra and Fatehpur Sikri in India. For the Arabs of the desert, the Semitic dislike of imagery fell on fertile ground.

[12] Ibid., 1:135.
[13] Ibid., 1:144.
[14] Ibid., 1:124.
[15] Ibid.

Fig. 1. Example of representational imagery in Islamic art: Muḥammad on the celebrated night ride (Miniature, Iran, A.D. 1320–1325). Detail of miniature rephotographed by author.

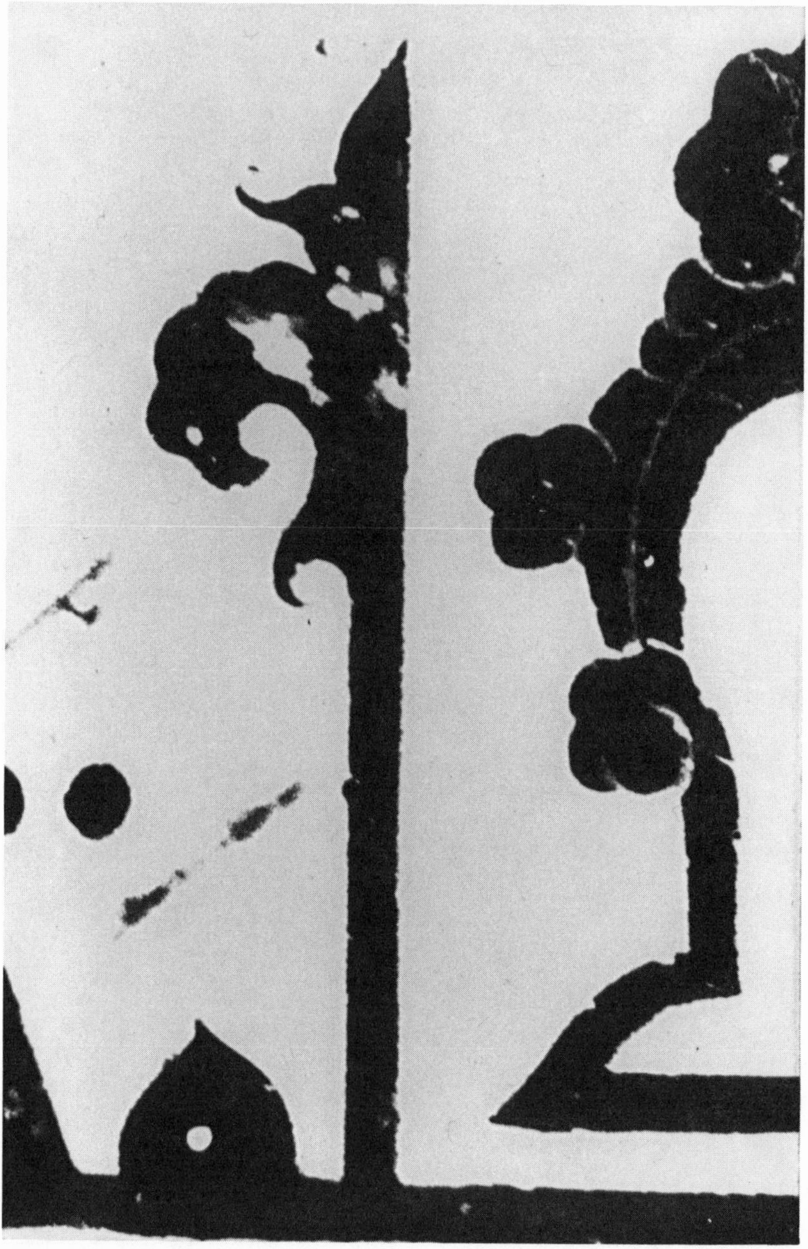

Fig. 2. Florid Kufic script (fourteenth-fifteenth century Qurʾān). Reprinted with permission from Abdelkebir Khatibi and Mohammed Sijelmassi, *The Splendor of Islamic Calligraphy* (New York: Rizzoli, 1976).

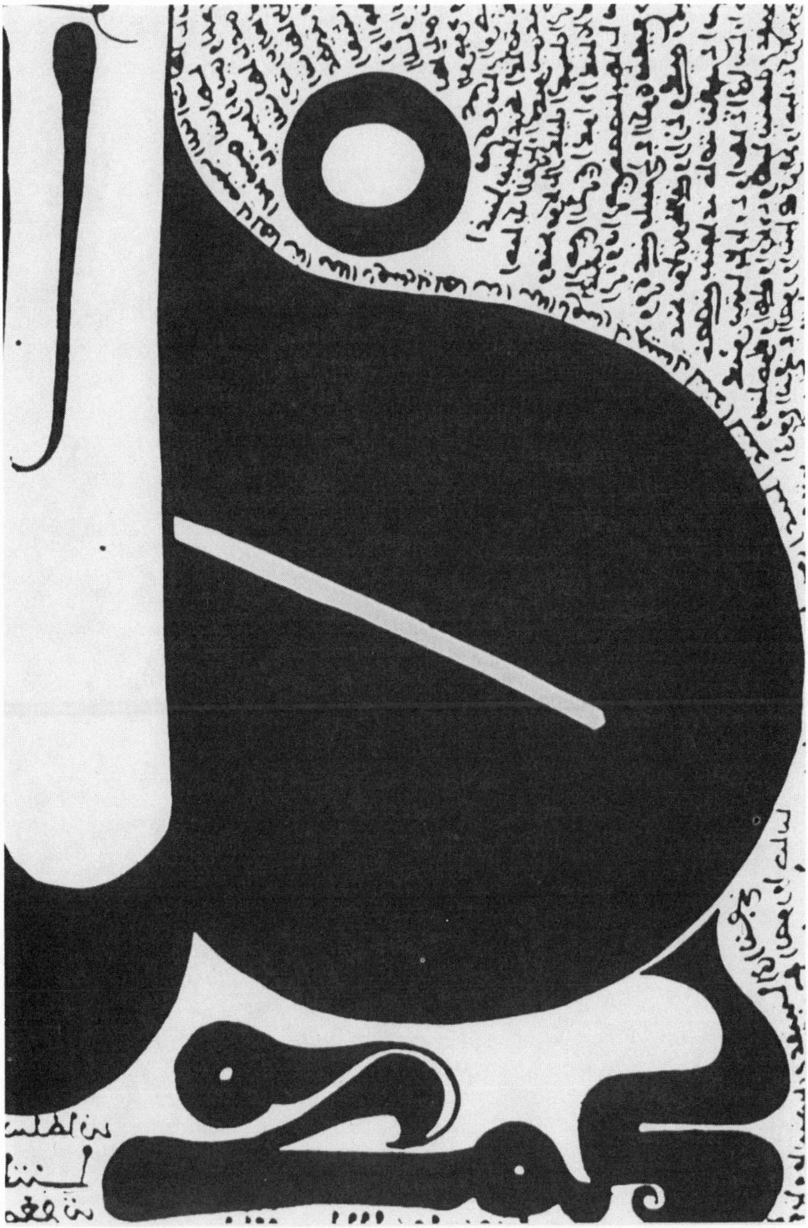

Fig. 3. Calligraphy within and around the name of Allah (Qandusi-Morrocan, 1828). Reprinted with permission from Abdelkebir Khatibi and Mohammed Sijelmassi, *The Splendor of Islamic Calligraphy* (New York: Rizzoli, 1976).

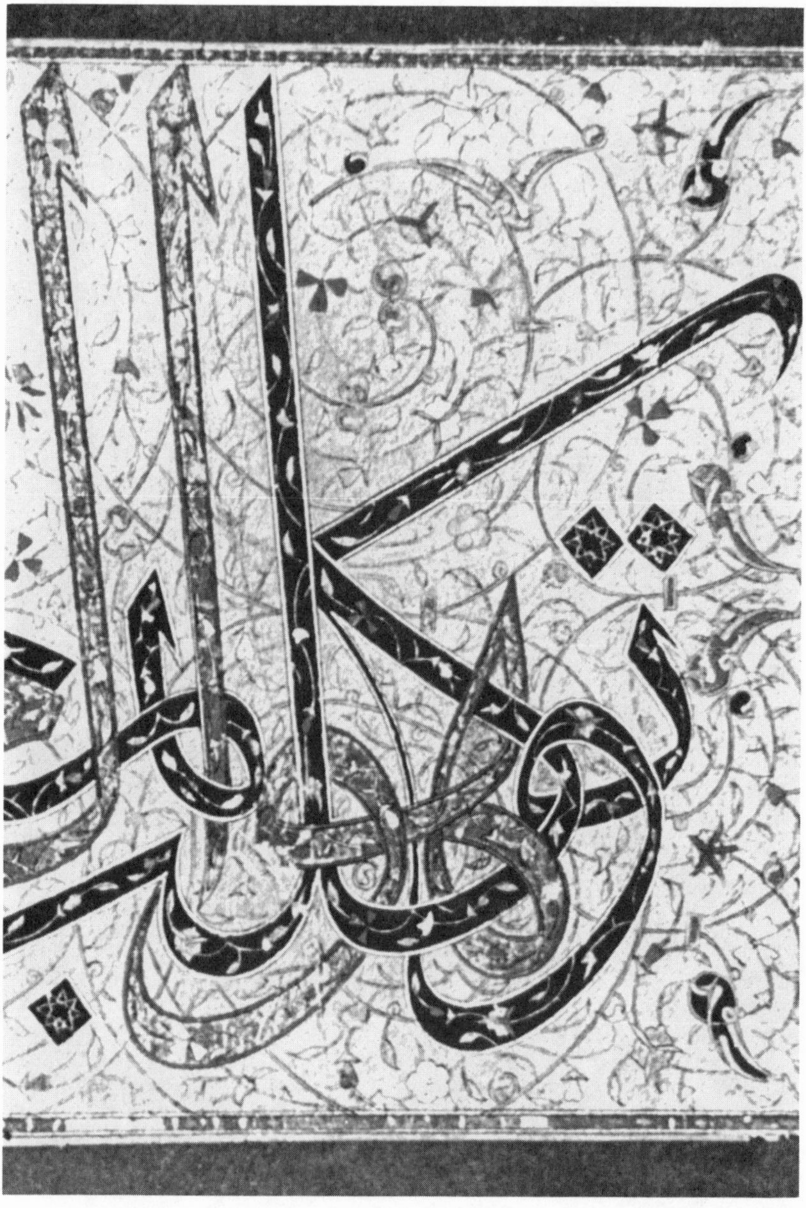

Fig. 4. The calligraphy of color: a celebration of the letters (Taʾliq script, sixteenth century, Nijaburi). Reprinted with permission from Abdelkebir Khatibi and Mohammed Sijelmassi, *The Splendor of Islamic Calligraphy* (New York: Rizzoli, 1976).

Fig. 5. Book cover: calligraphy and geometrics ennoble earthly matter. Detail photographed by the author.

Fig. 6. Calligraphy, decoration, architecture: inseparably entwined columns and arches in the Mosque of Cordoba. Photograph by the author.

Fig. 7. The continuing window, gate, doorway of geometry. (Masjid-i-Shah, Isfahan, Iran). Photograph by the author.

Fig. 8. The celestial dome: The Dome of Two Sisters in the Alhambra. Photograph by the author.

David Noel Freedman

The Formation of the Canon of the Old Testament

The Selection and Identification of the Torah as the Supreme Authority of the Postexilic Community

FREEDMAN SHOWS HOW THE focusing of Israel's religious outlook in the postexilic period on the divinely revealed law (Torah) led to a new scriptural canon, one in which the Pentateuch was detached from the following history writings (Joshua through 2 Kings) and the latter were attached to the prophetic writings to give a Scripture composed of Law and Prophets, in contrast to the earlier canon that had been composed of Primal History and Prophets. In this new canon the holy law was given an independent status suited to a time when Israel's religion was, under the leadership of Ezra, shifting from a historical mode (that is, divine acts in human history) to the mode of law (that is, divine words or commands to regulate the behavior of the human community). By segregating Torah from the rest of scripture, thus "identifying" it, Ezra enhanced the figure of Moses as prophet/lawgiver. Thus did the fusion of religion and law in the life of ancient Israel, with the consequent increasing focus upon holy law as the basis of that nation's relationship with God, come to be reflected in the way the present-day Bible is organized.

David Noel Freedman is the Arthur F. Thurnau Professor of Biblical Studies at the University of Michigan and Director of the Program on Studies in Religion. He is also the endowed Professor of Hebrew Biblical Studies at the University of California, San Deigo.

He received his Th.B. from Princeton Theological Seminary and is an ordained Presbyterian minister. His Ph.D. is from Johns Hopkins University in Semitic languages and literature. In addition to authoring numerous works in biblical studies, Professor Freedman has been the driving force behind many of the century's major biblical projects, including the *Anchor Bible Dictionary*, and the *Anchor Bible Reference Library*.

This presentation arises out of an effort to answer a relatively simple question, which turned out to be not so simple. Moreover, the ramifications turned out to be more interesting and perhaps more important than the original question and its answer. The question is briefly: Where did the Pentateuch (that is, the Five Books of Moses) come from, or How did the Torah become the primary canon of the Hebrew Bible? Why just these five books, not more and not fewer? When did this momentous event take place, and under what circumstances and by whose authoritative decision?

Before attempting to answer this multiple-choice question or even discuss it, I must explain the connection between this rather technical question concerning the canon of the Hebrew Bible and the theme of "religion and law." The response is both clear and simple: The Torah of the Hebrew Bible is the classic example of this theme—the wedding or interweaving of religion and law, that is, religion understood primarily in the categories of law, or law understood as the epitome or summation of religion, its essential expression. Thus, in dealing with the question of the Torah as canon and especially as law, I inevitably and quite deliberately enter the domain of religion and law.

The paper falls into two parts: the first deals with the question of the origin and emergence of the Pentateuch as the law par excellence, the primary canon of the Hebrew Bible, while in the second part I will consider the rationale and intentionality of the decision to equate or identify law with canon (of sacred scripture). The mutually reinforcing roles of law and religion are exemplified in the traditions concerning Moses who stands preeminently in both spheres: as the chief prophet of the Hebrew Bible and as the supreme lawgiver. In the person of Moses and in the achievement attributed to him, namely the Torah, the roles, tasks, contents, and purposes of religion and law are found intertwined and blended.

The Torah, which in its present form (not its substantial content, which is earlier) may date anywhere between the eighth and fifth centuries B.C.E. (and most likely to the seventh and early sixth centuries), constitutes the principal legacy of the ancient Near East to the western world in the realm of religion and law.

The Origin and Emergence of the Pentateuch: Torah (Law)

I think the tradition is both reasonable and plausible that associates the promulgation of the Torah as divine law transmitted through Moses to Israel with the efforts and undertakings of Ezra and Scribe, aided and abetted by Nehemiah the Governor around the middle of the fifth century B.C.E. Whether or not the "Law" that he read from the pulpit on the solemn occasion recorded in Nehemiah 8 was the whole Pentateuch or only selected portions of it, or some sort of summary with explanations, does not affect the discussion here, since I believe that the entire Pentateuch had long since been compiled, completed, edited, and published, and thus would have been available to this worthy scribe. In other words, his work was that of selection and presentation rather than compilation, much less editing or composing.

The result was to shift a literary boundary line from its original rational and plausible position between the books of Kings and the book of Isaiah to another position, between the books of Deuteronomy and Joshua. While such a shift may seem minor or inconsequential, it had momentous implications for the community addressed by Ezra, and even greater ones for the indefinite future. I can summarize this slight action in the following way: In my judgment, in the middle of the sixth century B.C.E., the Hebrew Bible, the first biblical canon, consisted of the Primary History (the books from Genesis through Kings) and a supporting collection of prophetic works. The Primary History (as I have tried to show elsewhere)[1] was the basic Bible, the story of God and his people Israel, which ran from the very beginning of everything until the demise of the kingdoms of Israel and Judah toward the end of 2 Kings. It must have been compiled and completed in its present form not earlier than 560 B.C.E. and not later than 540 B.C.E. (but I think that the actual date was much closer to the earlier figure than the later one). In fact, I believe that the final sentences of 2 Kings are a statement of the date and place of publication, shortly after the accession of Awil-Marduk, the heir and

[1] "The Earliest Bible," *Michigan Quarterly Review* 22/3 (1983) 167–75 (repr. in Michael P. O'Connor and David Noel Freedman, eds., *Backgrounds for the Bible* [Winona Lake, IN: Eisenbrauns, 1987] 29–37); "The Law and the Prophets," *Congress Volume: Bonn 1962* (Supplements to Vetus Testamentum 9; Leiden: Brill, 1963) 250–65.

successor of the great Nebuchadnezzar, as king of Babylonia. The collection of prophetic books, which included Isaiah 1–33, Isaiah 36–39, Jeremiah, Ezekiel, and as many as nine of the Minor Prophets (excluding the last three in the canonical collection, Haggai, Zechariah, and Malachi), was produced at about the same time (for example, Jeremiah ends with the same chapter with which 2 Kings ends) to provide supporting data and elaborative details concerning the role of the prophets in the period beginning in the first half of the eighth century B.C.E., when the Assyrian threat first materialized on the northeastern horizon, and ending with the tragic events including the end of the southern kingdom, the capture of Jerusalem, and the captivity of the leading people. Equally, if not more importantly, however, the collection shows the firm conviction of the same prophets that in spite of the overwhelming disaster for the nation, there would be a future for them, a return and restoration more glorious than anything they had experienced in the past.

In effect, I believe that what Ezra did was to redivide these two great works and produce instead the familiar, present-day arrangement of the Hebrew Bible. Instead of Primary History and Prophetic Corpus, which I postulate for the content and order of the books of the canon in the middle of the sixth century, the result of Ezra's action gives the Torah or Pentateuch, and the Prophetic Corpus now divided between Former Prophets (the balance of the Primary History, including Joshua-Judges-Samuel-Kings) and Latter Prophets (also four books: Isaiah [now including both 1 and 2 Isaiah, all 66 chapters], Jeremiah, Ezekiel, and the book of the Twelve [including Haggai, Zechariah, and Malachi as well as the earlier nine]). The line of division has been moved from the logical separation between narrative and prophecy, that is, between the end of Kings and the beginning of Isaiah, to a somewhat artificial one between Law and Prophecy, that is, the end of Deuteronomy and the beginning of Joshua, where there is no obvious separation, since the book of Joshua has been organized consciously and deliberately to be contiguous and continuous with Deuteronomy. In short, an artificial but extremely significant wedge was driven into the Primary History to create a new and decisive entity: Torah, the Law of Moses. Inevitably it contains the life of Moses as well, but the emphasis here is on the teaching of Moses, expressed in a variety of forms including especially legal codes.

I believe there were excellent reasons for making the change at that time and in those circumstances, but the question is a complicated one, first requiring a consideration of an intermediate pattern of arrangement of the canon before taking up the determination of the present order of the books and their divisions. Indeed, one may wonder whether I have not unnecessarily complicated and confused matters by proposing the hypothesis about the Primary History and a sixth century canon. Some scholars have indeed suggested as much to me, but the basic problem is hardly of my making, and it would remain to be dealt with even if my suggestions were dismissed or ignored, which by and large has been their fate. It has long been recognized (especially since the classic and seminal work of Martin Noth in describing and delimiting the so-called Deuteronomic History, a major literary work that included the books from Deuteronomy through Kings) that the book of Deuteronomy was tied in various literary and linguistic ways to the books that followed rather than to the books that preceded.[2] So it has become customary now to speak of a P (Priestly) work, which runs from Genesis through Numbers, and a D (Deuteronomic) work, which runs from Deuteronomy through Kings. If one accepts this analysis of the major components of the Primary History, then the creation of a Pentateuch including the four books of the P work and only the first book of the D work must be explained equally as the deliberate decision to shift an established boundary from one place to another. In other words, in order to attach Deuteronomy to the Tetrateuch, it must have been detached from the literary work to which it previously belonged. Such a decision, based upon whatever considerations, which is contrary to the literary structure of both works and which no doubt opposes the intention of the earlier compiler or editor, requires investigation and explanation. So I must return to an analysis of the important political and literary developments of the century from the compilation and publication of the First Bible until the emergence of the canon of the Law and the Prophets as the central units of the Hebrew Bible.

Shortly after the publication of the Primary History and the first prophetic collection around 560 B.C.E., Cyrus the Persian king began his meteoric career of conquest and the consolidation of a vast empire. For the Judahites in captivity in Babylonia, this development, including specifically the capture of Babylon in 539 B.C.E., would ultimately mean redemption and release, return, restoration, and renewal, a new beginning in the old land. So dramatic was this reversal of fortunes, and so unexpected in spite of the widespread anticipation of the end of the Babylonian hegemony and a possible return of the exiles (as it

[2] "Martin Noth, *A History of Pentateuchal Traditions* (Englewood Cliffs, NJ: Prentice Hall, 1972); *The Deuteronomistic History* (JSOT Supplement Series 15; Sheffield: JSOT Press, 1981); the latter work is a translation of pp. 1-110 of *Überlieferungsgeschichtliche Studien* (Tübingen: Max Niemeyer, 1957).

turned out the details were vastly different) that it was necessary to produce a new literature to account for and cope with the new situation unfolding before their eyes. Extraordinary things were happening and even more remarkable things were about to happen, so an array of new prophets appeared in order to proclaim the new age and to link it up with the former times and the transition through which they were living.

Beginning with Second Isaiah (which includes chaps. 34-35 and 40-66) and continuing and concluding with Haggai, Zechariah, and perhaps Malachi, the prophetic collection was supplemented and enlarged to bring the story of Jerusalem and its Temple full circle with the renewal of the Jerusalem community and the rebuilding of the Temple. In this way the prophetic canon was brought to completion, while another great historical work was produced to accommodate the new developments: the Chronicler's Work. This narrative, which shares thematic and stylistic features with the P work, constitutes in major part an alternative version of the Deuteronomic History. I have written elsewhere about the date, provenience, purpose, and contents of this work and there is no need here to repeat those points.[3] Briefly stated, however, I believe that this work in its original or perhaps an early form was produced at the time of the rebuilding of the Temple (between 520 and 515 B.C.E.) and was intended to support the claims of the returned exiles to preferred status in the restored community and to encourage them in rebuilding the Temple and renewing the city. It would have included most of 1 and 2 Chronicles (especially the narrative sections beginning with the death of Saul and accession of David in 1 Chronicles 10 and continuing through 2 Chronicles) and then the first three chapters of Ezra and possibly some material from the accounts before chap. 7. With its emphasis on the kingdom of Judah, the house of David, the city of Jerusalem and its Temple, as well as the strict omission of the northern kingdom from consideration, it may have been meant as a replacement for the Primary History itself, or at least a revised version of the history of the monarchy. It, along with the prophetic canon, would have been used by the returning exiles to validate their claims upon the land, the city, and the Temple. The effort to rewrite or revise the classic history of Israel did not entirely succeed, but the Chronicler's work, ultimately supplemented by the memoirs of Ezra and Nehemiah, constituted the framework of a third circle of literature in the canon. Such books as the Psalter, Proverbs, and others that could be associated with the house of David (for example, Ruth, Song

[3] The Chronicler's Purpose," *Catholic Biblical Quarterly* 23 (1961) 436-42.

of Songs, Ecclesiastes) were included, as well as those that dealt with the fortunes of the sacred city and its Temple (for example, Lamentations and, later, Daniel).

Sixty years later, Ezra the Scribe came from Babylon with a revised agenda. The hopes and expectations of the early arrivals had only been fulfilled in part, and circumstances clearly were altered. The concentration on the revival of the kingdom and the reinstatement of the royal house clearly was misplaced and possibly dangerous. Ezra supplemented the Chronicler's Work with his memoirs, and those of Nehemiah were also attached. Whatever their personal relations (they had a tendency to speak of their own labors without mentioning or recognizing the contribution of the other, but that is hardly a compelling reason to date them in different generations, much less in different centuries), they were colleagues and partners in the work of reformation. By this time there were subtle but significant changes in emphasis and outlook: The traditions of the house of David were of the greatest value, especially in connection with the restored Temple, because David had organized everything in preparation for its building in the first place, and its music and liturgy besides. Its actual construction was carried out by Solomon, and it is no accident that these two kings dominate the whole of the books of Chronicles, with lesser attention given to their descendants. But that was all in the past; for the present the proper attitude was to remember the past, not to await or expect, much less to plan or plot the restoration of the monarchy or of the dynasty at this time. With the passing of Zerubbabel and perhaps his son-in-law El-natan, the house of David surrendered its executive post, the governorship, and it remains only a genealogical list of names in the time of Ezra and Nehemiah (cf. 1 Chronicles 3, esp. vv 19–24). Ultimate earthly authority would be lodged in the Persian empire, while limited autonomy would be the most that could be expected, at least at present. At the same time, the life of the community could and would be ordered in accordance with the precepts and regulations of the great ancient lawgiver, Moses the man of God. Internal arrangements and practices would be governed by these laws, while external matters would be regulated by the masters of the empire.

The province, or subprovince, should be and would be administered by the returned exiles, a high priest of the house of Aaron and a governor of Judahite descent, but they would be responsible in temporal affairs to higher authority vested in the satraps and ultimately the emperor himself. There was no place for a king of the house of David, even though members of the royal house doubtless survived and could be identified at that time, and for some time thereafter. In the initial phases of the return, a scion of the house of David, Zerubbabel, served as governor of Judah and Jerusalem, but not as king. Even this compromise apparently failed, because no son or descendant of Zerubbabel was named governor after him. It is possible, on the basis of recently published seal inscriptions to determine that a successor of Zerubbabel was El-natan, the husband of a woman named Shelomit, who in turn may have been the daughter of Zerubbabel (cf. 1 Chron 3:19).[4] After that person, however, the connection with the house of David vanishes and subsequent governors are simply appointed officials for varying terms. Among them, of course, is Nehemiah, who has no royal claims or pretensions whatever. With the relegation of the house of David to obscurity by the end of sixth century B.C.E., the time had also come to assign thoughts about or hopes concerning this dynasty to the pages of past history or to an indefinite and far-off future, and to put these in language that would not alarm the neighboring peoples or disturb the imperial authorities.

I summarize these developments in the following manner. Israel, in its long history, could count two great heroes among the many who served their country well: Moses the founder of the nation and the leader during the critical transition period from bondage in Egypt to occupation of the promised land; and David, who came at a critical juncture in the nation's history, and firmly and finally established its independence and suzerainty over an extended territory. The Primary History gives an essentially balanced, if slightly prejudiced, picture of the two men and their far-reaching attainments. For the period of the monarchy, especially in Judah, and for the period when these works were being published, the house of David constituted an actual and perhaps viable means of independence and self-rule, as well as a potential threat to existing authorities. In the prophets, as well as in the Chronicler's Work, the house of David received special attention and was the bearer of aspirations and expectations for the future. The same could not be said for Moses, whose house had vanished long since, and whose work was enshrined in a book. As it turned out, he was the authentic alternative, since he posed no threat to external authorities, but could provide a structured way of life for survivors under foreign rule.

The pendulum swung one way with the returnees and their leaders and prophets toward the end of the sixth century, and then in the opposite direction in the days of Ezra and Nehemiah. Neither

[4] Carol L. Meyers and Eric M. Meyers, *Haggai, Zechariah 1-8* (Anchor Bible 25B; Garden City, NY: Doubleday, 1987) 12-13; Nahman Avigad, "Bullae and Seals from a Post-exilic Judean Archive," Qedem 4 (1976) 30ff.

prophets nor pretenders play any role in the plans or strategies of the latter. On the contrary, for Ezra, the life of the community would be shaped and structured by the domain of Moses, and only indirectly, that is in the liturgy of the Temple, by that of David. In making the momentous decision to separate the Torah from the Former Prophets, or to extract the Pentateuch from the Primary History, Ezra (if he is the one who made the decision) thus created not just an anomalous literary work, but shifted the focus and target of biblical religion from an essentially historical mode (that is, divine acts in human history) to the mode of law (that is, divine words or commands to regulate the behavior of the human community). While the inclusion of the book of Genesis, which is hardly a book of law, reflects the original concern for historical continuity in the larger work (the Primary History, an argument strengthened by the notable connections between Genesis and Joshua in terms of promise and fulfilment, present in the larger work, but disconnected in the creation of the Pentateuch), and the narrative of the other books of the Torah tells the dramatic story of Israel's beginnings from deliverance from bondage in Egypt until the settlement in Transjordan, the emphasis in the Torah is clearly on the spoken word, the once-for-all and unchangeable command of the living God, the covenant Lord who imposes a pattern of believing and behaving on his people, the variety of written codes governing all the aspects of faith and practice, life and works, through examples and general statements.

On the one hand, therefore, Ezra's aim was to exalt the rule of law and the role of Moses as mediator of the covenant by which the people were to live. That Moses was in fact not a king and founded no dynasty, regardless of the authority that he actually wielded or of dynastic claims made by his descendants, made him a much more useful and attractive figure and symbol in the difficult and delicate situation in which Ezra and the people found themselves, than David, who was a king and had a dynasty, members of which were alive and could be identified at that time. Along with the idea of exalting the status of Moses and especially his role as lawgiver, there was the strategy of diminishing or distancing David as a role model. As conqueror of the surrounding territories and creator of the Israelite empire, as founder of a dynasty that had ruled in Jerusalem for more than 400 years and whose descendants might rule again, David was not the person to inspire confidence in the neighbors or trust in the eyes of the authorities. The choice for a person like Ezra, as well as for Nehemiah, was both inevitable and congenial. Without disturbing the existing documents already part of the canon of Holy Scripture, but only by moving the boundary marker between the parts, Ezra was able to focus the spotlight on Moses as prophet and lawgiver, and thereby to achieve a shift in the definition and delimitation of biblical religion, with the most serious consequences for the present and the future. At the same time, the figure of David was not so much diminished as obscured. He remained a great hero of the past, and a less well-defined hope for the future, but meanwhile there would be no emphasis on the possibilities of the present, or any serious talk of a restoration of the monarchy. Henceforth, law would be seen as, and at, the heart of biblical religion, the law revealed through Moses at Mount Sinai, while history and prophecy would be less central and play supporting roles. Nothing was lost, which is the secret of the canonical process, but some elements were shifted, and priorities rearranged. Over time, Judaism would move in a variety of ways, but the essential ingredients were preserved and available. For the present, the dominant component was Moses and law; in the future there could be a revival of prophecy and David, that is, the Messiah ben-David, who would restore the kingdom and its glory.

Similarly, Ezra or his editor and scribe supplemented the Chronicler's Work with an appendix containing his memoirs and those of his contemporary and collaborator, the civil governor, Nehemiah, thus redirecting a document that emphasized national independence, the dynasty of David, and the temple of Jerusalem, so that finally that work would conform to the newly revised but ultimately ancient pattern. What finally counts for Ezra and his colleagues is neither national independence nor monarchy, but the intimate relationship of the people with their God, mediated by Moses, that existed before either nationhood or kingship and had outlasted both. This relationship was established and is governed and regulated by the individual commands and precepts of a holy God, who has chosen to put his name and his glory in the midst of this tiny but precious community. Without rejecting the prophets and their dreams, or the Davidic dynasty and the hopes and expectations associated with it, Ezra nevertheless relegated those to the wings, and cleared the center of the stage for the Torah above all, for Moses the founder and the lawgiver, for the divine words he and he alone communicated.

Before turning to the second part of the paper, I pause briefly to summarize the first part:

I. The First Bible (ca. 560 B.C.E.)
  A. The Primary History (including Genesis through Kings)
  B. The Prophetic Corpus (associated with the Primary History)
    1. First Isaiah (chaps. 1–33, 36–39)
    2. Jeremiah (including chap. 52)

3. Ezekiel
4. Minor Prophets (including the first nine books)

(The First Bible, which may have included other books as well, such as the Psalter and Proverbs, was compiled not earlier than 560 B.C.E. and not later than 540 B.C.E.)

II. The Second Bible (ca. 518 B.C.E.)
 A. The Primary History
 B. The Prophetic Corpus
  1. The Three Major Prophets
   a. Second Isaiah combined with First Isaiah to produce the full book: Isaiah 1–66. Chapters 34–35 and 40–66 were composed, compiled, and combined with First Isaiah in the two decades between the First Bible and the Edict of Cyrus in 539 B.C.E. The timetable apparently was determined by a calculation of the years of a jubilee from the time of the destruction of the Temple (587 B.C.E.) until the expected return and restoration in 538 B.C.E.
   b. Jeremiah
   c. Ezekiel
  2. The Twelve Prophets
   a. The first nine books, as above
   b. Haggai, Zechariah, and Malachi added before the completion of the Second Temple in 515 B.C.E. The last date given in these books is the 4th year of Darius in Zechariah 7 = 518 B.C.E.

(No doubt the Second Bible included other works as well, including especially the following:)

 C. The Chronicler's History
  1. 1 & 2 Chronicles
  2. Ezra 1–3, down to the resumption of work on the Second Temple under the supervision of Zerubbabel.

III. The Third Bible (ca. 430 B.C.E.)
 A. The Torah (= Law). I hold the isolation of this work from the larger Primary History and its identification as the primary and central authority within the Bible to be the achievement of Ezra as recorded in Ezra–Nehemiah.
 B. The Prophets
  1. The Former Prophets
   a. Joshua

b. Judges
c. Samuel (including 1 & 2 Samuel)
d. Kings (including 1 & 2 Kings)
2. The Latter Prophets
a. The three major prophets
1) Isaiah (1–66)
2) Jeremiah (1–52)
3) Ezekiel (1–48)
b. The Twelve Prophets
1) The nine earlier books
2) The three later books
C. The Writings
1. The Chronicler's Work
a. 1 & 2 Chronicles
b. Ezra–Nehemiah. (The latter chapters of Ezra and Nehemiah were derived from the memoirs of the two men, and incorporated in the work during the latter part of the fifth century. The horizon does not extend beyond the reign of Artaxerxes I, 464–424 B.C.E., or Darius II, 423–404 B.C.E.)
2. The other books
a. Psalms
b. Proverbs
c. Job
d. The Megillot (Rolls). The collection no doubt included books such as Ruth, Song of Songs, and Lamentations. I would hesitate to make a judgment about books such as Ecclesiastes and Esther.

Moses as Apostolic Prophet and Lawgiver

In the first part of this paper, I have proposed that Ezra, in effect, created or at least identified the Torah (that is, the Pentateuch) by extracting it from a larger work, thereby spotlighting and focusing attention on the figure of Moses as both the founder of the nation and its primary and principal lawgiver. It is nevertheless important to note that the tradition concerning Moses' role in these areas is both old and widely distributed among the sources. The last thing I wish to do is give the impression that Ezra invented the tradition or exaggerated the role assigned to Moses in the thinking of Israel. Whatever one makes of the documentary hypothesis as it relates to the Pentateuch, the representation of Moses as founding father and lawgiver, leader of the Exodus and the Wilderness Wanderings, chieftain in battle and judge of his people, prophet and revealer of Yahweh, is essentially the same in all of the sources, with only minor variations or differences in emphasis and terminology. Even if the Hebrew word for prophet (*nābîʾ*) is anachronistic when applied directly to Moses, it was clearly understood that he performed the function and fulfilled the role of one who receives the word of God, is commissioned to deliver it to the people, and does so in accord with the divine command. He is the principal human figure in the dramatic story of Israel's deliverance from bondage in Egypt, the wanderings in the wilderness, its victories in the plains and plateaus of Transjordan, and initial settlement there, pending the invasion of the West Bank.

Moses and his Torah (cf. Deut 33:4) represent, therefore, the initial and enduring combination of law and religion—religion and law—which has been the major contribution of the ancient Near East, and more particularly of the biblical tradition, to Western culture and civilization. The tradition of written law is an old one in the Near East, going back much earlier than any conceivable date for Moses. Furthermore, legal codes and their sponsors are invariably associated with religious authority and sanction, so I cannot argue for the originality or uniqueness of Moses and Torah on that basis. There is innovation and novelty, but they lie in the nature of the combination, the interfusion of the elements, rather than in the idea that law and religion have something to do with each other.

In viewing the data from inscriptions and other archaeological finds, one observes that a sizable number of such law codes have been preserved, although generally in fragmentary form, the most famous and important being that of Hammurabi, the fourth king of the first dynasty of Babylon, who may be dated around 1750 B.C.E. This extensive code of laws deals with a number of subjects and covers a variety of cases, which are also treated in the Bible, as well as in other codes. Earlier codes are known in both Semitic and Sumerian; the format and general content must go back into the third millennium and possibly the early part of it. Often the code is promulgated by the king, who is shown or described as presenting it to an appropriate deity. The purpose clearly is to claim divine sanction for the code and its administrator, and to lend authority both to the provisions and to those who are expected to enforce them. The codes are exemplary in character, designed to illustrate the principles of justice and the manner of its execution. Evidently each domain, whether law or religion, is intended to support and reinforce the other. The law appeals to religion for authority and sanction, while religion finds in law its appropriate expression and implementation, whereby the sacral requirements are met, and the presence or threat of force ensures conformity and submission to the demands of religion. Each seeks from and contributes to the other in order to strengthen both, at least insofar as institutional interests are concerned.

This constant and repeated association no doubt contributed to the rule of law and widespread conformity to the social and political regulations of the times and places. Such a combination tended to ensure domestic tranquillity and a certain measure of security for all members of the society. But it was designed and exploited by those in power to preserve the status quo, and it was frankly intended to benefit those who exercised authority in both spheres. The essential difficulty lay in the fact that such law and such religion were essentially pragmatic instead of being principled, and could easily serve, as they often did, the interests of autocratic and oppressive governments. The notion of a principle of law or ethical behavior independent of and higher than those who had power was either not recognized at all, or included as a mere rhetorical flourish. In the long run, the system proved to be of benefit primarily to those by whom it was designed and operated, rather than for those who especially needed to be protected by its application: the poor, the alien, the bereaved, and the afflicted.

The same could be said of legal codes and instruments instituted by kings and rulers of later times, such as Justinian or Napoleon, both of whom sponsored famous and long-enduring codes of law. In these latter cases, the codes inevitably reflected the influence of the biblical tradition in modifying or qualifying their formulation and application, but the major components remain much the same: To the extent that the king or ruler is directly involved in the codification or enforcement of the regulations, the basic interest of the state in social control and the reinforcement of its power remains dominant. Religion provides the means by which that authority is sanctioned and sanctified, while the religious establishment is itself served and enhanced by the power of the state.

The emergence of Moses as leader and lawgiver is, however, a new and different phenomenon. It is no accident that Moses is never called a king (in spite of Deut 33:4–5, which must be understood as referring to God as king, not Moses), and never associated with the political structure of a monarchy as are most if not all of the so-called lawgivers of the ancient Near East (the traditions of Greece and Rome may reflect a different experience and understanding of the role of law and relationship to religion and vice versa). Moses was not a political leader seeking the sanction of religion, nor a religious leader seeking the power of the state to enforce his rules, but a prophet, one called by God and commissioned by him to speak in his behalf and perform the tasks assigned to him. The authority behind the authorities in both spheres is Yahweh himself, who rules over both law and religion, over the state and the religious order.

The role of prophet as lawgiver is unique in the person of Moses, and specific for the biblical tradition. Thus, law is not independently developed or derived from political and social or economic areas and elements. It is not established or imposed by powerful groups in society, but proceeds from religion, is itself the expression of religious truth and revelation. Religion is embodied in law, just as law is the mechanism by which religion rules over and operates in the lives of its adherents. If one believes that with Moses and the Torah a new element was introduced into the world, especially of the ancient Near East, then in what ways did the Mosaic society, early Israel, differ from its neighbors? The question is not as easily answered as one should or might suppose. Superficially, at least, and in many details Israel was hardly distinguishable from the other peoples, and this circumstance is reflected in the numerous clauses in the codes, both biblical and nonbiblical, dealing with similar and conventional circumstances and situations, such as the ubiquitous and irrepressible goring ox. All too often, as well, Israel did not attain to the level of behavior demanded of it by its religion, and was no better—and sometimes even worse—than its neighbors. Nevertheless, a new kind of society was visualized and initiated by Moses, and it is described and circumscribed in the legal sections of the Torah. Obedience to the commandments is for the sake of God and not for the sake of a king. Any national enhancement or success would be a serendipitous by-product, not a goal of conformity to the requirements. To love God and one's neighbor adequately summarizes the purpose and function of law in Israelite society, and at the same time it is the epitome of religious devotion and obedience.

In the solemn compact between God and his people based upon the prior act of divine grace in delivering his people from bondage in Egypt, that is, redeeming them from slavery and thereby acquiring them as a personal possession (Hebrew *sĕgullā*), a weighty obligation thereby rests upon the whole body politic and distributively on each individual. The latter is bound not only to obey as a person, that is, to govern his or her personal behavior in accordance with the stipulations, but to act responsibly as a member of the community, which is ultimately answerable to the divine suzerain for its actions, including those of its individual members. The latter responsibility, as also the former, varies with the status and skills, the possibilities and actualities of each individual. Of the one to whom much has been given, much will be expected; but balancing that rather austere guideline is the one that says that little will be asked of the one to whom little has been given. Thus, those in positions of power, wealth, and leadership, will be held more strictly to account than many others. At the same time, special protection and assistance are promised to those outside, those who are deprived, those who are afflicted—in short, the victims of society.

Beneath the superficial resemblances between Israel's covenant and the codes of other nations, which are inevitable and understandable, and alongside the details that relate to time and place and local circumstances, there is a central and visible difference, a plan and a goal: to establish an equitable society on earth, one in which the sense of purpose and spur to action derive from a profound acknowledgment of divine authority, and a firm commitment to the service and worship of the deity who has made his will known. The whole pattern of behavior would be governed by these principles: from the basic level of conformity to the rules of what is permitted on the one hand and what is prohibited on the other, to the highest level of fulfillment of the commandments of love, as expressed in the admonishments of Deut 6:4–6 and Lev 19:18 (and others). The summary of these obligations, as offered on more than one occasion in the New Testament, attests the centrality and ultimacy of the duty to love God with all one's heart and soul and mind, and to love one's fellow human being as oneself.

The legacy of Moses and his Torah to the Western world is the merger of law and religion, the inseparable joint expression of the divine will, communicated by his prophet. If true religion involves the right relationship between humanity and deity, then the law is the way in which that relationship is defined and regulated. There is, after all, the inescapable factor of obligation and obedience. Such a relationship, biblically understood, cannot be purely mystical, romantic, or privately personal; it must be ethical, moral, and social. It must be regulated by law, but the law must be in accordance with the divine will and interest, and not merely a social contract meeting the needs or accommodating the interests of humans.

What I have said of Moses and his Torah applies as well to others in the same tradition. Prophet-founders of religious communities are also the lawgivers for those groups. The occurrence of such phenomena outside of the Bible, the appearance of individuals in the role of prophets and founders, and as revealers and lawgivers, enhances the validity of the view proposed here: that Moses as lawgiver reflects a different pattern for the association of religion and law in the formation and preservation of a particular community. I have already indicated that Jesus was seen by at least some of his followers as a lawgiver in the pattern of Moses, but transcending him (especially in the Gospel of Matthew, in which the teachings of Jesus are deliberately set in contrast with those of Moses). While there has been a good deal of debate about the Law, its validity and its applicability in the new Christian dispensation, and while there has been a great deal of discussion of St. Paul's supposed antinomianism, Jesus as supreme lawgiver, and the Christian community as functioning under divine law, has always been the prevailing view in the Church, and remains so.

I see a similar phenomenon in Islam, in which the Prophet Muḥammad is not only the founder of a new community based on the exclusive worship and service of Allah (equivalent of Hebrew *ʾĕlōah*, one of the designations of the God of Israel), but its lawgiver as well. The same kind of union or combination of religion and law is present in Islam as I have noted for Judaism and Christianity, in which the founder-prophet is also the revealer and lawgiver.

Finally I call attention to the same sort of development in the history of Christianity. In diverse times and places, prophetic figures have appeared and communities devoted and dedicated to these leaders, seen as revealers and lawgivers, have arisen. Here I can mention that uniquely American phenomenon, Joseph Smith, who was the prophet-founder of a new society, the Church of Jesus Christ of Latter-day Saints (popularly known as Mormons), and also its principal lawgiver. In an effort to maintain both contiguity and continuity with the past, the pattern of prophet-leader who is also lawgiver has been preserved in this community of faith, so there is a steady procession of "prophets" who are empowered to modify existing laws or proclaim new ones. In self-reforming and self-renewing fashion, this structure reflects the dynamic association of religion and law, established initially by Moses with his Torah.

Shalom M. Paul

Biblical Analogues to Middle Assyrian Law

MOST OF THE ESSAYS in this volume have endeavored to bring to light ideas about holy law and the inseparability of religion and law as developed *within* the Bible or the Jewish and Islamic religious traditions. Paul moves into the larger Near Eastern setting within which biblical ideas emerged and presents some aspects of the interaction between the Bible and that larger setting, thus reminding the reader that even holy law does not develop in isolation from legal traditions in the surrounding environment. Specifically, Paul looks at four biblical passages (Deut 25:11–12, Isa 47:1–4, Ezek 23:24–25, Lev 24:10–23) in which he finds analogues to specific sections in the Middle Assyrian Laws. Although these analogues do not indicate wholesale borrowing, they are extremely important in elucidating the background and understanding of the biblical passages studied here.

Shalom M. Paul recently became chairman of the Department of Biblical Studies at the Hebrew University of Jerusalem. He received his Ph.D. in Oriental Studies from the University of Pennsylvania. His publications include *Studies in the Book of the Covenant in the Light of Cuneiform and Biblical Law*. He has written on various aspects of ancient and biblical law, the Near Eastern background of the Bible, biblical archaeology, and prophetic literature. His commentary on the book of Amos will appear in the *Hermeneia* series.

Full-scale studies dedicated to the comparison of biblical and Middle Assyrian Laws began with the almost simultaneous publication of two independent works: E. Jacob, "Die altassyrischen Gesetze und ihr Verhältnis zu den Gesetzen des Pentateuch," and E. Ring, *Israels Rechtsleben im Lichte der neuentdeckten assyrischen und hethitischen Gesetzesurkunden.*[1] Ever since the discovery of MAL, reference to these laws has been made in biblical commentaries, primarily comparing them to legal provisions in the books of Exodus, Leviticus, and Deuteronomy. Among the most widely discussed and compared laws may be mentioned, for example, Exod 21:22-25 and MAL A:21 and 50-52 (the case of assault causing the miscarriage of a pregnant woman), Exod 22:15-16 and Deut 22:23ff. and MAL A:55-56 (the laws of seduction and rape), Lev 20:13 and MAL A:20 (homosexuality), Lev 20:10 and Deut 22:22 and MAL A:14-16 and 22-24 (adultery), Deut 22:13ff. and MAL A:18 (slander). Comparisons to some of these as well as to other analogues, with linguistic and formulistic notes, can also be found in my work, *Studies in the Book of the Covenant in the Light of Cuneiform and Biblical Law.*[2] Moshe Weinfeld also makes an occasional remark on the relation between MAL and Deuteronomy: "Some of these humanistic laws have their parallels in the ancient Near-Eastern Codes but without the special overtones found in Deuteronomy. Especially salient in this respect are the affinities to the Assyrian Laws, a fact which may not be without significance for the background of the composition of Deuteronomy. . . . Unlike other Biblical codes, Deuteronomy preserved a series of family laws similar to those in the Middle-Assyrian laws."[3]

After all the investigation of these laws, it seems that the general conclusions drawn by Ring still ring true: though there are "mehr oder weniger stark analogue Zeuge" between biblical and Middle Assyrian legal collections, nevertheless there are very few that are

[1] Jacob: *Zeitschrift für vergleichende Rechtswissenschaft* 41 (1925) 319-87; Ring: (Leipzig: Harrassowitz; Stockholm: Fock, 1926). Middle Assyrian Laws (hereafter, MAL) are numbered in accordance with the text and translation in G. R. Driver and J. C. Miles, *The Assyrian Laws* (Oxford: Clarendon, 1935; repr. with corrections Darmstadt: Scientia Verlag Aalen, 1975) 380-453. For MAL in general see, in addition to Driver and Miles, G. Cardascia, *Les Lois Assyriennes* (Paris: Cerf, 1969); see also P. Koschaker, *Quellenkritische Untersuchungen zu den altassyrischen Gesetzen* (Mitteilungen der vorderasiatisch-ägyptischen Gesellschaft 26/3; Leipzig: Hinrichs, 1921) 24; and Ring, *Israels Rechtsleben*, 37-38.

[2] (Vetus Testamentum supplement 18; Leiden: Brill, 1970) 39-40, 62, 71-73, 96-98, 113.

[3] *Deuteronomy and the Deuteronomic School* (Oxford: Clarendon, 1972) 292 and n. 2.

actually identical.[4] He continues "Irgend welche Übereinstimmungen zwischen den in Frage kommenden Gesetzen in rein formeller Hinsicht sind nicht vorhanden, sondern die Analogien umfassen ausschliesslich die reele Seite der Bestimmungen."

The purpose of this paper is not to rediscuss the examples cited above but rather to (1) draw further attention to a legal case cited in Deuteronomy, then (2) to extend the scope of inquiry to prophetic literature, where the background of two verses will be interpreted in the light of laws from the Middle Assyrian compilation, and, finally, (3) to draw a previously unnoticed comparison between a legal precedent in Leviticus and a Middle Assyrian harem edict.

Deuteronomy 25:11-12 and MAL A:8

One of the biblical laws frequently noted as being analogous to MAL is found in Deut 25:11-12:[5]

> *Kî-yinnāṣû ʾănāšîm yaḥdāw ʾîš wĕʾāḥîw wĕqārĕbâ ʾēšet hāʾeḥād lĕhaṣṣîl ʾet-ʾîšāh mîyad makkēhû wĕšālĕḥâ yādāh wĕheḥĕzîqâ bimĕbušāyw. Wĕqaṣṣōtâ ʾet-kappāh lōʾ tāḥôs ʿênekā.*

> If two men get into a fight with each other and the wife of one comes up to save her husband from his antagonist and puts out her hand and seizes him by his genitals, you shall cut off her hand; show no pity.[6]

The uniqueness of this prescription lies in its being the only specific example of the application of corporal mutilation mentioned in Israelite law outside of the thrice-repeated *lex talionis* (Exod 21:23-25; Lev 24:19-20; Deut 19:19, 21).[7] One scholar has contended that strictly

[4] Ring, *Israels Rechtsleben*, 111. For additional notes on the relationship between the Bible and MAL, see R. Yaron, Review of *Les Lois Assyriennes*, by G. Cardascia, *Biblica* 51 (1970) 549-57.

[5] Cf. also the last law discussed in this paper, Lev 24:10, and also, Exod 21:22.

[6] Note the paronomastic repetition of *yad*. The verb *heḥĕzîq* + *b* signifies some sort of violent seizing or grasping. The position of this law immediately after the case of the nonconsummated levitical marriage may partially be due to a similarity in phrasing: v 5: (*kî-yēšĕbû*) *ʾaḥîm yaḥdāw* and v 11: (*kî-yinnāṣû*) *ʾanašîm yaḥdāw ʾîš wĕʾāḥîw*; v 5: *ʾēšet-hammēt* and v 11: *ʾēšet hāʾeḥad*. For other semantic ties within Deut 25:4-12, see C. M. Carmichael, *The Laws of Deuteronomy* (Ithaca: Cornell University, 1974) 232-40, and "Treading in the Book of Ruth," *Zeitschrift für die alttestamentliche Wissenschaft* 92 (1980) 248-66. For a uniquely untenable interpretation of the connection of the laws, see J. T. Norman, Jr., "The Muzzled Ox," *Jewish Quarterly Review* 70 (1980) 172-75.

[7] However, the punishment of mutilation of the hand is applied in Hammurabi's Law Code (LH) 195, for a son who has struck his father; LH 218, for a physician who

speaking the principle of retaliation is not involved here, since the female offender is not punished by the same injury as she inflicted.[8] According to a different view, the reason that her hand is cut off is because it is assumed that she is still holding on to the scrotum and refuses to let go.[9] Yet another commentator argues that the punishment actually does apply the principle of retaliation since the *kap* of the woman is interpreted as referring to the corresponding female genitalia in two other passages: Gen 32:26, 33 and Cant 5:5—all three supposedly referring to the male or female scrotum or labia.[10]

All of these very dubious interpretations can be rejected out of hand. This regulation is actually an example of talionic extension or vicarious talionic punishment of the peccant member. For other examples, see LH 116, 195, 210 and 230 and MAL A:50 and 55. Since the "injury of the testes cannot be applied to the woman . . . , the *jus talionis* is modified in the sense that the same member of the attacker is punished which directly caused the injury."[11] The incident itself is obviously not one of frequent occurrence and its applied punishment is, as stated above, unique to biblical legislation. But it does have its analogy in MAL where a similar law appears:

> If a woman has laid hand on a man [*šumma aššitum qāta ana aʾīlim tattabal*—note the cognate expressions: Assyrian *qāta ana . . . wabālum* and Hebrew *šālĕḥâ yād b*], [and] a charge has been brought against her, she shall pay thirty minas of lead [and] shall be beaten twenty stripes with rods (MAL A:7).

> If a woman has crushed a man's testicle in an affray [*ina ṣalti* = Hebrew *yinnaṣû*], one of her fingers shall be cut off. And even though a physician has bound it up, if the other testicle has become affected along

---

has caused a patient's death or destroyed his eye; LH 226, for a brander who cut off the slave mark of someone else's slave without the consent of the latter's owner; and LH 253, for one who was hired to cultivate another's field and stole the seed and fodder. For *lex talionis*, see my *Studies in the Book of the Covenant*, 73-77.

[8] B. S. Jackson, *Essays in Jewish and Comparative Legal History* (Leiden: Brill, 1975) 83 n. 57.

[9] Jacob, "Die altassyrischen Gesetze," 362.

[10] L. Eslinger ("The Case of an Immodest Lady Wrestler in Deuteronomy XXV 11-12," *Vetus Testamentum* 31 [1981] 269-81, esp. 272-73, 277) interprets this law in a novel fashion, as the deuteronomic moralistic comment upon Jacob's wrestling match by the Jabbok River. See also his "More Drafting Techniques in Deuteronomic Laws," *Vetus Testamentum* 34 (1984) 221-26.

[11] E. Roth, "Does the Thorah Punish Impudence? Notes to Deuteronomy XXV 11-12," *Études orientales à la mémoire de Paul Hirschler* (ed. O. Komlós; Budapest: N.P., 1956) 20.

> with it and becomes inflamed,[12] or if she has crushed the other testicle in the affray, they shall tear out [*inappulu*] both [*kilallūn*] her . . . (MAL A:8).

Since the text is broken at this very point, the identification of the exact member of her body that is subject to mutilation is open to question. The guidelines for resolving the issue are to be found in the Assyrian *kilallūn* 'both', a nominative dual, and the verb that designates the punishment, *napālu* 'to gouge out', otherwise employed in connection with the gouging out of the eyes.[13] Thus, E. Ebeling followed by T. J. Meek assumes that the text originally had [*inē*]*ša* 'both her eyes'.[14] However, much more preferable, due to the sexual injury involved, is the restored reading of V. Scheil followed by Cardascia, [*tulē*]*ša* 'her breasts'.[15]

The severity of the punishment in MAL A:8 is most likely due to the fact that she has destroyed the man's procreative ability.[16] She, in turn, is made to suffer in retaliation the mutilation of her sexual organs.

Despite the somewhat external similarities of the biblical and Assyrian laws—a woman grabbing the male private parts during a brawl and the punishment of the mutilation of a hand or a finger[17]—several significant differences still exist between them. In MAL the

[12] For the various possibilities of translation, see Driver and Miles, *Assyrian Laws*, 385, 460; Cardascia, *Les Lois Assyriennes*, 108; *The Assyrian Dictionary of the Oriental Institute of the University of Chicago* (hereafter, *CAD*; Chicago: University of Chicago, 1956-), vol. E, p. 295 ("*erimu*"); W. von Soden, *Akkadisches Handwörterbuch* (Wiesbaden: Harrassowitz, 1959-1981) 241 ("*eri*[*m*]*mu*"). See also Koschaker, *Quellenkritische Untersuchungen*, 24, and Ring, *Israels Rechtsleben*, 37-38.

[13] See *CAD* N/1, 273, 275 for *napālu* and *nuppulu*.

[14] E. Ebeling, "Altassyrische Gesetze," in H. Gressmann, *Altorientalische Texte zum Alten Testement* (2d ed.; Berlin: de Gruyter, 1926) 412-22; Meek, "The Middle Assyrian Laws," *Ancient Near Eastern Texts Relating to the Old Testament* (hereafter, *ANET*; ed. J. B. Pritchard; 3d ed.; Princeton: Princeton University, 1969) 181.

[15] V. Scheil, *Recueil de lois assyriennes* (Paris: Geuthner, 1921) 10. Cardascia, *Les Lois Assyriennes*, 108-9. So too *CAD* K, 356, which inadvertently omits putting the word "breasts" in brackets. The problem with Driver and Miles's restoration, [*dīdē*]*ša* 'her [nipples]', is that *dīdū* does not appear in Akkadian with either the meaning of 'breasts' or 'nipples' (see *CAD* D, 136).

[16] The punitive severing of the breasts is also found in LH 194, which pertains to a wet nurse who, after a child has died in her care, undertakes to nurse yet another son without the knowledge of the child's parents. The verb there, however, is *nakāsu* 'to sever' and not *napālu* 'to gouge out'. Cf. Cardascia, *Les Lois Assyriennes*, 109; Driver and Miles, *Assyrian Laws*, 30-31.

[17] The severing of a finger is also found in MAL A:9, where a man has in some way assaulted a married woman, and in B:8, where a man has encroached upon his

woman is directly involved in the brawl from the outset, and the law is primarily concerned with the injury itself.[18] The deuteronomic legislation, on the other hand, pertains to a woman who enters the fight at a later stage and then only in order to save her husband, who is one of the combatants. The law is not concerned whether or not she has caused any permanent damage to the male.[19] Its emphasis is placed upon a "breach of modesty."[20] She has touched the male's pudenda, referred to euphemistically as *mĕbušāyw,* and thus her crime is considered so shameful and so severe that the law ends with the expression *lōʾ tāḥôs ʿênekā* 'show [her] no pity'. This injunction also appears as a part of three other laws in Deuteronomy: 13:9 (regarding idol worship), 19:13 (one who premeditatively commits

---

neighbor's boundary. For the latter, see Driver and Miles, *Assyrian Laws,* 303. For the cutting off of the *kappu* 'arm, hand' (= Hebrew *kap*), in Mesopotamian royal documents, see *CAD* K, 187.

[18] For a possible example of the application of this injunction, see C. H. Gordon, "A New Akkadian Parallel to Deuteronomy 25:11-12," *Journal of the Palestine Oriental Society* 15 (1935) 29-34, who refers to E. Chiera, *Excavations at Nuzi* (Harvard Semitic Series 5; Cambridge: Harvard University, 1929) 43. See also A. Saarisalo, *New Kirkuk Documents Relating to Slaves* (Studia Orientalia 5/3; Helsinki: Societas orientalis fennica, 1934). In this tablet a wife of a slave intervenes in a fight between two men and inflicts a bodily injury on one of them. After the injured party indicts her, and four witnesses testify against her, she refuses to undergo the ordeal of the oath of the gods and is found guilty. Her punishment, along with the standard fine of livestock, is the amputation of one of her fingers. The similarities are very apparent. The only questionable item is the member of the male body she injured. The text states that, "She put her hand on the *aḫu* [of the male] and blood was let." Gordon translates this as 'loin' and is followed by S. E. Loewenstamm (*Encyclopaedia Biblica* [Jerusalem: Bialik, 1962], 4:610-11 [Hebrew]) who interprets *aḫu* (literally, 'arm, side') as a euphemism. It must be admitted, however, that such a euphemism is otherwise undocumented. Driver and Miles's interpretation of *aḫu* as 'brother' is highly untenable; see their "Ordeal by Oath at Nuzi," *Iraq* 7 (1940) 135.

[19] Weinfeld (*Deuteronomy and the Deuteronomic School,* 292-93) correctly criticizes Loewenstamm's assumption as to the inner connection of MAL A:7 and 8, explaining the one by the other. MAL A:7 does not mention the male privy parts, and only MAL A:8 states that the incident occurred during an affray.

[20] See Weinfeld, *Deuteronomy and the Deuteronomic School,* 292. See also the quote by A. Dillmann in S. R. Driver, *Deuteronomy* (International Critical Commentary; Edinburgh: Clark, 1895) 285: "Immodesty, even when extenuating circumstances are present, is to be checked as stringently as possible." Cf. D. Daube, "The Culture of Deuteronomy," *Orita* [Ibadan] 3 (1969) 36-37, who cites this law as part of the book's "shame culture." So, too, Carmichael (*Laws of Deuteronomy,* 234) states that Deuteronomy is "only concerned with the shamefulness of the woman's act." Cf. Carmichael, "A Ceremonial Crux: Removing a Man's Sandal as a Female Gesture of Contempt," *Journal of Biblical Literature* 96 (1977) 332: "The law is not concerned, unlike some Assyrian laws, with any damage the woman may do to the genitals of her husband's opponent. Its concern is solely with the shamefulness of her deed."

murder and flees to an asylum), and 19:21 (one who testifies falsely); cf. also Deut 7:16. As Weinfeld states, "Whenever there is a danger that the punisher would be lenient or even unwilling to perform the punishment the author uses לא תחוס עינך 'you must show (him) no pity'.[21] The purpose of all these laws is to purge Israel of all "evil things."

Isaiah 47:1-4 and MAL A:40

In chap. 47, Deutero-Isaiah launches into a satiric tirade and taunt song against "Fair Maiden Babylon." This "Mistress of Kingdoms" (v 5) who, in her undaunted and supercilious arrogance, presumptuously declares, "I am, and there is none but me" (vv 8, 10), believes that she "shall always, forever and ever, be the mistress" (v 7).[22] Led astray by her very own skill, she is destined to be dethroned, humiliated, despised, and reduced to the lowest of all menial classes:

> Get down, sit in the dust,
> Fair Maiden[23] Babylon.[24]
> Sit[25] dethroned on the ground,[26]
> O Fair Chaldea. Nevermore[27] shall they call you
> "Tendered and Pampered" (v 1).[28]

Nothing other than the "Decline and Fall of the Babylonian Empire" is being described here. Or as the Talmudic adage would have it: "from the loftiest height to the pits [lit. 'deepest pit']" (*b. Ḥag.* 5b). Yet

[21] Weinfeld, *Deuteronomy and the Deuteronomic School*, 2.

[22] Read *gĕvāret ᶜad* as one expression, against the Masoretic division; *ᶜad* parallels *lĕᶜôlām*. See D. N. Freedman, "Mistress Forever, A Note on Isaiah 47:7," *Biblica* 51 (1970) 538. The Qumran scroll reads *ᶜôd* for *ᶜad*.

[23] On *bĕtûlā*, see my "Virgin, Virginity," *Encyclopaedia Judaica* (Jerusalem: Keter, 1971), 16:160-61. The description is also applied to Zion, 2 Kgs 19:21, Isa 37:22, Lam 2:13; to Judah, Lam 1:15; to Israel, Jer 18:13, 31:4 [Heb. 3], 21 [20], Amos 5:2; to Egypt, Jer 46:11; and to Sidon, Isa 23:12.

[24] For Hebrew *bābel* in parallel to *kaśdîm*, see Isa 48:20.

[25] Note the repeated imperative *šĕbî* for emphasis.

[26] Compare the Baal text in Ugaritic literature (tablet 67, col. 6, lines 11-14): *apnk.lṭpn.ʾil / dpiʾd.yrd.lksi.yṯb / lhdm.wl.hdm.yṯb / lʾarṣ*: "Straightway Kindly El Benign / Descends from the throne, / Sits on the footstool; / From the footstool, / And sits on the ground" (see H. L. Ginsberg, "Poems about Baal and Anath," *ANET* 139). Note the similarity of the theme and wording in the Hebrew and Ugaritic: *rdy* (Hebrew) and *yrd* (Ugaritic), *ksʾ* and *ksi*, *šby* and *yṯb* (each twice), and *šby lʾrṣ* and *yṯb lʾarṣ*. This is then followed in the Ugaritic myth by a series of mourning rites.

[27] *Kî* is probably emphatic here.

[28] Cf. Deut 28:54, 56.

even with this precipitous descent, she has not yet reached the nadir of her disgrace. The prophet continues to address the former queen sarcastically with the following desultory description, all uttered in the form of short and succinct commands:

> Grasp the handmill and grind meal!
> Remove[29] your veil!
> Strip off your train! Bare your thigh!
> Wade through rivers!
> Your nakedness shall be uncovered,
> and your shame shall be exposed.[30]
> I will take vengeance;[31]
> I shall not be entreated,[32] says[33]
> our Redeemer—Lord of Hosts is his Name—
> the Holy One of Israel (2-4).

A review of the catalogue of the maiden's menial duties reveals the following:

1. *Qĕḥî rēḥayim wĕṭaḥănî qāmaḥ*:[34] 'Grasp the handmill and grind meal.' The grinding of grain is one of the allotted tasks of a slave, for both a male (Samson, Judg 16:21) and a female: "And every first-born in the land of Egypt shall die, from the first-born of Pharaoh who sits on his throne to the first-born of the slave girl who is behind the mill-stone" (Exod 11:5). Note once again the polar opposites: from throne to stone! (cf. Job 31:10, Lam 5:13).
2. *Ḥeśpî-šōbel*[35] *gallî-šôq ᶜibrî nĕhārôt*: 'Strip off your train, bare your thigh, wade through rivers.' The reference here is to the degradation endured by the captives deported to alien lands. As they demeaningly trip across the waters, instead of being ferried across as befits royalty, they raise their skirts on high, thus uncovering their shame to all. Compare the illustration on the

[29] *Gallî* also appears twice in v 2. It means to 'uncover, reveal'. Then comes the climactic third occurrence, *tiggāl*, in v 3.

[30] Cf. Isa 20:4; Jer 13:22, 26, Nah 3:5.

[31] For the idiom *lāqaḥ nāqām*, see also Jer 20:10.

[32] Read *lōᵓ ᵓeppāgaᶜ*. For *pgᶜ* with this meaning, cf. Gen 23:8, Isa 53:12, Jer 7:16, 27:18, Job 21:15, Ruth 1:16.

[33] For *ᵓādām*, read *ᵓāmar*, and cf. LXX.

[34] Note that the letter *ḥ* appears in each of these four words.

[35] The Qumran Isaiah Scroll has simplified the *hapax legomenon* by reading *ḥśwpy šwlyk*. For *šōbel*, see G. R. Driver's suggestion ("Difficult Words in the Hebrew Prophets," *Studies in Old Testament Prophecy Presented to Theodore H. Robinson* [ed. H. H. Rowley; Edinburgh: Clark, 1950] 58): "flowing tresses."

bronze doors of Balawat of the women of Dabigi who, as they are being led away captive by Shalmaneser III, are portrayed as lifting their skirts.[36] Thus from head (*gallî ṣammātēk*) to toe their body will be uncovered and revealed.

3. *Tiggāl ʿerwātēk gam tērāʾeh ḥerpātēk*: 'Your nakedness shall be uncovered, and your shame shall be exposed.' The fair maiden is further demeaned and debased by having to suffer the public humiliation of an adulteress. Compare Ezek 16:35–37 (discussed further below): "Now then, O harlot . . . because your nakedness was exposed in your harlotry with all your lovers . . . I am gathering all your lovers . . . all you loved and all you loathed; I am gathering them against you from all around. I will expose your nakedness to them and they shall gaze upon your nakedness." Thus measure for measure, or member for member: Since she is accused of *wattiggāleh ʿerwātēk,* her punishment shall be *wĕgillêtî ʿerwātēk* (cf. also Hos 2:12).

In the midst of these humiliating punishments, the prophet also commands Maiden Babylon: *gallî ṣammātēk*[37] 'remove/uncover your veil'. For the significance, and understanding of this act, one must turn to the Mesopotamian legal sphere. Though no mention of the practice of veiling is found in Babylonian texts, it is the subject of MAL A:40, marking the distinction of different social classes of women.[38] Married women and women of the upper classes must be veiled in public (lines 42–57), for veiling is the privilege of the respectable and distinguished lady. So, too, a concubine, *esirtu,* must be veiled when she accompanies her mistress in public (lines 58–60).[39] A hierodule(?), *qadištu,* on the other hand, is forbidden to veil herself unless she is married and then it becomes obligatory (lines 61–65).[40] However, a common prostitute, *ḫarimtu* (lines 66–76), and an ordinary slave girl, *amtu* (lines 88–93), are not permitted to be veiled

[36] See A. Jeremias, *Das Alte Testament im Lichte des alten Orients* (3d ed.; Leipzig: Hinrichs, 1916) 640, picture 281.

[37] For *ṣammâ,* see Cant 4:1, 3; 6:7.

[38] See the discussion of this law in Driver and Miles, *Assyrian Laws,* 126–34. On p. 127 they state that although there is "no corresponding law in the Babylonian code, [the] veiling, if it was obligatory in Babylonia, must have been part of the customary but unwritten law of the land."

[39] This is "not intended as a privilege for the girl but obviously as a protection for the mistress," Driver and Miles, *Assyrian Laws,* 128. Cf. Cardascia, *Les Lois Assyriennes,* 204.

[40] See the comments in *CAD* Q, 48–50, which refrains from translating *qadištu* as 'hierodule', as is commonly accepted, but rather, 'a woman of special status'.

under any circumstances. If they do veil themselves, they are severely punished: The man who arrests her (the prostitute) shall take her clothing (but not her jewelry); she is beaten with the rod fifty times, and pitch is poured over her head. (The last is a "mirroring punishment" reflecting her crime: the pitch covering her face represents the veil that she illegally donned.)[41] One who has seen a veiled harlot and has not arrested her is himself, in turn, punished. He is beaten with the rod fifty times, his clothing taken, his ears pierced, a cord is passed through them and tied behind him, and he must do a full month's labor for the king (lines 77-87, 94-106).

As for a slave girl who veils herself, she shall have her ears cut off and her clothing taken from her. One who has seen a veiled slave girl and not apprehended her suffers the same punishments as mentioned above.

The intention of the laws is quite clearly to distinguish the respectable women from the harlots and the slave girls.[42] The latter, as a sign of their inferior status, must remain unveiled at all times. This then is precisely what is being referred to by the prophet. In between the catalogue of punishments that designate a slave's status and a harlot's status, he declares that Maiden Babylon must remove her veil, which characterized her former position of dignity as a free woman. Now she is categorically reduced to the shameful status of both a common harlot and slave alike.[43]

Ezekiel 23:24-25 and MAL A:4

Ezekiel 23 is an allegory featuring two female *dramatis personae* who represent the two kingdoms of Israel: Oholah personifies Samaria and

[41] Driver and Miles, *Assyrian Laws,* 130; Cardascia, *Les Lois Assyriens,* 205.

[42] On veiling in the ancient Near East, see M. Jastrow, "Veiling in Ancient Assyria," *Revue archéologique,* 5th series, 14 (1921) 209-38; A. Jeremias, *Das Schleir von Sumer bis Heute* (Der alte Orient 31:1/2; Leipzig: Hinrichs, 1931). R. de Vaux, "Sur le Voile des Femmes dans l'Orient Ancien," *Revue biblique* 44 (1935) 397-412, concludes his study, "Le voile est donc à la fois un signe d'appartenance et une garantie" (p. 411). Tamar in Gen 38:14-15 (according to de Vaux) was covered up not because it was a custom of prostitutes, but simply in order not to be recognized. For a study of the practice in Greece, see C. M. Galt, "Veiled Ladies," *American Journal of Archaeology* 35 (1931) 373-93, who, upon examining the archaeological evidence concludes that veiling was the prevailing custom in Athens: "Greek ladies were veiled as brides when walking in the street, in certain religious acts, and in mourning." He refers also to the comment of Plutarch (*Moralia* 232c), concluding that the "real motive for veiling was the desire on the part of husbands to hide a possession from the gaze of other men."

[43] The study by R. Martin-Achard, "Esäie 47 et la tradition prophétique sur Babylone," *Prophecy: Essays Presented to Georg Fohrer* (ed. J. A. Emerton; *Zeitschrift*

Oholibah, Jerusalem. These two degenerate sisters have dedicated themselves from their youth to the practice of harlotry—harlotry being the metaphor for constantly changing alliances with foreign nations. Their biography consists of one unmitigated and unrelenting tale of lascivious adultery. Though the elder sister's whoredom eventually brought about her own demise, her young sibling did not heed the lesson of history, but rather persisted in her reckless and feckless conduct unabatedly. Her wanton and unbridled lust impels her to consistently change allies as a prostitute switches lovers. Yahweh, in utter disgust, repudiates her in the same manner that he did her younger sister. This, however, only adds more fuel to the heat of her burning desire for indulging in harlotry. Yet the day of eventual reckoning is not far off. Her sentence and punishment are imminent. Since she has degraded herself to the practice of heathens, Yahweh shall hand her over to her heathen paramours, who, as her judges, shall execute judgment according to their own prescriptions of law. Yahweh declares,

> I will entrust your punishment to them, and they shall inflict their punishments on you. . . . They shall cut off your nose and ears. . . . They shall strip you of your clothing and take away your dazzling jewels. . . . They shall take away all you have earned from your toil and leave you naked and bare. . . . They shall punish them with the punishments for adultery . . . for they are adulteresses (Ezek 23:24-26, 29, 45).

It should first be noted that several of these themes are already present in chap. 16—the parable of the unfaithful wife portrayed in the metaphor of a nymphomaniacal adulteress.[44] Since she indulged in fornication, she shall be indicted and sentenced to a violent death. The prophet declares in the name of Yahweh that he is gathering about her all of her lovers, both those she has loved and loathed. She will be publicly degraded by being exposed in her nakedness (Ezek 16:37). Then following her conviction, she will be handed over to her former paramour peers who shall act as her executioners. They shall first strip her of clothing and jewelry and then summarily execute her by stoning and finally hack and sever her corpse limb by limb (vv 39-40).[45]

---

für die alttestamentliche Wissenschaft supplement 150; Berlin: de Gruyter, 1980) 83-105, does not refer to this practice at all.

[44] See M. Greenberg, *Ezekiel 1-20* (Anchor Bible 22; Garden City, NY: Doubleday, 1983), *ad loc.*

[45] Stoning is "a public mode of punishment expressing the outrage of the community" (Greenberg, ibid., 287, citing the Hebrew study of H. Cohen, על עונש

The public naked exposure of a harlot is also attested elsewhere in the Bible (Jer 13:22, 26; Ezek 23:10; Hos 2:12; and Nah 3:5). And the stripping of a wife who leaves her husband for another man is well known from Nuzi.[46] A Jewish Aramaic incantation sending forth Lilith naked, thereby divorcing her, has also been frequently cited in this connection.[47]

The punishment upon which we would like to focus our attention is the corporal mutilation of the nose and ears of the adulteress—a punishment unknown from Israelite law but quite common in Mesopotamia, documented both in the legal corpora as well as in the Assyrian military annals.[48]

The dismemberment of both the nose and the ears is found twice in the Hittite Laws: no. 95 prescribes it as the punishment for a slave caught stealing goods from a house; and no. 99, for a slave who sets a house on fire.[49] LH 205 exacts the punishment of the cutting off the ear only in the case of a slave who strikes the cheek of a free man. Mutilation of the nose and/or ears is also prescribed several times in MAL. According to MAL A:4 if a slave receives property stolen by a woman from her husband, "They shall cut off the nose [and] ears of the male or female slave." The husband, in turn, has the option of also cutting off his wife's ears. If, however, he lets her go free, without

---

הסקילה [Ramat-Gan: Bar-Ilan University, 1962]). For the stoning of an adulteress, see Deut 22:21, 24 and Ezek 23:47. See also Loewenstamm, "מיתות בית דין," *Encyclopaedia Biblica* (Jerusalem: Bialik, 1962), 4:947–48 [Hebrew].

[46] See C. Kuhl, "Neue Dokumente zum Verständnis von Hos. 2:4–15," *Zeitschrift für die alttestamentliche Wissenschaft* 52 (1934) 102–9; C. H. Gordon, "Hos. 2:4–5 in the Light of New Semitic Inscriptions," *Zeitschrift für die alttestamentliche Wissenschaft* 13 (1936) 277–80.

[47] J. Montgomery, *Aramaic Incantation Texts from Nippur* (Philadelphia: University Museum, 1913) 190 (no. 17). The practice is also reported by Tacitus to have been current among the ancient Germans (*Germania* 19).

[48] For mutilation and other corporal punishments, see R. Haase, "Körperlich Strafen in den altorientalischen Rechtssammlungen," *Revue internationale du droit de l'antiquité* 10 (1973) 55–75. Compare also the Egyptian "Judicial Papyrus of Turin," dated to the end of the reign of Rameses III (ca. 1164 B.C.E.), where in a trial for conspiracy the accused had their noses and ears cut off "because they had abandoned the good instructions given to them" (J. A. Wilson, "Egyptian Documents," *ANET* 215). R. Borger, *Die Inschriften Asarhaddons, Königs von Assyrien* (*Archiv für Orientsforschung* supplement 9; Graz: E. Weidner, 1956) 106:24, documents an example of mutilation in Assyria: the (hands), nose, eye, and ear of anyone who fled from his master were cut off. See also the multiple references to military inscriptions under the entries "*batāqu*," "*ekēmu*," and "*nakāsu*" in the corresponding volumes of *CAD*. For another example of the mutilation of the ear in Assyrian legal practice, see E. Weidner, "Hof- und Harems-Erlässe assyrischen Könige aus dem 2. Jahrtausend v. Chr.," *Archiv für Orientsforschung* 17 (1954–56) edict no. 21, 287:104. For the amputation of both the nose and ears, see edict no. 5 (273:26). Cf. also MAL A:4.

[49] See A. Goetze, "The Hittite Laws," *ANET* 193.

cutting off her ears, the slave likewise is released from the similar punishment. MAL A:5 stipulates that if a married woman steals property over the value of 5 minas of lead from the house of another, her husband may ransom her, but he also cuts off her ears. If he does not opt to ransom her, the owner of the stolen property cuts off her nose. MAL A:24 pertains to the case of a woman who deserts her husband and enters the house of another Assyrian and stays with the mistress of that house for three or four nights without the master of the house being aware of her presence. If the woman is subsequently caught, her husband may take her back, but he still cuts off her ears. The ears of the woman with whom she stayed are also then cut off. MAL A:40 similarly prescribes the cutting off of the ears of a female slave who veils herself. The final law in the first tablet of MAL, A:59, also mentions penalties that the husband may inflict upon his wife, including damaging her ears.

Of special importance, moreover, is MAL A:15: If a man has caught his wife with another man *in flagrante delicto,* and he is prosecuted and convicted, both are put to death, without any liability attaching to the deceived husband.[50] If, however, he brings the couple to the king or to the judges and they are convicted, the husband has three options from which to choose: he may put his wife to death, and then kill the lover; he may allow his wife to go free and thereby pardon the paramour as well; or—and this is very significant—he may employ the punishment of mutilation, cutting off his wife's nose and then correspondingly make the other man a eunuch.[51] The reason for the disfigurement of the nose is apparently to make her the object of abhorrence, since any damage to her ears can be concealed by her hair.[52] Thus it becomes clear that according to MAL one of the several ways whereby adultery is punished is by the mutilation of the nose.[53]

[50] For MAL A:15, see Driver and Miles, *Assyrian Laws,* 45-46, and Koschaker, *Quellenkritische Untersuchungen zu den altassyrischen Gesetzen,* 39-42.

[51] Cf. LH 129, where if the two are caught *in actu,* they are bound together and thrown into the water. If the husband spares his wife, the king may spare his subject (cf. also LH 130-32, 155-56); for the corresponding Hittite laws, see nos. 197-98, where the husband also may kill or spare the adulterers. For other systems, cf. Driver and Miles, *Assyrian Laws,* 46 n. 5. For the stringent biblical laws on the subject of adultery, which make the crime an absolute wrong incapable of pardon by human agency (cf. Lev 20:10, Deut 22:23-24), see Greenberg, "Some Postulates of Biblical Criminal Law," *Yehezkel Kaufmann Jubilee Volume* (ed. M. Haran; Jerusalem: Magnes, 1960) 11-12. See also my *Studies in the Book of the Covenant,* 37, and n. 5, with additional bibliography.

[52] So Driver and Miles, *Assyrian Laws,* 48. See the quotation from Diodorus Siculus in n. 53 below.

[53] On facial mutilation of women, see Diodorus Siculus's statement concerning the Egyptians: "Severe also were their laws touching women. For if a man had violated

This then is of significance for the understanding of the passage in Ezekiel. For there it is explicitly stated that the adulteress is to be punished according to the laws of her paramours (23:24). And one of the nations frequently listed as consorting with both sisters is Assyria (in vv 5, 7, and 9 with Oholah; in vv 12 and 23 with Oholiba—cf. also 16:28). Israel thus is condemned to suffer, for the crime of adultery, a punishment meted out by her very lover, the Assyrians.[54]

Leviticus 24:10-23 and Assyrian Harem Edicts

Leviticus 24:10-23 is an independent pericope within the Holiness Code that consists of a narrative framework (vv 10-13, 23) embodying

---

a free married woman, they stipulated that he be emasculated, considering that such a person by a single unlawful act had been guilty of the three greatest crimes, assault, abduction, and confusion of offspring; but if a man committed adultery with the woman's consent, the laws ordered that the man should receive a thousand blows with the rod, and that the woman should have her nose cut off, on the ground that a woman who tricks herself out with an eye to forbidden licence should be deprived of that which contributes most to a woman's comeliness" (*Diodorus of Sicily* [trans. C. H. Oldfather; Loeb Classical Library; London: Heinemann, 1933] 271, §I:78:4-5). For studies on adultery, see W. Kornfeld, "L'adultère dans l'Orient Antique," *Revue biblique* 57 (1950) 92-109; D. Daube, "Origin and Punishment of Adultery in Jewish Law," *Studia Patristica* (ed. K. Aland and F. L. Cross; Texte und Untersuchungen zur Geschichte der altchristlichen Literatur 64; Berlin: Akademie, 1957), 2:109-13; Loewenstamm, "The Laws of Adultery and Homicide in Biblical and Mesopotamian Law Corpora," *Beth Miqra* 13 (1962) 55-59, and 19 (1964) 77-78 [Hebrew; Eng. trans. in Loewenstamm, *Comparative Studies in Biblical and Ancient Oriental Literatures* (Neukirchen-Vluyn: Neukirchener, 1980) 146-53, 171-72]; Weinfeld, "Israelite and Non-Israelite Concepts of Law," *Beth Miqra* 17 (1964) 58-63 [Hebrew]; M. Falasca, "L'evoluzione della pena dell' adulterio del diritto penale ebraico," *Euentes Docete* 18 (1965) 246-65. Loewenstamm (*Beth Miqra* 13) raises some serious reservations against Greenberg's view ("Some Postulates"), both from the Mesopotamian as well as from the biblical texts.

[54] In view of the fact that this is an established Assyrian practice it would seem to be a bit hasty to delete the phrase *kol-bĕnê ʾaššûr* 'all the Assyrians', from v 23 as an "interpretive" or "elaborative addition," as do W. Zimmerli (*Ezekiel 1* [Philadelphia: Fortress, 1979] 474-75, 486, 488) and many other moderns. From another perspective entirely, see R. Zadok, "West Semitic Toponyms in Assyrian and Babylonian Sources—Appendix II: The Unger Prism ('Nebuchadnezzar's Court Calendar') and Ezek. XXIII, 23ff.," *Studies in the Bible and the Ancient Near East* (S. E. Loewenstamm FS; ed. Y. Avishur and J. Blau; Jerusalem: Rubinstein, 1978) 178-79 [English vol.]. Zadok points out that the arrangement of the Babylonian regions in the Unger Prism correspond in general to those mentioned in Ezekiel 23. He comments, "'All the sons of Assyria' possibly refers to the greater area of Assyria which was in Babylonian hands." He further remarks that the term "all the sons of Assyria," rather than merely "Assyria," is "probably due to the fact that this geographical designation is much wider than Assyria proper and includes Upper Mesopotamia, Syria, Phoenicia and Palestine as well" (p. 178).

a series of legal statutes (vv 14-22).[55] The narrative, set within the desert sojourn of Israel, recounts a specific incident and its *ad hoc* judgment, which serves as a legal precedent normative for all similar cases in the future.[56] The test case involves a brawl that broke out (*wayyinnāṣû*) between a full Israelite and a half Israelite (one whose mother was Israelite but father an Egyptian).[57] During the affray the half Israelite uttered blasphemy, and for this offense he was brought to Moses and then placed under custody until a divine oracle would decide the proper judgment. The verdict was as follows: "Take the blasphemer outside the camp and let all who were within hearing lay their hands upon his head and let the whole community stone him" (Lev 24:14). According to this ruling blasphemy affects not only the speaker but infects the hearers as well.[58] This contamination is transferred back to the guilty party by the ritualistic laying of hands upon him. He is then summarily executed by stoning—a public execution that eradicates the stain from the community.

The definitive general prescription is then handed down. It differentiates in severity between one 'who blasphemes his God' (*yĕqallēl ʾĕlōhāyw*) and one who 'pronounces the name YHWH' (*wĕnōqēb šēm-YHWH*); the former "shall bear his guilt/be liable for his penalty" and the latter "shall be put to death." This is followed, in turn, by a series of *lex talionis* legislation and concludes by reporting the execution of the blasphemer in accordance with the principles cited above.

At the very beginning of this case it is stated that the half Israelite "pronounced the Name in blasphemy" (v 11).[59] The difficulty of the first verb, *wayyiqqōb* (whether it is to be derived from *nqb* 'to mark,

[55] See the standard critical commentaries on Leviticus. K. Elliger, *Leviticus* (Tübingen: Mohr, 1966) 330, calls it a "Gesetzesätiologie."

[56] See J. Weingreen, "The Case of the Blasphemer," *Vetus Testamentum* 22 (1972) 118-23, and the comments on the article by J. B. Gabel and C. B. Wheeler, "The Redactor's Hand in the Blasphemy Pericope of Leviticus XXIV," *Vetus Testamentum* 30 (1980) 227-29. Both studies pertain to whether the P redactor extended or narrowed the definition of blasphemy in his legislation. For an earlier study, see H. Mittwoch, "The Story of the Blasphemer Seen in a Wider Context," *Vetus Testamentum* 15 (1965) 386-89.

[57] Cf. the similar procedure recounted in another test case, Num 15:32-36.

[58] See J. Milgrom, "Leviticus," *The Interpreter's One Volume Commentary on the Bible* (ed. C. M. Laymon; Nashville: Abingdon, 1971) 83-84.

[59] "Because of the derogatory context the P author does not even write 'Yahweh' and substitutes 'Name'" (Milgrom, "Leviticus," 82). This is the only place in the Bible where "the Name" stands as a surrogate for the Tetragrammaton, YHWH, except for a partial exception in Deut 28:58. It becomes a standard substitute in rabbinic literature. See below, n. 63.

specify, designate' or *qbb* 'to curse'[60] is resolved by reference to v 16, where the root *nqb* appears twice: "He who enunciates/designates [*wĕnōqēb*] the name YHWH," and "when/if he has enunciated [*bĕnāqĕbô*] [the] Name."[61] Note that the Septuagint and Vulgate add *YHWH* after "Name"; and the Samaritan reads *hšm* 'the Name').[62] This specific and deliberate enunciation of the unique name of YHWH takes place as part of the individual's "curse"[63] and thus forms an hendiadys—the supreme blasphemy, a curse in which the name of YHWH is specifically pronounced.[64]

A remarkable and, as yet, unnoticed parallel to this prescription (which may also shed light on the antiquity of the biblical material) is found in the Assyrian harem edicts from the time of King Ninurta-apal-ekur (1192/91-1180/79 B.C.E.).[65] These edicts afford an interesting behind-the-scenes look into harem life and its concomitant female squabbles. The following decree was issued by the king for his palace:

> *lu aššāt šarri lu sinnišāti mādātu*[66] [*ša---itti*] *aḫāʾiš idukkāni*[67] *ina ṣaltišina šu*[*m il*]*i ana mašikte*[68] *tazzakrūni napšāte ša Aššur it*[-][69] *inakkisu* (lines 56-58).

[60] Most commentaries and translations interpret the verb as 'he cursed', deriving it either from *qbb* or assuming that *nqb* is an alloform of *qbb*. See also W. Schottroff, *Der altisraelitische Fluchspruch* (*Wissenschaftliche Monographien zum Alten und Neuen Testament* 30; Neukirchen-Vluyn: Neukirchener, 1969) 28. For the Talmudic discussion on whether to derive the verb from *nqb* or *qbb*, see *b. Sanh.* 56a. On *nqb* see L. Koehler and W. Baumgartner, *Lexicon in Veteris Testamenti Libros* (Leiden: Brill, 1985) 678-79.

[61] For *nqb* + *šēm* (within different contexts), see Num 1:17; Isa 62:2; Ezra 8:20; 1 Chr 12:32, 16:41; 2 Chr 28:15, 31:19. Compare, similarly, Nabatean *nqwbyn bšmhn*; see J. J. Rabinowitz, "A Clue to the Nabatean Contract from the Dead Sea Region," *Bulletin of the American Schools of Oriental Research* 139 (1957) 14.

[62] See also the comments of A. Geiger, *Urschrift und Übersetzungen der Bibel* (2d ed.; Frankfurt: Wahrmann, 1928) 273-74; Elliger, *Leviticus*, 330, 333-34.

[63] Cf. Targum Onqelos *wpryš* and Septuagint's *eponomasas*. Cf. *m. Sanh.* 7:5, "The blasphemer is not culpable until he expressly pronounces [*yprš*] the Name." The expression *šm hmpwrš* becomes a standard surrogate for YHWH in rabbinic literature.

[64] For other related prescriptions regarding the misuse of YHWH's name and the "cursing" of God, see Exod 20:7 and 22:27. H. C. Brichto (*The Problem of "Curse" in the Hebrew Bible* [Philadelphia: Society of Biblical Literature, 1963] 143-47), in the course of his discussion of *qll*, misconstrues the target of abuse, and assumes that it is not the deity but the full Israelite. He later concludes (p. 164) that there is a total absence of blasphemy in the Bible (cf., however, Weinfeld, *Deuteronomy and the Deuteronomic School*, 241 n. 2). From a different perspective altogether, see my "Daniel 3:29—A Case Study of 'Neglected' Blasphemy," *Journal of Near Eastern Studies* 42 (1983) 291-94.

[65] Weidner, "Hof- und Harems-Erlässe," 279-80 (edict 10).

[66] Weidner, ibid., reads *ma-ṭa-a-tu* and translates "niedere [Frauen]." He is followed by von Soden, *Akkadisches Handwörterbuch*, 635 ("*maṭû*"). This, however,

> [Should] either the wives of the king or the other women [of the harem] fight with each other, and during their quarrel utter/invoke the name of the/a god blasphemously; they will cut the throat of the one who has [ ] the god Aššur.

Note the very interesting similarities between the Akkadian and biblical reports. First, the two protagonists, male or female, are engaged in a brawl: Hebrew *wayyinnāṣû,* from the root *nṣh,* is the semantic cognate equivalent of Akkadian *ṣaltu.* Second, in both, one invokes the name of his/her god, first mentioned by Hebrew *haššêm* and Akkadian *šum ili* and then explicated as *YHWH* or *Aššur,* in a blasphemous fashion (Hebrew *wayyiqqōb . . . ʾet-haššēm wayqallēl* is analogous to Akkadian *šum ili ana mašikte tazzakrūni*). And third, both offenders are punished by death—one by stoning, the other by having his throat cut.[70]

Another decree of this same Assyrian king that has biblical echoes is found in the very next edict, which extends the crime invoking the name of a god to include the king as well:[71]

> [*šu*]*m šarri ina ṣalti la* [*izakkar šu*]*m ili lu la izakkar . . . šum ili ana la kitti* [*. . . tazakk*]*rum* [. . .] *la uballuṭuši* (lines 61-63).

---

would create an unnecessary *hapax legomenon,* since the feminine of the adjective *maṭû* is *maṭītu* 'low in status'. The correct reading is cited several times in *CAD*; cf. *A,* 1:164 ("*aḫāmeš*"); A/2, 464 ("*aššatu,*" § *m*); M/1, 22 ("*mādu,*" 'several, many'). Compare, for example, *Archives royales de Mari,* vol. 10: *Correspondance féminine* (ed. G. Dossin and A. Finet; Paris: Geuthner, 1978), text 129, lines 8 and 17: *sinnišātim mādātim ittišama isabbik* '[the sick woman] infects other women with her'.

[67] For the idiom, *dâku* (*itti*) *aḫāmeš* 'to fight', see *CAD* D, 42.

[68] For *mašiktu,* see *CAD* M/1, 323-24 ("*masiktu*"). For the use of the verb in the reviling of someone's name, cf. *Musée du Louvre—Départment des antiquités orientales: textes cunéiformes* (Paris: Geuthner, 1910), vol. 1, text 29, line 39: *aran šumni damqam ina ālini umassaku* 'as punishment for reviling our good reputation in our city'.

[69] Weidner ("Hof- und Harems-Erlässe," 280) reconstructs *it-t*[*a-re-ra-ni*] from *arāru,* which he admits "ist nur ein Versuch." However, in Akkadian *arāru* does not refer to an offense committed by a human against a deity. The same is also true of Hebrew *ʾrr,* which only has the deity as the subject, never as the object (compare especially Exod 22:27, where one is forbidden to *qll* God and to *ʾrr* a chieftain). See Brichto, *The Problem of "Curse",* 77-117, esp. 115: "the subject of the active verb *ʾrr* is always the Deity or an agency endowed by God or the society with unusual power" (cf. p. 217; for the Akkadian, see pp. 115-17). Weidner's other suggestion, however, based on the verb *tamû* 'to swear' is possible. E. Reiner, on the other hand, suggests deriving the verb from Akkadian *nazāru* 'to blaspheme, to curse the gods' (oral communication; see *CAD* N/2, 139).

[70] Stoning represents a communal public execution throughout the Bible.

[71] Weidner, "Hof- und Harems-Erlässe," 280-81 (edict 11).

> One must not [invoke the na]me of the king in a brawl. One must verily not [note the emphatic *lu la*] invoke the name of the/a god [in a brawl]; [If one invok]es the name of the/a god falsely, they must not spare her.

This combination of blasphemy and reviling involving God and king is also found in 1 Kings 21 where Naboth is falsely accused of "reviling God and king" (*bērăktā ʾĕlōhîm wāmelek,* vv 10, 13), for which crime he is subsequently stoned. Such a coupling of *lèse-majesté divine* along with *lèse-majesté humaine* can be found also in MAL.[72] Immediately following MAL A:1 (which pertains to the crime of sacrilege, that is, stealing from the temple), MAL A:2 continues with a law prescribing that "if a woman . . . has uttered blasphemy [*šillata taqtibi*][73] or spoken sedition/insolence [*mikit pî tartešši*],[74] that woman shall bear her liability [*aranša tanašši* = *nāśāʾ ḥeṭĕʾô* of Lev 24:15].[75]

[72] For the topical association of arrangement, see Driver and Miles, *Assyrian Laws,* 20, and Cardascia, *Les Lois Assyriennes,* 47.

[73] For this idiom and its biblical counterpart, see the discussion of Dan 3:29 in my article cited in n. 64 above.

[74] For this idiom, see O. R. Gurney, "A Tablet of Incantations against Slander," *Iraq* 22 (1960) 226 n. 6 (line 12); W. G. Lambert, *Babylonian Wisdom Literature* (Oxford: Oxford University, 1960) 312–13; *CAD* M/2, 105; and von Soden, *Akkadisches Handwörterbuch,* 657 (line 5).

[75] For yet another accusation of blasphemy that is uttered during a brawl, see MAL tablet N. The law refers to one who has blasphemed and profaned the temple. If he is proven guilty, his punishment is, along with corvée duty plus *40 ina ḫaṭṭe imaḫḫuṣuš* 'they shall beat him 40 blows with a rod' (not in Driver and Miles, *Assyrian Laws;* see Meek, "The Middle Assyrian Laws," *ANET* 188). For this exact punishment compare MAL A:18 and Deut 25:3 (*ʾarbāʿîm yakkennû*). If, however, the charge is not proven, the accuser suffers the same punishment in a retaliatory fashion. See Weidner, "Das Alter der mittelassyrischen Gesetzestexte," *Archiv für Orientsforschung* 12 (1937–39) 53; Cardascia, *Les Lois Assyriennes,* 334–35; and the notes of Koschaker cited in both. See also *CAD* B, 127–30 ("*barû/burrû*").

Delbert R. Hillers

Rite: Ceremonies of Law and Treaty in the Ancient Near East

HILLERS'S CONTRIBUTION to this volume stands out as unique. All other authors have explored biblical, Jewish, and Islamic notions of holy law and of the inseparability of law from religion. In doing so, they have all, with the exception of Bernard Jackson, focused their attention to written (statutory) law as found in scripture or codes; even Jackson, while shifting the focus to judicial procedure, has included written law in his discussion. Hillers, in contrast, goes entirely beyond the realm of scriptures and codes and explores formularies relating to everyday legal transactions in the ancient Near East. His source is the Elephantine documents. In researching those documents he has come to see everyday legal life in the ancient Near East as essentially secular: the formularies represent a performative use of language (as explained by the British philosopher John Austin). In other words, the formularies accomplished transactions necessary for everyday life without a dependency on religious notions (evocation of deity, etc.), which entered in only occasionally to fill in certain gaps.

Delbert R. Hillers is W. W. Spence Professor of Semitic Languages at Johns Hopkins University. His best known work is *Covenant: The History of a Biblical Idea*; he recently completed *Lamentations* in the Anchor Bible and *Micah* in the Hermenia series.

The usefulness of the term *rite* is that it expresses in a compressed way one aspect of the relation of religion and law. It is defined in *Black's Law Dictionary* as "duly and formally, legally, properly, technically."[1] Another definition is given by Lewis and Short: "According to religious ceremonies or observances; . . . with due religious observance or rites, according to religious usage."[2] Even if it is not difficult to see how the one sense arose out of the other, the existence of a word that means variously "legally" and "according to religious ceremonies" may suggest that, when one looks at law and religion together, it may be appropriate to adopt an approach to their relation from the side of ritual or ceremony.

As far as I know, this is not the usual approach. When scholars in branches of Near Eastern studies have tried to explain the nature of religion or law, or of the two of them together, it has usually been done from a more philosophical point of view and at a very fundamental level, disregarding minutiae of a formal sort. The legal material discussed tends to be from statutes, not from documents. The best known attempt of this kind is the influential brief study *Law and Covenant in Israel and the Ancient Near East* by George Mendenhall. He begins by drawing a distinction between value systems and ways of putting those systems into effect, between legal policy and legal techniques, with religious obligation—expressed in the idea of a covenant between God and his people—the source of community policy in law.[3] Mendenhall sharpens the basic contrast in his later essay "Religion and Politics as Reciprocals," where the essential contrasts between religious covenant and law are expressed in a concise chart.[4] In his own way, the Assyriologist J. J. Finkelstein also stresses "fundamental assumptions" about the law that prevailed in Mesopotamia—underlying principles that Finkelstein calls "conceptual postulates."[5] Ancient laws about the classic case of the goring ox are said to "arise out of, and reflect, a cosmological outlook," which Finkelstein proceeds to delineate. The Old Testament scholar

[1] Henry Campbell Black, *Black's Law Dictionary* (4th ed.; St. Paul, MN: West, 1951) 1491.

[2] Charlton T. Lewis and Charles Short, *A Latin Dictionary* (Oxford: Clarendon, 1879).

[3] (Pittsburgh: Biblical Colloquium, 1955) 3-5 and passim.

[4] "Toward a Biography of God: Religion and Politics as Reciprocals," *The Tenth Generation: The Origins of the Biblical Tradition* (Baltimore: Johns Hopkins University, 1973) 200.

[5] *The Ox That Gored,* ed. Maria Ellis (Transactions of the American Philosophical Society, 1981) 5, 39. See also his "The Goring Ox: Some Historical Perspectives on Deodands, Forfeitures, Wrongful Death, and the Western Notion of Sovereignty," *Temple Law Quarterly* 46 (1973) 169-290.

Albrecht Alt went at the problem of the nature of law in the ancient world in a different way: by studying the way individual statutes are formulated in ancient collections of laws, resulting in a sharp distinction between apodictic and casuistic law, which in turn were supposed to be characteristic, respectively, of ancient Israel and of her rival Canaan.[6] Whatever the validity of Alt's views, he is clearly more interested in fundamental attitudes about law and their expression in statutes than in the history of legal ceremonies and instruments.

Without wishing to challenge the usefulness of these more profound approaches to ancient law and religion, I will take an alternate route, beginning with the use of ceremonies or rituals in ancient legal life, including the making of treaties. Perhaps a view from this side will enrich or clarify the conception of *(a)* the intricate way in which ancient law related to the sphere of the gods and *(b)* human concern for ritual.

Anthropologists are in dispute about a satisfactory definition of *ritual* or *ceremony*.[7] My understanding of ritual—a working understanding—is close to that of Victor Turner: "prescribed formal behavior for occasions not given over to technological routine, having reference to beliefs in mystical beings or powers."[8] I prefer to use ceremony as a broader term, not restricted to the religious realm; a ceremony, in my usage, will not necessarily have "reference to beliefs in mystical beings or powers."[9] I understand Turner's "prescribed formal behavior" to include both words and actions. In the broadest sense, any of the formalities of the law, including merely verbal behavior such as the drafting and witnessing of an instrument in traditional stereotyped language, may be regarded as ceremonial behavior, so in part I will discuss the formulary of ancient Near Eastern law; but I shall take as my starting point those formalities involving some kind of action by the participants. With reference to the actions and gestures performed in ceremonies, writers on this subject frequently use the term "symbolic." For Barbara Myerhoff this

[6] "The Origins of Israelite Law," *Essays on Old Testament History and Religion* (trans. R. A. Wilson; Garden City, NY: Doubleday, 1968) 101–71; originally *Die Ursprünge des israelitischen Rechtes* (Berichte über die Verhandlungen der Sächsischen Akademie der Wissenschaften zu Leipzig, Philologisch-historische Klasse, 86/1; Leipzig: S. Hirzel, 1934).

[7] See, for example, the discussion by Jack Goody, "Against Ritual," *Secular Ritual* (ed. Sally F. Moore and Barbara G. Myerhoff; Assen/Amsterdam: van Gorcum, 1977) 25–35.

[8] *The Forest of Symbols: Aspects of Ndembu Ritual* (Ithaca, NY: Cornell University, 1967) 19.

[9] This is the usage advocated by Mary Gluckmann and Max Gluckman, "On Drama, and Games and Athletic Contests," *Secular Ritual*, 227–43.

seems to be the essence of a ceremonial act: "rituals can be distinguished from custom and mere habit by their utilization of symbols."[10] A part of my discussion will question the total appropriateness of the terms symbol and symbolic in these contexts. My selection of illustrative material on ceremonies of law will come mostly from the Hebrew Bible and the Aramaic papyri from Upper Egypt; on the side of treaty and covenant I will discuss Dennis McCarthy's application of the word symbolic to the Semitic terminology used for treaty making and show that ceremony has a performative role in covenant, as it did in legal ritual.

Performative Ritual in the Aramaic Papyri

The Elephantine papyri are for the most part the miscellaneous papers of a colony of Jewish mercenary soldiers in the service of the Persian king stationed at Elephantine, an island by Syene (Assuan) in Upper Egypt.[11] Among the dozens of papyri are many legal documents: conveyances of property, contracts of various kinds, documents relating to loans and the settlement of renunciation of claims, marriage contracts, affidavits, and documents of manumission. Since all fall within the fifth century B.C., these are toward the end of the flourishing period of ancient Near Eastern law, rather than the beginning of it. Not long after the time of these documents, Alexander's conquest of the Near East inaugurated a radically different set of political conditions, so that ancient legal traditions either disappeared or survived only in a different setting.

Although these documents are late, they may claim unusual interest because they seem to be closer to real law than the older "codes" of laws and similar materials that have so often been the focus of attention in discussions of law and religion. In most cases there is no reason to doubt that the terms of these contracts would have been enforced by the court (the Persian governor and his associates) in case a dispute arose. However, there is some justification

[10] "We Don't Wrap Herring in a Printed Page: Fusion, Fictions, and Continuity in Secular Ritual," *Secular Ritual,* 199; the whole discussion on pp. 199–200 is valuable.

[11] The recently published papyri from Saqqara, evidently not far removed from the Elephantine papyri in date, contain many legal documents (the editor lists eighteen), but they are on the whole much more fragmentary than the Elephantine papyri and hence more difficult to interpret. In addition, they reflect a non-Jewish community. They do not seem to challenge the general picture of the relation of law and religion drawn here. See J. B. Segal, *Aramaic Texts from North Saqqara* (London: Egypt Exploration Society, 1983).

for doubting whether certain provisions were really valid. Thus Reuven Yaron, one of the principal and pioneer students of the legal aspects of these texts, expresses doubt about the enforceability of clauses in a legal document that asserts its own genuineness and condemns divergent documents as forgeries: "We should like to know what force a court would give to such a clause."[12] On the whole, however, the Elephantine documents are close to the law in the sense of what the courts *do*. In contrast to the so-called codes of law, which were almost never cited in court, these documents would have been introduced in court to decide, for example, whether Yehoyishma really owned the house where she was living, or whether the woman Tamut was slave or free.

On examination, this sizable body of legal material contains little by way of ceremony or religious ritual, in the sense in which these terms are used here. Presently I will qualify that statement and deal with exceptions, but as a generalization it is true. The law of the Aramaic papyri is secular and mundane. These mercenary soldiers were Jews of some sort, greatly concerned about their temple and its service, but there is little mingling of religion with their legal life. They buy and sell houses and movable property, sell or free slaves, marry or enter other important contracts, all without much reference to religion and with little use of any ceremonial observances other than the preparation of the proper written forms. The law appears here as autonomous and competent to achieve its goal of regulating practically all kinds of human affairs.[13]

The one ceremonial and religious observance referred to rather often is the taking of an oath. One fragmentary papyrus records the kind of oath sworn: "Oath of Menahem b. Shallum b. Hodaviah . . . by Yaʾu the god, by the temple and by ʿAnathyaʾu, and spoke to him saying. . . ." [14] Another document shows the setting of the oath in court procedure. A certain Dargman had laid claim to land owned by one Mahseiah; the case came before the Persian judge Damidata and his fellow judges. The judge made the present owner, Mahseiah, take an oath by Yaʾu (his god), which he did. The court then compelled Dargman to abandon his claim in a "deed of renunciation": "You have sworn to me by Yaʾu, and have satisfied my mind about this

[12] Reuven Yaron, *Introduction to the Law of the Aramaic Papyri* (Oxford: Clarendon, 1961) 29–30.

[13] On the "striving of the law for independence and autonomy" in various historical periods see Edgar Bodenheimer, *Jurisprudence: The Philosophy and Method of the Law* (Cambridge: Harvard University, 1962) 173–74.

[14] A. Cowley, *Aramaic Papyri of the Fifth Century B.C.* (Oxford: Clarendon, 1923; repr. Osnabrück: Otto Zeller, 1967) no. 44, lines 1–4.

land."[15] As Yaron notes, all the references to oaths at Elephantine are to oaths of clearance, as distinguished from promissory oaths.[16]

These oaths, for all their invocation of various divine names, do not seriously alter the picture of an autonomous, secular law; indeed, the employment of the oath may be thought to reinforce that picture. At certain points the legal system confronted an inability to act on the basis of ordinary evidence, but was unwilling simply to abandon all hope of regulating affairs and hence had resort to ceremony and religion. This is not allowed to get out of hand, however, for the oath is ordered by the judge, evidently taken in his presence, written up in a legal document, and assented to by the plaintiff. In short, ceremony and rite appear here as legal *techniques.* As stated at the outset, it probably has been more common to think of religion, including the idea of covenant with God, as stating broad policy, and of law as a lower order of thing, consisting of techniques for carrying policy into effect. But the use of oath at Elephantine may be viewed as showing this view turned upside down, with an independent and competent legal sphere achieving its ends, if necessary, by resort to religion as a device.

At this point it seems useful to illustrate the same situation in ancient Israel. In the midst of other legal material, the biblical writer turns his attention to unsolved homicide: the case of a person found slain in the open country, with the identity of the slayer unknown (Deuteronomy 21). Obviously this might have been a serious threat to the peace of the community, but it is also obvious that the law could not deal with the situation in ordinary ways. So resort is had to ritual. The elders of the town closest to the corpse take a heifer and ceremonially break its neck beside running water; they then wash their hands over the heifer and formally assert their innocence. Looking aside from the question of how this ceremony fits with Israelite practices for purging away guilt, I note that this case again illustrates that ritual might be a technique for filling in gaps in the law. As Moshe Weinfeld notes, the ritual act is not carried out by priests, although they are present, but by the elders and judges (magistrates); the ceremony is clearly thought of as part of legal life, not part of ordinary sacrificial praxis.[17]

Returning to Elephantine legal documents, I find them at first reading to be relatively austere, practically devoid of the color and liveliness of ceremony, with a language totally adapted to the mun-

[15] Ibid., no. 6, lines 11–12.

[16] Yaron, *Law of the Aramaic Papyri*, 32.

[17] *Deuteronomy and the Deuteronomic School* (Oxford: Clarendon, 1972) 210–11.

dane affairs it embodies—a conclusion that must be modified somewhat when the phrases and clauses of the formulary are subjected to historical and comparative study. Yohanan Muffs has shown that practically every feature of the Aramaic legal language at Elephantine is descended from antecedents in cuneiform law.[18] The closest relative, not surprisingly, is the law of the Neo-Assyrian empire, the political power that was dominant when the Aramaic language advanced to the status of being the official language of the empire. But the history stretches far back beyond that, so that individual features of this legal system may be traced back through Aramaic texts to Akkadian documents, and beyond that to Sumerian forms of speech. This great antiquity of important parts of Elephantine law certainly calls for notice; in addition, another feature emerges from historical study. Mere words and phrases at Elephantine turn out to be allusions to what were in earlier times ceremonial acts connected with the law: postures and gestures and comings and goings that were as binding in law as the verbal forms that accompanied them or later replaced them.

With respect to the antiquity of the formulary used in Elephantine, it would be interesting to inquire seriously and in detail whether the oldest private law as a whole had the same nature as the laws of Elephantine, that is, autonomous, secular, striving for universality, and employing rituals of any kind only sparingly and for well-defined purposes. Such an inquiry is impossible here, both because it is largely in the province of cuneiform studies and because the discussion would have to take in the many complexities arising out of varying local traditions and out of the cultivation in different places of ritual practices not met with at Elephantine (such as the ordeal, the sacred lot, and the conduct of legal matters by so-called "temple judges" in sacred places).[19] All the same, it would appear from the summary discussions of cuneiform specialists that the formulary developed at an early stage, for cuneiform law remained substantially

[18] *Studies in the Aramaic Legal Papyri from Elephantine* (Studia et Documenta ad iura Orientis Antiqui pertinentia 8; Leiden: Brill, 1969; repr. New York: KTAV, 1973).

[19] Muffs, ibid., 12, notes that earlier interpreters of the Elephantine Aramaic legal documents approached them from the vantage of later legal traditions, such as Talmudic law, or as a self-contained entity (e.g., Yaron); his own approach, the Assyriological, is the only one that commends itself for my present purpose. See Arnold Walther, *Das altbabylonische Gerichtswesen* (Leipziger Semitistiche Studien 6/4–6; Leipzig: Hinrichs, 1917) on temple judges. In his view the temple judges were not actually clergy; from a time earlier than the first dynasty of Babylon the administration of law was almost entirely out of the hands of priests, except for administration of some oaths.

the same throughout the long history and wide extent of Mesopotamian civilization.[20] If correct, such an observation is perhaps deserving of emphasis, especially for biblical scholars, who may be accustomed to leaving the documentary side of law out of account, because of the differing nature of the legal material in the Bible.

Leaving this question aside, I pursue the second observation made above, namely, that the documents from Elephantine contain references to formal ritual acts, even if the reference has become only metaphorical. The general form of these Aramaic documents is of a first-person oral declaration before witnesses: "On such and such a date A said to B, 'I have come to thy house, etc.' This was written at the dictation of A. Witnesses thereto: C, D, E, etc." Within this subjective framework, whose antecedents in cuneiform law Muffs has traced, occur references to ceremonial acts by the speaker or other parties to the agreement. For example, the most elaborate of the known Aramaic marriage contracts reads:

> I have come to thy house and asked of thee the woman Yehoyishma (by name), thy sister, for marriage. And thou didst give her to me. She is my wife and I am her husband from this day forth unto forever. And I have given thee as the *mohar* of thy sister Yehoyishma silver [1 karsh]. It has gone in to thee [and thy heart is satisfied there]with.[21]

Whether or not the acts referred to were really carried out as late as fifth-century B.C. Egypt (they certainly were at some earlier time, before the formulary was fixed), there were prescribed ceremonial steps in getting married: the visit by the bridegroom to the father or male relative's house, the formal asking for the woman in marriage, the father's assent, the declaration by the groom, and the presentation of the *mohar*. Even the superficially abstract terms used in sale contracts turn out, on detailed examination, to have a more colorful background. In other kinds of documents, a phrase that may be rendered "we have renounced claim to . . ." had to do originally with the physical removal of a former owner from property once his; as Muffs notes, at Nuzi "the seller lifts his foot from his property and

[20] For example, A. Leo Oppenheim, *Ancient Mesopotamia* (Chicago: University of Chicago, 1964) 280–81; note Oppenheim's judgment on the persistence of the essentials of the formulary: "Radical changes in style occur rarely and only in marginal or late text groups" (p. 281).

[21] Emil G. Kraeling, ed., *The Brooklyn Museum Aramaic Papyri: New Documents of the Fifth Century B.C. from the Jewish Colony at Elephantine* (New Haven: Yale University, 1953; repr. Salem, NH: Arno, 1969) no. 7, lines 3–5.

places the foot of the buyer in its place."[22] There are other gestures of distancing oneself (Akkadian *ireteq*, Aramaic *rḥq*). Possibly, too, the statement by the seller "my heart is satisfied" with the price of some property may go back to a more gestural, concrete situation where payment was originally made in grain to be consumed by the seller.[23] When Meshullam freed his slave Tepmet, he said: "You are freed from shadow to sunlight . . . you are freed unto God."[24] This unexpectedly vivid bit of phraseology has its explanation in a whole cycle of gestures, words, and ceremonies of manumission in the ancient Near East, which consistently associate manumission with passage from darkness to light. In some localities it also involves anointing a slave's head with oil, facing him toward the sun, and "cleansing his forehead."[25] Since, at Elephantine and elsewhere, the language of legal documents contains only historical allusions to these ceremonies, I conclude that in Near Eastern law there was a general movement away from acted-out ceremony to written-out verbal formulas.

Even in this regard, however, it is important not to misinterpret the earlier ceremonies. In my opinion, Muffs does so when he says of Elephantine: "Many metaphorical terms seem to be terminological metamorphoses of early symbolic-magical actions"; or, with reference to sales of land, "All of these symbolic gestures magically effectuate the severing of old ties and claims and the creation of new ones."[26] In reality there is nothing magical about these rituals, and it misses the mark to call them symbolic. A much more useful term is the one coined by the British philosopher John L. Austin: performative. Austin's pioneering discussion of this aspect of human communication had to do primarily with speech—with "performative utterances"—but his first example was of a ritual combining word and action: the christening of a ship ("I name this ship the Queen Elizabeth"), surely accompanied by the traditional bottle-smashing.[27] Austin's point about this kind of speech—and I would say, ritual—was that it

[22] Muffs, *Aramaic Legal Papyri from Elephantine*, 21.

[23] Ibid., 110–11.

[24] Author's own translation of Kraeling, *Brooklyn Museum Aramaic Papyri*, no. 5, lines 9–10.

[25] The exact sense of the last phrase is not well understood. On facing the sun see Muffs, *Aramaic Legal Papyri from Elephantine*, 110, and Delbert R. Hillers, "*Berît ʿam*: 'Emancipation of the People,'" *Journal of Biblical Literature* 97 (1978) 175–82.

[26] Muffs, *Aramaic Legal Papyri from Elephantine*, 110 and 21.

[27] J. L. Austin, *How to Do Things with Words* (2d ed.; ed. J. O. Urmson and Marina Sbisa; Cambridge, MA: Harvard University, 1962).

actually accomplishes what it states. The naming of the ship is not a separate act from the ritual; you name a ship exactly by saying "I name this ship X." In English the words "now" and "hereby" often accompany performatives, which typically take the form of a first-person singular in present tense.

To apply this to my subject, I would improve on Muffs's way of putting it by saying that the early rites lying behind later Aramaic terms are performative; publicly and ritually removing the foot from property you once owned, as the same sort of thing others did in the same circumstances, did not *symbolize* the renouncing of a claim, it *was* the renunciation. It was not magic, it was business, and it was legal.[28]

There is a linguistic aspect of this that cannot be dealt with fully here, but may be mentioned. Just as in English one most typically casts performative utterances as first-person singular presents, so in various Semitic languages there are characteristic tenses used: the preterit in Akkadian and the perfect in Arabic, Hebrew, and Aramaic.[29] In these cases, instead of the normal rendering of a verb in past tense, it is necessary to translate as a present, for example, "I divorce [*śnʾt*] Asḥor my husband."[30] Therefore, perfects involved in the originally gestural performatives of sale and quittance must be translated as "I hereby give . . ." or "We hereby renounce claim . . ."; this in turn reflects on the nature of these ceremonial acts. My conclusion is simply that even if in ancient law there is a movement away from accomplishing things by gestures, this is not deeply

[28] The anthropologist S. J. Tambiah treats this subject, ritual as performative, but his discussion seems to miss the point. He contrasts ritual (magical) acts, which are performative, with "scientific activity" as having "positive" or "creative" meaning but not being subject to verification. But whatever the case may be with a magical act, it is obviously possible to verify whether a ritual was performed, and hence in appropriate cases whether a ship has been named, a house sold, or a man married. See S. J. Tambiah, "Form and Meaning of Magical Acts: A Point of View," *Modes of Thought* (ed. Robin Horton and Ruth Finnegan; London: Faber and Faber, 1973) 199–229.

[29] See Wolfgang Heimpel and Gabriella Guidi, "Der Koinzidenzfall im Akkadischen" (*Zeitschrift der Deutschen Morgenländischen Gesellschaft* supplement 1; Wiesbaden: Franz Steiner, 1969) 148–52, and Werner Mayer, *Untersuchungen zur Formensprache der bablyonischen "Gebetsbeschwörungen"* (Studia Pohl: Series Maior 5; Rome: Biblical Institute, 1976); the latter contains a lengthy discussion of "Der Koinzidenzfall im Akkadischen" (pp. 183–201) and includes many examples from other Semitic languages, with references to previous scholarly discussions. (These works were called to my attention by my colleague, Dr. Jerrold S. Cooper.) The present writer's forthcoming discussion of Hebrew performatives will carry the study farther in that area. Muffs shows some awareness of this use of the perfect tense in Aramaic (*Aramaic Legal Papyri from Elephantine*, 32 n. 2).

[30] Cowley, *Aramaic Papyri*, no. 15, line 23.

significant of a fundamental change in attitude, but more of a recognition of the convenience of literate ways of doing things. To use the terminology of Lucien Lévy-Bruhl, it is improbable that this is evidence for a movement from the prelogical to the logical; what is attested is a change from the preliterate to the literate.

CEREMONY IN ANCIENT NEAR EASTERN TREATIES

The making of treaties in the ancient Near East leaves the sphere of what is strictly legal, for the treaty or covenant apparently depended much less on any existing social group for its enforcement than was true in the case of a legal contract. It often was intended to create a new social grouping, and appealed to celestial powers as witnesses and enforcers. Treaties and the religious covenants modeled after them also made a rather rich and free use of ceremonies and gestures. The best known of these is the slaying of a selected animal, giving rise to Semitic phrases such as *kārat bĕrît* (Hebrew) or *gĕzar ʿădayyaʾ* (Aramaic), which have close counterparts in the classical languages (*horkia temnein*; *foedus icere* or *foedus ferire*). Other treaty ceremonies include eating together, drinking from the same cup, and mutual anointing with oil.[31] Even though the treaty and covenant area of ancient political and religious life is something rather different from legal life, at the same time, the use of ceremonies in the one may clarify or modify views in the other area.

Dennis McCarthy has written extensively about treaty and covenant; I take his views as the focus of attention here, not because of their vulnerability but, on the contrary, because he has written expertly and intelligently about the rites surrounding ancient treaties. In McCarthy's presentation the word *symbolic* recurs frequently. Thus the Sinai covenant is said to have been "a relationship based on various symbolic rites enacting union."[32]

McCarthy proceeds from this point of view to draw a significant contrast between Hittite treaties and later Syrian and Assyrian treaty usage, where a much greater emphasis is placed on "substitution rites"—rites in which the swearer of an oath is identified with various animals or objects that are ceremonially destroyed or mutilated, the

[31] See the vassal treaties of Esarhaddon: "(if) you establish this treaty before the gods who are placed (as witnesses), and swear by the laden table, by drinking from the cup, by the glow of fire, by water and oil, by touching one another's breast. . . ." (§13; trans. Erica Reiner, *Ancient Near Eastern Texts Relating to the Old Testament* [ed. J. B. Pritchard; 3d ed.; Princeton: Princeton University, 1969] 536).

[32] Dennis J. McCarthy, *Treaty and Covenant* (Analecta Biblica 21a; Rome: Biblical Institute, 1978) 15.

idea being that the swearer will be treated so in the event he or she plays false. The purpose of these vivid ceremonies is said to be psychological, working through the oath-takers' religious fears: "The rites are simply a form of curse, made graphic and acted out so as to impress the mind more and to be more effective." These rites, most commonly that of killing an animal, "accompanied" covenant-making. The Semites, especially, put an emphasis on the rite over against the word, the latter being characteristic of the Hittites. In McCarthy's view: "We have then, two sub-groups in the treaty family, the Hittite with its historical section, and the Syrian-Assyrian with its curses and substitution rites."[33]

A. Leo Oppenheim is more outspoken on this subject than McCarthy. What I politely call covenant ceremonies Oppenheim calls "primitive and ritualistic practices" meant "to illustrate, in a crude way, the fate of any offender." They correspond to magical practices, and are "primitive" and "barbaric."[34]

This conception that the rite of slaughter in covenant-making is essentially symbolic leads McCarthy into a rather lengthy discussion of what the blood might symbolize. He takes issue with E. Bickerman, who held that the blood is a divine element released when the victim is slain, thereby giving a special force of mystic communion to the contrasting parties and their union.[35] In my own opinion, McCarthy's views on this point are better founded than those of Bickerman, but this kind of argument runs the danger of missing the point that arises from comparing treaty practice to legal practice.

Legal practice too, as shown above, at times involved ceremonies: eating, anointing, making of gestures, and pronouncing of words. But these are in this context primarily performative or operative—not symbolical. For example, to set a slave facing the sun and to anoint him within that impressive ceremony might well invite reflection on the symbolism involved, but the practical and overriding point was that the ceremony *did* something: it made a person free. And the ordinary slave might well have been content with a mere document giving the verbal equivalent of the rite.

It seems to me that ordinary treaty rites must be understood in the same way, especially the most common of them—killing an animal in an act of self-cursing. This is very old and widespread, extending beyond the Semitic-speaking world. Like a ceremony of marriage or a

[33] Ibid., 92, 151.

[34] *Ancient Mesopotamia,* 285.

[35] McCarthy, *Treaty and Covenant,* 94; Bickerman, "Couper une alliance," *Archives d'histoire du droit oriental* 5 (1950/51) 133–56.

formula of sale, it fulfilled a need that societies felt repeatedly: to join separate groups together for certain purposes and to have a mutually recognized act to do this. Other attested covenant rites would have functioned the same way: as performative ceremonies to achieve important social goals. If in certain areas, at certain times, ceremonies (always *accompanied* by words in any case) are wholly and partly replaced by verbal formulas, this is not surprising, in view of parallel developments in the law. It may be questioned whether this represents any fundamental conceptual shift. It would be equally unsurprising to find a metonymic shift in the development of the idiom: to *cut* a covenant.[36] A comparable development is found in Akkadian expressions having to do with *kanāku* 'to seal'. Although the verb originally refers to a physical act, it comes to refer to the social or legal reality brought about by the ceremonial act, hence 'to give or receive under seal, to transfer property by means of a sealed document'. An example cited by the Chicago Assyrian Dictionary is "the field which my father gave with a sealed document to his daughter."[37] This signals the strong possibility that the phrase 'cut a covenant', superficially so pregnant with symbolic meaning, is instead a very faded metaphor.

I argue, then, that just as there is good deal of unity in the ancient Near Eastern legal formulary over the ages and in widespread areas, so treaty forms constitute, in McCarthy's phrase, "a basic unity."[38] If so, then perhaps in this sphere also the presence or absence of acted-out ceremonies does not signal a fundamentally different way of proceeding.

To sum up, I argue that ceremonies should not be thought of as accompanying, or reinforcing, the making of treaties and covenants, but as operative, performative elements. And, while maintaining a distinction between treaty and law, I would stress more strongly than has been done certain elements and developments that they have in

[36] On this, see the somewhat labored discussion of McCarthy, *Treaty and Covenant*, 91-92.

[37] *eqlu ša PN abua ik-nu-ku-ma ana mārtišu iddinu* (*The Assyrian Dictionary of the Oriental Institute of the University of Chicago* [Chicago: University of Chicago, 1956-], vol. K, p. 141). The verb also comes to mean 'to obtain a sealed document from a debtor'.

[38] "The Treaties: A Basic Unity" is the title of an extensive section (pp. 122-40) of McCarthy's monograph. Gene M. Tucker, "Covenant Forms and Contract Forms," *Vetus Testamentum* 15 (1965) 487-503, draws a sharp distinction between the forms of contracts and covenants, but this valid distinction does not rule out resemblances in other respects, such as the existence of a standard form.

common. If everyday law appears from the beginning as something rational and mundane (appealing to ceremony and religion as only one of its techniques), then the sphere of treaty-making is not altogether different.

In my student days, I remember being amused by a reference to the ancient Babylonians' love for legal red tape. Now I take a different view. An important element in the first growth of civilization, its spread, and its endurance, was the development of forms of law, documentary or ceremonial, which must have made an enormous contribution to order and stability in human affairs.[39] The Hebrew Bible itself contains a unique tribute to legal forms and rites in the book of Jeremiah, a passage that I call (with a little exaggeration), a "hymn to a conveyance." At the very end of Israelite national life under her own king, with Nebuchadnezzar's army surrounding Jerusalem, the prophet Jeremiah bought a field in order to keep it in the family:

> And I bought the field at Anathoth from Hanamel my cousin, and weighed out the money to him, seventeen shekels of silver. I signed the deed, sealed it, got witnesses, and weighed the money on scales. Then I took the sealed deed of purchase, containing the terms and conditions, and the open copy, and I gave the deed of purchase to Baruch the son of Neriah son of Mahseiah, in the presence of Hanamel my cousin, in the presence of the witnesses who signed the deed of purchase, and in the presence of all the Jews who were sitting in the court of the guard. I charged Baruch in their presence, saying, "Thus says the Lord of Hosts, the God of Israel: 'Take these deeds, both this sealed deed of purchase and this open deed, and put them in an earthenware vessel, that they may last for a long time.' For thus says the Lord of Hosts, the God of Israel: 'Houses and fields and vineyards shall again be bought in this land.' " (Jer 32:9-15)

The description is detailed enough (approaching the tedious) to allow the conclusion that this was done *rite*—formally and legally—even with the sort of double document that contemporary legal practice required. Oddly but appropriately, prophetic vision for the restored society of the future takes the form of hope for a revival of legal routine.

[39] Moore and Myerhoff stress the ordering function of ritual in their introduction to *Secular Ritual*: "collective ritual can be seen as an especially dramatic attempt to bring some particular part of life firmly and definitely into orderly control" (p. 3). This seems to apply in an even stronger way to the forms and ceremonies of law.

Izhak Englard

Religious Freedom and Jewish Tradition in Modern Israeli Law—A Clash of Ideologies

THE FINAL TWO CHAPTERS in this volume put the reader in touch with the modern world and, in particular, with a conflict that is raging in many parts of the world between traditional forces, which wish to revive and enforce the fusion of religion and law, and liberal ideology, which wishes to separate religion and law. The two chapters concentrate upon Israel as a special case. Englard shows that the ideal of religious freedom creates special problems in Israel and explains the inner logic of the religious factions that are eager to enforce the traditional Jewish law. These factions understand freedom along lines that reflect not only Jewish but also Islamic-Ottoman tradition: religious freedom is a freedom for communities, not a freedom for individuals. Liberal factions in Israel who have embraced a more individualistic conception of religious freedom are thus a challenge to the very fabric of Israeli society.

Izhak Englard is the Bora Laskin Professor of Law at the Hebrew University of Jerusalem, and former Dean of the Faculty of Law. He received his doctorate of law from the University of Paris. He has served as Director of the Harry Sacher Institute for Legislative Research and Comparative Law, and as Director of the Israel Matz Institute for Research in Jewish Law. His published works deal with the law of torts and the role of religious law in the Israeli legal system. He has held visiting appointments in the United States, Italy, and Switzerland.

Modern Israeli law faithfully reflects the fundamental problems created by the clash between the orthodox Jewish religious outlook and secular liberal philosophy.[1] The specific problem in Israel is caused by the contrast between the basic tenets of liberal ideology, which is accepted in principle by the great majority of Israeli citizens, and the Jewish religious tradition, which is based on different foundations. I shall first make an attempt to outline some basic ideas of rabbinic Judaism concerning freedom of religion, and then to examine the actual legal situation of Israel as a manifestation of the clash between these conflicting ideologies.

The Jewish Religious Tradition and the Idea of Freedom of Religion

First a preliminary remark of caution: it is certainly bold, if not foolhardy, to try to summarize in a few lines any fundamental topic in a tradition as longstanding and rich as Judaism. Moreover, there always exists the real danger to succumb to the temptations of one's own convictions and treat the literary sources in a tendentious way. Indeed, neither the spirit of apology nor that of polemics are advisable companions in approaching any given cultural and religious tradition. Having duly warned myself of the manifold pitfalls in the endeavor, I shall nevertheless try to give a succinct account, as objectively as possible, of some central principles in rabbinic Judaism that touch upon the problem of religious freedom.

The perspective of Judaism is essentially theocentric. It is not the happiness or well-being of the individual or the community that constitutes, in itself, the ultimate end of human existence. Human-

[1] When speaking of Jewish religion, I shall refer exclusively to rabbinic orthodox Judaism, in view of the fact that it is this movement—representing the great majority of believing Jews—that confronts the State. Reform and Conservative Judaism, to the extent they are present on the political scene, ordinarily side with the State in the latter's conflicts with the rabbinical establishment over the implementation of liberal values. There is no need to expound here the foundations and principles of modern liberalism, which emphasizes the values of freedom of conscience and freedom of religion. Moreover, the widespread contemporary notion of the secular nature of State implies the ideas of religious pluralism and tolerance.

kind, the creature of god, achieves purpose and personal fulfillment in adhering to God. Hence, the central notion is that of service to God, which is conceived in Judaism as the task of conducting one's life according to the precepts laid down by the positive religious tradition. This nomistic tradition is characterized by a comprehensive and detailed set of rules of behavior of a predominantly legal nature (Halakah). Serving the Creator by abiding by the religious commandments is the absolute value in face of which no contrary human value system can be considered legitimate. Judaism attaches considerable importance to the heteronomous understanding of the obligatory nature of religious norms. The believing Jew is required to act under the conscious acceptance of the binding nature of the precept *qua* religious, and hence divinely ordered, command. This fundamental principle is pithily expressed in numerous sources, one of which is the talmudic saying of Rabbi Hanina: "He who is commanded and does fulfill the law stands higher than he who is not commanded and fulfills it" (*b. ʿAbod. Zar.* 3a, and elsewhere). The required motivation is therefore not one of personal conviction regarding the substance of the rule of conduct, but the consciousness of the heteronomous significance of God's command and its obedient acceptance as an act of faith.

Humanity, created in the image of God, is endowed with freedom of will and hence is held responsible for its deeds. However, the Jewish person is not viewed as an isolated individual, seeking personal perfection, but as an integral part of a larger community—the Jewish people. This collective body has entered into a special relationship with God by means of a formal covenant. Under the covenant the Jewish people and each Jewish individual has assumed a special commitment towards God and the law. In the light of these few but central points of the Jewish religion, I shall now examine the fundamental elements of the actual problem of religious freedom.

The idea that the Jewish people occupy a special position vis-à-vis God, being charged with particular duties and responsibilities (cf. Amos 3:2), has a direct influence upon their relationship with the non-Jewish world. Judaism has withdrawn from proselytism, since it has always rejected the notion of *extra Ecclesiam nulla salus.* It would, however, be erroneous to draw the conclusion that normative Judaism (as seen in Halakah) ignores the Gentiles. Being necessarily a universal system—in view of the absolute nature of the divine lawgiver—Jewish law, indeed, comprises rules of conduct intended for Gentiles. These so-called seven noachide laws are much less numerous than the precepts applicable to Jews (traditionally numbered 613). But it remains a historical fact that most Jewish people in the postexilic diaspora did not try in practice to act outside their ranks in order to convince Gentiles of the truth of the Jewish faith.

The resulting acquiescence in a pluralistic world is not grounded upon any ideology demanding the recognition of a basic right of religious freedom. It is rather the corollary of a division of functions between the Jewish people and the other nations. This divinely ordained partition does not detract from the non-Jew's ability to achieve full salvation. It admits, therefore, a certain measure of pluralism in religion, subject to the observance of a number of fundamental principles, as established in the framework of the above mentioned noachide laws. Among these universally binding principles one finds the prohibition of idolatry. The latter, which has actually become a legally defined concept, constitutes in the eyes of Jewish law an intolerable criminal activity, exceeding by far the boundaries of legitimate religious pluralism. Thus the essence of Judaism has been defined as the radical and complete negation of idolatry.

Let me return to the problem of the individual Jew's freedom of religion. From a purely religious point of view, one can hardly conceive the existence of a *natural right* of freedom of conscience in the modern secular meaning of that term. Humans standing before God have no *right* to act contrary to the ultimate purpose of their very existence. In the framework of an essentially theocentric conception, humankind's duties and not its rights take the foremost place in its relationship to divinity. Human rights can prevail only on the level of interhuman relations. The Jewish religious notion of individual freedom has been pertinently defined by Rabbi Aharon Lichtenstein:

> Personal liberty retains its immense significance—not, however, as an inalienable civil or natural right but rather as an essential factor, both an instrument and a condition, in the quest for beatitude. From a religious perspective, neither the concept nor the content of liberty resembles the secularist's *jus naturalis*. It is not a lack of restraint but a capacity for self-realization; not a freedom *from* but a freedom *to*. For the Jew, liberty is the power to realize his spiritual potential as an individual—as a being existing in special relation to God—and as a member of a community endowed with a unique historical destiny and charged with a singular commitment. Its ultimate point of reference lies beyond the order of rights or goods, on a plane where freedom and servitude are no longer polar opposites as man realizes himself in service to God. "They are My slaves, for I have taken them out of the land of Egypt" (Lev 25:42); and yet, "there is no free man but he who engages in Torah" (*m. ʾAbot* 6:2).[2]

[2] "Religion and State: The Case for Interaction," *Judaism* 15 (1966) 391–92.

The individual's freedom of choice constitutes, no doubt, a vital element in the performance of an act of faith. The fulfillment of a commandment does not possess its full religious significance if it is not accompanied by a sincere and profound internal conviction. Religious motivation is essential in the accomplishment of religious duties. But in the framework of Judaism one cannot deduce from the motivational requirement the existence of a principle of religious freedom. The pronounced nomistic nature of rabbinic Judaism tends to emphasize the legal dimension of religion. Hence, the service of God in terms of Halakah does not require merely the accomplishment of acts of faith, but also a minutely regulated external conduct, which covers almost all aspects of human life. The legalist character of Jewish religion is, in essence, the manifestation of the intimate connection between the individual and the collective group. The individual is not supposed to aspire after personal salvation outside the community. This is a highly dialectical relationship charged with strong tensions, since the behavior of the individual influences the fate of the whole community and vice versa. This mutual responsibility has found its expression in the talmudic saying: "All of Israel are the guarantors of each other" (*b. Šebu.* 39a).

The idea that the violation of religious precepts endangers the welfare of the whole community is deeply rooted in Judaism; it actually constitutes the leitmotif in the Bible. It is, therefore, understandable that Judaism emphasizes the external behavior of a person, though the actor's state of mind may be of highest importance for the religious perfection of his or her actions. In my opinion, this insistence upon preestablished actual and concrete human conduct in given circumstances constitutes one of the great contributions of Judaism to culture. True, it is hoped, and to some extent presumed, that the habit of righteous conduct will eventually produce a change of heart with the actor and induce him or her to the required internal motivation (*b. Pesaḥ.* 50b). But the community's foremost duty is to assure the actual implementation of religious precepts. The solid core of Jewish tradition is constituted by an extensive and comprehensive body of rules of external conduct. The search for abstract concepts and for underlying principles behind the rules of the system has been relegated to a second place, permitting in practice a considerable amount of ideological pluralism. The rationalistic approach to religion could thus legitimately coexist with mysticism, each endeavoring with its own methods to elaborate the foundations and significance of religious precepts (*mitzvot*).

Given these fundamental traits of rabbinic Judaism it can hardly come as a surprise that the idea of coercion is not foreign to its philosophy. The assumption of an ultimate suprahuman end to human existence, the notion of mutual responsibility, and the importance of concrete behavior—all militate in favor of the coercive enforcement of religious precepts. As a matter of fact, talmudic sources mention not only the obligation of both the individual and the community to prevent forbidden activities, but also the legitimacy of using force in compelling a person to perform a religious act of purely ceremonial nature (*b. Ketub.* 86a).

It would, however, be too simplistic to conclude that under Jewish law forcible compulsion of religious behavior is the habitual and recommended way of government. The rabbinic sources dealing with the issue by way of principle did not countenance the reality of modern society. They most likely presupposed the existence of a community of believers, where the societal sanctions were directed against the deviant individual who basically considered himself or herself to be a member of that community. Today's situation differs substantially: Jewish society is pluralistic; a large section of it is secular-minded, or at least rejects the obligatory force of the entire rabbinic tradition. The rejection in principle of the validity of Jewish religious law by substantial parts of Jewry calls into question the assumptions of the traditional approach. Moreover, it renders illusory the hope that lies behind an effort to bring about a change of heart through the actual enforcement of the religious norm. The practical impossibility to achieve through physical force a change of inner conviction constitutes, from a religious point of view, an important element that transcends purely tactical considerations. It draws into question the very justification of the use of force, at least in relation to the accomplishment of acts that require for their religious significance a measure of freedom of choice. The contradiction between legal coercion and the requirement of freedom of will is a well-known topic in rabbinic literature. Indeed, in this connection one of the most authoritative rabbinic scholars of this century has stated that "where the religious tribunal knows with certainty that the person on trial does not want to submit and it is obvious with all that coercion will be useless because he will prefer to die rather than to give in, then it will be prohibited to raise a hand against him."[3] It has been argued that in the same line of ideas, coercion is religiously inadmissible in contemporary society against nonorthodox people who adhere to different moral convictions. In any event, the rejection of religious coercion is not based upon any notion of freedom of religion. It is the outcome of considerations of a purely utilitarian nature: the results do

[3] Meir Simḥah Kahan, *ʿor Sameah: ʿal Kol Sefer Mishneh Torah* (Warsaw and Riga, 1902-26; repr. 4 vols. in 2, Jerusalem, 1982), 2-20.

not justify the means. Moreover, the application of force may prove to be even counterproductive in view of the expected violent reactions of people hurt in their innermost convictions. Social reality is, and has always been, a most legitimate consideration in the application of Jewish religious law. Today, this reality comprises the fact that the principles of freedom of conscience and religion are of almost universal acceptance.

Religious Freedom in Israeli Law

The foundation of the State of Israel in 1948, the fulfillment of an age-old aspiration of the Jewish people, brought into focus the clash between Jewish tradition and liberal ideology. The fundamental issue was now over the nature of the newly established Jewish State, in particular the place of religion in that state.

That Israel has never had a formal constitution is directly relevant to the issue of religious freedom. Hence, the problems of civil rights in general, and freedom of religion in particular, do not arise in a constitutional framework, as they do in most countries of the world. Parliament is sovereign, in an identical way as practiced in the United Kingdom. Civil rights are upheld through the judicial review exercised by the High Court of Justice.

Freedom of religion and freedom of conscience is mentioned in the Israeli Declaration of Independence, which, although not a legally binding document, serves as an important guideline in the construction of laws. A formal legal provision protecting certain basic rights has been received into Israeli law from Mandatory legislation. However, the relevant provision not only lacks higher constitutional validity, but has been rather narrowly constructed by Mandatory courts. Thus, according to an early decision of the Mandatory court, the law's principal intention is to protect the *collective* freedom of religion.[4] As a matter of fact, the historical Ottoman system of recognized religious communities concerned mainly the internal autonomy of the various ethno-religious communities. The system has been maintained, in principle, by the State of Israel in relation to non-Jewish communities. These communities enjoy organizational autonomy and freedom of worship. The above mentioned nonproselytic attitude of Judaism is no doubt a factor congenial to peaceful coexistence with other religious denominations. In this respect, no serious conflicts have been experienced between the liberal outlook

[4] Criminal Appeal 109/35, *Attorney General v. Shanti,* Collection of Judgments (ed. Rotenberg), vol. 8, p. 651.

and the traditional Jewish conception. Both agree that freedom of worship be granted to adherents of other religions. The only clashes between Jews and Christian churches in Israel have been due to missionary activist Protestant sects whose methods have aroused resentment. The repeated allegation that some sects had attempted to attain their end by exploiting the economic straits of poor Jewish families, provoked legislative intervention. An amendment to the Penal Law criminalizes the practice of giving or receiving material benefits in connection with change of religion.[5] The legislation stirred some angry reactions from Christian and secular circles, but as expected it remained without any practical effects. It is noteworthy to mention in this context that change of religion as such is permissible under Israeli law, which regulates some formal aspects of the conversion.[6]

The major problem is, therefore, not the freedom of worship or freedom of religion, but freedom from religion. The relative autonomy of the religious community vis-à-vis the State does not guarantee the freedom *from* religion. To the contrary, the legal powers given to the established religious community may severely infringe upon the civil rights of its individual members. Thus, under Israeli law, no member of a recognized religious community can effectively leave it, except by way of a formal change of religion. The major problems of freedom from religion are experienced by the Jews, who are all subject in matters of marriage and divorce in Israel to rabbinical law and jurisdiction. The absence of civil marriage is strongly resented by nonorthodox and secular Jews, who pretend to be exempt from religious law. It would exceed by far the limited scope of this paper to go into the most complex and intricate details of the legal situation in respect to matters of personal status. Suffice it to remark that the laws in this regard are full of internal contradictions that are the outcome of compromises concluded in the wake of the clash of ideologies. The compromises are not merely the result of contrasting political forces; their ambivalent nature reveals a deeper sense of ideological insecurity common to both sides. The great majority of Jewish citizens, be they agnostic nonbelievers or critics of Orthodox law, would like the State to preserve its Jewish particularity. But they are at a loss as to how to translate this "Jewishness" into the language of reality without affecting the secular nature

[5] Penal Law Amendment (Enticement to Change Religion) Law 5738–1977, 32 L.S.I. 62.

[6] Religious Community (Change) Ordinance of 1927.

of the State. It is a fact that historically Judaism has always been marked by religious elements. The attempt to isolate purely cultural aspects inside the heritage of Judaism encounters, in my opinion, insurmountable obstacles, since the religious dimension is of the very essence of Judaism.

The dilemma of many of the believing Jews in Israel is of no minor gravity. They regard the return of the Jewish people to its homeland and the establishment of an independent polity as profoundly meaningful religious events. They aspire to a complete identification with the country's political-national system and participate in the government. But despite this commitment they find themselves unable to accept with equanimity the basic secular character of the State—which is an undeniable fact in view of the actual government. The reality of a secular Jewish State creates for the believing Jew difficult ideological problems: How to accomplish in this inconvenient framework the collective religious mission of the Jewish people? How to fulfill the eternal commitment created by the divine covenant? From a religious point of view the Jewish State should be the instrument for the accomplishment of that mission. Moreover, many believing Jews are convinced that the nonobservance of religious precepts jeopardizes the very existence of the independent Jewish State. On the other hand, many have recognized that the prospect of effectively enforcing religious law upon a nonbelieving population by means of secular agencies is a hopeless task with frustrating effects. Moreover, many religious people have been won over by such liberal ideas as freedom of conscience and free choice in religious matters. They reject intuitively coercive methods aimed at forcing individuals to practice religion.

The ambivalence in the feelings of the adherents to the two opposing ideologies has facilitated the making of political compromises. The keystone of the entire structure of state-religion relations is the principle of status quo. The term figures in the coalition agreements that are the basis of the religious parties' participation in the government. The concept implies, in principle, that nothing should be modified in this sensitive area. An additional important factor of the continued existence of the status quo principle is the fear of an open social conflict that is likely to shatter national unity.

There can be no doubt that the actual legal system based upon the status quo violates the principle of freedom from religion. In particular, in the field of marriage and divorce nonbelievers and nonorthodox people are required to perform religious acts according to rabbinic law. In reality, the status quo has undergone important changes both by judicial and legislative interventions aimed at attenuating some of the harsher effects of religious law. The general framework of religious jurisdiction has, however, remained intact.

This dilemma of religious Jews—who on the one hand accept the liberal tenets of modern democratic society and on the other hand believe in the traditional idea of mutual responsibility for the implementation of religion—has created in practice a most interesting distinction between individual and collective behavior. The main thrust of religious parties is not to coerce individuals to observe religious practices but to prevent the State from taking measures that violate religious law. The emphasis is on the public aspect of the State's activity, which has symbolic character in the eyes of the religious Jew. The wish to identify with the Jewish State leads to the demand that the government should not infringe upon those legal characteristics that have become symbols of the "Jewishness" of the State. The choice of the relatively few topics that are considered by the people as symbolic of the Jewish nature of the State appears rather arbitrary in view of the great number of religious precepts in Judaism. But once such symbols have emerged, the religious groups concerned are prepared to fight for them to the last, however little their practical importance may be.

Among the few topics charged with symbolic religious value and affecting the principle of freedom from religion are the following three: marriage and divorce, observance of Sabbath, and dietary laws (*kashrut*). In all these fields the reason behind enforcement of Jewish law upon the population is not so much concern for the individual's salvation, but for the community's. Thus, the general legal recognition of civil marriage would be considered an official declaration of the secular character of the Jewish State. Hence, the manifold attenuations of the rigors of religious law, achieved indirectly by various legal techniques, have not provoked any acute political conflicts. As long as the formal symbol is preserved, the loss of substance is disregarded.

One encounters the same phenomenon in relation to the Sabbath and dietary laws. There is no question of imposing upon the individual citizen the observance of the strict rules of Jewish law. The religious parties aim at preventing the government from violating them in its official activities. Thus, for example, public transportation is motionless in most parts of the country on Saturday, but taxi services are available.

In conclusion, the compromises are frequently of a curious sort and the whole system is replete with inner contradictions. The ambivalence of the actual solutions is the result of the adoption of conflicting ideologies. The basic principle of freedom of religion is generally recognized but it clashes with the desire of preserving the Jewish nature of the State and national unity.

In practice, the principle of individual freedom of religion is safeguarded, except in relation to those public topics that have acquired symbolic value. It appears that religious people, too, are basically convinced that the most promising way of implementing religious values is not state-compulsion but education and dialogue. Moreover, the sensibility of nonbelievers for the protection of religious freedom has considerably increased over the last decade.

J. Clifford Wallace

Israeli and American Conceptions of Religious Freedom: A Response to Izhak Englard

WALLACE UNDERTAKES a comparative study of the American and Israeli legal systems with special reference to the issue of religious freedom. He concludes that, while the Establishment Clause of the American constitution works well for Americans and represents a cherished principle of American life, such a provision in law would not be appropriate to Israel's situation. He also suggests that Americans may have something to learn from the Israeli experiment in religious democracy.

J. Clifford Wallace is a United States Circuit Judge, sitting on the Ninth Circuit Court of Appeals. He has served as an adjunct professor of Law at the J. Reuben Clark Law School at Brigham Young University, the University of San Diego School of Law, and the California Western School of Law. Judge Wallace has published articles in several law journals.

In responding to Izhak Englard's interesting and intriguing paper on the clash of ideologies in modern Israeli law in the context of religion in the law, I claim no special expertise in philosophy, religion, history, or political science. My exposure to Israel last year was brief, but rewarding. I can best respond by considering some of the salient legal issues presented by Englard's paper. His detailed and fascinating description and analysis of the interaction between Jewish religious law and secular law in Israel presents lessons both for the Israeli legal system and for our own American system of justice. Englard succinctly summed up some of the salient features of the Israeli legal system as they affect religion and its practice. Initially, I would like to point out the more important contrasts between the Israeli and American systems, and then discuss what lessons each system may learn from the experience of the other, as far as the interaction of religion and law is concerned.

Contrasts Between the Israeli and American System of Law

The most obvious difference between the Israeli and American systems of law centers on the legal source of "religious freedom." In America, it is the first amendment to the Constitution that guarantees the free exercise of religion and the freedom from government-established religions, or excessive governmental entanglements with religious institutions. Since Israel lacks a constitution, Israeli law does not have this type of firm basis on which to place religious freedom. Therefore, the legal bases of the freedoms and laws to which Englard referred must either be statutory or the product of a common law grounded in the principles expressed by the Israeli Declaration of Independence or the early Mandate legislation.

This difference in legal basis has several important ramifications for a comparative analysis. First, the lack of a firm textual framework for analysis contributes to uncertainty in judicial determinations of religious freedom issues. Second, the lack of a firm textual basis may well indicate a lack of a political consensus among various groups about the proper place of religion in the framework of human rights. It would appear that this lack of consensus, and the concomitant desire to avoid conflict, are partially responsible for the development of the status quo policy as discussed by Englard.

Even if the current substantive law on the relationship between religion and the state were embodied somehow in the Israeli constitution, however, significant differences would remain between the two legal systems. The starkest difference in the substantive law between the two systems is the conscious absence of an Israeli establishment clause or something similar in design. The first amendment to the United States Constitution provides that "Congress shall make no law respecting an establishment of religion." Unquestionably, this language was intended by the Framers to prevent the development of a national state religion, such as the Anglican Church of England. While there is currently much debate about what other meanings are contained in the establishment clause, there is no doubt about its initial meaning. This stark difference in the substantive law of the two nations, however, is not especially relevant in the comparative discussion for an equally obvious reason. The United States never was intended to be a nation tied to a particular religion, while Israel was expressly intended to be a Jewish state from the outset; an intent evidenced by Jewish ritual and liturgy for the past two thousand years. The absence of a blanket establishment clause in Israeli law, therefore, is consistent with the overriding goals and purposes of that nation.

The most interesting contrast between the two substantive systems of law lies in their different treatment of the concept of "free exercise of religion." Both nations guarantee to their citizens a legal right to practice the religion of their choice. To this extent, the two systems are the same. But, as Englard pointed out, the Israeli concept of free exercise is a guarantee of freedom to recognized groups rather than an absolute right guaranteed to individuals: the right is essentially a collective right of recognized religions to conduct their business without interference. The added dimension of an individual religious right, present in the United States, is absent or subordinate in Israel.

The collective basis of free exercise in Israeli law, however, presents curious anomalies that do not appear in the American system. Englard observes in his paper that the Jewish religious law in Israel is rabbinical law—the law of Halakah. Moreover, he also points out that nonorthodox Jews, Jews who are members of the Conservative and Reform movements, and Jews who are purely secular in practice usually side with the government in religious conflicts. Although this is, I believe, an accurate statement, it ignores the legal ramifications of the rabbinical tradition. If one is a member of the Jewish religion, one is obliged to conform to the rabbinical interpretation of that religion. Marriages, divorces, and conversions that do not conform to or are not sanctioned by rabbinical authority are not recognized. Particularly in the field of marriage, this leads to measures designed to circumvent Jewish law (for example, foreign marriages).

Englard proceeds to observe that this result is consistent with traditional Jewish law and its conceptual understanding of coercion as a means to enforce behavioral norms. The larger ramification of this tradition, however, is that Jews who do not share the strict halakic interpretations of Jewish law are inhibited from practicing their variety of Judaism. In this respect, the free exercise of religion on an individual level has been abridged by the collective freedom of religion.

The collective right to freedom of religion also has created another anomaly. By treating religions as collective units, it becomes necessary to define the relationship between those units. Hence, situations arise like the one referred to by Dean Englard—legislation restricting proselytizing by forbidding the transfer of material benefits in connection with conversion. Thus, the freedom *from* religion manifests itself as the freedom of one religion from the influence of another religion. In the United States, where the freedom of religion is based on the individual, a laissez faire free market exists between the various religions. Freedom from religion in America manifests itself in precisely the opposite fashion—as the freedom from regulation regarding choice of religion or interaction between religions.

The religious courts in Israel support the collective structure of religious law. But this is not an Israeli invention. On the contrary, it reflects the merger of Middle Eastern and Western thought. Although this result is mandated as a matter of Jewish law, the collective structure of the religious court system in Israel does not appear to be mandated by Halakah. It stems from a colonial device used to facilitate ease of administration over a subject territory. Both of the two most recent colonial powers to occupy Israel, the Ottoman and British Empires, reserved the administration of personal law—the law of marriage, divorce, and succession—to recognized religious tribunals. Thus, the overall structure of the Israeli religious court system is not the result of a Middle Eastern tradition, but is a colonial theory inherited from prior rulers.

Lessons from the Israeli Law System

My principal focus, however, is not to highlight the differences between the substantive law of the two legal systems, but to discuss influences. Because I am focusing on a legal system established in the recent past, it might be helpful to speak not only of past influences manifested in present institutions, but also of present influences that offer the possibility of future institutional change as a result of contemporary comparative analysis. I will begin with the lessons that the American system of justice can draw from the Israeli experience as it relates to the interaction of law and religion.

The Israeli experience sheds some light on one of the great legal controversies in contemporary American jurisprudence. Debate rages over the scope and meaning of the free exercise and the establishment clauses, but particularly over the meaning of the establishment clause.

The recent Pawtucket creche case (in which the Supreme Court held that a nativity scene in a public place did not violate the establishment clause) and the recent uproar over school prayer (exemplified by the Alabama silent prayer statute), illustrate the legal manifestations of what has been an ongoing scholarly debate.

There are two major schools of thought on the establishment clause issue. The "accommodationist" school of thought argues that the Framers of the Constitution only intended to prohibit Congress from establishing a religion, or from aiding established religions in a discriminatory fashion. They argue that the historical evidence surrounding the constitutional convention and the ensuing debate over the Constitution and the Bill of Rights, combined with judicial interpretations of the first amendment over the first one hundred years since its ratification, support this view. Under the accommodationist theory, the several states have the power to enact legislation favoring one religion over another, or even to establish their own, official religion. In fact, several of the original states had such official religions at the time the first amendment was adopted. The major tenet of this perspective is that the first amendment is not incorporated into the fourteenth amendment, and thus does not apply to the states but only to the national government. Accommodationists often argue that other constraints operate to control the state governments and to prevent abuses—for example, the guarantees of equal protection, due process, and privileges and immunities embodied in the fourteenth amendment.

The second perspective, the "separationist" school, advocates a diametrically opposed position. Under the separationist theory, a "wall of separation" exists between church and state, with the term "state" including both the national and state governments. The separationist school also resorts to historical evidence to support its argument, particularly selected writings of James Madison and Thomas Jefferson. Moreover, it relies strongly on the last thirty-eight years of Supreme Court precedent, since *Everson v. Board of Education* was decided in 1947. The separationists argue that the only means of truly protecting religious freedom is by strictly separating secular government functions from religious institutions. In contrast to the accommodationist school, the separationist school relies heavily on the incorporation doctrine, and argues that the fourteenth amendment applies the Bill of Rights to state governments to justify its position that the states also are prohibited from interacting with religious institutions.

The conflict between these two theories has provoked vociferous and occasionally acrimonious debate among scholars, politicians, and theologians. Proponents of both schools tend to engage in somewhat hyperbolic discussion, predicting dire consequences to the fabric of American society if prayers are or are not allowed in public schools, or if parents who send their children to parochial schools are or are not permitted a tax deduction for their tuition payments. Which school of thought is correct as a constitutional matter is for the Supreme Court to decide. It can be argued that a national consensus on this issue has never been crystal clear, and that the leaders of our country when the Bill of Rights was adopted had reservations about both interpretations. Which school is correct as a matter of social policy, however, is certainly a matter open to debate.

What the Israeli experience teaches Americans about this issue, however, is that both schools of thought may wish to reconsider their predictions about what will happen if either social and constitutional agenda is adopted. The great lesson that Israel represents is that a pluralistic democracy can survive and even flourish in the presence of an official, sanctioned majority faith. At least in the present circumstances facing Israel, an establishment clause may not be a necessary prerequisite for democratic pluralism. This should serve to take the edge off the debate on this issue because the very survival of this republic is not at stake. Although the edge may be off, this does not mean that the debate is unimportant. The circumstances facing Israel are dissimilar to those facing most countries. When national survival from severe military and economic pressures is the first priority, with other issues falling far behind, many concerns are not vital enough to cause majority dissatisfaction. Peace may be the only real method of testing the interaction between social and religious institutions of Israel.

At the very least, however, the Israeli experience suggests that separationists may wish to reconsider their assertions that pluralism will suffer irreparably if the state becomes actively involved in the religious arena. This is not necessarily the case. Israel as a state entity is intimately involved in the daily life of its citizens, enforcing certain norms of halakic behavior. Religious parties with religious agendas abound in the Knesset, the Israeli parliament, and have emerged in recent years as the critical component in any ruling coalition. And yet, as the influence of these parties and the rabbinate has grown, the vigor of democracy and public interest in the political process has not diminished. On the contrary, it has increased, leading to some of the most vocal internal criticism and soul-searching that Israel has faced since its inception. The result is a thriving, if somewhat fractured, western democratic and pluralistic society.

The Israeli experience also may cause the accommodationists to rethink their criticisms of separationist views when they suggest that the moral fabric of America is somehow endangered by the absence of a closer relationship between church and state, or that this moral fabric would be enhanced if closer relations were effectuated. While the official state religion of Israel is rabbinical Judaism, the majority of its citizens are not Orthodox. In addition to nonorthodox religious Jews, a sizeable percentage of Israelis are completely nonreligious, secular Jews whose primary commitment is to Zionism and fulfillment of their Jewishness through Jewish culture. There is also a substantial Christian and Moslem population. Whether the lives of these nonorthodox Jews and non-Jews are more or less moral depends not so much on whether the State is more or less active in its halakic observances or whether the religious parties have more or less influence, but upon the dictates of their own consciences. While this result may be due in part to the nature of coercion in Jewish law, as Englard has pointed out, it illustrates that when the freedom to practice one's own religion and follow one's own conscience exists the official religious activities of the State have much less effect on the morality of the individual or of society as a whole.

In summation, American legal scholars may wish to consider not only whether the free exercise clause is absolutely necessary to the healthy existence of a pluralistic democracy, but also whether the Israeli experience teaches that the establishment clause is not necessarily indispensible. Israel should be viewed from this perspective as a great experiment in religious democracy, an experiment that, like the American experiment in democracy, has been largely successful.

Lessons from the American Law System

To say that an establishment clause is not indispensable to the existence of a pluralistic democracy, however, is not to say that it is undesirable. The controlling factor, of course, is the extent to which the state, in the exercise of its relationship between itself and religious institutions, impinges on the individual's rights to free conscience and to practice his or her own religion. This may be an influence that Israel can receive from the American experience.

As I mentioned earlier, one of the problems and potential conflicts in the Israeli system is the differential treatment of nonorthodox Jews in certain legal relationships. When one of these individuals wishes to marry, divorce, or convert in a manner dictated by his or her beliefs but not strictly according to halakah, they must do so in a manner that circumvents the religious courts that have exclusive legal jurisdiction with regard to those subject areas. The persistence of such individuals in foreign marriages and other circumventions is not surprising if one concedes that their beliefs are sincere and that their interest in following Halakah in such matters is outweighed by their personal objectives.

A second problem that seems to concern many Israelis is the unequal treatment of individuals of different religions in identical personal legal matter. While each religion may be treated equally in allowing it to establish courts for certain aspects of law, the religious courts naturally enforce different substantive law based on different religious concepts, resulting in unequal treatment of individuals from different religious communities. Although religious equality is guaranteed to each religion, it is not guaranteed to each individual.

Some have supposed that eventually these problems will cause serious and perhaps troubled reassessment in Israel. It is here that the American experience may be helpful to Israel. The Constitution embodies the American compromise on the issue. Under our Constitution as interpreted by the courts, one body—the Supreme Court—has the final word on the scope of religious freedom. As a direct result of the constitutional foundation of religious freedom, this volatile issue has been discussed in a controlled fashion, and the social change that is reflected by American first amendment law took place relatively smoothly over a period of two centuries. While these issues sparked much spirited debate and continue to do so, disrespect for the institutions of justice never has been a problem. The arguments always have been over constitutional interpretation of an accepted, known and defined principle. The arguments rarely involved challenges to the legal system as a whole. As a result, America has survived changes in its law of religion and state with barely a ripple in the structure of the legal system. This process promotes stability in judicial decision-making, and increases the respect among the population for the entire judicial system.

A constitution, like the establishment clause itself, is not essential for a pluralistic democracy. After all, both Israel and the United Kingdom exist without one, and both have official religions. Unlike the United Kingdom, however, the involvement between the Israeli government and religion is much more intense and explicit. Under these circumstances, the question arises whether Israel would benefit if the basis for religious freedom were defined in a manner that would channel debate into the substance of religious freedom, and away from the structure of the judicial system.

Conclusion

Whatever the result of these deliberations and whatever the solution to the dilemmas presented to the citizens of Israel, the happy news is that they will be accommodated within the framework of a democratic institution. Somehow, its citizens will come to grips with how to maintain the unique "Jewishness" of their country without sacrificing democratic values, even among the Jews themselves. This task presents a great challenge to Israel, but that nation has a history of overcoming tremendous difficulties. The meeting of this challenge, however, may become another historical chapter that will influence the West.

Index of Biblical References

Index of Extra-biblical Jewish Sources

Index of Qurʾānic References

Subject Index

Grateful acknowledgment is given to the copyright holders named below for permission to use the illustrations that appear in Jo Milgrom's article, pp. 263ff.

Fig. 1, p. 266: Reproduced from H. Swarzenski, *Monuments of Romanesque Art* (Chicago: University of Chicago, 1967) fig. 309.

Figs. 2 and 3, pp. 267 and 268: Reproduced from A. Kampf, *Contemporary Synagogue Art* (Philadelphia: Jewish Publication Society, 1966).

Fig. 4, p. 269: Reproduced from E. R. Goodenough, *Jewish Symbols in the Greco-Roman Period* (Princeton: Princeton University, 1964), copyright © 1964 Princeton University Press.

Fig. 5, p. 270: Reproduced from E. R. Goodenough, *Jewish Symbols in the Greco-Roman Period* (Princeton: Princeton University, 1964), by permission of the Yale University Art Gallery.

Fig. 6, p. 273: Reproduced from B. Shahn, *Alphabet of Creation* (New York: Schocken, 1964), by permission of Pantheon Books, a division of Random House, Inc.

Fig. 7, p. 275: Reproduced from M. Podwal, *A Book of Hebrew Letters* (Philadelphia: Jewish Publication Society, 1978), by permission of Georges Borchardt, Inc., copyright © 1978 by Mark Podwal.

Fig. 8, p. 276: Reproduced from M. Podwal, *A Book of Hebrew Letters* (Philadelphia: Jewish Publication Society, 1978), by permission of Georges Borchardt, Inc., copyright © 1978 by Mark Podwal.

Fig. 10, p. 281: Reproduced from Benn, *Visions of the Bible* (Tel Aviv: Sinai, 1954).

Fig. 11, p. 282: Reproduced from E. Wiesel, *The Golem* (illus. by M. Podwal; New York: Summit, 1984), by permission of Georges Borchardt, Inc., copyright © 1983 by Mark Podwal.

Fig. 12, p. 283: Reproduced from R. Cook, *The Tree of Life* (New York: Avon, 1974).

Fig. 13, p. 285: Reproduced from M. Podwal, *A Book of Hebrew Letters* (Philadelphia: Jewish Publication Society, 1978), by permission of Georges Borchardt, Inc., copyright © 1978 by Mark Podwal.

Fig. 15, p. 289: Reproduced from M. Cordovero, *Pardes Rimmonim,* by permission of the Jewish National and University Library, Jerusalem.

Fig. 16, p. 290: Adapted from B. W. Holtz, ed., *Back to the Sources: Reading the Classic Jewish Texts* (New York: Summit, 1984), by permission of Simon & Schuster, Inc.

Fig. 17, p. 293: Reproduced from *Old Jewish Manuscript Calendars* (Tel Aviv: W. Turnowsky & Sons).

Fig. 18, p. 296: Reproduced from the title page of *Portae Lucis,* by Gikatilla (Augsburg, 1516), by permission of the Jewish National and University Library, Jerusalem.